The Relational Subj

More and more social theorists are now calling themselves 'Relational Sociologists', but they mean entirely different things by this term. It can cover anything from reductionist methodological individualism to a form of holistic sociological imperialism that deems all our relations to be exclusively 'social'. The majority, however, endorse a 'flat ontology', dealing exclusively with dyadic relations. Consequently, they cannot explain the context in which relationships occur despite there being no such thing as context-less action. It also means that the outcomes of relationality can be explained only as the result of an endless series of 'transactions', whose aggregation would somehow account for social stability and change. The approach of this book is quite different, in regarding 'the relation' itself as an emergent property, with internal causal effects upon its participants and external ones on others. A second difference is that many of these 'Relationists' appear unaware that analytical philosophers, such as John Searle, Margaret Gilbert, and Raimo Tuomela, have spent twenty years trying to vindicate a concept of the 'We' that gives rise to commitment, cooperation, and collective action; one that also generates deontic rights: obligations, rights, and duties. Uniformly, they have worked on different versions of shared intentionality. In this book, however, 'We-ness' is held to derive from subjects' reflexive orientations towards the emergent relational 'goods' and 'evils' they themselves generate – then affecting their actions in a couple, a work group, sport's team, orchestra, voluntary association or social movement. Both authors could be called 'Relational Realists', but we have something to offer to Realism too, which, despite its humanism, has failed to explore the 'Relational Subject'.

PIERPAOLO DONATI is Professor of Sociology and Director of the Centre of Studies on Social Innovation (CESIS) at the University of Bologna, Italy.

MARGARET S. ARCHER is Professor of Sociology and Director of the Centre for Social Ontology at the University of Warwick.

The Relational Subject

PIERPAOLO DONATI AND MARGARET S. ARCHER

CAMBRIDGE
UNIVERSITY PRESS

CAMBRIDGE
UNIVERSITY PRESS

University Printing House, Cambridge CB2 8BS, United Kingdom

Cambridge University Press is part of the University of Cambridge.

It furthers the University's mission by disseminating knowledge in the pursuit of education, learning and research at the highest international levels of excellence.

www.cambridge.org
Information on this title: www.cambridge.org/9781107513952

First published 2015

A catalogue record for this publication is available from the British Library

Library of Congress Cataloguing in Publication data
Donati, Pierpaolo, 1946–
The relational subject / Pierpaolo Donati and Margaret S. Archer.
pages cm
Includes bibliographical references and index.
ISBN 978-1-107-10611-6 (hardback) – ISBN 978-1-107-51395-2 (paperback)
1. Intergroup relations. 2. Interpersonal relations. 3. Social interaction.
4. Sociology. I. Archer, Margaret Scotford. II. Title.
HM716.D66 2015
301 – dc23 2015001681

ISBN 978-1-107-10611-6 Hardback
ISBN 978-1-107-51395-2 Paperback

To all those who by pursuing mutual concern and reciprocity, generate relational goods for the flourishing of a new civil society

Figures

Acknowledgements

The list of friends and colleagues who have given us support and helped us to clarify and combine our thinking is very long indeed. However, a very special debt is owed to Doug Porpora for his enthusiasm for our project and his excellent judgement about how to improve our text.

PART I

1 *Introduction Relational Sociology: reflexive and realist*

PIERPAOLO DONATI AND
MARGARET S. ARCHER

The rationale for this book

Increasingly, theorists of many different persuasions are presenting themselves as 'Relational Sociologists'. Yet it is difficult to see how there could be a sociological theory that was not concerned with relations in some sense of the term. The problem is that those appropriating this adjective for their theorizing mean very different things by it: ontologically, epistemologically, and methodologically. When Relational Sociology is proclaimed as a 'manifesto', the expectation is that its signatories will be endorsing at least the main planks of an 'explanatory programme'; but even this is not the case. Moreover, 'manifestos' issued in any domain are promissory notes; what they promise is to perform a task better than did their predecessors. The trouble here is that the best known versions of 'Relational Sociology' – largely North American – do not even address the scope of this enterprise as traditionally conceived in the discipline.

Sociology came into being to seek answers to four questions about the social order: 'Where have we come from?', 'What is it like now?', 'Where is it going?', and 'What is to be done?' These are all realist questions: there is a real social world with real properties inhabited by real people who collectively made the past and whose causal powers are already shaping the future. One way in which Weber expressed the vocation of sociology was to discover why things are 'so' and not 'otherwise'. In other words, the purpose of the discipline was explanatory. Both authors of this book situate themselves uncompromisingly in this tradition and in their previous works have struggled to contribute something to answering all four key questions. This distinguishes us from nearly all of those today who term themselves 'Relational Sociologists' and who retreat further and further from trying to explain anything. We can illustrate this most pungently by simply asking: 'What do those proclaiming their approaches to be distinctively "relational" contribute to our understanding of what is happening today in our one global society?' We are not exigently demanding a grand theory, but more modestly asking for a statement of their explanatory programme.

In our view, as the economic crisis of late modernity became entrenched, it accentuated the incongruity between the cultural 'ideal' of Individualism and the structural influences that preceded, precipitated and prolonged this state of affairs in the economy, which are irreducible to individualistic terms. The excesses of unregulated global finance capitalism were met by an intensification of bureaucratic regulation on the part of enfeebled nation states when implementing their politics of austerity, which further accentuated the incongruity. This is encapsulated in the generalized acceptance in the developed world that structurally 'there is no alternative' to the financialized economy, whilst simultaneously scapegoating particularly rapacious individuals (bankers) for its damaging consequences. Hence, the old oscillation between individualism and collectivism that had dogged modernity re-presented itself in yet another guise. This is the backcloth to the present book. We start from the assumption that behind the complex interactions generating the current crisis, what is at issue is the central nucleus of Western modernity: its characteristic compromise[1] between individualism, which ironically goes hand in hand with its characteristic collectivism, as manifest in the *'lib/lab'* nature of government and governance that oscillate between the two.[2]

More pointedly the book is concerned with the way in which the social sciences have reflected the same ambiguity and incorporated it into their theorizing. Both authors, sometimes writing together, have

[1] 'Compromise' results from situations where *incompatible* cultural and structural factors that are *necessarily* related to one another, i.e. representing a 'constraining contradiction' (Margaret S. Archer, *Culture and Agency: The Place of Culture in Social Theory*, Cambridge, Cambridge University Press, 1988, pp. 148–153).

[2] This peculiar combination of individualism and collectivism is at the basis of the arrangement that in the following chapters will be called the *lib/lab* configuration of modern society: see P. Donati, *Relational Sociology. A New Paradigm for the Social Sciences* (London: Routledge, 2011), p. 48; *Sociologia della riflessività. Come si entra nel dopo-moderno* (Bologna: Il Mulino, 2011), pp. 221–294.

criticized interpretations of the intensified morphogenesis in the Western world as a process of destructuring in which contingency, complexity, uncertainty, and risk are captured by the trope of liquidity.[3] We remain convinced that there are generative mechanisms that underlie the current state of affairs, but that is not our focus in this text. Instead, we concentrate upon the parallel crisis in current social theorizing, particularly as concerns the social subject – both singular and collective.

In a nutshell, we regard the European shift towards political centrism (where government and opposition are increasingly indistinguishable, where the practice of politics is without conviction and the preoccupation is with tactics rather than strategy) as having its parallel in social theory. Generically, this is the move towards 'central conflation',[4] in which the problems of Structure and Agency and of objectivism and subjectivism are supposedly 'transcended'; flows replace structures, narratives displace culture, and human plasticity makes the fluidity of our putative serial re-invention homological with the equally putative liquidity of the social order.

What is the connection with the conceptualization of human subjects, both singular and collective, that are central to this book? Not so very long ago the conflicting claims of individualism and collectivism dominated the philosophy of social science in the embattled positions of methodological individualism versus holism. Until quite recently *homo economicus* pursuing 'his' lone and individual preference schedule through instrumental rationality confronted *homo sociologicus* as 'organizational man', the puppet of rule and role requirements. Neither has become extinct despite postmodernism's proclamations of the 'death of the subject'. Rather, the equivalent of political centrism was again fostered. The 'institutionalized

[3] For our latest contributions see the three books edited by Margaret S. Archer (Dordrecht: Springer): *Social Morphogenesis* (2013), vol. 1; *Late Modernity: Trajectories towards Morphogenic Society* (2014), vol. 2; *Generative Mechanisms Transforming Late Modernity* (2015), vol. 3.

[4] Margaret S. Archer, *Culture and Agency*, chapters 2, 3, and 4, and *Realist Social Theory: The Morphogenetic Approach* (Cambridge: Cambridge University Press, 1995), pp. 79–89. Bourdieu provided a clear statement of central conflation in the first sentence of *The Logic of Practice* (Cambridge: Polity Press, 1990), p. 25 (italics added): 'Of all the oppositions that artificially divide social science, *the most fundamental, and the most ruinous is the one that is set up between subjectivism and objectivism.*'

individualism'[5] (of Ulrich Beck rather than that of Talcott Parsons) presented us with *homo inconstantus*, a subject freed from traditionalism's 'zombie categories' of class and gender, now enmeshed in a plethora of bureaucratic regulations yet free to embrace their self-reinvention, change their identities, and rewrite their biographies according to current whim and devoid of durable commitment, thus yielding *provisional* men and *pro tem* women. With a handful of exceptions,[6] the human subject's real, objective capacities for flourishing and liabilities to suffering faded into sociological insignificance. What remained was the 'ability' of fluid subjects to make what they would of social liquidity. Such was the 'transcendence' of the central problems of social theory in the hands of the central conflationists.

Breaching the theoretical tenet that every social phenomenon comes in a SAC and can only be explained by unpacking its contents – 'Structure', 'Culture', and 'Agency' – and examining their interplay, these main constituents of the social order were increasingly conflated with one another.[7] For the majority of social theorists, the resulting soup had one distinctive flavour: despite its colouring, the pervasive taste of the *social* – after all ingredients had been through the Moulinex.[8]

Although this tendency fell short of homogenizing different theoretical approaches, it became an increasingly potent strand of thinking within them. With little exaggeration, this trend could be called 'the socialization of everything personal'. The 'Individual' – who had remained robust since the Enlightenment – was the obvious victim and one whose demise we welcome. However, there is a crucial difference between insisting that the social order was not only 'outside' us but also 'within' us and the insidious assumption that the social

[5] Ulrich Beck and Elizabeth Beck-Gernsheim, *Individualization: Institutionalized Individualism and Its Social and Political Consequences* (London: Sage, 2002).

[6] Charles Taylor, *Human Agency and Language* (Cambridge: Cambridge University Press, 1985); Andrew Sayer, *Why Things Matter to People: Social Science, Values and Ethical Life* (Cambridge: Cambridge University Press, 2011); Christian Smith, *What Is a Person?* (Chicago: Chicago University Press, 2010).

[7] D. V. Porpora, *Restructuring Sociology: The Critical Realist Approach* (Cambridge: Cambridge University Press, 2015 forthcoming).

[8] Colin Campbell (in *The Myth of Social Action*, Cambridge: Cambridge University Press, 1996) had traced precisely the same misguided transformation of all 'action' into 'social action'.

infiltrated every nook and cranny of the human person, thus reduced to zombie status. Most sociologists could agree that thinking in terms of the 'Individual and Society' – as many teaching modules used to be entitled – implied a highly misleading separation of the two. Nevertheless, some of us resisted the steady encroachment of the social upon human personhood and the progressive reduction of personal properties and powers that it implied. Our resistance was just as strong towards the parallel implications for 'structure' and 'culture' entailed by this tendency to endorse central conflation. These similarly underwent the erosion of their distinctive properties and powers, which were reduced to the products of 'interaction' among (over-) social agents. In turn, this subtracted *sui generis* constraints, enablements, and sources of motivation from structure and culture alike, as these became the plasticine of interaction. Pushed to the extreme – and not all were such extremists – the result was a sociology of 'actants' and their networks making up a social world with a completely flat social ontology.

Certainly, there are 'old' representatives of this position (interpretivists) and 'new' ones (actor-network theorists), but we are more concerned by the less articulated and generally rather diffuse creeping forward of this tendency. Let us consider some of its indicative traits before we come to the growing popularity of the label 'Relational Sociology'.

To begin with, we note the *grounding* of 'Relational Sociology' in the revival of George Herbert Mead, especially his view that selfhood is completely derived from the social order and subsequently regulated by the 'generalized other'. However, in the nascent globalized world that he detected, early in the twentieth century, Mead also feared that the 'generalized other' could not survive the loss of familiar geo-localism.[9] In addition, note that Mead was a theorist who fully endorsed 'emergence', although this is rarely mentioned by those rediscovering him. After all, the defence of emergent properties and powers is subjected to widespread hostility, in part at least, because this concept is the

[9] Mead admits that 'the community in its size may transcend the social organization, may go beyond the social organization which makes such identification possible. The most striking illustration of that is the economic community. This includes everybody with whom one can trade in any circumstances, *but it represents a whole in which it would be next to impossible for all to enter into the attitudes of others*' (George Herbert Mead, *Mind, Self and Society*, Chicago: Chicago University Press, 1934, pp. 326–327; italics added).

strongest bulwark against those denying the relative autonomy, temporal priority, and causal powers of Structure and Culture in relation to Agency. In equal part, this is because the relations between human agents are also denied the power to generate emergent relational phenomena themselves. In this connection, Part II of this book is devoted to how the capacities and liabilities of human persons are affected by the structural and cultural contexts into which we are ineluctably born and that we necessarily have to confront. Part III examines our ineradicable human powers to transform these unavoidable, inherited aspects of our natal contexts.

Neo-liberalism, centricism, and central conflation

North-American 'Relational Sociology' is marked by two distinct responses to the liberalism of modernity and the neo-liberalism of late-modernity: virulent antagonism towards the Individualist patrimony of pre-twentieth century social thought and uncritical receptivity towards the destructured portrayal of late modernity as fluid flows and formless complexity, which does sterling service in muting the critique of mutating capitalism.

First, its refusal to tackle the macro-level at all and its failure to recognize any distinctive properties and powers of emergent social structures (which it shares with the revival of neo-pragmatism)[10] means that the machinations of financialized banking, multinational corporations, digital technology, climate change, warfare, and so on are subjected to silence, as are associated failures in health care delivery[11] and growing differentials in income distribution. Of course, the studied absence of these major politico-economic features of the USA's social landscape makes the endorsement of 'destructuration' considerably easier.

Second, and more directly relevant to this book, is the conceptualization of the social 'relationship' – or rather its absence. People do not stand in close relations with one another – as friends, parents, fellow workers, team players or supporters, members of the same church

[10] See Neil Gross, who deals with this problem by invoking the (supposed) homology between the three 'levels': N. Gross, 'A Pragmatist Theory of Social Mechanisms', *American Sociological Review*, 74 (2009), 358–379.

[11] The world's most expensive, yet the mortality rates for children are the highest in the developed world. Doug Porpora, *Restructuring Sociology: The Critical Realist Approach*.

or voluntary association, and so forth. Instead of warmth, caring, and commitment, which motivate their actions, generating 'relational goods'[12] and promoting social integration, they feature as nodes in networks of connectivity or represent its 'holes'. There is no coalescence into groups, significant to the subjects involved; no social movements committed to any cause and hostile to their opponents, and no parties or interest groups with social agendas. In place of personal concerns and collective conflicts, social relations are merely the site of an infinite series of 'transactions'. What a transaction is remains without definition and is as indefinite as 'everything'. As a portmanteau term, it certainly steers clear of the foundational imagery of the exchange of equivalents – of apples for bananas – in classical economics but fails to reveal when a transaction is successful (or a failure) and under what conditions and with what consequences. In all the approving references to transactional relations, without love or hate or even instrumental indifference, we find an overzealous reaction formation against the heritage of modernity's individualism. Persons are shorn of their intrinsic personal powers, but the social relations that now subsume those previously attributed to the individual in no sense generate recognizable human relationships. Instead, we are increasingly encouraged to become anti-humanists.

The connection between neo-liberalism and individualism is well-known in the history and philosophy of political economy, dating back to the utilitarians and *philosophes*[13] and constantly receiving new shots in the arm throughout the twentieth century. This needs no rehearsing. Neither does its percolation into social theorizing as the philosophical individualism that accounted for the resilience of methodological individualism. Specifically, rational choice theory and rational action theory are its fully fledged representatives. The pernicious irony was that intensified attacks upon the individual and upon emergence left millennial forms of Relational Sociology without the conceptual resources to mount a critique upon the damaging consequences of neo-liberalism.

[12] P. Donati, 'Capitale sociale e beni relazionali: una lettura sociologica delle reti associative a carattere cooperativo', in V. Pelligra (ed.), *Imprese sociali. Scelte individuali e interessi comuni* (Milan: Bruno Mondadori, 2008), pp. 135–153.

[13] C. Gide and C. Rist, *A History of Economic Doctrines* (London: G. Harrap, 1932 [1915]).

An important forerunner as to where this version of Relational Sociology would end was Giddens' 'structuration theory', as the acme of 'central conflationism'.[14] The bridge was that 'structure' and 'agency' were systematically elided and held to be even analytically inseparable, as each necessarily drew upon the other in the conception, conduct, and consequences of any action. This was followed by Giddens' work on 'self and society' in late modernity developing his notion of the 'pure relationship', which remained a relation only as long as the two participants derived personal satisfaction from it.[15] All the same, some kind of subject remained, if the capacity for subjective 'personal satisfaction' did, just as some kind of *virtual* structure and culture did, if they were elements that could be drawn upon. As a theoretical backcloth, structuration theory might have been more prominently foregrounded in relational sociology were it not contaminated by Giddens' venture into *realpolitik* in publishing his *Third Way*.

Instead, the same assumptions were taken from other sources, most importantly Bourdieu – after his works arrived in translation. Even Beck's version retained too much of the human subject because he stressed progressive 'individualization'. The latter was induced by the free flow of information and media representation, meaning that 'traditional' categories guiding self-direction, such as class and status or norms and values, were superseded by new notions of 'living a life of one's own', serial personal reinvention, familial experimentation, and kaleidoscopic biographical revision.[16] This preoccupation with the individualized 'life of one's own', negotiated and renegotiated among our new 'precarious freedoms', was held to underpin various contributions to the major loss in social solidarity: the attenuation of intergenerational social solidarity, the demise of the durable family, the reduced salience of class (now a 'zombie category'), indifference to party politics, and the vanishing of normative consensus. For the Becks, 'the human being who aspires to be the author of his or her life, the creator of an individual identity, *is the central character of our*

[14] Margaret S. Archer, 'Morphogenesis versus Structuration', *British Journal of Sociology*, 33 (1982), 455–483; *Realist Social Theory: The Morphogenetic Approach* (Cambridge: Cambridge University Press, 1995).

[15] A. Giddens, *Modernity and Self-Identity: Self and Society in the Late Modern Age* (Cambridge: Polity, 1991).

[16] J. Beck and E. Beck-Gernsheim, *Individualization* (London: Sage, 2002).

time.'[17] Thus 'institutionalized individualism'[18] was held to be 'becoming *the social structure of second modern society itself*.'[19] Even this was a step too far in allowing the human being the personal power to 'make a life' and to remain the 'central character' in the social drama.

Somewhat surprising, given his 'adoption' as their founding father within Relational Sociology, is the stance of Norbert Elias towards individualism. He himself chose to sum up his fifty years of theorizing under the title *The Society of Individuals*.[20] In it, his thought pivots on the 'we-I' balance and its shift from the hegemony of the 'we' in tribal and classical civilizations towards the 'I' of late modernity (the last essay is dated 1987).[21] What is surprising is that in 1987 Elias still looked forward to increased system integration and in his last years foresaw, 'before the process of integration into a tightly knit worldwide network of states has fully begun, a greater chance of individualization'.[22] The result was an upbeat interpretation of 'networked individualism', whose hallmark 'is that people function more as connected individuals and less as embedded group members'.[23] This 'is the era of free agents and the spirit of personal agency'.[24] We have no reservations about the existence of a general association between liberal market economics and individualism; indeed, Archer has underlined that modernity is closely linked to 'Autonomous Reflexivity' as the dominant mode practised and that its practitioners are instrumental rationalists who come close to resembling Rational Man.[25] However, there is a very important caveat.

17 *Ibid.*, pp. 22–23, italics added.

18 *Ibid.*, 'Preface', p. xxi. 19 *Ibid.*, p. xxii.

20 Norbert Elias, *The Society of Individuals* (Oxford: Basil Blackwell, 1991).

21 'Whereas previously people had belonged . . . to a certain group for ever, so that their I-identity was permanently bound to their we-identity and often overshadowed by it, in the course of time the pendulum swung to the opposite extreme. The we-identity of people, though it certainly always remained present, was now often overshadowed or concealed in consciousness by their I-identity'. *Ibid.*, p. 197.

22 *Ibid.*, p. 169. The thinking is very similar to Mead's at the end of *Mind, Self and Society*; whilst Mead's hopes were pinned on the League of Nations, Elias dreams of world government. The difference is that whilst Mead saw the growth of international trade as terminal for the reach of the 'generalized other', Elias seems to hope for the development of a global humanistic 'we'.

23 *Ibid.*, p. 12. 24 *Ibid.*, p. 19.

25 Margaret S. Archer, *Making Our Way Through the World: Human Reflexivity and Social Mobility* (Cambridge: Cambridge University Press, 2007), chapter 5.

That was only the case until towards the end of the twentieth century. It was only the case whilst ever the remnants of 'mutual regulation' between system and society lasted, underwriting some degree of overall integration. It ceased to be the case when multinational and finance capitalism broke free of national bounds and cast off the shackles of geo-local restraint: of the unions, of accountability to parliament, of the law of 'the land' and of normative regulation. The unfettered pursuit of the *situational logic of competition* intensified as the last bonds were shed that had tied national institutions together into an imperfect form of system integration, but sufficient to have produced the post–Second World war 'golden years'.

Ironically, for all its covenantal Meadianism and its celebration of Elias, North American Relational Sociology was distancing itself further and further from neo-liberalism's 'individual', eventually producing yet another version of the 'death of the Subject'. With it, certain questions were struck off the sociological agenda: 'What is a person?', what makes for being human and human well-being? in what do human suffering and flourishing consist, beyond the bio-physical level? This 'missing person', capable of initiating and sustaining human relationships and generating relational goods (and evils), means the price they paid was an inability to account for 'who' entered into their myriad 'transactions', 'why' they did so, and with 'what' consequences. In other words, the 'flat ontology' of North American Relational Sociology in the new millennium had effectively eliminated the Subject (by its anti-humanism) and the 'social structure' (through its so-called anti-substantialism). Consequently, they had disabled themselves from producing an account of the current economic crisis in terms of 'dyadic, transactional networks between actants'.

These considerations have been introduced because they inflect much of what styles itself as 'relational social theory', one that goes with the flow, plunging deep into embracing social liquidity. Differences within this relatively new camp will be touched upon as this introduction proceeds, but it is important to underline what distinguishes our approach from that whole camp.[26] We believe

[26] One that rarely recognizes Donati's foundational work which predated them all. See: Donati, *Introduzione alla sociologia relazionale* (Milan: FrancoAngeli, 1983) and *Teoria relazionale della società* (Milan: FrancoAngeli, 1991).

that this is distinctive in the following ways, ones that justify our Relational Sociology being qualified as both Reflexive and Realist.

What distinguishes our contribution from other versions of Relational Sociology?

1. We acknowledge that robust singular selves – not individuals – are necessary preconditions for subjects to form relations and thus, to the Relational Subject and Relational Sociology.
2. We advance distinctive concepts of what counts as a 'Relational Subject' and what constitutes relationality, according an important role to *Collective Reflexivity* in both.
3. We endorse a stratified ontology of the 'Relational Subject': as an 'I' with a Lockean continuous sense of self; a 'Me' whose natal social placement is involuntary and who accrues further objective social characteristics through the positions assumed as the life course proceeds; and a 'We' deriving from voluntary relations with others, a relationality that has *sui generis* properties and powers, irreducible to although continuously dependent upon those of others.
4. We defend an emergentist conception of relationality, which generates real and causally efficacious – but not 'substantialist' – emergent properties that unite this approach with Critical Realism. (Henceforth, those who reject emergence will be referred to as *Relationists.*)
5. We work at the micro-, meso- and macro-levels, instead of placing a Big Etcetera after our dyadic analyses. Moreover, we do not view these levels as homological, precisely because they are distinguished by the existence of distinctive properties and powers.
6. We are overtly engaged as critics of late modernity because it is hostile to the *flourishing* of the 'Relational Subject', be he/she uniquely singular or constituting a collective subject at any of the three levels. Conversely, Relationists turn their backs upon Eudemonia at any level.

Western culture continues to purvey the myth that 'where there is a will, there is a way'[27] and is regularly updated with exemplars from

[27] *Where There Is a Will, There Is a Way* is a didactic book published in 1869 by Michele Lessona, modelled on the work *Self-Help* by the British writer Samuel Smiles well before F. Nietzsche theorized the superman's will to power.

entertainment and business. Currently, it is the 'Steve Jobs cultural model'; the paradigmatic example of an individual who prevails against the cut-throat competition of the global market because he believes in his own capacities and talents; he does not have to answer to anyone, other than to himself and his own objectives, accepts risks against all odds, and achieves phenomenal success and celebrity. The movie of this American dream, as realized in Silicon Valley is paralleled by the East Coast film version of Mark Zuckerberg's lone rise to fame and fortune, with both reflecting the anthropology that the human being is self-determined, whatever the conditions of society in which he/she lives.

Late-modern society is replete with images and messages that systematically repress any idea of our relations with 'others' being decisive for the purposes of our individual existence. In cultural representations of our behaviour, the part played by other people is usually portrayed as merely contingent and random. In other words, relations do not have their own existence; they are not the object of care and consideration in and of themselves. Consider those using public transport, and we become aware that relations with others are to be carefully avoided or choreographed by Goffmanesque strategies. Encounters should not only be brief but impersonal; that is one role of political correctness. The idea that my space/place in the world depends on relations with others is not perceived as a support and frequently a resource, but is essentially considered to be an intrusion from which I must free myself as quickly as possible.

Late modern society is systematically based on immunization *against* social relations and leads to the repression of social relations. The inability of individuals to acknowledge social relations has become the illness of the century (the endemic disease of self-referentiality). This absence of social relations 'retaliates' by causing distress and disorientation for the self, which increasingly experiences isolation, poverty (in a vital sense), and a lack of support in everyday life. To emerge out of loneliness becomes an enormous enterprise – and often a hopeless one.

When we become aware of all of this, social change can begin. New processes aimed at re-evaluating relations with others emerge. One discovers that working in a team is more efficacious and gives more satisfaction, on condition that the task is not coercively imposed or that one's collaboration with others is not exploitative. We rediscover

Contents

family and friendship bonds as relations that, despite constituting obligations, nevertheless give a meaning to one's life that no other relation can supply. A growing number of people are realizing that they can achieve their goals only through new forms of association and new social movements. Justice and social solidarity require a vision that puts the needs and rights of all members of a community in relation with one another. We discover, in short, that we are all profoundly interdependent. The decisions, choices, and actions of each of us are not purely individual acts, but are arrived at in relation to and with others. It is unrealistic to think of them as the simple expressions of an autonomous Self. We realize that, in reality, each of us lives in a condition of dependence and interdependence with many other people without whom we could not be what we are and desire to become.

Each individual's biography is to be found enmeshed in relations with significant others and with the nonsocial world. The human person is not a self-sufficient entity: he/she is a '*subject-in-relation*,' where social relations are partly *constitutive* of personhood, whilst allowing that they are not exclusively so (see chapter 3).

However, in the social sphere, we are all in the same boat, in the sense that we depend on one another. And so the question becomes: how is this boat constituted? We call it the We-relation, but how is this relation generated? How should the relation be constituted in order to be fulfilling rather than alienating for those involved?

Our answer to the question about how the social relation that humanizes the person should be construed and conceptualized is the following: such social relations should be an expression of the Self as a 'Relational Subject'.[28] We want to explore the idea that a valid answer to the increasingly unbound morphogenesis of Western society[29] consists in being able to recognize and to foster the emergence of social subjects who no longer correspond to the ideal types of individualistic or collectivistic modernity.

In the social sciences, there has always been an abundance of literature that addresses the fact that 'the individual' in him/herself is a

28 A formal definition comes later.

29 Archer (2007), 'The Ontological status of subjectivity: the missing link between structure and agency', in Clive Lawson, John Latsis, and Nuno Martins, *Contributions to Social Ontology* (London: Routledge, 2007); Archer (ed.), *Social Morphogenesis*; Archer (ed.), *Late Modernity. Trajectories towards Morphogenic Society* (Dordrecht: Springer, 2014).

problematic entity. The individual's sociality as an intrinsically social animal has been affirmed since Aristotle. Nevertheless, during the long history of human thought, the social character of human individuality was often lost, as Horkheimer and Adorno observed.[30] With modernity, the nature of this sociality increasingly became a problem in itself. In brief, modernity has called natural sociality into question and replaced it with an artificial sociality. On the one hand, some have considered the individual to be hypersocialized by social and cultural structures, that is, an overestimation of sociality (methodological holism). On the other hand, some have thought of the individual as a hyposocialized, autonomous subject, which is to say, an underestimation of sociality (methodological individualism).

From the advent of modernity onwards, the individual has become the object of increasingly complex and contradictory conceptualizations: at times, the individual has been considered as completely autonomous and, at other times, as completely dependent; at times, he or she has been treated as *ens realissimum* and, at other times, as a phantasm; in the end, the individual became a mere 'point of reference for communication'.[31]

It is banal to point out that individuals exist because there is a social context that generates them and supplies their means of subsistence. No human individual is a monad because each person is in relation with other persons. But modern thought has not produced a sociological paradigm capable of adequately expressing the relationality to which we refer. In short, the notion of a 'social subject' has oscillated between individualism and collectivism.[32]

Our collaboration dates back over two decades, but because its products have appeared at least as frequently in Italian as in English, it is not surprising that only a few have fully appreciated its relational effects! We can summarize these as our development of the synergy between Donati's pioneering statement of Relational Sociology

[30] M. Horkheimer and T. Adorno, 'Individual', in id., *Aspects of Sociology* (Boston: Beacon, 1973), chapter 3.

[31] Niklas Luhmann, 'Sozialsystem Familie', *System Familie*, 1 (1988), 75–91.

[32] An emblematic author, in this connection, is Alain Touraine, who began by exalting the role of collective subjects in the 1960s, later to emphasize the return of the individual with a study on the Self. See A. Touraine and F. Khosrokhavar, *La recherche de soi. Dialogue sur le sujet* (Paris : Fayard, 2000).

and Archer's morphogenetic framework for social realism.[33] In 1991, Donati, talking about the so-called 'postmodern era', wrote: 'what happens is understandable as social morphogenesis under conditions of high complexity'.[34] He suggested discarding the grand narratives of the past and restarting from the very basic concept of social relation and, soon after, linked this to a two-way exploration of social morphogenesis. The latter offered a dynamic without which theorists simply listed a taxonomy of successive social formations without (excepting Marx) providing robust explanations of what accounted for these transitions.

The explanatory paradigm of social morphogenesis[35] appeared to be particularly suited to providing a way out of these difficulties in that it is better able than other approaches to give an account of how the objective and subjective factors, internal or external to a given society, combine and interact with one another so as to generate a society (or sector of it) that is different from the preceding one. As is well known, the morphogenetic approach was conceived as an explanatory framework for the transformation of social and cultural structures as a process that is continuously mediated by human agency, with agents themselves becoming transformed in the course of social transformation.

From Archer's point of view, one initially honed on David Lockwood's[36] distinction between system and social integration, it had become increasingly clear that social integration entailed much more than the presence or absence, the promotion and defence of vested interests, their articulation, organization, and confrontation (i.e. conflict theory). Donati's introduction of Relational Sociology[37]

[33] We would like to note that both of these were first formulated throughout the 1980s and not at the much later dates usually cited by commentators. Donati's work suffers from its appearance in Italian (as is still evident in that Relationists only cite his 2011 book in English). Archer's suffers from wrongfully making her a 'disciple' of Roy Bhaskar, when in fact the first statements of both their approaches appeared simultaneously in 1979.

[34] Donati, *Teoria relazionale della società*, p. 11.

[35] Margaret S. Archer, *Social Origins of Educational Systems* (London: Sage, 1979); 'Morphogenesis versus Structuration', *British Journal of Sociology*, 33 (1982), 455–483; *Realist Social Theory: The Morphogenetic Approach* (1995).

[36] D. Lockwood, 'Social Integration and System Integration', in G. K. Zollschan and W. Hirsch (eds.), *Explorations in Social Change* (Boston: Houghton Mifflin, 1964), pp. 244–257.

[37] P. Donati, *Introduzione alla sociologia relazionale* (1983) and *Teoria relazionale della società* (1991).

offered a much richer resource for answering the question of what, in fact, bound people together than did any 'third person account'[38] imposed by the sociologist. This issue became even more important as Archer explored and advanced Subjective Reflexivity as the element linking 'Structure and Agency'. In shorthand, further planks strengthening the bridge making for our collaboration include 'Relational Reflexivity', our shared preoccupation with the Common Good, and more recently our theoretical interrogation of the conditions under which a 'morphogenic' social formation might realize it.

The present contribution seeks to deepen the analysis of the process of social morphogenesis in the light of a generalized theory of the social relations that mediate between the initial phase (at time T1) and the final phase (at time T4) of each morphogenetic cycle. Another way of putting this is that the present text focusses firmly upon the T2–T3 stage and understanding it more comprehensively than in terms of the manifest cut and thrust between groups pursuing or defending their objective interests (both material and ideational) as subjectively defined under their own descriptions.

'*Being in relation*' is an ontological expression that has three analytical meanings: (i) it says that, between two (or more) entities there is a *certain distance* which, at the same time, distinguishes *and* connects them; (ii) it says that any such relation *exists*, that is, it is real in itself, irreducible to its progenitors, and possesses its own properties and causal powers; and (iii) it says that such a reality has its own *modus essendi* (the modality of *the* beings who are *inside* the relation which refers to the internal structure of the social relation and its dynamics) and is responsible for its emergent properties, that is, relational goods and evils. These three meanings are analytical, because – from an empirical viewpoint – every relation contains all these aspects, which are closely interlinked.

The fundamental thesis of this work is that the morphogenesis of society comes about through social relations, which are connectors that mediate between agency and social structure. The generative mechanism that feeds social morphogenesis resides in the dynamics of social relations. However, in order to capture this phenomenon adequately, it is necessary to invoke a general theory of social

[38] Margaret S. Archer, *Making Our Way Through the World: Human Reflexivity and Social Mobility* (Cambridge: Cambridge University Press, 2007).

relations, which is presented here from the point of view of Relational Sociology.

Donati's relational theory of society came into being in order to critique not only methodological individualism and methodological holism but also the failures of formalist approaches in the field of social network analysis.[39] These failures have been pointed out by many other authors, including White[40] and Azarian.[41] With respect to these authors, his approach is characterized by its attempt to deepen understanding of the change in social relations as a process that takes place within social morphogenesis and which Archer terms 'the double morphogenesis'[42] (an integral part of the process but one rarely accentuated by readers). This we now call the 'relational order of reality.'

The differences between 'Relationism' and our European approach to relations

The difference between our theory, as advanced in this book, and that of other authors lies in the fact that, contrary to radical constructionism, we maintain that there are close links between the social relation as responsible for weaving the social fabric and as the expression of human nature – *in potentia* – that develops in a biophysical environment as well as a social one. The majority of authors who expound a Relational Sociology – such as, for example, Emirbayer,[43] White,[44] and Crossley[45] – reduce the relation to a transaction, to a narrative (the telling of stories), or to a network effect, and so forth. These are interrelated; thus, following Emirbayer and White, Crossley argues that social worlds 'comprise' networks of interaction and relations. It

39 Donati, *Teoria relazionale della società*, chapter 2.

40 H. White, *Identity and Control: How Social Formations Emerge* (Princeton NJ: Princeton University Press, 2008 [1992]).

41 R. Azarian, 'Social Ties: Elements of a Substantive Conceptualization', *Acta Sociologica*, 53 (2010), 323–338.

42 The 'double morphogenesis' refers to the fact that by engaging in actions to bring about social transformation, agents are themselves changed in the process (e.g. becoming regrouped, occupying new roles, having different positions upon society's distributions of scarce resources, and pursuing different goals from in the past and usually from one another).

43 M. Emirbayer, 'Manifesto for a Relational Sociology', *American Journal of Sociology*, 103 (1997), 281–317.

44 H. White, *Identity and Control.*

45 N. Crossley, *Towards Relational Sociology* (London: Routledge, 2011).

seems that society is like a 'space' where relations happen over time. He asserts that relations are lived trajectories of iterated interaction, built up through a history of interaction, but also entailing anticipation of future interaction. To him, sociologists should focus upon evolving and dynamic networks of interaction and relations conceived as transactions. In our opinion, this approach avoids any analysis from within social relations, their own internal constitution, and ultimately does not deal properly with the 'nature' of social relations.

Conversely, we treat social relations as a reality that interweaves elements deriving from nature (both the nature that is internal to human beings and that which is external, biophysical nature and material culture)[46] with effects deriving from the structural and cultural contexts and networks linking agent/actors.

In recent years, Relational Sociology has received increasing attention at the international level. Generally speaking, scholars have built upon the previous theories of White and/or Emirbayer. In the first case, Relational Sociology has been elided with structuralist network analysis.[47] In the second case, scholars have denied the emergent character of social relations, reproducing the misapprehension contained in Emirbayer's "Manifesto for a Relational Sociology" (1997) that speaks of a 'transactional' (not properly relational) sociology. We leave aside the 'figurational sociology' developed by Norbert Elias not because of its irrelevance, but because it does not provide a specific ontological and epistemological theory of social relations as such, despite Elias having explored many social phenomena as social relations.

Nevertheless, there are some important overlaps between these two lines of development from which we dissociate our approach.

(a) Neither 'connectivity' (in networks) nor 'transactions' (between people) *necessarily* entail social relations. Anyone can be 'connected' to some source (for instance, a journal, a retail outlet, or a charity) simply by being placed on a distribution list, which are frequently sold between enterprises and therefore indicate no

46 See Peter Dickens, *Society and Nature. Towards a Green Social Theory* (New York: Harvester Wheatsheaf, 1992).

47 See for instance Reza Azarian, *The General Sociology of Harrison White*, Dept. of Sociology, Stockholm University, 2003; R. Azarian, 'Social Ties: Elements of a Substantive Conceptualization', *Acta Sociologica*, 53 (2010), 323–338.

wish to belong on the part of recipients or interest in the contents received. 'Cold calling' is an even more blatant practice and example. There are no social relations at all between the population of recipients and that of senders. Relationally, such 'connectivity' is no greater than that between the aggregate of people who have been confronted by the same advertising hoarding. Similarly, 'transactions' is also a polysemic term which does not *necessarily* invoke or depend upon social relations. Its first dictionary referent (from the Latin *transactio*, *transactor* being a broker) is to 'a piece of commercial business done; a deal' (*OED*). Here, again, someone can buy and sell stocks and shares online, transacting without any contact with another at all. Similarly, if a public speaker convinces us that his/her argument is good, in what sense is this a transaction when even our acceptance remains unknown? At the other extreme, when a couple confesses their love for one another, this is relational, but what has been transacted? Equally, when people join a voluntary association (for a variety of motives), what is the deal? Ontologically, we need to give more attention to the relationship itself rather than subsuming all relations under an abstract noun such as 'transactions'.

(b) Network analysis in general enables the detection of patterns, often of practical utility – from the identification of isolates in the school playground to the movement of populations within an area, region, or state. But, to be so, some cause or generative mechanism has to be invoked in explanation of the pattern.[48] The same is the case for Emirbayer, whose 'Manifesto' contains multiple references to 'patterns' and 'patterning'. Both types of usage are confined to the level of the event and, in avoiding a stratified ontology that seeks for what causes the event (including actual aspects of it that defy experiencing), they are glaringly empiricist.[49] White himself later came to realize that network analysis can be an important tool to study how social ties among nodes can produce different

[48] Margaret S. Archer (ed.), *Generative Mechanisms Transforming Late Modernity*, Dordrecht, Springer, 2015.

[49] See Douglas Porpora on structures construed as patterns: 'Four Concepts of Social Structure', *Journal for the Theory of Social Behaviour*, 19 (1989), 195–212, and 'Why Don't Things Change? The Matter of Morphostasis', in Margaret S. Archer (ed.), *Generative Mechanisms Transforming Late Modernity* (Dordrecht: Springer, 2015), pp. 172–193.

structural outcomes, but he omits the cultural and agential dimensions of social relations. That is why, subsequently, Fuhse and others[50] have turned to a different approach that tries to free network analysis from these limitations, in order to detail some of the basic mechanisms of network formation such as the building up of relational expectations. In doing so, Fuhse has come to treat social relations according to Luhmann's view of relations as mere communications,[51] which, as another form of reductionism, does not change the approach to social relations in which networks remain linkages between nodes instead of networks of relations.

(c) Both transactions and 'snapshots' of networks in Relational Sociology are usually weak on interactive processes and how change over time is produced.[52] Especially when the issue is not geographically confined, such as 'inequality', the flat ontology leads some like Emirbayer simply to assert that repeated transactions result in practices that 'crystallize' into equalities or inequalities. Discussing immigrants, he maintains that the recently arrived acquire control over a valuable resource (e.g. information about employment opportunities), hoard their access to it (e.g. by sharing it only with others in their personal networks), and develop practices that perpetuate this restricted access (e.g. by staying in touch with their places of origin through frequent correspondence and visits home). *Hard, durable differences in advantages and disadvantages then crystallize around such practices. Unfolding transactions, and not preconstituted attributes, are thus what most effectively explain equality and inequality.*[53] Is this present-tense account plausible? Do 'preconstituted attributes', such as having a degree or a transferable skill, a job waiting for the migrant, or a friendship group of those well established in the host country, make no difference? Can any group of immigrants be treated as objectively homogeneous? All cannot visit 'home' and subjectively all do not think of it

50 Jan Fuhse and Sophie Mützel (Hrsg.), *Relationale Soziologie. Zur kulturellen Wende der Netzwerkforschung* (Wiesbaden: VS Verlag für Sozialwissenschaften, Springer Fachmedien, 2010).

51 Jan Fuhse, 'The Communicative Construction of Actors in Networks', *Soziale Systeme: Zeitschrift für soziologische Theorie*, 15 (2009), 85–105.

52 This need not be the case; Nick Crossley, for example, tracked network changes over time and supplemented this methodology with ethnographies of subjects (*Towards Relational Sociology*, London: Routledge, 2011, chapter 9).

53 M. Emirbayer, 'Manifesto for a Relational Sociology', 293, italics added.

as such, and neither may have anything to do with their 'unfolding transactions'.

Powell and Dépelteau,[54] leaning on Emirbayer's theory, have proposed a sort of handbook of the many different versions of Relational Sociology that the latter calls 'fighting words' whose defence requires 'epistemological vigilance'.[55] In fact it reads as a frenzied rhetoric for 'radical relationality', without coherence or consistency. The rhetoric behind this theoretical jihad simply corrals any past contributions – from Barnes and Bloors' 'strong programme', Marx, Foucault, Bourdieu, Garfinkle, Dorothy Smith, and Latour – that might increase the decibels of the clarion call. This is more like 'product placement' than serious theorizing; most of the above have been strenuously critiqued by those they have opposed, but theirs is a book of assertions rather than arguments.

In their introduction, Powell and Dépelteau certainly recognize that 'relational sociologists are more likely to emphasize how individuals are always-already enmeshed in relations of interdependency with others and cannot be understood, even theoretically, apart from their relational contexts.'[56] But they strongly argue against the emergent character of social relations, claiming that the latter do not possess any *sui generis* reality and therefore any causal properties of their own. They maintain that social relations are 'nothing more than patterns in the actions of individuals, patterns in the ways that individuals are constrained by each other's actions and are therefore dependent on one another.' Dépelteau 'advocates a single-level ontology in which relations are simply the transactions between interdependent individuals'.[57] Powell takes a subversive position by proposing a '*radical relationism*' according to which 'all phenomena, including individuals themselves, be understood as composed of relations'. Rather

[54] Christopher Powell and François Dépelteau (eds.), *Relational Sociology. Ontological and Theoretical Issues* (New York: Palgrave Macmillan, 2013); François Dépelteau and Christopher Powell (eds.), *Applying Relational Sociology. Relations, Networks, and Society* (New York: Palgrave Macmillan, 2013).

[55] M. Emirbayer, 'Relational Sociology as Fighting Words', in C. Powell and F. Dépelteau (eds.), *Relational Sociology. Ontological and Theoretical Issues*, p. 211.

[56] C. Powell and F. Dépelteau, *Introduction to Relational Sociology. Ontological and Theoretical Issues*, p. 2.

[57] *Ibid*, p. 9.

than relations being emergent from human action, humans themselves, social structures, and indeed non-human actors and forces all emerge from relations. Thus, human beings and all other phenomena are figurations. Relations are processes that can best be conceptualized as work, that is as transformative action. 'In this nonhumanist framework, the distinction between "social" and "natural" phenomena is arbitrary and anthropocentric; all social relations are also natural and vice versa. Structure and Agency appear not as two distinct types of phenomena but as two complementary and ultimately equivalent epistemological frameworks for understanding the same phenomena. This framework abolishes subject-object dualism and therefore employs reflexivity rather than objectivity as the standard of validation for truth claims.'[58] Anti-substantialism and anti-humanism are the tracks along which Powell launches his project of a new radical 'Relational Sociology'.

These editors state that their aims are epistemological but, in fact, are more often ontological. This boils down to the fundamentalist claim that everything is relational in some sense (which is uncontentious) to the mightily contentious claim that this consequently makes everything social. Ontological differences between 'Structure and Agency' (as bearers of different properties and powers) are (again) transcended, this time by the extravagant oxymoron that 'any given phenomenon is entirely, completely structured, and at the same time entirely, completely agential'.[59] All distinctions are fundamentally invalid, including those necessary to (any definition of) causal analysis, to be replaced by the play 'of what we call cause and effect, without requiring the separation entailed by these concepts'.[60] As intentionality, commitment, validation, worth and truth itself are rudely brushed off, the 'flat monism of radical relationality'[61] brings us back to the primitive post-modernism where the academic merely 'plays with the pieces' (Baudrillard).[62] Ultimately, the key to all this self-indulgent relativism

58 *Ibid*, p. 10.

59 C. Powell, 'Radical Relationism', in C. Powell and F. Dépelteau (eds.), *Relational Sociology. Ontological and Theoretical Issues*, p. 198.

60 *Ibid.*, p. 196.

61 *Ibid.*, p. 202. Powell has been the focus above, since Dépelteau simply engages in a distasteful personalization, flailing around without concern for accuracy even in his quotations (see p. 173, where we are even told the citation is 'word for word'!).

62 J. Baudrillard, 'On Nihilism', *On the Beach*, 6 (1984), 24–5.

is that at no point do these editors ever engage with an empirical problem in an attempt to explain it; the real world and perhaps especially the relations (very varied in kind and importance) making for the current crisis or for climate change or for practices such as human trafficking impose no discipline upon the intellectual posing of these rebels without a cause or a conscience.

In the end, Powell and Dépelteau recognize that they have not been able to define an ontological and epistemological framework for a coherent and readily identifiable Relational Sociology, since they have only been able to juxtapose various theories. They conclude by saying that Relational Sociology should be understood as a 'language game'.[63]

The relativist conclusion of this self-proclaimed handbook reveals its profound weaknesses. It seeks to persuade social scientists to regard the social relation in conflationary terms, and as an indeterminate notion. Moreover, the *eschaton* (ultimate reality) of a society loses its human qualities, in particular human freedom and intentionality, because the subject who bears them is lost, not as a casualty but through the militant anti-humanism of these editors. On the contrary, we claim that the human subject, as dependent on social relations as s/he might be, is or at least can be the proper subject of personal and Relational Reflexivity on objective reality.[64] The Relational Subject is able to distinguish her/himself from the objective and objectified social forms that are generated in social processes.

The morphogenesis of society and the role played by relational forms

What are 'social relations'?

For Donati's Relational Sociology, society does not 'have' relations but '*is*' relations.[65] Society is the product of associative and dissociative relations that arise from societal structures and cultures and how

[63] 'It is a handbook to the language games we are playing, and an invitation to join in': C. Powell and F. Dépelteau, *Introduction to Relational Sociology. Ontological and Theoretical Issues*, p. 12.

[64] See Andrew Collier, *Being and Worth* (London: Routledge, 1999) and *In Defence of Objectivity* (London: Routledge, 2003).

[65] P. Donati, *Teoria relazionale della società*, pp. 80–86; *Relational Sociology. A New Paradigm for the Social Sciences*, pp. 3–7.

human action continuously alters them. It is a matter of understanding how the structural dynamic of relations creates a relatively enduring social formation that is different from others because the generative dynamics of the relations that characterize it are different. The ultimate objective is to understand and explain the links that exist between the social morphogenesis of the relations that make for a given society or social form and the emergent structures that qualify a concrete society or social form as different from others.[66] First, however, it is necessary to get 'inside' the social relation.

If we conceptualize the social relation as reciprocal actions between Ego and Alter in a social context, the relation can be regarded either from the *subjective* side (of Ego and Alter, respectively) or as an *objective* reality existing between the two.

A) From the subjective point of view, Max Weber's definition has remained classic and is the origin of all action or 'actionistic' sociologies: the 'social relation is to be understood as a behaviour of more than one individual reciprocally established according to its content of meaning and oriented in conformity. The social relation therefore consists exclusively in the possibility that one acts socially in a given way (endowed with meaning), whatever the basis on which this possibility rests.'[67] Note that Weber does not attribute its own reality to the relation. What he stresses are two individuals and their actions, which conform to one another in certain ways by giving meaning to the action. For him, the meaning of the relation resides in the individual and does not have a causal relation with its object.[68] The social relation with others does not have its own meaning; it is only a subjectively understood symbolic reference (*refero*) for those involved.

[66] See Archer (*Social Origins of Educational Systems*, 1979, new edition 2013) for a morphogenetic analysis of how state educational systems came about with emergent centralized and decentralized relational organizations and what difference this made to processes of educational change in the next cycle of morphogenesis.

[67] Max Weber, *Economia e società* (Milan: Comunità, 1968), vol. I, pp. 23–24.

[68] For Weber's followers, meaning is a complex form of ideation that is elaborated by the subject him/herself, taking into account his/her life experiences. It is thus a relation that a subject has with a 'subjectively understood' object; for this reason, no causal relation exists between subject and object.

B) From the objective point of view, the relation is understood as a bond, connection or reciprocal tie between Ego and Alter. In this case, the relation is seen as the product of the objective conditioning that 'ties' Ego and Alter together. This bond (the *religo*) was analyzed by Emile Durkheim, in particular, who distinguished two main forms of it: mechanical solidarity (due to uniformity of consciousness given a low division of labour) and organic solidarity (the greater individualization of consciousness and strong interdependencies, in the wake of an intensified division of labour). In contrast to Weber, individual subjectivity does not feature as other than a resultant.

C) Here it is proposed to connect the *refero* and the *religo*, that is, to see them as interwoven dimensions giving rise to an emergent effect: the relation as the 'effect of reciprocity',[69] which is held to be a generative mechanism that operates through a combinatory mode (i.e. as 'combined provisions'[70] or, if preferred, as 'internal relations') of the symbolic-psychological axis (the Weberian *refero*) and of the instrumental-normative axis (the Durkheimian *religo*).[71]

In short, from analysis of the classical sociologists the following three semantics of the social relation are derived:

(i) the semantics of the relation as *refero*, that is, as a symbolic reference starting from a motivation to understand meanings;[72]

(ii) the semantics of the relation as *religo*, that is, as a bond, deriving from the structural connection constituted by norms and means;[73]

(iii) the generative semantics of the relation as an emergent phenomenon (relational effect). Here the relation between Ego and Alter is understood as an effect of reciprocity that produces a

[69] Georg Simmel (*The Philosophy of Money*, London and New York: Routledge, 2014 [1907]) uses the term *Wechselwirkung*, which is usually translated into English with the terms 'interaction, correlation, reciprocity, interdependency, interplay, reciprocation, reciprocal action'.

[70] 'Combined provisions' is a juridical expression indicating that two norms must be interpreted and applied together in that the one is necessarily combined with the other.

[71] P. Donati, *Teoria relazionale della società*, chapter 4.

[72] Here the entire sociology of Max Weber is decisive (in particular, his research on the Protestant ethic and the spirit of capitalism).

[73] Here the entire sociology of Emile Durkheim is decisive (in particular, his theory of the division of labour).

form (its own reality) endowed with its own properties and causal powers,[74] which requires making reference to the specific social context in which these interactions take place. Interactions always take place in a relational context (but it must be noted that, although relations themselves also always take place in a structural and cultural context, that context cannot be reduced to relations, in the same way that a relation cannot be reduced to its communicative content, since the former is the context of the latter). The context can define the social relation as a simple event (for example, a person asks for a beer in any pub, pays, and leaves), or as a bond created through multiple reiterations over time (for example, the relation between a patient and his long-standing doctor), or a bond that derives from ascriptive factors (for example, the relation between parents and children).

The relation as generative mechanism

Social morphogenesis begins within relations, and it is through relations that new social forms are generated. It is through social relations that contradictions and complementarities between the elements that compose the relation are, or are not, realized in varying ways and degrees.[75]

Morphostasis results when reciprocal action in social relations has a reproductive character based on negative feedback and usually reliant upon 'Communicative Reflexivity'.[76] Conversely, morphogenesis comes about when the relation involves the reflexivity of subjects, in either the autonomous or meta-reflexive mode, and entails positive feedback, in particular, relational feedbacks. A relational feedback differs from individual positive feedback (which is a personal variation introduced by Ego into the relationship with Alter), because it has transformatory consequences – however small – for the relational structure of the participants' network. It operates when the subjects perceive that their relational structure is a reality that influences

[74] Here the entire sociology of Georg Simmel is decisive (in particular, in his works on the philosophy of money and social differentiation).

[75] Margaret S. Archer, *Social Origins of Educational Systems*, and *Culture and Agency: The Place of Culture in Social Theory*, pp. 219–226 and 258–273.

[76] Margaret S. Archer, *Structure, Agency and the Internal Conversation* (Cambridge: Cambridge University Press, 2003).

them for good or for evil as Relational Subjects. It is thus not simply activity-dependent, as must necessarily be the case, but also has to be subjectively (though fallibly) recognized as such. Then, the agents can attempt to reproduce or modify the relational structure of their network. They can stabilize it, change it, or destroy it, depending on the kind of reflexivity that governs the feedbacks, and providing of course reflexivity is not fractured or merely expressive.

As such, the relation has properties and powers that generically surpass 'social interactions' (which have an *événenemental* character: they are pure 'events'). Among various properties and powers of relations to be accentuated are at least two that are connected to one another.

First, the social relation is intrinsically reflexive, in the sense that it 'is always bent back' on to the subjects that are in the relation. However, reflexivity can be minimal, impeded, distorted, or fractured and in that case so, too, will be the relationality between the agents/actors. Precisely because they 'are (i.e. they exist, from the Latin '*ex-sistere*', which means being *out* of themselves) in relation', agents/actors must think and act *into* the relation between them. The structure of the relation is reflexive in that the axis of the *refero* (as discussed earlier) is not only a symbolic reference to the goal that Ego and Alter intend to realize (since they 'are in relation'), but is also a bending back of what emerged from the interactions based upon the prior motivations of the participants, followed by deliberation about some new course of action to be undertaken. It is in this process that the ethical value of the relation resides, in as much as the relation demands a 'response' (responsibility), that is, as part and parcel of being accountable to oneself and to others for the outcomes of interactions. To say that relations have an ethical dimension, simply means that relations – as actions – have a moral value because what they mean to the subjects is a good or an evil or a mixture of both (besides its objective consequences).

Second, and in parallel, this means that the social relation can never work purely mechanically because it has a ternary, not binary, structure. Automatic mechanisms are binary (stimulus-response) and do not have their own purposes (intentionality), whereas the social relation – if and insofar as its configuration constitutes a *generative* mechanism – *contains a human finalism* – one that may or may not be realized because of other countervailing mechanisms that are at play. Obviously, *qua* relationship it is not a given that the relation's finalism corresponds to the ends of the singular subjects who are in a given relationship, even when they are in agreement. On the contrary, it is highly probable that the outcome caused by the relation is distanced from the particular goals (wishes, expectations, etc.) of the singular subjects involved, precisely because it is an emergent effect that mediates between subjects. Nevertheless, in order for subjects to sustain a generative relation, they must acknowledge a finalistic dimension to their relation. That finality may simply be to continue enjoying the products of their relationships (e.g. on-going friendship or to hone a team's performance with the aim of winning the sport's top trophy).

The tasks of Part I

Part I answers the question: what is a Relational Subject? As yet, a formal definition has not been given because we fully acknowledge that this concept is hard to grasp, precisely because it involves something quite different from the notions embedded in Western individualism or collectivism (both politically and philosophically). However, we are certainly not the first academics to have wanted something different from both that is not some kind of compromise between them. In advance of us, certain distinguished analytical philosophers sought to achieve the same task with the notion of the 'Plural Subject', a concept intended to meet the same desiderata and one we do not dismiss as a 'Third Way'. We respect their efforts and have to engage with them, otherwise there is no justification for introducing yet another concept – that of the Relational Subject. However, as will be seen in the next chapter, our main reservations about the Plural Subject concern the absence of *emergence* in the form of 'relational goods and evils', the absence of *reflexivity* about the conduct of joint action, and the final absence of any conception of the *morphogenesis* of how relations begin, the course they take, and the effects of the outcomes to which they give rise. These three features are central to our concept of the Relational Subject. Thus we hope that the critique that follows of the Plural Subject also usefully serves to enable readers to gain a realistic sense of what the Relational Subject is, in a way that formal definitions cannot do. We also have a debt towards these philosophers because the three whose work we examine quite closely – John Searle,[77]

[77] J. Searle, *The Construction of Social Reality* (New York: Simon & Schuster, 1995).

Margaret Gilbert,[78] and Raimo Tuomela[79] – all exemplify the power of everyday examples to speak more directly to any reader than does lengthy exegesis. It is no accident that we have tried to take this leaf out of their books and articles. However, for those who also require formal definitions we present ours:

> The term '*Relational Subject*' refers to individual and collective social subjects in that they are '*relationally constituted*', that is, *in as much as they generate emergent properties and powers through their social relations.* These relational goods and evils have internal effects upon the subjects themselves and external effects upon their social environments.

To all five of us, joint action – when entailing collaboration, co-operation, or joint commitment – are not satisfactorily explained in individualist terms, namely as aggregates of the 'like-minded' (those sharing the same personal beliefs, aims, concerns and so forth) who somehow come together. The response of these three philosophers is to work upon the commonly used expression, 'We think', and to maintain that, in one way or another, this is an expression of *shared intentionality*. The subjects involved intend to engage in the same action (joint action) without this deriving from some putative collective entity such as a 'group mind'. Thus, how collective intentionality can be conceptualized as underpinning 'We-thinking', without appealing to such dubious entities, is the task they all address.

We tackle this generic problem quite differently, by focussing upon the *shared orientation* of the subjects involved to the emergent consequences that they themselves generate through their relationship. They can produce both 'relational goods' and 'relational evils', and their *shared orientation* is towards extending the former and eradicating the latter, without any guarantee that they will be successful or that their relation will not break down in the process. For the participants to be orientated towards a particular emergent good or evil does not assume that they have the same thoughts in their heads or any version of 'We-thinking' because their personal intentions will be singular and can diverge in terms of intentionality. As will be seen, this is where both *realism* and *reflexivity* come into play in our account of the Relational Subject; *realism* because the subjects in relation are *oriented* to the

78 M. Gilbert, *On Social Facts* (London-New York: Routledge, 1989).

79 R. Tuomela, *Philosophy of Sociality: The Shared Point of View* (Oxford: Oxford University Press, 2005).

emergent products generated by their relation; *reflexivity* because each participant exercises the mental ability of all normal people to consider themselves in relation to their (social) contexts and vice versa.[80] In our argument that follows, we circumscribe this basic definition to refer only to those elaborated features of the agents' contexts that their relationship has been responsible for generating.

We recognize that the notion of the Relational Subject could be problematic for most of today's social sciences, which continue to oscillate between methodological individualism and holism. This book indicates another path that is not situated midway between the individual (the Self) and the whole (the social system), nor is it a mixture or a bridge between the two, but is located on another stratum of reality. This plane is the 'relational order of reality.' Our basic thesis is that *the subject is social in that he/she is relational.* To maintain that the subject is relational means that he/she is part of a 'We' that is not a super-ordinate entity but is, instead, a relation.

[80] Margaret S. Archer, *Making Our Way Through the World: Human Reflexivity and Social Mobility*, p. 4.

2 *The Plural Subject versus the Relational Subject*

MARGARET S. ARCHER AND PIERPAOLO DONATI

In ordinary life, we, *qua* individuals, often speak in the plural referring to a 'We'. People say: we had lunch together, we went on holiday together, we wrote a book together, we furnished our house together, we had the same opinion about that, and so on and so forth. This 'we' is a term whose referent remains unspecified and serves only to indicate who was involved in an event. Its reality is taken for granted in everyday life. If one asks people to say what constitutes the 'we' they are talking about, most likely they will indicate a number of individuals and/or give a list of names, starting or ending with I myself. In ordinary language use, the 'we' appears to refer to an aggregate of people, seemingly wanting, doing, or thinking the same thing.

However, most philosophers and social scientists agree that the 'we' cannot be a simple aggregate of individuals who are supposed to share an idea, an action or a purpose. There must be more than that, but when they try to give an explanation of what lies behind the 'we', they also differ greatly in their accounts of it. The understanding of what constitutes the 'we' – in terms of intentions, beliefs, opinions, attitudes, orientations, thoughts, and actions – is crucial in comprehending most, though not all, aspects of the social. Therefore, it becomes essential to reach a clearer and sounder view of the 'we' as a social subject.

In this chapter, we begin (please, note that whenever one of us speaks each of us does so as part of a 'we') by considering the notion of the 'Plural Subject', which has received a lot of attention as a generic answer to the question about who and what the 'we' is that is so influential in social life. We want to show that the explanations of 'Plural Subject' theorists are both ill-founded and inadequate for the job. Thus, we put forward an alternative theory, which introduces the 'Relational Subject', as a more complex and robust concept of what a 'we-subject' is. From the sociological viewpoint, phrases such as 'we think' or 'we act' can and should be analyzed within a conceptual framework that regards them as emergent effects, relational in kind and existing and developing over time. It is argued that their (morphogenetic) development depends upon the degree of Relational Reflexivity possessed by those agents who belong to any particular 'we'. The relational reality of the 'we' – its ontology – becomes understandable if and only if both methodological individualism and holism are rejected from the outset.

Much of this chapter aims at making the notion of the 'we' more reflexive, thus precluding any kind of reductionism and firmly setting it apart from those theories that reduce it to a set of individuals acting collectively. The 'we' is built up by agents through their enduring relationality, which has its own reality and therefore its own properties and powers, namely, to generate the Relational Subject. A better understanding of these dynamics can help us to distinguish the different ways in which the 'we' influences social life and produces its own *sui generis* outcomes. Our main claim is that, in order to understand the constitution and vicissitudes of the 'we', the social sciences need to adopt a relational approach based upon a social ontology of relational realism.

On Plural Subjectivity and the Relational Subject

What does 'we think' mean and what turns upon its different meanings?

The Plural Subject rests on the collective concept of 'We thinking' and it stands or falls with this notion. 'We think', as used by ordinary people in everyday conversations about their beliefs, intentions, and actions (as in 'We're going to dinner together'), has intrigued many analytical philosophers in the last two decades. Why has the use of the first person plural (along with the possessive pronoun 'our') recently become so significant to them, given that such grammatical forms have a long history in most languages?[1] For some, the simple fact that 'we' make statements about 'our' shared intentions (beliefs, goals, identities and actions, agreements and acceptances) has become the lynch-pin for understanding and explaining our 'sociality' itself, at the most

[1] Variations in how these forms are linguistically encoded from language to language do not seem to have any bearing on the arguments advanced or their criticism here.

micro- to the most macro-levels. From these grammatical origins, theories of 'joint', 'collective' or 'plural' thought and action have been developed by many prominent analytical philosophers (including Michael Bratman, Margaret Gilbert, John Searle, and Raimo Tuomela). Most of them hold that the theories they have advanced on the basis of 'we thinking' do the biggest of jobs: nothing short of redefining the subject-matter of social science and its appropriate mode of explanation.

That is why it is worth coming to grips with what 'we think' means, and it does not mean the same thing to the four exponents just named. As social theorists we will be critical of both their foundational views of human sociality and the explanatory programmes they advance for dealing with the social order. We will be yet more contentious and maintain that endorsement of and extrapolation from 'we thinking' are not profitable paths for social theorists to follow. Instead, we suggest that taking the 'Relational Subject' seriously does solve many of the difficulties that the above theorists have confronted. Relations and relationality are central to sociology (and other social sciences), whereas the analytical philosophers who have been intrigued by the 'we think' issue have also attempted to use it as the basis from which the social order can be derived by deductive logic.

How does the fact that people often say 'we think' provide a springboard for the conceptualization of human sociality and the understanding and/or explanation of the societal order? Analytical philosophers are not homogeneous in how they construe 'we think', but for all it provides the key to major aspects of the social: to 'co-ordination' for Bratman, to 'co-operation' for Searle, to 'commitment' for Tuomela, and to 'obligation' for Gilbert. All variously see 'we think' as being deontic – the generic source of 'rights', 'duties', 'obligations', 'authorizations', 'requirements', 'permissions', and so on, and this is how the springboard to the societal level works.

In case we are held to exaggerate the ambitious nature of at least three of these four projects in redefining the basis of 'sociality' and then rooting their accounts of the 'societal' in it, let these philosophers express their ambitions in their own words.[2] Searle states his

[2] Michael E. Bratman alone ('Shared Intention', *Ethics*, 104 (1993), 97–113) explicitly declines to discuss shared intentionality at the institutional level (e.g. 'The Philosophy Department intends to . . .').

ontological aim as being: '[t]o construct an account of social and institutional reality'.[3] Tuomela considers that he is writing about 'the conceptual resources and philosophical prerequisites that a proper understanding and explaining of the social world requires' presenting 'almost a philosophical "theory of everything" in the social world relying on the 'we-perspective'.[4] Gilbert's claim is that 'analysis of our concepts of "shared" action" discovers a structure that is constitutive of social groups as such . . . going for a walk together may be considered as a paradigm of social phenomena in general.'[5] Later on, she amplifies this statement: 'I believe that the concept of joint commitment is a fundamental social concept – perhaps *the* fundamental social concept'.[6]

An 'action' replay of the 1950s debate in philosophy of social science

In many ways the different contributions of these four philosophers over the last twenty years replicate the major controversy of the 1950s and 1960s between defenders of methodological individualism, the protagonists of holism, and a number of those who settled, sometimes uneasily, for a position 'in between', frequently termed methodological collectivism.[7] The earlier debate (see Brodbeck and O'Neill)[8] concerned social structure, its ontology, and the propriety of irreducible 'group variables' (structural or cultural) figuring in causal explanations. The more recent debate has, as it were, transferred attention from 'Structure' to 'Agency'. Resemblances do not stop there because *all the positions taken up in the earlier debate are reproduced in the later one, without being superseded or supplemented.* The omission of emergence remains glaring. Instead, 'structure' is quite

[3] J. Searle, *Making the Social World* (Oxford: Oxford University Press, 2010), p. 60.
[4] Raimo Tuomela, *The Philosophy of Sociality* (Oxford: Oxford University Press, 2010), pp. vii–viii.
[5] Margaret Gilbert, *Living Together* (Lanham, MD: Rowman and Littlefield, 1996), p. 178.
[6] *Ibid.*, p. 366.
[7] Archer, *Realist Social Theory: The Morphogenetic Approach*, pp. 33–64.
[8] May Brodbeck (ed.), *Readings in the Philosophy of the Social Sciences* (New York: Macmillan, 1971); John O'Neill (ed.), *Modes of Individualism and Collectivism* (London: Heinemann, 1973).

literally pushed into the 'Background'. That controversial term and manoeuvre of Searle's[9] – duplicated by Manicas[10] – has stimulated a debate in its own right, but it is not the one with which we engage here.

Where the meaning of 'we think' is concerned, the one rejected by all four analytical philosophers is 'aggregate individualism'. That is the position where 'shared'[11] thought denotes nothing more than a summation (an average or majority view) of what those involved in an issue happen to think *qua* individuals, such as the results of an attitude survey. Of course, none of the four deny that we all have individual thoughts, beliefs, and commitments that are the reasons for (some of) our actions,[12] and no more do we.

a. Bratman's conventional Methodological Individualism

The methodological individualist 'slot' in the earlier debate is represented by Bratman, who avows that his 'approach to shared intention is broadly individualistic in spirit.'[13] To him, 'we think' means that we can indeed have a shared intention with another, such that two people intend to paint the house together, which, if all goes well between them, results in the joint action by which the house gets painted. In rejecting 'aggregate individualism', he argues: 'On the one hand, it is clearly not enough for a shared intention to paint the house together that each intends to paint the house. Such coincident intentions do not even insure that each knows of the other's intention or that each is appropriately committed to the joint activity itself. On the other hand, a shared intention is not an attitude in the mind of some super-agent

[9] J. Searle, *The Construction of Social Reality* (London: Penguin, 1995), pp. 127–147.

[10] Peter T. Manicas (*A Realist Philosophy of Social Science*, Cambridge: Cambridge University Press, 2006) relegates structural and cultural properties to being 'materials at hand', without the capacity to exert causal powers but also without giving any explanation of why some are within easy reach of certain actors but out of reach for others.

[11] 'Joint' or 'shared' are used as the most neutral terms available because some (like Bratman) would jib at the word 'collective' and only Margaret Gilbert fully endorses the 'Plural Subject' concept as holistic.

[12] Raimo Tuomela (*The Philosophy of Sociality*) has given the most effort to distinguishing between what he terms the 'I-mode' of thought and action etc., exercised by a singular person (or 'privately' as he prefers to put it) and the 'We-mode' (also exercised by persons in the singular, hence his preference for the terminology he uses).

[13] Bratman, 'Shared Intention', p. 112.

consisting literally of some fusion of the two agents. There is no single mind which is the fusion of your mind and mine.'[14] Bratman argues that neither shared intentions nor joint action necessarily entail such a group agent, and only Gilbert is willing to appropriate the term holism and to defend mental fusion under certain conditions.

Bratman tackles the fundamental problem for the individualist, namely that *I* cannot intend to *J*, where *J*-ing is a *joint* performance. The separate thoughts of two individuals, even if both want to *J together* (walk, shop, or marry), is insufficient even though 'my conception of our *J*-ing can function in my plans in ways similar to my conception of my own *A*-ing', whatever the latter project may be.[15] A shared intention requires not only that I intend we *J but also* that I know you too intend that we *J*. Even if they do know this of one another – or believe they do – that does not require the pair to have (or even aim at having) a shared conception of how they are to paint the house together. Because some notions would be contradictory (painting it blue all over or entirely red), negotiation about and coordination of the sub-plans of each is also necessary. It takes the willingness of both satisfactorily to mesh their sub-plans for a shared intention[16] to be said to exist (which is similar to the *relationists'* transactions). If the pair do get the house painted as a 'we' through their joint action, 'they do not, or need not, go so far as to constitute anything deserving to be called *a novel plural subject*, with its own distinctive states of intention. Joint action is just that: the joint and intentional production of some effect.'[17]

b. Searle's weaker Methodological Individualism

Searle also begins with a straightforward rejection of aggregative individualism: collective intentional behaviour '[c]annot be analysed as just the summation of individual behaviour'.[18] During the twenty years he has been writing on 'we intentionality' – for him the most important aspect of 'we think' – he has made low-key asides implying an

[14] *Ibid.*, p. 98. [15] *Ibid.*, p. 102.

[16] For his precise formulation see Bratman, *ibid.*, p. 106f.

[17] Philip Pettit and David Schweikard, 'Joint Actions and Group Agents', *Philosophy of the Social Sciences*, 36 (2006), 30.

[18] J. Searle, 'Collective Intentions and Actions', in Philip R. Cohen, Jerry Morgan, and Martha E. Pollock (eds.), *Intentions in Communication* (Cambridge, MA: MIT Press, 1990), p. 401.

allegiance to methodological individualism. The following can stand as his summary statement: 'the general demands of '"methodological individualism" do not require that we-intentions be reducible to I-intentions, because the requirement that all intentionality exist in individual brains does not imply that the content that exists in the individual brains cannot exist in a plural grammatical form.'[19] Two people cleaning the yard together can each have in their separate heads the thought that 'We are cleaning the yard'. Why does he hold that supplementing our individual mental repertoires by this irreducible 'we' element is possible and preferable?

Three reasons are given. These appear problematic in themselves, and in combination they sit uneasily with methodological individualism. First, Searle criticizes attempts to reduce 'We intentionality' to 'I intentionality' plus something else, usually mutual beliefs. For example, in Bratman earlier, the addition was called 'knowledge' (taking the form 'I know that you, too, intend that we'). Because we cannot get inside anyone's head but our own, I cannot 'know' this of you; it must constitute a belief about you. So, too, by extension must notions of 'common knowledge' and of matters being 'out in the open'. Searle's objection is that the 'we intend' (to clear the yard together) means that I intend to do it in the belief that you, too, intend it do it and this results 'in a potentially infinite hierarchy of beliefs. "I believe that you believe that that I believe . . . ," and so on'.[20] Presumably, this infinity of beliefs about beliefs rules out any resting place from which a shared intention could emanate, although Searle does not actually state this conclusion.

Second, to Searle, another major difficulty with a procedure reliant upon beliefs about beliefs 'is that it does not add up to a sense of *collectivity* [whereas] the crucial element in collective intentionality is a sense of doing (wanting, believing etc.) something together.'[21] Third – again a separate point, despite the sentence running straight on – 'and the individual intentionality that each person has is derived *from* the collective intentionality that they share.' Does this mean, 'I would only want to do some yard clearance if we do it together'? If so, this does not seem to be an *a priori* matter but one that is empirically variable. These are the reasons Searle uses to claim that (in relation to clearing

[19] J. Searle, *Making the Social World*, p. 47.

[20] J. Searle, *The Construction of Social Reality*, p. 24.

[21] *Ibid.*, pp. 24–25.

the yard together), each of the two heads contains the plural form of intentionality – 'We intend'.

Because our notion of the 'Relational Subject' does not entail 'we think' in any version whatsoever (see the section entitled 'How Relational Subjects generate relational goods and evils'), neither does it become entangled with the foregoing issues. Nevertheless, it may be useful to indicate why the three points that Searle makes central to his case seem to be misguided and that his final point sits uneasily with canonical methodological individualism.[22]

As concerns Searle's first argument about the infinite regress of mutual beliefs, we simply point out that the difficulties of knowing for sure what someone else believes is part of the fallibility of all our knowledge claims, and yet people do have reasons to hold certain beliefs sufficient for them to act upon them.[23] The latter may provide a terminus short of infinity for strategies such as Bratman's. In any case, Searle's dissatisfaction with this type of account, or with Bratman's token of it, provides no justification for his directly imputing 'we think' into two heads. The mutual and reciprocal intentionality of our 'Relational Subjects' does not depend upon *their thinking the same thing*, that is literally 'being of one mind' or, as Gilbert puts it, intending 'as a body'. However intriguing Alter's thoughts may be to Ego (if romantically involved, during a business deal, or betting at cards), they remain Alter's and *vice versa*.

Second, the importance of the *sense of collectivity* or the feeling of togetherness, for which a sociological case can indeed be made and we will be making one, is not logically entailed by Searle's 'we think', because he agrees someone can be misguided or mistaken in thinking it. Thus, he admits that 'collective intentionality in my head can make a purported reference to other members of a collective *independently of the question whether or not there are such members*.'[24] In that case, the 'we' is wrongly projected because there is no 'we' to which 'we think' or 'we intend' refers or can refer. (Such cases of wish-fulfilment – or whatever they may be – also undermine the derivative status assigned above to 'I think'). Thus, it is admitted that 'I may

22 The canon is taken to be J. W. N. Watkins, 'Methodological Individualism and Social Tendencies', in May Brodbeck (ed.) *Readings in the Philosophy of the Social Sciences* (New York: Macmillan, 1968).

23 Andrew Collier, *In Defence of Objectivity* (London: Routledge, 2003).

24 Searle, 'Collective Intentions and Actions', p. 407 (italics added).

be mistaken in taking it that the "we" in "we intend" actually refers to a we.'[25] It is therefore in order to ask what makes 'we intending' something necessarily plural? We concur with Pettit and Schweikard's response: 'Not the fact that a number of people instantiate it, since Searle allows that I may instantiate such a state in the mistaken belief that others do so too. So what then? We see no answer in Searle's work and find his position on this issue inherently obscure.'[26] What we suggest in the section entitled 'How Relational Subjects generate relational goods and evils' is that there is no need to get into this position. Moreover, if 'cooperation' and feelings of 'togetherness' are at stake, the position adopted must also be capable of dealing with the obverse feelings of antipathy and uncooperativeness – and not merely as unintended consequences.

Third, we do not see any sociological grounds upon which personal intentions should be held to be derivative from collective intentionality.[27] His defence of the latter is confined to intentional states where I am doing something only as part of our doing something. Such doings are not restricted to the informal (sweeping the yard together), but include playing in a football game or in an orchestra, or taking part in a ballet.[28] As purported examples in which 'I only intend as part of our intending',[29] these are not watertight. Whilst it can be true that 'We want to win the game, play the symphony,' and so on, it is not necessarily the case that this constitutes collective intentionality. Quite different individual intentions are compatible with these joint actions. For example, particular people may play in the hope of being talent spotted, or, in a different kind of play, one actor, dancer, or instrumentalist 'upstages' others for personal reasons. Thus, genuine collective intentionality would imply

25 Searle, *ibid.*, p. 408. 26 Pettit and Schweikard, *ibid.*, pp. 31–32.

27 Antti Saaristo's defence of this position by means of Tuomela's 'we-mode' thinking falls short. See A. Saaristo, 'There Is No Escape from Philosophy: Collective Intentionality and Empirical Social Science', *Philosophy of the Social Sciences*, 36 (2006), 42. He maintains that in the we-mode, 'I figure out what is *our* goal in the situation at hand and what is *our* best means for achieving that goal, and then form a we-intention of the form "*We* will do X". Only when I have reached this stage do I *derive* my individual-mode intention from the we-intention.' In this case, 'I' have merely 'derived' 'my' intention from the one that 'I' have imputed to the collectivity!

28 Searle, 'Collective Intentions and Actions', pp. 402–403.

29 Searle, *The Construction of Social Reality*, pp. 23–4.

a commitment to joint action, but the former cannot be deduced from the latter.[30]

Moreover, these examples all invoke 'choreography', by means of a score, a script, or the rules of the game, which partly regulate players' movements. Searle holds these to belong to the 'Background' (as do the skills of the actors), that is the context necessary to understand what they are doing. Conversely, *accounting* for how the situations or contexts in which interaction takes place came to be shaped that way is part of our explanatory programme, which is both diachronic and synchronic. A 'Background' of rules, roles and resources cannot just be 'wheeled in and out' like stage scenery. Their existence and the form they take calls for sociological explanation because there is no action without a context and the latter partially shapes the former (by affecting motivation, imposing constraints, and affording enablements). However, the admission that the 'Background' needs to be brought in to provide adequate explanations sits uncomfortably with any claim to be working in conformity to methodological individualism. 'Background' features cannot be assumed *a priori* to be reducible to individual terms.

c. Tuomela's Methodological Collectivism

Unifying Tuomela's contributions is the notion that the 'social world cannot be adequately studied without making use of the distinction between the notions of having an attitude and acting as a group member versus as a private person'.[31] The former corresponds to what he calls 'we-mode thinking and acting' and the latter to 'I-mode' thought and action. Initially, this distinction has intuitive appeal, especially for those of us brought up on 1950s social psychology about how differently individual subjects believe and behave when they become part of

30 Ultimately, however, Searle's supposed super-ordinate status for collective intentionality rests either upon biology: 'The biologically primitive sense of the other person as a candidate for shared intentionality is a necessary condition of all collective behavior and hence of all conversation' ('Collective Intentions and Actions', p. 415), or later upon a more Habermasian view of language: 'once you have a shared language you already have a social contract . . . language is constitutive of institutional reality' (*ibid.*, pp. 62–63) because he stresses 'the social character of the communication situation, the conventional character of the devices used' (*ibid.*, p. 80). Thus, the presumed tendency towards human cooperation is admitted not to be derivative from collective intentionality.

31 Tuomela, *The Philosophy of Sociality*, p. 46.

small groups. The 'individual' who works in the 'I-mode' is not defined but seems to be the kind of instrumental rationalist who appears in the 2×2 tables of game theorists. Whatever else they may be, these individuals are not 'Relational Subjects'.

Aggregate individualist explanations are reserved for those interacting in the 'I-mode': 'In the case of I-mode groups, there is only "aggregated", although possibly conditional, private responsibility for what a member does'.[32] I-mode thought and action certainly does not preclude joint actions, such as two motorists coming from different directions who jointly move the log that blocks the road for both drivers. Because we-mode groups are based on voluntary membership, by a person 'signing on as a member' and accepting the group's basic goals, beliefs, norms, and practices, this appears to be straightforward methodological individualism. Tuomela reinforces this impression when he states: '[s]ocial groups are not agents in an ontological sense' and 'a group cannot literally have an attitude'.[33] It thus comes as a surprise when he writes that the 'concept of we-mode in itself contains the notion of group (and expresses part of the group-perspective). *It is a holistic institutional notion*'.[34] This is because '[t]hinking or acting for a we-mode reason (group reason) entails thinking or acting *for the group*' (idem). Indeed, he states that members 'act as one agent'. Nevertheless, Tuomela seems most properly characterized as a methodological collectivist, one who basically follows May Brodbeck's[35] advice to eliminate 'group variables', unless they are indispensable for explanation, and Mandelbaum's[36] counsel to translate them into individual terms whenever possible. Hence, for Tuomela, the 'group member level is, as it were, an appropriate translation or re-description of the group level.'[37]

We-mode thinking entails various interconnected concepts in addition to we-mode intentions (such as, 'We will perform joint action X together'). There are we-mode reasons, especially collective commitment to the group's 'ethos', which 'glues' members together, and the 'collectivity condition', which involves group members necessarily 'standing or falling' together. Of these, the 'central assumption' and,

32 *Ibid.*, p. 12. 33 *Ibid.*, p. 10. 34 *Ibid.*, p. 14 (italics added).

35 May Brodbeck, *Readings in the Philosophy of the Social Sciences.*

36 Maurice Mandelbaum, 'Societal Facts', in John O'Neill (ed.), *Modes of Individualism and Collectivism* (London: Heinemann, 1973), p. 229.

37 Tuomela, *ibid.*, p. 47.

thus, the core meaning of 'we think' to Tuomela 'is that the members of a group share an ethos, E, that consists of contents such as goals, beliefs, values, standards and norms',[38] which they should accept, satisfy, maintain, and promote.

If the 'we-mode' hangs upon behaving towards the group 'ethos' in the above ways, then its acceptability turns upon the answers to two questions: (i) What kinds of intragroup relations are held to bring about and sustain this conformity? (ii) Is there a *consistency of contents* making up the group 'ethos' such that members can be said to share them, where sharing stands for all the forms of normativity held in common as listed earlier? These are two separate questions: (i) is posed at the Socio-Cultural level and is about the extent of intragroup consensus and (ii) at the level of cultural systems and about the coherence of the ideas involved.[39]

To ask about consensus within the group is crucial to the meaning of 'we think', given that Tuomela has also agreed that '[g]roups may have goals and interests that members do not have and that may even conflict with the members' goals and interests'.[40] In addition, there may be compromises that 'no single member finds privately acceptable'.[41] Pettit's[42] discussion of the 'discursive dilemma' that can result in this situation under majority voting conditions[43] cannot just be dismissed as 'perhaps not very representative of group decision-making' (*idem*). This simply begs the question of what would count as 'representative', and it is doubtful whether that question makes sense sociologically. In any case, what 'I think' differs from what the group says 'we think'. Under what circumstances this can arise requires reference to the *prior* Constitution (in both senses) of the group and the empirical relations at work within it.[44]

38 *Ibid.*, p. 18. 39 Archer, *Culture and Agency*, and see Chapter 5.
40 Tuomela, *ibid.*, p. 38. 41 Tuomela, *ibid.*, p. 59.
42 Philip Pettit, *A Theory of Freedom: From the Psychology to the Politics of Agency* (Cambridge: Polity Press, 2001).
43 Pettit illustrates this dilemma by supposing that three people, A, B, and C, are asked to generate a common body of judgements by majority vote on each issue: whether p; whether if p, then q; and whether q. He demonstrates that the group may find itself committed to holding that p; that if p, then q; and that not-q.
44 P. Donati, *Social Subjectivities and the Complex of Citizenship in Advanced Societies: A Relational Theory of Collective Action*, paper presented at the 30th International Conference of the IIS, Kobe (5–9 August 1991), and *La cittadinanza societaria* (Rome: Laterza, 2000), pp. 197–228.

Question (ii) asks whether the ethos of a group is ever sufficiently coherent to form a basis for the 'we-mode' of thinking to be meaningful as presented by Tuomela. If an 'ethos' denotes a shared set of practices and understandings, a view common enough with regard to culture though one we hold to be misguided,[45] the Roman Catholic Church fails to meet these two criteria of *sharedness*. This is despite the existence of its Magisterium (formal and binding teaching authority), which most normative groups lack. 'Practices', from the sexual norms advocated in *Humanae Vitae* to the liturgical norms endorsed by the Second Vatican Council, are respectively widely ignored or hotly contested. 'Understandings' are equally problematic. At every Sunday Mass it is the duty of the faithful to say the Creed, but were it broken down into its component propositions, the most diverse array of understood meanings would result. Were Tuomela to respond that all the same those at Sunday Mass still stand up and say the same words, we would reply that this is to slide from observing an overt 'sharing' of ideas into the assumption of a collective ideational 'ethos', one just as unhelpful as assuming that all American pupils who daily salute the flag mean the same thing by doing so. Thus, what, 'we think' in 'we-mode' thinking remains elusive.

d. Gilbert's Holism

Precisely the opposite is the case for Gilbert. Since her doctorate *On Social Facts* (1978 and the eponymous book 1989), Durkheim has been her guide for defining the range of *social* phenomena. Thus, her answer to the question, what makes a population a social group, is when it is a Plural Subject and not an aggregate; a Plural Subject being a Durkheimian 'synthesis *sui generis*'.[46] Gilbert has consistently called herself a holist and continues to regard this debate about human sociality as 'the question of individualism versus holism'[47] – the only two positions she acknowledges in social ontology.[48] Hence, the concept

[45] Margaret S. Archer, 'The Myth of Cultural Integration', *British Journal of Sociology*, 36 (1985), 333–353; Archer, 'Collective Reflexivity: A Relational Case for it', in C. Powell and F. Dépelteau (eds.) *Relational Sociology: From Project to Paradigm* (New York: Palgrave Macmillan, 2013), pp. 145–161.

[46] M. Gilbert, *Living Together*, p. 268.

[47] M. Gilbert, *Sociality and Responsibility: New Essays in Plural Subject Theory* (Lanham, MD: Rowman and Littlefield, 2000), p. 155.

[48] Because Tuomela regards 'we intentionality' as *definable* in terms of individual predicates (*The Philosophy of Sociality*, p. 119), he registers as an Individualist

of a joint commitment as applied to a Plural Subject 'is a holistic one in the following sense: it cannot be analyzed in terms of a sum or aggregate of personal commitments',[49] although she has no truck with dubious entities such as 'group minds'.

The meaning of 'we think' (intend, belief, act) is explicitly holistic because a Plural Subject *arises directly from a joint commitment*, which 'is the commitment of two or more individuals considered as a unit or whole.'[50] This Plural Subject is constituted by its 'we thinking', because those involved subscribe to p 'as a body' (e.g. 'we eat in the cafeteria after the departmental meeting'), without this custom necessarily being or becoming the goal of any of them. 'We think' is thus derivative from the 'joint acceptance' (voiced or unvoiced) that constitutes the Plural Subject. Its heritage is avowedly in social contract theory, and if that has succumbed to the objection at 'there was no such agreement', Gilbert suggests that '[I]f actual contract theory is rejected, plural subject theory should be explored in its stead. Plural subject theory may be the truth in actual contract theory'.[51] Despite the plausibility of her everyday examples about how people start to walk together or have coffee together, we find this less than convincing in the absence of any sociological account of the causes of origin and those of continuation of such 'contracts'. Agreements involve human relationships, relations have histories, and their trajectories can transform original agreements into their contraries, yet Gilbert can be said to offer at most a 'one step account'.

This she seems to hold sufficient because it is a 'giant step', given the deontic power of initial commitments to create lasting obligations. The 'obligations arising from [an] agreement are simultaneous and interdependent'[52] in the strong ontological sense that they cannot exist without one another and thus have no 'parts'. Obligations form reasons for action, justifications for expectations, and rightful sources of reproach because they cannot be rescinded unilaterally. They are also constitutive of social ties and bonds – Gilbert reminds us that 'obligation' derives from the Latin *ligare*, 'to bind'[53] – because 'a joint commitment *unifies* people in a very real way... When we share an

on Gilbert's binary scheme – there being nowhere else for her to put him – despite the *explanatory* powers he assigns to the 'we-mode'.

49 Gilbert, *Sociality and Responsibility*, p. 3.

50 Gilbert, *Living Together*, p. 2.

51 Gilbert, *Sociality and Responsibility*, p. 97.

52 Gilbert, *Living Together*, p. 292.

53 *Ibid.*, p. 295.

intention it is ours: the intention we uphold together by virtue of a unifying joint commitment'.[54] But, do obligations simply unify, and does Durkheimian social solidarity accompany these forms of social interdependence? Etymologically, 'obligation' comes from the Latin *ob-ligare* – not only *ligare* – where the 'ob' ('against') gives the word the meaning of a *constraint.* Therefore an obligation is not fundamentally a unifying joint commitment, but a relationship of duties that may go *against* the desires, needs, attitudes, and so forth of the individuals involved. The latter, of course, can also be in agreement to accept the constraint. We have an obligation to pay taxes, but for most people this is not usually a *unifying* joint commitment.

Indeed, Gilbert acknowledges this when maintaining that lasting obligations cannot be reduced to individual commitments and that that 'members all now recognize an obligation to act in the light of the plural subject's goals, beliefs, and principles of action, even when their personal goals and so on are at odds with these. A striking corollary of this is that a member's actions may often be explained without any reference to his or her own personal goals, values, or principle of action'.[55] It is not that individual subjects cease to have personal views, but the constraints on voicing them are strong and encourage, instead, the expression of what 'we think'. As the member of a Plural Subject, stating one's own views must be prefaced by a self-deprecating 'Personally'. Voicing it may incur the suspicion of no longer being 'one of us', which can inhibit private thoughts doubting the group view, and lead to selective nonperception of evidence hostile to it (in a scientific research team, for example). 'Hence there is a significant initial cost in every case of mooting an idea that runs contrary to a collective belief'.[56] The price of bucking the consensus can be cumulative and, thus, 'we think' has causal powers affecting the individual subject and the overall outcome (in the above case, the state of scientific knowledge).

We have difficulties with this account, specifically about *how* groups influence their members (not *that* they do so). First, from the previous paragraph it seems that 'we think' dominates what 'I think', but that 'I do think' has to be presumed *in order for* group pressure to be exerted. However, Gilbert gainsays this when she notes 'that it is not obvious

[54] Gilbert, *Sociality and Responsibility*, p. 31.
[55] Gilbert, *Living Together*, p. 268.
[56] Gilbert, *Sociality and Responsibility*, p. 42.

that coming to use the pronoun 'we' correctly in the plural subject sense presupposes prior mastery of the pronoun 'I''.[57] Yet, without the continuous sense of self expressed by the 'I', how can a subject know that a given 'we think' (out of the many uttered) applies to him or to her and thus should be appropriated and asserted, unless he or she knows that it comes from 'my' group of which 'I' am a member?

When Gilbert continues that 'plural subject theory does not obviously require self-consciousness or striving conceived as personal to precede the understanding that one is a group member', this compounds confusion (as in Baier).[58] Elsewhere,[59] it was argued that the 'Me' we become involuntarily at birth (a member of one of the sexes or having a particular nationality) has social implications that are only learned gradually. But an 'I' is required to gain this understanding and reflexively to define one's stance towards it (for instance, 'I do/don't think of myself as a girl'). Conversely, actively to endorse being/becoming part of a 'We' does entail (some) personal election or ratification. (See Chapter 3.) How else do Gilbert's Plural Subjects come into being without someone who concludes an agreement by giving his or her assent, who says 'I agree'? Moreover, when some member of a group (a research team) declares 'I disagree', it may indeed be the case that to explain the dynamics (of producing innovation) requires attending closely to that individual.[60]

Second, in promoting the Relational Subject we also feel that contractual agreement has wrongly been assigned primacy over human relationality. Rather, we hold that it is through *jointly acting together* that subjects become jointly committed to one another [or the exact reverse], not that it is because of them being jointly committed that they act jointly act together [or against each other]. This is the burden of Donati's studies of local associations and therapeutic interventions.[61]

57 Gilbert, *ibid.*, p. 113.

58 Annette Baier, *The Commons of the Mind* (Chicago: Open Court, 1997).

59 Archer, *Being Human: The Problem of Agency* (Cambridge: Cambridge University Press, 2000).

60 John Greenwood, 'The Mark of the Social', Social Epistemology, 5 (1991), 221–232, quotation p. 226.

61 See Donati. *How to cope with family transitions when society becomes an unbound morphogenesis*, in E. Scabini and G. Rossi (eds.), *Family Transitions and Families in Transition* (Milan: Vita e Pensiero, 2012), pp. 29–47.

It is reinforced by Sheehy's[62] critique illustrated by four prisoners who are rowing a boat to make their escape. They share the belief 'I am escaping' and that it entails 'we are escaping', given they are literally in the same boat and reluctantly form a group. Yet, here, 'a group is formed through the ways in which individuals interrelate and interact, and group-constituting patterns of relations are not necessarily those in which the kinds of beliefs essential to the intentionalist thesis will feature.'[63] We are going to present just such a relational account as the substitute for any version of 'we thinking'. The four versions of 'we think', briefly examined earlier, also share four major difficulties that are summarized next. Each represents a challenge that our relational realism must be able to surmount.

Noting the absences: what Plural Subject accounts lack

Sociality is not held to generate emergent properties and powers

Space precludes entering the debate about emergence in the philosophy of social science but, as Critical Realists, we endorse the concept[64] and will use it in the following sections. *The point of drawing the close parallel between the different positions from which 'we thinking' has been presented in the section entitled 'An "action" replay of the 1950s debate in philosophy of social science' and those taken up in the 'old debate' about social ontology in the 1950s and '60s was to*

62 Paul Sheehy, 'On Plural Subject Theory', *Journal of Social Philosophy*, 33 (2002), 377–394.

63 *Ibid.*, p. 384.

64 We are writing as mainstream Critical Realists, and CR holds that where emergent properties and powers are generated by social relationships these are irreducible to their components. For instance 'rent' derives from the landlord-tenant relationship, because a property owner without a tenant does not receive 'rent', nor can the tenant pay 'rent' to him/herself. What a child learns from his/her parents is irreducible to the behaviour of his/her parents, because it depends on the qualities of their relationship. The productivity of a corporation is not reducible to the sum of the productivity of its workers (or their personal sociability), because it is the product of their relations. Emergent social relations are relatively autonomous from their components (elements), but continuously activity-dependent and often concept-dependent upon them; relational properties can exercise causal powers without these being manifest as empirical regularities because of the intervention of contingency and countervailing powers in the open system that is society.

show that nothing has changed and that 'emergence' continues to be excluded.[65]

We regard the social subject as being neither singular nor plural but relational – as is the case for all instances of emergence. First, the concrete singularity of persons originates through relations (with nature, artefacts, and people); second, social activities are ineluctably relational throughout life and, third, it is in relationships that new social properties and powers are generated. The latter include relational goods (trust, commitment, common projects, and certainly togetherness) and also relational evils (their opposites). Significantly, relational evils never feature in the Plural Subject literature, and their absence constitutes a 'beneficent bias' in the authors' overviews of social life.

One key point we will be making (in the section entitled 'How Relational Subjects generate relational goods and evils') is that the Relational Subject can orient his or her actions (goals, intentions, commitments) to such emergent goods and evils rather than interpersonally (or institutionally), as in all four positions examined. In short, *Relational Subjects can achieve a 'we-ness' without our needing to invoke 'we thinking' as a necessary mechanism or mediatory process.* Indeed, we ourselves explicitly deny that the workings and effects of 'we-ness' entail (i) sharing the same beliefs or coming to do so (Bratman); (ii) positing that we have the same thoughts in our heads (Searle); (iii) having achieved a mutual agreement and sharing a common ethos (Tuomela); or (iv) arriving (explicitly or tacitly) at a joint commitment (Gilbert).

Presentism: relations have no past or future

The four accounts examined are almost exclusively present tense. In none do the examples of social relations given have a history. 'We think' is discussed without any diachronic account of how 'we' came to 'think' such and such or to be in a position to do so. Furthermore, in the present tense, the resulting joint actions are not acknowledged to entail relational dynamics. Searle's cooks who regularly make béarnaise sauce together[66] simply continue pouring and stirring in a frozen time frame; one or the other never suggests that pouring more

[65] Although we would consider Gilbert to be an 'emergentist', given the irreducibility of the properties and powers assigned to the effects of 'obligation' once generated, she herself makes only rare references to 'supervenience'.

[66] Searle, 'Collective Intentions and Actions'.

slowly or stirring faster might enhance their cooperation or the end product. Yet, joint action is rarely nonreflexive, nondiscursive, and free from learning. These are the aspects of ordinary social relations through which the future is forged in the present through incremental – or innovative – changes. Alternatively, they can also result in growing boredom and a future preference for shop-bought sauce. Searle's illustrations are more like stills from silent movies than everyday life.

Moreover, outcomes are never allowed to be generative: those regularly walking together (with enjoyment, for we don't do so out of obligation alone) never start buying boots and becoming hikers. Nor are outcomes ever degenerative in their consequences: no one comes to think that another action replay of the departmental meeting in the cafeteria is more than they can take, begs off, and is simply indifferent to being reproached. Indeed, to court a merited reproach may be used reflexively to end uncongenial relationships ('If I don't turn up, he'll get the message'). Instead, present relations have no futures to these philosophers, yet the future is forged in the present: each motion passed by a group or its response to the circumstances confronted 'today' subtly contributes to shifting that group's ethos and to the group itself expanding or dwindling 'tomorrow'.

These dynamics, making for morphostasis or morphogenesis in social relations at all levels, including the collective subjectivity of the 'we', will be examined in the section entitled 'How Relational Subjects generate relational goods and evils'. There, we will try to resist the notion that people simply 'drifting' into joint action suffices as an adequate account of its relational origins or that to talk of cooperation 'evolving' is a satisfactory explanation – by biological metaphor – of their future relational trajectories.

The neglect of Reflexivity

In this literature devoted to 'we thinking', where the authors reviewed are agreed that the phenomenon cannot be construed as the aggregate of individual thinking, the practice of reflexivity is almost completely ignored. Is this because our four philosophers regard it as a wholly self-referential (and therefore individual) practice? If that is the case, we are in straightforward disagreement with them because one of 'the jobs'[67]

[67] Norbert Wiley, 'The Sociology of Inner Speech: Saussure meets the Dialogical Self', paper presented to the American Sociological Association, August 2004, p. 9.

that reflexive deliberations perform for their practitioners is to enable them to consider themselves in relation to their social circumstances, to their social relations themselves, and to review their future courses of action in the light of reflexivity itself. Undoubtedly, 'presentism' (b) helps to deprive reflexivity of this major task. Nevertheless, because many of the examples these authors give involve joint action that takes time to accomplish and may result in failure (two people trying to start a car together) and none deny that 'I think', it is curious that neither party attempting to get the car going ever seems to volunteer reflexive suggestions about how it might be better done. After all, if one of these works, 'we' might come to think differently!

This is puzzling because if, indeed, 'we think', then the possibility that 'we think reflexively' seems at least to merit consideration. Why can some thought be placed inside more than one head but, seemingly, not mental deliberations? Ironically, it will be we who support 'Relational Reflexivity' and not the Plural Subject theorists. We will venture that 'collective reflexivity' exists when and where two or more parties are reflexive about the emergent features of their relationship (as part of their social circumstances) that, under (a), our four authors have foreclosed by their rejection of emergence itself.

We work in terms of the *different kinds* of relational goods and evils that are emergent at various levels of the social order (from interpersonal goods to the Common Good) towards which subjects can orient their actions. In this way we seek to turn the tables in the section entitled 'How Relational Subjects generate relational goods and evils', without resorting to 'we thinking'.

The problem of scope

As highlighted at the start of this chapter, 'we think' is not simply about interpersonal relations for these four analytical philosophers. It is a springboard doing a lot of work for them at the macro-societal level. The difficulties we have with this procedure are threefold. First, there is simply far too much extrapolation from arguments honed on the dyad to the macroscopic level of social institutions. Second, despite Simmel having stressed that the triad introduces possibilities unknown in the dyad (for example, ways other than brute force by which two can *justify* ganging up on one), there is an in-built assumption amongst Plural Subject thinkers of homology between micro- and macro-levels. Third, and most important, analytical philosophy furnishes *logical derivations* rather than *causal accounts* of large-scale social phenomena. Were this possible, the contributions of social science would indeed be as redundant as it is generally treated to be by these philosophers.

The concept of the Relational Subject

The issue

A subject is, first and foremost, an agent and actor apprehended in his or her singularity as a human person. Indeed, the human being qualifies and distinguishes him/herself with respect to all other living beings by being a person who possesses a continuous sense of self *and* his/her own subjective reflexivity.[68] This enables human subjects to define their personal concerns (what matters most to them) and to consider these in relation to their social circumstances and vice versa. The problem that the human and social sciences must address is that of understanding and explaining how this subjective singularity starts to be formed from the moment the newborn begins to interact with the external world, that is, the world of nature, material culture, and people with whom he/she enters into relation, something that happens even before birth.

Relational realism tries to avoid both subjectivism and its opposite, which today is represented not only by positivism ('objectivism'), but above all by "relational*ism.*" For Relational Sociology, to hold that subjectivity consists of the person's "consciousness" (or Mind) alone, as rationalist and idealist thinkers assert (from Descartes to Hegel and after) is reductionist because no subject is an isolated monad. Equally, it is reductionist to maintain that consciousness exists only in so far as it is formed by its relations, as relational*istic* thinkers would have it, based on arguing that the relation has *ontological priority* over the existence of consciousness (Laflamme; Emirbayer; Vautier).[69]

[68] Archer, *Being Human: The Problem of Agency.*

[69] S. Laflamme, *Communication et emotions. Essai de microsociologie relationelle* (Paris: L'Harmattan, 1995); M. Emirbayer, 'Manifesto for a Relational Sociology', *American Journal of Sociology*, 103 (1997), 281–317; C. Vautier, 'La longue marche de la sociologie relationnelle', *Nouvelles perspectives en sciences sociales: revue internationale de systémique complexe et d'études relationnelles*, 4 (2008), 77–106.

When Donati[70] stated of the social order that, '*in the beginning, there is relation*', he did and does not mean that the relation *determines* consciousness. Consciousness (or Mind) is itself an emergent reality. What the statement is intended to underline is that consciousness must necessarily relate to 'an' Other (and 'otherness') than the Self, and it is only through relations that it can develop and function. Thus, consciousness is also a 'related' reality, like every social phenomenon. But this does not mean that relations 'create' consciousness.

The relational realism that we endorse holds that *personal* subjectivity consists in consciousness (or Mind), which operates in relation to itself through the external world that it encounters. Consciousness and relationality are necessary to one another, without the latter having ontological priority over the former because they exist as relatively autonomous and distinct from one another. Consciousness and its *relata* do not emerge simultaneously (in which case we would be endorsing central conflation between the subject and his/her context). Rather, they emerge through different temporal phases in which consciousness and relations influence each other in turn. Human subjectivity and the external context are different strata of reality that reciprocally condition each other over time through the phases constituting the morphostasis/morphogenesis schema.[71]

In what way and to what extent do the relations that the individual establishes with the 'outside' (everything that is not-I) influence the subject and the constitution of his/her personal and social identity? When we speak of the 'Relational Subject', this refers to the human person apprehended in making these relations and being made by them. As soon as we consider the human individual 'in relation' to others and otherness (people and things), we grasp a 'relational I' that not only acts and is involved as a Self in these relations, but is itself elaborated (as the Me, the We and the You) in/through/and with these relations.

What is "social" in the Relational Subject?

Each human being is relational by nature, but relations are created in time and space, that is, in situated sociocultural contexts. 'Human selfhood, as the reflexive consciousness of the Self, is not a substance in

[70] P. Donati, *Relational Sociology. A New Paradigm for the Social Sciences* (London and New York: Routledge, 2011), pp. 25–27.

[71] Margaret S. Archer, *Social Origins of Educational Systems* (London: Sage, 1979) and *Realist Social Theory: The Morphogenetic Approach*, 1995.

and of itself lacking relations, but is constituted by relations with other human subjects and relations experienced in the natural and practical order'.[72]

In order to understand how the person in the social order is a 'Relational Subject', above and beyond the simple Aristotelian assertion that man is a political animal and exists only in society, we need a more sophisticated conception of social relations that is lacking in classical thought. To say that the human individual exists only because he/she was conceived and raised by other human beings and also needs other people in order to live and flourish is banal. This says little or nothing about how the human individual is effectively shaped (configured) in as much as he/she is a concrete and situated 'relational being'. The problem is to understand how *social* relationality helps to mould the human individual's personal and social identity as well as agency.

When the personal I (the continuous sense of self) fully encounters the social realm in the form of the *Me, We*, and *You*, it is necessary to understand these as different aspects of social identity and what relations are implied by them and established with them.[73] The relations established between the Self and the *Me, We, You* are very different from one another. An analysis of these dynamics is taken up in the next chapter.

A Relational Subject is a subject who exists only in relation and is constituted by the relations that he/she cares for, that is, the subject's concerns. By this we do not claim that the social relation is a subject in and for itself, but rather that the relation has its own (*sui generis*) reality because it possesses its own properties and causal powers. Such relationality (the relation as a real emergent) is *activity-dependent*, but has its own *structure*,[74] the exercise of whose causal powers

72 Archer, *Being Human: The Problem of Agency*; A. Malo, *Io e gli altri. Dall'identità alla relazione* (2010). Here we deal only with social relations, but those with the natural order and the practical order (material culture and the skill to deal with it) are equally ineluctable.

73 Archer, *Being Human: The Problem of Agency*; Donati, *La conversazione interiore: un nuovo paradigma (personalizzante) della socializzazione*, Introduction to Margaret S. Archer, *La conversazione interiore. Come nasce l'agire sociale* (Trento: Edizioni Erickson, Trento), pp. 9–42.

74 P. Donati, *Sociologia della relazione* (Bologna: il Mulino, 2013) and *Morphogenic Society and the Structure of Social Relations*, in Margaret S. Archer (ed.), *Late Modernity. Trajectories towards Morphogenic Society* (Dordrecht: Springer, 2014), pp. 143–172.

acts back upon the constituents (Ego and Alter) of the relation itself.[75]

It is not universally the case that those constituting the *social* relation (*Ego* and *Alter*) personally reflect on how the relation between them is generated or can be altered by their actions. The relation and its properties can remain implicit and latent. In the social world something akin to what occurs in the physical world happens. We do not see light, we see *with* light. In the same way, in the social world we often do not 'see' relations, we 'see' *with* relations, which themselves remain 'unseen'. However, we argue that it is possible both to be and to become aware of relations and that people have a greater awareness of relational goods and evils than they often acknowledge – under their own descriptions.

The underlying question is what do we mean by the word 'social' when we use it in the expression 'social relation'. The term 'social' is notorious for its ambiguity and riddled with misunderstandings. In general, it is used as a synonym of 'collective', in the sense of an aggregate of individuals. But here, instead, we use it as a synonym of 'relational'.[76] To say that something or someone is social means that it is relational, in the sense that it is a social existent (pertaining to the *social* order and not to other orders of reality, precisely in that it is defined by social relations).[77] Obviously, we can and do have many relations that are not primarily social.

To clarify this point, it is worthwhile remembering that the social is usually understood in the following two ways:

(i) as resulting from actions or exchanges between individuals who orient themselves to one another; here the social is understood as an aggregate effect of a multitude of individuals who produce a collective result.[78]

[75] P. Donati, 'Critical Realism, as Viewed by Relational Sociology', in A Maccarini, E. Morandi, and R. Prandini (eds.), *Sociological Realism* (London: Routledge, 2011), pp. 122–146.

[76] Donati, *Relational Sociology. A New Paradigm for the Social Sciences*.

[77] Emmanuele Morandi, 'Introductory Outlines to Pierpaolo Donati's Relational Sociology. Part 1', *Journal of Critical Realism*, 9 (2010), 208–226 and 'Introductory Outlines to Pierpaolo Donati's Relational sociology. Part 2', *Journal of Critical Realism*, 10 (2011), 100–121.

[78] C. J. Uhlaner, '«Relational Goods» and Participation. Incorporating Sociability into a Theory of Rational Action', *Public Choice*, 62 (1989), 253–285.

(ii) or as the structure that overshadows (orchestrates) individuals and makes them think and act in a certain way.[79]

If one adopts either of these two meanings of the 'social', *it is not possible* to conceive of the 'Relational Subject'. In the first case, the relation is reduced to a flat aggregate lacking structure or one that produces an entirely contingent structure (effectively, upward conflation by aggregation is endorsed); in the second case, the relation is reduced to a structure lacking agency (entailing downward conflation by substituting *träger* for subjects).

It is thus necessary to arrive at another meaning of 'social', and we propose that:–

(iii) The social be understood as a distinct stratum of reality, different from an aggregate reality and from that of a structure overshadowing the agents and actors, yet which profoundly affects them precisely because it consists of irreducible relations.

However, it is necessary to distinguish our concept from that of others who share the idea that the analytical unit is the social relation. To us, the irreducibility of relationality means that it is neither upwardly nor downwardly reducible to individuals nor to structures conceived as 'wholes' that determine individuals. For various reasons that will be discussed later, we do not concur with those authors who declare themselves to be 'relational' but who, in reality, propose a 'transactional' sociology because they conceive of the social as nothing more than '*transactions*' between individuals (Emirbayer) in networks constituted by dyadic relations (Crossley).[80] The defects of such

[79] Mary Douglas, *How Institutions Think* (Syracuse, NY: Syracuse University Press, 1986). On the various meanings of social structure, see D. V. Porpora, *The Concept of Social Structure* (New York: Greenwood Press, 1987) and 'Four Concepts of Social Structure', *Journal for the Theory of Social Behaviour*, 19 (1989), 195–211.

[80] Crossley argues that social worlds '*comprise*' networks of interaction and relations. He asserts that relations are lived trajectories of iterated interaction, built up through a history of interaction, but also entailing anticipation of future interaction (N. Crossley, *Towards Relational Sociology*, London: Routledge, 2010). To him, social networks comprise multiple dyadic relations which are mutually transformed through their combination. On this conceptual basis he builds a Relational Sociology which aims at overcoming three central sociological dichotomies – individualism/holism, structure/agency, and micro/macro – that are utilized as a foil against which to construct

transactional sociologies are principally twofold: in the first place, because they conceive of social relations as mere interactions or exchanges between individuals, they do not acknowledge the *sui generis* reality of the relations themselves and, in particular, the reality of the social structures constituted by those relations, which are not merely transactional outcomes; second, because they reduce the relation to an interaction or multiple interactions, they endorse some form of central conflation between individuals and social and cultural structures.[81]

We speak of a Relational Subject, whether individual or collective, when social relations enter into the constitution of the personal identity of whoever is involved, that is, it becomes one of their constellation of concerns. The Relational Subject does not exist if this is not the case. For example, as discussed later, the couple is a Relational Subject if and to the degree that the personal identities of the two partners are (partly) defined through their relationship as a couple, whereas the doctor-patient or buyer-seller relation does not constitute a Relational Subject because their relation does not enter into the two actors' personal identities but remains external to them.

The validity of the relational (neither transactional nor relationalistic!) perspective can be seen at different levels in 'collective' social subjects: on the micro level (for example, in the couple relation), on the meso level (social associations and organizations), and on the macro level (for example, in citizen/State relations), as discussed in Part III of the book.

The concept of personal and collective (social) Relational Subjects

The term 'Relational Subject' refers to individual and collective social subjects in that they are '*relationally constituted*', that is, *inasmuch as they generate emergent properties and powers through their social relations.* The term 'Relational Subject' refers to both the singular social subject and the collective social subject given the role that the relation

the case for his Relational Sociology. Crossley argues that neither individuals nor 'wholes' – in the traditional sociological sense – should take precedence in sociology. Rather sociologists should focus upon evolving and dynamic networks of interaction and relations conceived as transactions.

[81] Archer, *Culture and Agency*. Part I introduces the three forms of conflation.

with 'the' Other (and Otherness) plays in defining and redefining identity, whether personal (the identity that the 'I' has for itself) or social (the identity that the 'I' has for 'Others').

Obviously, this comes about in different ways depending on whether the subject is individual or collective. Where the singular subject is concerned, the relation to the Other enters into the individual consciousness and plays a part in the internal definition of that particular Self. In collective subjects, relation to 'the' Other alters the network of relations between the members of the collective subject and, therefore, also the processes that lead to discernment, deliberation, and dedication on the part of the collective subject when it acts as a collective subject.

The term 'collective social subject' thus denotes one that is constituted by internal relations between the individuals forming it and by the external relations that they maintain with others as expressed by the 'We'. However, left there, the We could remain merely an abstract concept, a pure symbol, an idea or ideal. In contradistinction, we insist that a 'relational social subject' exists only when this We is a *real* relation (*a We-relation*).

If it is relatively easy to think about and describe the *individual* Relational Subject, understanding and explaining the *collective* Relational Subject is rather more complex. The difficulty resides in the fact that – properly speaking – only individual persons '*think*' (reflect). Extending the concept of the single human individual's reflexivity to a social group (of primary or Corporate Agents) appears to be problematic.[82] Nevertheless, we hold that this is possible, under certain conditions and this is what is distinctive about our approach (see the section entitled 'How Relational Subjects generate relational goods and evils') Specifically, we maintain that in order to understand how the reflexivity of a collective (social) subject – termed *Relational Reflexivity* – is possible, it is necessary to adopt a specific sociological approach, namely 'relational realism'.

The I that converses with itself inside its own Mind results in thinking, evaluating, and planning its courses of action through its own deliberations, which will influence the subject's external relations. But

[82] Margaret S. Archer, 'Introduction. The Reflexive Re-turn', in Margaret S. Archer (ed.), *Conversations About Reflexivity* (London and New York: Routledge, 2010), pp. 1–13; P. Donati, 'Modernization and Relational Reflexivity', *International Review of Sociology*, 21 (2011), 21–39.

does something qualitatively different result if the subject is reflexive about his/her social *relations as such*? That is, as opposed to thinking directly about her particular boss or boyfriend. People make this distinction in everyday conversation: 'She's a fair supervisor, but we don't make a good team' or 'He's a nice guy but we don't bring out the best in one another'. We hold that deliberations *on the relation per se* will influence the production of social phenomena in a qualitatively different way, generating a specific range of outcomes.[83]

Let us take the example of a musician in an orchestra when he reflects on the quality of his personal performance as distinct from what he thinks *about* (and *within*) the performance of the orchestra as a whole and, from this standpoint, evaluates his own performance: are these two ways of reflecting the same thing? This is the problem of the 'Relational Subject'. If the musician thinks only about himself, he will consult his personal model of perfection and nothing more (in an exercise of Autonomous Reflexivity). If he thinks about his own contribution to the orchestra, he will seek how best to 'adapt' his performance to the other players' performances (in an exercise of

[83] We assume that the internal conversation is relationally constituted, which means that the Self dialogues with itself in relation to the (social) context. Such activity has a double analytical dimension: (a) the self-referent relation of the I (when I ask myself 'who am I?'), as an operation of differentiation, and (b) the relation between the Self and its environment (its internal environment = body, and its external environment = outer world; this is a *connection* operation) where the Self is a Me, We, You. This is the '*normal*' (first order) activity of personal reflexivity, in which *the Self sequentially redefines itself as a Me, We, You through its relationality to the context*. In *the second order (b)*, there can be situations in which the relationality to the context is refused (denied, erased) or suspends its own effects (usually, forms of detachment from the social world). To be reflexive about the relation *per se* is the operation that avoids falling into the lack of relationality; *it is the exact opposite of the refusal or suspension of thinking of the relation to the context as an issue in itself*. It pushes the 'normal' internal conversation further to the extent that *it implies a second order activity* (i.e. reflecting on the relation to the Other as an outcome irreducible to the actions of Self and Other). In fact, in this case, the Self does not only (first order operation) reflect on itself through its context (as a Me, We, You) (what shall I do in relation to the context), but *redefines its relationality* ('a different relationship is needed independently of my own internal concerns as the second order operation'), and therefore, *by taking the relation to the Other as a third element (the tertium* Donati 2011: 13) *the Self redefines its context not as a matter of personal preferences (I wish/want/need to change the context), but as a demand or invitation coming from the We-relation, if certain outcomes are to be achieved.*

Communicative Reflexivity). If, instead, he reflects *on* the orchestra's performance and about how this performance could be improved were the musicians to relate to each other in a different way, he will seek to alter the performance of the whole orchestra, that is, he will seek to produce a different emergent effect – a better performance by the orchestra. In this latter case, we can speak of the player practising Meta-reflexivity.[84]

However, it is necessary to distinguish between individual and collective Meta-reflexivity. The Meta-reflexivity of single musicians has certain repercussions on the orchestra, but only those attributable to singular persons and their aggregate effects. It becomes collectively relational when each musician looks (relates) to the orchestra's conductor who – in this metaphor – represents and interprets the *We-relation*. Then, Meta-reflexivity works as the reflexivity of the 'collective subject', operating with regard to what is deemed (fallibly) to be relationally possible and relationally best *for the performance given by all the players considered together*. Although the metaphor refers to a real situation (shared by team leaders, heads of departments, etc.) our point is emphatically not about 'leadership' being necessary for collective reflexivity. That would be an oxymoron because it depends upon the conductor's interpretation (in the illustration) and thus reverts to being individual. Rather, the point is about the *orientation of all the musicians to the collective performance*. A collective orientation to a collective 'output' is the core of collective reflexivity. Another way of putting this is that that group is oriented to the relational goods it produces, to maintaining or improving upon them – and to eradicating any relational evils detected in their collective performance. It is predicated upon that performance being a (relational) emergent and thus not only endorses the stratified realist ontology for academic analysis but maintains that Relational Subjects are realists in their practical, everyday lives in so far as they *orient their actions to relational goods/evils*.

Thus, to speak sociologically about 'collective subjects' is to refer to groups of individuals who act 'collectively' in the sense of constituting

[84] The dominant modes of practising reflexivity were developed on the basis of empirical research by Margaret S. Archer: *Structure, Agency and the Internal Conversation* (Cambridge: Cambridge University Press, 2003); *Making Our Way Through the World: Human Reflexivity and Social Mobility* (Cambridge: Cambridge University Press, 2007); *The Reflexive Imperative in Late Modernity* (Cambridge: Cambridge University Press, 2012).

a collectivity that evaluates objectives (discernment), deliberates about realizing its common concerns (deliberation), and commits itself to achieving them (dedication).[85] Examples of collective subjects are the couple, the family, a voluntary association, a cooperative, a labour union, a political party, a foundation, a local community, and a social movement. Both in common parlance and in scientific studies, it is claimed that these collective groups evaluate, deliberate and 'act' as 'subjects'.

The same issue arises as it did for singular persons with respect to these collective subjects. Namely, how can we capture and conceptualize the 'internal subjectivity' of the We, of these collective subjects as they evaluate, deliberate, and act in themselves, and when they evaluate, deliberate, and act in relation to other (individual or collective) subjects? Here, we will advance 'Relational Reflexivity', without having any truck with the 'group mind' and in opposition to the main solution on offer – the Plural Subject.

How Relational Subjects generate relational goods and evils

Relational goods are emergent, being generated and sustained by the subjects constituting them, and possess their own properties and powers: to motivate, to facilitate, and to constrain the parties involved in them and to affect matters beyond them. When reflexivity is relational, it does not differ in kind from the modes practised by singular subjects and conforms to the general definition: reflexivity is 'the regular exercise of the mental ability, shared by all normal people, to consider themselves in relation to their (social) contexts and *vice versa*'.[86] Relational Reflexivity focuses upon that important tract of anyone's social context at any given time, namely that which is made up of human relationships (as opposed, for example, to a person's relation to his/her natural environment, to the skills they seek to develop or the technology they use, about which they can be reflexive but not in a socially relational sense).

Nothing hangs on the term 'context', which is used for its neutrality, given that some term is essential because there can never

[85] Archer, *Being Human: The Problem of Agency*. The DDD scheme is treated in more detail in Chapter 4.

[86] Archer, *Making Our Way Through the World*, p. 4.

be 'context-less action'. If preferred, 'situations', 'circumstances', or 'environment' can be substituted and dispute about the *ontological constitution* of all four referents be postponed for the time being. The term used is irrelevant to the main point, at least for all who rightly eschew the 'ontic fallacy', namely that how things are determines how we see, think, and talk about them. The point being made is that people are necessarily reflexive about their 'context' or 'circumstances' when they ask themselves quotidian questions (in internal or external conversation) such as: 'What shall we have for dinner?', 'Do I need to visit the dentist?', or 'Can one of us get back from work in time to pick the kids up from school?'. Obviously, subjects' reflexive deliberations are exercised under their own epistemic descriptions, as is the case for all thought and talk. Social reflexivity refers to Relational Subjects being reflexive about their social relationships, as analytically distinct from their relations with other orders of natural reality.[87]

Epistemologically, agents can misconstrue their social relations, including failing to take them into account, in which case they pay the price uncomprehendingly (in terms of deteriorating or broken relationships). Intrinsically, this is no different from someone miscalculating the size of mortgage that they think they can service every month, then falling into arrears and finally seeing the property being repossessed. If this is not to come about, both contexts require learning and applying new knowledge that could result in more satisfactory outcomes for the subjects involved.

Dwelling upon how actors or agents come to learn *about* and then reflexively work *with* the relational emergents they produce and have produced may sound unduly abstract and a long way from people's everyday behaviour. In fact, the thought and actions involved are just as down to earth regarding reflexivity as some of the homely examples adduced by the analytical philosophers when discussing the Plural Subject. Take John Searle's instance of the two people who agreed to clear the yard together, in order to note some of ways in which it lacks

[87] It is held that human beings have relations with the natural order and the practical order as well as with other persons and groups (Archer, *Being Human: The Problem of Agency*), but constituted as we are and the world being as it is, this cannot be otherwise. However, theorists can disagree about the relative importance of the three orders – as do subjects. What they cannot do is to collapse the three orders into the social alone.

quotidian instances of 'Relational Reflexivity' – and the consequences of these omissions.

First, once the compact to tackle the yard has been concluded, there is no mention of reflexive monitoring of either the self or the other in terms of how they play their parts. No helpful suggestions or critical comments appear to pass between the pair. Yet, perhaps the tempers of both and the state of the yard would be improved by changing their division of labour. Second, because human subjects are what Charles Taylor terms 'strong evaluators',[88] our internal conversations provide a variety of unvoiced commentaries as the task proceeds. We evaluate the other ('Why does he leave brooms and buckets all over the place?'), ourselves ('I'm going to need a break soon'), the working relationship ('We're getting through this faster than I expected'), the outcome ('The yard does look much better!'), and the impact of their collaboration upon their relationship itself (varying from 'I'll never do that kind of thing with him again' to 'Didn't we make a good team'). In real life, crude cooperation is not enough and any old sloppy performance will not do, because we are reflexive about ourselves, the other, the relation, and its outcome, though nothing need be openly said.

Third, the two parties have to assume that each has an intention-in-action with the same goal, the same 'collective B',[89] but the story does not end there. The relational experience they have been through together and the result jointly produced also have consequences with which Searle's 'presentism' cannot deal.[90] If the pair conclude that they have worked enjoyably together and made for a more agreeable yard, they may both be ready and willing to 'up' their 'collective B' ('Let's tackle the junk room next', which is met by 'Sure, and then we could have a go at the garage'). Conversely, a bad afternoon of snapping and snarling without much to show for it could eliminate anything resembling 'collective B' from the plans they moot in the future and will not have enhanced their relationship.

[88] Charles Taylor, 'Self-Interpreting Animals', in his *Human Agency and Language* (Cambridge: Cambridge University Press, 1985), pp. 35–76.

[89] J. R. Searle, *Making the Social World* (Oxford: Oxford University Press, 2010), p. 52.

[90] Others do make more though not detailed references to overt 'negotiations' of various kinds. For example, Bratman talks about the 'meshing of sub-plans' and Gilbert of both 'compromise' and 'fusion'.

In sum, *non-reflexive* portrayals of subjects and *presentist* accounts of their relational activities exclude much that is important in their doings and forego capturing anything about their relationship's trajectory in the future. Yet, the example just used was proffered by Searle as an instance of 'we thinking', in which for him the feeling of togetherness is 'crucial'. As we have hinted, however, joint action may have, or at least contribute to, the opposite outcome and sentiments. That is, we have started to signal that joint action can also lead to deteriorating relationships, and have done so in order to rectify the 'beneficent bias' that permeates the Plural Subject literature. Nevertheless, we are actually in agreement with Searle about the importance of 'we-ness' to all but the most reclusive of subjects. (Even in their case, we would want to discover whether or not the onset of extreme social withdrawal had some relational precursor.) However, we regard 'joint agreement', 'collective commitment', and 'shared intentionality' as unconvincing bases, not simply for the supposed 'we think' phenomenon, but for explaining and understanding 'we-ness' as real and important in social life. When people experience and express this feeling, we ourselves are not willing to consign it to the status of 'qualia'. Consequently, the onus is on us to advance a different account, and we will offer a realist one based upon the notion of relational emergence.

Relational goods and 'We-ness'

Our version of 'we-ness' does not rest upon any version of 'we think' but, rather, upon the concept of 'relational goods' (we will come to 'relational evils' later on in the section entitled 'The vicissitudes of Relational Subjects: relational evils'). These are goods generated from the *relations between* subjects, ones that remain continuously activity-dependent and concept-dependent upon those involved but cannot be reduced to individual terms. Significantly, reductionist philosophers of social science have often treated our relations as individual predicates,[91] which has to be an oxymoron since one property of a relational good is that it cannot be divided and parcelled out among its generators. When a couple separates or divorces, the

[91] To Watkins, acceptable individual predicates can include 'statements of about the dispositions, beliefs, resources and *interrelations of individuals*' (J. W. N. Watkins, 'Methodological Individualism and Social Tendencies', 270–1). Italics added.

parties can and usually do divide up their worldly goods – including their children – but ontologically their relational goods cease to exist with the separation of the two people responsible for generating them.

Relational goods have causal properties and powers that *internally* influence their own makers. They are known – under their own descriptions – by the parties involved. That is, by those diachronically responsible for their emergence and synchronically for their reproduction, elaboration, or destruction. The fact that they can only be known under subjects' own descriptions certainly implies that Relational Subjects can be wrong about their relationships, as about anything else. Nonetheless, their fallibility does not prevent them from *reflexively orienting* their own actions *towards* relational goods – and relational evils.

We start from the premise that 'relational goods' are desirable and desired by all (normal) people to some degree, again under their own descriptions. Of course, this does not preclude them from also seeking non-relational goods, such as health or wealth, insofar as these can be obtained non-relationally. Friendship is regarded as paradigmatic of 'relational goods' and is one that people desire nearly universally. Friendship varies in both degree and definition. Some talk unidimensionally about 'my Bridge friend/partner' and perhaps share little else together beyond regularly playing this particular card game. Among their other friends may be ones with whom their sharing is more extensive. Yet, regardless of matters of degree, these relationships can prompt the same reflexive thought that 'I mustn't let X down' or that 'X would enjoy hearing this'. Emergent features such as reciprocity, reliability, and consideration come into play.

In other words, friendship relations are deontic: creating obligations (to bid at Bridge according to conventions agreed upon by the partners), rights and duties, authorizations and embargos. They are causally influential: friendship can banish or mitigate feelings of loneliness, give the confidence or incentive to do something or go somewhere that a subject would not contemplate undertaking alone, and it can be divisive in prompting jealousy amongst others, and so on. (Our discussion does not include overstretched definitions of 'friendship', such as those on Facebook who address 'my one thousand friends', as these have no claim to be relationships.)[92]

[92] This is not to say that relations that matter cannot develop through socially interactive media.

One feature that friendship possesses, like all 'relational goods' and, indeed, other kinds of goods, is that subjects can and often do orient their actions towards it or in the light of it. Just as someone may reflect 'If I don't sell this now, it will be worth a lot more in the future', so, too, the same person might also consider 'I won't tell her that, it would be hurtful'. It is this latter kind of action that is fundamental to our conception of 'we-ness', but it takes a little working at to distinguish it from having good manners, being very considerate, or possessing what was once known as a 'kindly disposition'.

In opposition to 'presentism', we briefly introduced (in the section entitled 'The concept of the Relational Subject') those relations that generate 'relational goods' as ones that developed morphogenetically over time.[93] Relationships always arise in a context ('They met at university') and the subjects involved come from their own social contexts. In short, *there is no context-less relationship*, and neither can the context/s be relegated to the 'Background' because they are influential in the present as expectations, hopes or aspirations, motives and fears and, importantly, as networks of family and friends who remain active in subjects' lives. Important as this is,[94] we will dwell here on the generation of 'relational goods' and their consequences within the dyad, in order to parallel the Plural Subject approach, rather than upon how relationships are initiated.

Suppose that a serious relationship has developed between David and Helen during their time at university and that it is acknowledged between them.[95] They wish to be a couple after they graduate, but also need to shape a life for themselves once they leave university.[96] One of their unavoidable problems is that both have some (personal) idea about the life each would like to lead as a couple. Supposing these

[93] Relations themselves can be morphostatic, such as the Bridge partners who regularly play cards together but their friendship goes no further, or they can be entropic, but these are not of concern at present.

[94] Especially for the formation of personal reflexivity (Donati, *Sociologia della riflessività. Come si entra nel dopo-moderno*, 2011, and Archer, *The Reflexive Imperative in Late Modernity*, 2012).

[95] P. Donati, 'Engagement as a Social Relation: A Leap into Trans-modernity', in Margaret S. Archer and A. M. Maccarini (eds.), *Engaging with the World. Agency, Institutions, Historical Formations* (London: Routledge, 2013), pp. 129–161.

[96] Charles Taylor, 'Leading a Life', in Ruth Chang (ed.), *Incommensurability* (Cambridge, MA: Harvard University Press, 1997).

ideas are not blatantly incompatible, the question remains about how they can be forged into a life together. In this setting, Plural Subject theorists and Relational*ists* suggest that the couple gets down to the negotiating table and 'transact' their way forward. In short, there is no implication or indication that Relational Reflexivity is involved or that either David or Helen orients their thinking by reference to the 'relational goods' they are already generating.

It is certainly not the case that everyone does do so. After all, the goodness of anything compels neither that it be recognized, nor that it be received with gratitude, nor that efforts be made to maintain or to extend it. Good health, usually presumed to be an incontestable good, may be taken for granted and regarded rather like one's height as something relatively unchanging. However, the fact that Relational Reflexivity is not universal – whereas 'we think' is presented as a universalistic tendency – does not justify its neglect.

'Me-ness', 'Thee-ness', and 'We-ness'

Equally unjustified are contrary orientations whose universality is simply assumed and which presume to eliminate any need to make reference to 'We-ness'. The two generic versions of this practice will be called 'Me-ness' and 'Thee-ness' and are briefly touched upon before coming to our own notion of 'We-ness'.

'Me-ness' is most clearly illustrated by rational choice theory, by *homo economicus* used in neo-liberal economics and whose roots lie in classical utilitarian thinking. Confronted with any social decision-making situation, each actor seeks to maximize (or if need be satisfice) his or her own 'preference schedule'. These preferences themselves are not necessarily selfish or mercenary, but they leave their owners better off in their preferred terms. As an atomistic individual, 'economic man' has no social bonds that deflect him from instrumental rationality, unless these enter by the door of his own 'preference schedule'. Gary Becker has maintained that maximizing individual utility governs a person's choice of a spouse and warns against consorting with poorer people, because to fall in love and marry a poor spouse would damage personal utility.[97] This model cannot cope with the

[97] Gary Becker, *Accounting for Tastes* (Cambridge, MA: Harvard University Press, 1996).

human capacity to transcend instrumental rationality. Economic man remains mute and puzzled by the fact that we can devote ourselves to Aristotelian 'final ends', other than those inscribed in our preferences, which alone are held capable of moving us.[98] In sum, the 'Me-ness' of *homo economicus* precludes him from ever engaging in Relational Reflexivity; he remains a self-sufficient 'outsider' who simply operates in a social environment. As a subject, *homo economicus* only ever has what Martin Buber called *Ich-Es* (I-It) relations with Others.[99]

It is understandable why some are attracted by the 'Thee-ness' portrayed in Buber's *Ich-Du* (I-You) relations. Although Buber himself was critical of modernity for reducing those relationships in which the two parties reciprocally treat one another as 'You', this has not prevented generous claims being made for it in terms of hermeneutics. With considerable simplification, the argument is that David and Helen can succeed in forging a life together ('our' life as a couple after graduation) on the basis of hermeneutically entering into one another's aspirations for what kind of life that would be, given appropriate detachment on the part of both. Empirically – and assuming they are in love – it is quite likely that their external conversations together will cover this ground to the best of their abilities. But, these discussions cannot be a necessary condition for the source of 'We-ness'. The best of their abilities is not good enough because as subjects they cannot avoid the double hermeneutic. However hard the two try, they produce Alter's interpretations of Ego's self-interpretations and vice versa, doing so *seriatim* with no way out of this trap. Goodwill on both sides cannot extricate them from it, meaning that hermeneutics cannot provide a secure basis for forging a life that captures what the two people value most. In short, it cannot be a route to 'We-ness' that is not distorted by fallible interpretations and partial misinterpretations. Moreover, it cannot be a universal route because not all who set out to be couples will even try to take it (by holding serious conversations).

98 Margaret S. Archer, 'Homo economicus, homo sociologicus and homo sentiens', in Margaret S. Archer and J. Q. Tritter (eds.), *Rational Choice Theory: Resisting Colonization* (London: Routledge, 2000), pp. 36–56.

99 Martin Buber, *Ich und Du* (Berlin: Shocken Verlag, 1923, first translated into English in 1937).

Relational 'We-ness'

Let us approach 'We-ness', *jointly but severally* arrived at by a couple, David and Helen, as mediated through the reference both make to their relational goods. We will examine their attempt to answer the unavoidable question: 'Where are we going to live after graduation?' Most likely there will be contextual constraints that have to be factored in: the geographical location of the first posts they have obtained or hope to gain; where their family homes are located and the desires of David and Helen to be close to them or removed from them, which themselves may be different for the two; costs and availability of accommodation in various parts of the country; and so forth. Such contextual constraints are always *mediated* reflexively because they never act as hydraulic pushes and pulls with deterministic consequences. However, the outcome depends upon what form the reflexive deliberations take.

On the basis of 'Me-ness', David and Helen would each engage in their dominant form of *personal reflexivity*, define their own 'projects', and regard that of the other as another constraint that has to be dealt with in the attempt to maximize (or at least satisfice) their individual preference schedules. This formula is one that is likely to result either in an outcome of 'unequal utility' for the two parties or in a compromise that is sub-optimal for both because compromises entail concessions. It is certainly possible that later one of them may admit to not having been enthusiastic at first but now has come to like it, without this implying 'making the best of a bad deal'. Alternatively, it may serve to initiate a pattern of domination and subordination in their relationship as a couple or of dissatisfaction on both sides.

On the basis of 'Thee-ness', let us assume that David's and Helen's hermeneutic understandings attempt to 'see' the matter from one another's point of view and to give this parity of importance with their own through self-detachment. The trouble is that given the double hermeneutic and there being no way of escaping from it, our couple may again end up living somewhere or somehow that satisfies neither because their interpretive understandings of what matters to one another have both failed, at least to some degree. Consequently, not only does the couple live somewhere that both find wanting, but each remains puzzled at the discontent of the other whose (interpreted) concerns they had genuinely sought to accommodate. Having been

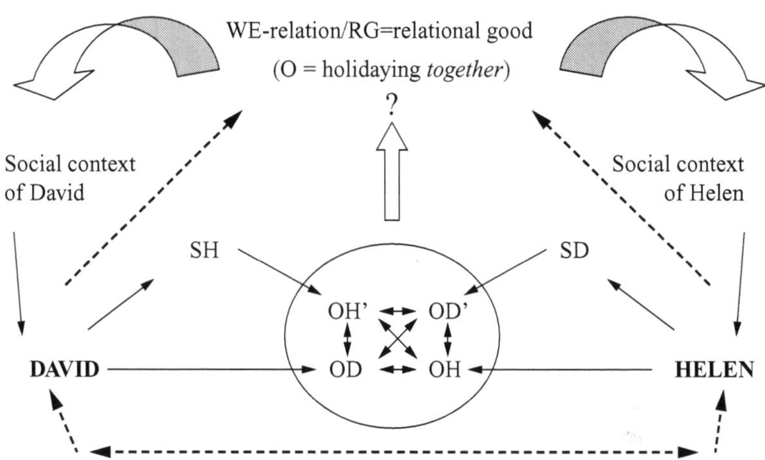

Key:
RG = Relational good as a we-relation
O = Object (the couple as a we-relation in action, generating a relational good, e.g. holidaying *together*)
SH = Helen as seen by David (as he thinks of her)
OH' = The object as David thinks that Helen sees it
OD = The object as seen by David
SD = David as seen by Helen (as she thinks of him)
OD' = The object as Helen thinks that David sees it
OH = The object as seen by Helen

Figure 2.1 The We-relation (relational good) of a couple (David and Helen)
Source: Modified from Donati, 'Engagement as a Social Relation: A Leap into Trans-modernity', in Margaret S. Archer and A. M. Maccarini (eds.), *Engaging with the World* (London: Routledge, 2013), by Archer.

through this hermeneutic process it becomes difficult for either to say 'Why on earth are we living here?' because each will think that it was the concerns of the Other that were responsible. In Figure 2.1 this is what happens if David and Helen are confined to their hermeneutic interpretations (indicated by the central circle).

On the basis of 'We-ness', answering where the couple are to live is approached in a different manner. Although allowance still has to be made for the constraints of work location and so forth, these do not determine the resolution of such issues as rural versus urban living, the choice between an apartment or a small house and garden, the importance of having shops and other facilities nearby, and so forth. Suppose, instead, they begin from *relational considerations*. That is, both tackle the problem neither self-referentially nor by orientation-to-the-Other but through deliberating on a different question, namely 'when and where do we have our best times together?' – those that they hope foreshadow their future life as a couple.

By reflecting upon 'our' best times together, their reflexivity is necessarily relational, and its referent is to the common goods they have already produced and thus know that they are capable of generating together. What the two summon up in their own heads will not be identical, for just as there is no 'we think', neither is there a mental process of 'plural reflexivity'. Nevertheless, their relational references will not be too disparate because the experiences that David and Helen each evoke were shared ones of mutual delight in what they did together and had probably been reinforced by their reminiscences. Note that in Figure 2.1, the couple could *in principle* circumvent hermeneutics entirely, by directly orienting themselves to the thought of their relational goods (represented by the dotted outer triangle). In this way – even though it is unlikely in practice for a young couple in love – their orientation does not have to be the result of a hermeneutic detour (represented by the central arrow).

Suppose each separately concludes that their weekends of walking in the countryside were their high points, the times that sealed their relationship. On that basis and with a view to extending their relational goods, Helen may tentatively venture that they should seek rural accommodation. David hesitates, not because he finds the project uncongenial, but he cannot drive and reflexively mulls over the difficulties of getting to and from work. Helen's tentativeness in voicing the proposal stemmed from her reluctance to remove herself from the proximity of her university friends. As they talk it over,[100] both are engaged in attempting to dovetail their other concerns *in the light of their relational goods*. Not only has their future as a couple (in this case) been promoted to become their ultimate concern, but it now arbitrates on the ordering of their other concerns, subordinating them but also evaluating them for compatibility with the furthering of their relational goods.

[100] Internal conversations can be externalized – with discretion – in ordinary conversation, without the subjects in question being Communicative reflexives.

David's practical reasoning is preoccupied with whether or not he can pass his driving test before the suggested relocation in the countryside. Helen's is concerned with how to maintain contact with her university friends and to form a network of 'village friends'. In short, they are far from having the same thoughts in their heads. Nevertheless, if both are wholeheartedly[101] committed to their future together, then their relational goods and the hope of extending them will be a motivational incentive for both to explore this rural *modus vivendi*. Note that in so doing, they have promoted the salience of their relational goods by allowing them to override the reservations stemming from 'Me-ness' and also that no 'Thou' consideration outweighs or distorts the achievement of 'We-ness'.

Were all to go well, their 'We-ness' would develop through the generation of further relational goods. Perhaps they discover that the rural area chosen has an active rambling club, which becomes a new network of 'ours'. Maybe they start to cultivate their garden, which represents a new and satisfying activity performed together that also connects them more closely with village life. Possibly they acquire a dog, and so on. If this is the case, they will have *elaborated their relational context* into one buttressing their *modus vivendi as a couple* because it will also have filtered out those old university friends who find their way of life uncongenial and filtered in some new friends to whom it is agreeable. If things continue to go well for the pair, this will have nothing in common with the spot-welding of Searle's 'we think', it will be unlike Bratman's 'meshing of sub-plans' because that assumes they already existed, whereas our pair are learning and discovering all the time. It does represent a collective agreement in Gilbert's terms, although not one glued together by (static) contractual obligations, but one that grows through relational morphogenesis.

The vicissitudes of Relational Subjects: relational evils

However, the scenario followed may differ from the felicific sketch above. When David repeatedly fails his driving test and gets home from

101 Harry G. Fankfurt, 'Identification and Wholeheartedness' in his *The Importance of What We Care About* (Cambridge: Cambridge University Press, 1988).

work late, Helen has found the waiting tedious because the network of village friends and activities she hoped for has failed to develop. As David begins to stay over with a colleague on the nights before early work meetings, Helen becomes lonely, aggrieved, and even suspicious. The trust they had built up as part of their relational goods begins to dissipate. Correspondingly, their 'We-ness' is wearing thin without this couple yet having come to the point of generating relational evils.

Remaining with the example of a couple, the major cause for the generation of relational evils is their failure to develop a *modus vivendi* together or the intervention of contingencies damaging their way of life. In the fictional case of Anna Karenina and her lover Vronsky, this downward trajectory develops because they experience the impossibility of severing themselves from the influence of their old social networks and yet find it equally impossible to embed themselves in any other. Some readers might respond that this was so obvious that the potentially adulterous couple should have been deterred by this common knowledge. Contrapuntally, Tolstoy presents 'doing adultery'[102] as a more nuanced enterprise in which such negative consequences – although not all – could be evaded. However, what is at issue is less adultery *per se* than how to shape a life together.

After Anna has given birth to Vronsky's child, rather than be separated by his military posting the couple leave for Europe, turning down her husband's offer of a divorce that would have enabled them to marry and assume some way of life within conventional Russian bounds. Seemingly, they believe that in being together they can be all-sufficient to one another. What they learn is that there cannot be a context-less relationship. Debarred from mixing with Russian émigrés of their own kind, both engage in a self-defeating 'Me-ness': Anna is initially happy to spend her time with her lover, but he is increasingly bored and seeks an outlet through pursuing his artistic talent, whose slimness is eventually recognized. They return to Russia as less of a 'We' than they left it, having shed their illusions that simply being together constitutes a *modus vivendi.*

[102] The two principals are flanked by Prince 'Stiva' Oblonsky (Anna's brother) and Princess 'Betsy', (Vronsky's cousin), both of whom pay much lesser prices for repeated adultery.

St Petersburg rapidly teaches them that there can be no home there for the pair as a couple. On the contrary, Vronsky can still move in Society and does so increasingly; Anna cannot, and relational evils engage between them as trust erodes. His increasing absences fuel Anna's jealous suspicions and corrode her belief in his love. He understands the social embargo upon her, but rather than facing this with her, he leaves Anna to learn it for herself. She insists on going to the theatre, where her status provokes public ostracism and a scene that brands her as an outcast.

When they then retreat to Vronsky's country estate, their relational evils intensify in the absence of any social context in which to form a *modus vivendi*. Anna tends to assume the role of the fallen woman in which their relationship has placed her – over-dressing and flirting with rare visitors. Vronsky distracts himself at first with his philanthropic project of building a hospital but soon reverts to absenteeism. As quarrels about his departures intensify, their attitudes towards one another become ones of boredom and jealousy, respectively. Both now want to marry in order to stave off the relational evils they are fuelling: Vronsky in the illusion of being able to live 'normally' and Anna to prevent him from leaving her. In other words, *both are oriented towards their negative relationality, which defines their desired courses of action.*

As her husband now refuses a divorce, the two are left to face their relational consequences. Perhaps Vronsky is tempted by his mother's machinations to marry him to a socially acceptable woman; at any rate, Anna believes so. The ensuing row shows that their mutual confidence has been replaced by the opposite. Believing that their relationship is now finished, Anna makes it so by dying under the wheels of a train. In fact, as a couple, it had never begun.

'Holding different, coordinated intentions in the pursuit of a common goal may turn out to be the closest that people can come to sharing an intention' writes Velleman.[103] As has just been illustrated, neither element can be achieved in the presence of relational evils that militate against both coordination of means and commonality of ends.

[103] Before seeking to argue otherwise on the basis of Gilbert's 'pooling of wills'. J. David Velleman, 'How To Share an Intention', *Philosophical and Phenomenological Research*, (1997), 29–50, quotation p. 35.

Equally, the framing of a common goal and the continuing dovetailing of intentions are reliant upon the on-going generation of relational goods and intentional orientations being formed with on-going reference to them, as David and Helen showed. In short, the 'We-ness' that is attained by Relational Subjects by virtue of their relationship – and one that Searle properly valued – will never be achieved by the Plural Subject.

PART II

Prologue: The sources of Relational Subjects and their resources

The likelihood is that Part I has raised as many questions as it has answered. Perhaps for some readers this stems from our decision to introduce our concepts through 'lifelike' and recognizable subjects in fairly common situations. We hope that this worked, but it does not dispense with the need for conceptual precision. In fact, a consequence of choosing this mode of presentation is that the more vivid the characters used for exemplification, the greater the eventual need to discipline them conceptually. An anecdote used to circulate about *Habits of the Heart*,[1] which excelled in pushing 'recognizability' much further than we have done with 'David and Helen'. Colleagues would reply to 'How are you?' by saying 'Oh, I'm having a very Brian-ish week'. All the same, no character vignette can replace the need to sharpen concepts into generalizable tools and to differentiate between a subject's circumstantial and particularistic features and those that pertain to the group or category that he or she is meant to exemplify. Conceptually, if one stands back from such vivid encounters (where the novel, film, and theatre outshine us), we sociologists are legitimately pressed to answer a range of issues about typicality, origins, historical specificity, causation, and so forth.

Our strategy in rounding out what is conceptually lacking is to condense these issues into a version of 'frequently asked questions' and responses to them. Because the issues themselves are complex and often require excursions into cognate areas, snappy answers are possible but not sufficient. In this Prologue to Part II, there are (at least) five FAQs arising from the previous text that the chapters constituting the second part of the book seek to answer. It may prove helpful to list them here and then to indicate briefly how they will be dealt with in Chapters 3–5.

[1] R. N. Bellah et al., *Habits of the Heart* (Berkeley: University of California Press, 1985).

1. Is the Relational Subject singular, plural, or both?
2. Is everyone a Relational Subject?
3. How do Relational Subjects arise?
4. Are there Socio-Cultural contexts that encourage/discourage the development of Relational Subjects?
5. What is the range of Relational Subjects in terms of the conventional subdivisions of the social order into micro-, meso-, and macro-levels?

Let's briefly examine these in the above order (although none of the questions is fully discrete), and indicate which of the following chapters responds to them in greater depth. First, 'Is the Relational Subject singular, plural, or both?' The basic answer is 'possibly all three', and it hinges upon the significance we attach to both 'relationality' and 'reflexivity', working in concert. Chapter 3 explicitly deals with how this is so. Generically, it is argued that that our formation as singular persons entails inescapable relations with all three orders of natural reality – natural, practical (artefactual), and social. In other words, our human selves *are relational through and through*, but our relationality is not confined to society's discursive order. This singular Relational Subject has the capacity to deliberate reflexively upon the relative importance of these three orders as far as he or she is concerned, but none can deem that establishing a liveable relation with all of the three is optional since survival is at stake. This is what makes all (normal) human beings generically Relational Subjects.

Collective Relational Subjects proper arise from any 'We' groupings that the generic subject electively joins in an expression of solidarity. This 'We' may be confined to a couple or extend to a Corporate Agent (a social movement, an organized interest group such as a union, or a 'cause' with its specific but explicit agenda). Such Corporate Agents fundamentally work by promoting an 'orientation' among their members towards 'relational goods' and 'evils' already generated, which does not entail singular Subjects taking the same stance as one another.

These latter and larger groupings also pack a special punch where societal or sectorial morphogenesis or morphostasis are concerned, exceeding those of aggregates of singular Subjects (as Primary Agents). Finally, it is the 'We's' that, relative to their success, serve to shape, modify and extend the social roles available to be sought and 'personified' by subjects as particular Actors. Thus, *relationality* accounts for the positioning of subjects in society, their participation in transformatory or reproductory social movements, and their adoption of a social role(s) that finally accords them strict social identity. Such an adoption crucially depends on the practise of *reflexivity* because each Relational Subject has to deliberate about which role(s) they (fallibly) consider will prove satisfying and sustainable.

Thus, the response to Question 2, 'Is everyone a Relational Subject?', would be an affirmative as far as the *generic* answer is concerned, for all must ineluctably forge some working relationship with the three constitutive orders of natural reality. However, that makes them a singular Relational Subject, whereas membership of a 'We' (or usually several of them – as wife/partner, member of union or professional association, active participant in a voluntary association – philanthropic, sporting, cultural, political, or religious) is the source of Collective Relational Subjects. Nevertheless, some people fail to develop a mode of reflexivity that enables them to bond in any lasting sense with a 'We', which is not regarded reductively or primarily as a psychological issue, but more importantly concerns their failure to have encountered 'relational goods' and having had greater acquaintance with 'relational evils'. Where the latter are serious, Fractured Reflexivity may ensue. It can be overcome, but when this is not the case it is often associated with relational deficits and precludes 'We' bonding. This is the point at which Chapter 3 segues into Chapter 4.

In responding to Question 3, 'How do Relational Subjects arise?' once more this hinges on our inter-related notions of 'relationality' and 'reflexivity'. Because the first relationships for most children derive from their natal backgrounds, primary socialization is of particular importance, but this process cannot be conceptualized in the early twentieth century fashion as 'passive internalization'. Thus, in Chapter 4 the concept of socialization is reconceptualized in a manner more appropriate to a world whose intensifying morphogenesis means that it cannot be captured as a largely passive internalization of consensual normativity, because that itself has been seriously eroded. This is so even within the natal environment, because multiple caretakers increasingly transmit 'mixed messages'. Instead, for the subject, socialization becomes *an active and necessarily selective process* of becoming engaged with the world. The quality of the relational goods/evils received in the home are presented as the main factor governing the dominant mode of reflexivity practised by the young subject:

'Communicative', 'Autonomous', 'Meta-', or 'Fractured'. That is, *providing* such influences are reinforced by subjects' other significant social relations. Consequently, it is the Relational Subject's 'concerns' (the things that matter most to each young person) that become their main compass for making their way through the world, but their realization continues to depend upon social relationality, though in the majority of cases upon *new* relations that promise different relational goods from those proffered (or not) within natal confines.

Question 4 asks 'Are there Socio-Cultural contexts that encourage/discourage the development of Relational Subjects?' Because our concept of the Relational Subject depends upon the working of 'relationality' and 'reflexivity' in combination, any long-term historical answer would be largely speculative in the absence of comparable empirical data. In the post–World War II period we focus upon qualitative changes and restrict statements about quantitative changes to ones of 'more' or 'less', although this could be remedied by appropriate studies of the 'baby boomers'. Overall, the impact of intensifying morphogenesis and the decreasing morphostatic conditions for the development and practice of stable relationality and routinized reflexivity ('Communicative' in mode), have rendered 'the reflexive imperative' increasingly pressing. This is because novel opportunities, unavailable in the parental generation, cannot be prepared for in the course of socialization. Yet they must be confronted by the socializand, who will meet with an increasing number of them. In parallel, the decline and replacement of many jobs, the diminishing of geolocality, of relatively homogeneous communities and neighbourhoods, of sex discrimination, of political parties aligned with social classes, and so forth, have created an equivalent 'relational imperative' to 'find' one's own partner and to constitute one's own relational network. Both features are documented for the last twenty or thirty years, and it is their interplay upon which we concentrate for generating differences in kind amongst contemporary Relational Subjects in the singular.

However, under most of the descriptive terms applied to late modernity – Knowledge, Information, Technological, Digital, or Risk societies – there is some consensus that the new drivers are cultural. Although this does not mean that structures have deliquesced into 'liquidity', leaving behind residual 'zombie categories', it does mean that the differences between structures (which, of course, exist in multinational and financialized capitalism) and culture pull further apart, producing new contestations between novel Collective Subjects. The most basic difference between the two is that cultural entities do not diminish in value when diffused, despite attempts to induce scarcity value through imposing intellectual property rights artificially. Hence new battle fronts open between the new Corporate Agents.

Cultural breakthroughs – most importantly the Internet – mean in a nutshell that a huge part of the world's cultural heritage is suddenly available for free – as a commons – to the populations of the developed world and increasingly so in developing countries. Simultaneously, mobile phones, as the most prized possessions of the young, have a parallel effect in potentially enlarging relational connectivity. As everyone knows, entrepreneurial commodification fast exploited the synergy between them in the form of social media (and the 'dark net'). This has impacted significantly upon the two features of 'relationality' and 'reflexivity'. To simplify greatly, on the one hand, it makes it faster and easier to mobilize demonstrations and to orchestrate social movements amongst strangers, just as it facilitates criminal rings engaged in human and drug trafficking or networks exchanging images of paedophilia. One question it raises is the need to differentiate clearly between the Socio-Cultural pressures (persuasion, normalization, mobilization, and recruitment) this represents and the simple availability of information (on anything from rose-pruning to bomb-making) that people increasingly employ. This is what Chapter 5 is about, and it has important consequences for the 'real relationality' that both of us see as essential, not only for the Relational Subject but also for explaining the loss of social integration in the developed world.

On the other hand, reflexivity is affected simultaneously. Proliferating digital devices absorb time and attention. Is this subtracted from the space in which to engage in reflexive deliberations, ones that concern 'what matters to me and to which "we(s)" I should elect to belong'? Does it distract from my and our concerns – and the business of dovetailing them and trying to realize them – substituting preoccupations with today's 'celebrity' doings or tomorrow's ephemeral scandals? If so, it promotes Expressive Reflexivity, quotidian and *événementalist*, encouraging 'drifting' through the future, accumulating the moraine of unconnected consequences of actions without a red thread of enduring concern or commitment linking them, rather than subjects assuming some governance over their life courses.

Already, we have moved away from this Prologue to Part II and, in merely considering the last question, 'What is the range of Relational Subjects?' have begun to stray into Part III. Yet, perhaps this is helpful in indicating that the two parts are indeed linked and that the micro-, meso-, and macro-levels are not merely conventional but that they raise unavoidable questions about upward and downward causation.

3 The Relational Subject and the person: self, agent, and actor

MARGARET S. ARCHER

No sociology can do without a concept of the human person. Even various forms of determinism or those who most determinedly pronounced the 'death of the subject' have such concepts: humans are taken to be fully malleable, mutable, and mouldable by 'social forces'. Those who view them as *träger* or fully permeable membranes simply conceptualize them in this way. This chapter deals with the different conceptions of personhood (usually) endorsed and advocated by some who call themselves 'Relational Sociologists' and those calling themselves 'Social Realists'. In my view, these two approaches are complementary and can work in synergy; otherwise this book could not have been written.[1]

In both approaches, 'personhood' is intended to cover the full gamut of concepts regularly used in social theory: 'selves', 'agents/agency' and 'actors'. In other words, the 'person' stands for the full human being. The generic dispute in social theory is about the balance of properties and powers that should be accorded to the 'social' rather than to the 'individual'. Both Realists and Relationalists are rather touchy about the term 'individual' because it is viewed as contaminated by its place in the history of thought and its association with neo-liberalism and 'individualism'. Relation*ists*[2] prefer to talk about 'selves', or 'persons as powerful particulars' (Rom Harré); Realists about people in their 'concrete singularity' (Roy Bhaskar). In themselves these terminological differences are not important and I will try to respect this shared squeamishness by not using the noxious term 'individual'.

What is important is whether or not our singular selves are credited with their own properties and powers – potentialities, liabilities,

[1] Margaret S. Archer, 'Critical Realism and Relational Sociology: Complementarity and Synergy', *Journal of Critical Realism*, 9 (2010), 199–207.

[2] I use 'Relationism' in the same way as Donati does in his chapters to distinguish those who reject emergence; 'Relational Sociology' or 'Relational Realism' are reserved for those who, like my co-author, endorse it.

capabilities, creativity, suffering, intentionality, and reflexivity *inter alia* – and where and how these are held to originate. At first glance, Relational*ists* and Realists appear to give the same answer. These originate from our human embodied constitution and life in the real world with which we necessarily have to interact in order to survive and, better, thrive. Thus, for example, Crossley writes of human-world interaction that 'We are practically connected. Practical involvement is our primary of being-in-the-world'.[3] Realists would assent: this is precisely what I argued in *Being Human.*[4]

However, the most contentious of concepts turns out to be 'the world' itself. To Realists, this signifies the whole natural world, constituted of nature, material culture, and social discourse, making for the natural, practical, and discursive orders with which humans ineluctably have to achieve accommodation. Conversely, for Relation*ists*, there is a slippage. Practice may be our 'primary mode' of being in the world, but primacy is quickly withdrawn from the world and attached to the discursive order. The effect is that singular subjects are cut off from direct contact with and influence from their interplay with the natural and the practical orders because these are mediated to them by the discourse of others. A parallel example of this kind of slippage is Colin Campbell's excellent *Myth of Social Action*,[5] where he traces how the broader Weberian concept of 'action' was sedulously truncated into 'social action'. This will be the subject of the main two parts of this chapter, after a brief and sympathetic glace at the heavy historical heritage of thought in which both approaches were unavoidably entangled.

However, let me give a warning note: neither approach can commandeer and monopolize the term 'relational'. Both are just as relational as one another. Where they differ are in *which relations* they will entertain, *whether one kind* is accorded priority, and therefore *which kinds of causal powers* are admitted and considered most influential. It follows that to preface any phenomenon, problem, proposition, or

[3] Nick Crossley, *Towards Relational Sociology* (London: Routledge, 2011), p. 75.
[4] Margaret S. Archer, *Being Human: The Problem of Agency* (Cambridge: Cambridge University Press, 2000). See chapter 4, 'The Primacy of Practice', pp. 121–153.
[5] Colin Campbell, *The Myth of Social Action* (Cambridge: Cambridge University Press, 1996).

proposed solution with the adjective 'relational' means little until it has been unpacked. After all, who would disagree that the whole universe is constituted by relations?

The background: modernity's man and society's being

The sociological problem of conceptualizing the person is how to capture someone who is partly formed by their sociality, but also has the capacity to transform their society in some part. The difficulty is that social theorizing has oscillated between these two extremes. On the one hand, Enlightenment thought promoted an 'undersocialized' view of the subject, one whose human constitution owed nothing to society and was thus a self-sufficient 'outsider' who simply operated in a social environment. On the other hand, there is a later but pervasive 'oversocialized' view of the subject, whose every feature, beyond the biological, is shaped and moulded by the social context. Singular subjects thus become such dependent 'insiders' that they have no capacity to transform their social environment.

Instead, if we are to understand and model each and every human person as *both* 'child' and 'parent' of society there are two requirements. First, social theory needs a concept of the person whose sociality does make a vital contribution to the realization of their potential *qua* human beings. Second, however, it requires a concept of the person who also possesses sufficient relatively autonomous properties and powers that he and she can reflect and act upon their social context, along with others like them, in order to transform it.

It is maintained that both the 'undersocialized' and the 'oversocialized' models of humankind are inadequate foundations for social theory because they present us with either a self-sufficient *maker* of society, or a supine social product who is *made*. This background to the chapter summarizes how these two defective models of the human being have sequentially dominated social theory since the Enlightenment, and to indicate their deficiencies for social theorizing. These are mirror images of each other, because the one stresses complete human self-sufficiency, whilst the other emphasizes utter social dependency.

In cameo, the Enlightenment had allowed the 'death of God' to issue in titanic 'Man'. The secularization of modernity was accompanied by an endorsement of human self-determination: of people's powers to come to know the world, to master their environment, and thus to control their own destiny as the 'measure of all things'. Not only does *'Modernity's Man'*[6] stand outside nature as its master; 'he' also stands outside history as the lone individual whose relations with other beings and other things are not in any way constitutive of 'his' singular self but are merely contingent accretions, detachable from 'his' essence. Thus the modern self is universally pre-given.

As the heritage of the Enlightenment tradition, *'Modernity's Man'* was a model which had stripped down the human being until he or she had one property alone, that of instrumental rationality, namely the capacity to maximize their preferences through means-ends relationships and so to optimize their utility. Yet, this model of *homo economicus* could not deal with our normativity or our affectivity, both of which are intentional – that is they are 'about' relations with the various orders of natural reality: nature, practice, and the social. These relationships could not be allowed to be, even partially, constitutive of who we are. Instead, the lone, atomistic, and opportunistic bargain-hunter stood forth as the impoverished 'model of man'.

On the one hand, some of the many things social with which this model could not deal were phenomena such as voluntary collective behaviour, leading to the creation of public goods, or normative behaviour, when *homo economicus* recognized his dependence upon others for his own welfare, and, finally, his expressive solidarity and willingness to share. On the other hand, one of the most important things with which this model cannot cope is the human capacity to transcend instrumental rationality and to have 'ultimate concerns'. These are concerns that are not a means to anything beyond them, but are *commitments which are constitutive of who we are* and thus the basis of our personal identities.[7] It is only in the light of our 'ultimate concerns' that our actions are ultimately intelligible. None of this caring can be impoverished by reducing it to an instrumental means-ends

[6] 'Man' and especially 'rational man' was the term current in Enlightenment thinking. Because it is awkward to impose inclusive language retrospectively and distracting to insert inverted commas, we reluctantly abide with the term 'man', as standing for humanity, when referring to this tradition.

[7] For a concise version of the argument, see Margaret S. Archer, 'Persons and Ultimate Concerns: Who We Are Is What We Care About', in E. Malinvaud and M. A. Glendon (eds.), *Conceptualization of the Person in Social Sciences* (Rome: Vatican Press, 2006), pp. 261–283.

relationship, which is presumed to leave us 'better off' relative to some indeterminate notion of future 'utility'.[8]

Nevertheless, this was the 'model of man' that was eagerly seized upon by social contract theorists in politics, Utilitarians in ethics and social policy, and liberals in political economy. *Homo economicus* is a survivor. He is also a colonial adventurer and, in the hands of rational choice theorists, he bids to conquer social science in general. As Gary Becker outlined this mission, 'The economic approach is a comprehensive one that is applicable to all human behaviour':[9] including choice of spouse, charitable giving, visiting aged parents, and which church is attended, besides specifically market behaviour.

However, the rise of postmodernism during the late twentieth century represented a virulent rejection of *'Modernity's Man'*, which then spilt over into the dissolution of the human subject and a corresponding inflation of the importance of society. Displacement of the human subject and celebration of the power of social forces to shape and to mould strips the subject of all personal properties and powers by rendering them as 'indeterminate material'. In Lyotard's words, 'a *self* does not amount to much',[10] and in Rorty's follow-up, 'Socialisation . . . goes all the way down.'[11] To give humankind this epiphenomenal status necessarily deflects all real interest onto the forces of socialization. People are indeed perfectly uninteresting if they possess no personal powers which can make a difference to themselves or to their social environment. What then becomes of human dignity or human rights?

The de-centring of the Enlightenment concept of the human being thus leads directly to an actual dissolution of the self, which becomes kaleidoscopically shaped by the flux of historico-cultural

[8] For a critique of Rational Choice Theory's 'model of man', see Margaret S. Archer, 'Homo Economicus, Homo Sociologicus and Homo Sentiens', in Margaret S. Archer and J. Q. Tritter (eds.), *Rational Choice Theory: Resisting Colonization* (London: Routledge, 2000).

[9] G. Becker, *The Economic Approach to Human Behaviour* (Chicago: Chicago University Press, 1976), p. 8. It seems regrettable that Becker termed this 'the economic approach' because of the erroneous implication that all economists endorse it.

[10] J-F. Lyotard, *The Postmodern Condition* (Minneapolis: University of Minnesota Press, 1984), p. 15.

[11] Richard Rorty, *Contingency, Irony and Solidarity* (Cambridge: Cambridge University Press, 1989), p. 185.

contingencies. References to the human person become indefinite, because contingency deprives him or her of any properties or powers which are intrinsic to humankind and inalienable from it. Consequently, to Foucault, 'Man would be erased, like a face drawn in sand at the edge of the sea.'[12]

Postmodernism has massively reinforced the anti-realist strand of idealism in social theory and thus given ballast to Social Constructionism. This is the generic view – endorsed by the *Relationists* – that there are *no* emergent properties and powers pertaining to human persons, namely ones which exist in between human beings as organic parcels of molecules and humankind as generated from a network of social meanings.[13] The model of *'Society's Being'* is Social Constructionism's contribution to the debate, which presents all our human properties and powers, apart from our biological constitution, as the gift of society. From this viewpoint, there is only one flat, unstratified, powerful particular, the human person – who is a site or literally a point of view. Beyond that, our selfhood is a grammatical fiction, a product of learning to master the first-person pronoun system, and thus quite simply a theory of the self which is appropriated from society. Constructionism thus elides the *concept of self* with the *sense of self*. We are nothing beyond what society makes us, and it makes us what we are through our joining society's conversation. *Society's Being* thus impoverishes humanity, by subtracting from our human powers and accrediting all of them – selfhood, reflexivity, thought, memory, emotionality, and belief – to society's discourse and particularly to culture.

What makes human subjects act now becomes an urgent question because the answer cannot ever be given in terms of people themselves; they have neither the human resources to pursue their own aims nor the capacity to find reasons good if they are not in social currency. This means that to the Constructionists people can only be moved by reasons *appropriated* from society and are thus effectively condemned to being *conventionalists*. Constructionists are unable to explain why some people (singularly and collectively) seek to replace society's rules,

[12] M. Foucault, *The Order of Things* (New York: Random House, 1970), p. 387.

[13] The best example of this model is provided by the work of Rom Harré. The leitmotif of his social constructionism is the following statement: 'A person is not a natural object, but a cultural artefact'. *Personal Being* (Oxford: Basil Blackwell, 1983), p. 20.

other than as permutations on what is socially given, or on what basis such change is sought.

The central deficiency of these two models is their basic denial that *our experiential relations with the nature of reality* as a whole makes any difference to the people that we become or even to our becoming people. *Modernity's Man* is preformed, and his formation, that is the source of his properties and powers, is not dependent upon his own experiences of reality. Indeed, reality can only come to him filtered through an instrumental rationality that is shackled to his interests – one whose own genesis is left mysterious. Preference formation has remained obscure, from the origins of the Humean 'passions' to the goals optimized by the contemporary rational chooser. The model is *anthropocentric* because man works on reality as a whole but reality does not work upon man, except by attaching risks and costs to the accomplishment of his preformed designs. In short, he is closed against any encounter with reality which could make him fundamentally different from what he already is, including both his formative and elective relations.

Similarly, *Society's Being* is also a model which forecloses direct interplay with most of reality. Here the whole of reality comes to people sieved through one part of it, 'society's conversation'. The very notion of being selves is merely a theory appropriated from society, and what people make of the world is a matter of permutations upon their appropriations. Again this model cuts persons (singular and collective) off from any experience of reality itself, one which could make them fundamentally different from what social discourse makes of them. Society is the gatekeeper of reality, and therefore all that we become is society's gift because it is mediated through it.

What is lost, in both versions, is the crucial notion of experience of reality; that the way matters are can affect how we are. This is because both anthropocentricism and socio-centrism are two versions of the 'epistemic fallacy', where what reality is taken to be – courtesy of our instrumental rationality or social discourse – is substituted for reality itself. Neither jointly nor severally can we live by the 'epistemic fallacy' for, had Hume been serious that we have no better reason to leave the building by the ground-floor door than through the second-floor window, that should have found him exiting through the latter half of the time. Instead, that which exists (ontologically) has a regulatory effect upon what we make of it and, in turn, what it makes of us – through our two-way relations. These effects are independent of our full epistemological penetration, just as gravity influenced us and the projects we could entertain long before we conceptualized it.

Relations between humanity and reality are intrinsic to the development of personal properties which are *necessary* conditions of social life itself. In brief, there is a transcendental argument for the necessity of a 'sense of self' to the existence of society. The continuity of consciousness, meaning a continuous 'sense of self', was first put forward by Locke.[14] To defend it entails maintaining the crucial distinction between the evolving *concept* of self (which is indeed social and variable) and the universal *sense* of self (which is not). This distinction has been upheld by certain anthropologists, like Marcel Mauss,[15] to whom the universal sense of 'the "self" (*Moi*) is everywhere present.'[16] However, there has been a persistent tendency in the social sciences to absorb the *sense of self* into the *concept of self* and thus to credit what is universal to the cultural balance sheet.

The best way of showing that the distinction should be maintained is a demonstration of its necessity – namely, that a *sense of self* must be distinct from social variations in *concepts of selves* because society could not work without people who have a continuity of consciousness. The demonstration consists in showing that for anyone to appropriate social expectations it is necessary for them to have a sense of self upon which these impinge, such that they recognize what is expected of them (otherwise obligations cannot be personally appropriated).

[14] Locke put forward a definition which has considerable intuitive appeal, such that a person was 'a thinking intelligent being, that has reason and reflection, and can consider itself as itself, the same thinking thing in different times and places' (*Essay* II, xxvii, 2). From Bishop Butler onwards, critics have construed such continuity of consciousness exclusively in terms of memory and then shown that memory alone fails to secure strict personal identity. See, for example, Bernard Williams, *Problems of the Self* (Cambridge: Cambridge University Press, 1973). A defence of a modified neo-Lockean definition is provided by David Wiggins, 'Locke, Butler and the Stream of Consciousness: and Men as a Natural Kind', *Philosophy*, 51 (1976), which preserves the original insight.

[15] To Marcel Mauss, the continuous 'sense of self' is universal. See M. Mauss, 'A Category of the Human Mind: The Notion of Person; the Notion of Self', in M. Carrithers, S. Collins and S. Lukes (eds.), *The Category of the Person* (Cambridge: Cambridge University Press, 1989).

[16] For Mauss, this constant element consists in the fact that 'there has never existed a human being who has not been aware, not only of his body but also of his individuality, both spiritual and physical.' *Ibid.*, p. 3.

Hence, for example, the individual Zuni has to sense that his two given names, one for Summer and one for Winter, apply to the *same* self, which is also the rightful successor of the ancestor who is held to live again in the body of each who bears his names. Correct appropriation (by the proper man for all seasons) is dependent upon a continuity of consciousness which is an integral part of what is meant by selfhood. No generalized social belief in ancestral reincarnation will suffice; for unless there is a self which (pro)claims *I* am *that* ancestor, then the belief which is held to be general turns out to be one which has no actual takers! This is incoherent for it amounts to saying that everyone knows what roles should be filled but that no one has enough of a sense of self to feel that these expectations apply to them. The implication for society is that nothing gets done. Human beings have to be determinate in this one way at least, that of acknowledging themselves to be the same beings over time. In other words, Zuni society relies upon a 'sense of self', even though concepts of the self, within Zuni culture, are unlike ours.

It should be noted that the two impoverished sociological models of the person, being briefly examined, are also themselves dependent upon a continuity of self-consciousness – of which they give no account. *'Society's Being'* needs this sense of self in order for a subject to know that social obligations pertain to her, rather than being diffuse expectations, and that when they clash it is she who is put on the spot (like Antigone) and has to exercise a creativity or decisiveness that cannot be furnished by the discursive canon. Unscripted performances, which hold society together, need an active subject who is enough of a self to acknowledge her obligation to write her own script to cover the occasion. Similarly, this continuous sense that we are one and the same being over time is equally indispensable to *'Modernity's Man'*. He needs this sense of self if he is consistently to pursue his preference schedule, for he has to know both that they are his preferences and also how he is doing in maximizing them over time.

Relations with the world or relations confined to the social order?

A major problem in examining 'Relational Sociology' is that those who appropriate the label are far from homogeneous or consensual. Certainly, all reject *'Modernity's Man'*, but since this repudiation is becoming more and more common among social (not economic) theorists it cannot serve as a differentiating feature. There is a tendency for *Relationists* to cluster more closely towards *'Society's Being'*, especially those who avow philosophical affinity with Wittgenstein. When these theorists turn to conceptualizing the *Relational Subject*, the thinkers upon whom they depend are uniformly those who have accorded the social order undisputed primacy over other orders of reality, to the extent that nature and practice *are filtered through* the social. For the rest of their days, neonate human beings cannot become other than they are *by means of their direct engagement* with the natural world or skilled involvement with their heritage of material culture. For example, this is the case for those who adopt Vygotsky as mentor (e.g. Rom Harré), or more frequently, George Herbert Mead (e.g. Nick Crossley).

However, this is not the case for all self-declared 'Relational Sociologists'. It does not appear so for Emirbayer,[17] who, despite his wealth of references, does not seem to be standing on the shoulders of any particular past giant. And it is certainly not the case for either of the present authors. Personally, I consider myself to be a 'Relational Sociologist' but one who stresses that all our human capabilities and liabilities (apart from the physiological) exist only *in potential* and, crucially, that their development – its direction or possible distortion – *depends on our relations with all three orders of reality*. There is much interplay between the consequences of our ineluctable relations with these three orders, and our task is to theorize them, but not by presuming that the social order is the universal filter of reality as a whole.[18] If some readers would be more comfortable in calling me a 'Relational Realist', so would I, because what I will be advancing is a *stratified ontology of the Relational Subject* (made up of the 'I', selfhood; the 'Me', primary agency; the 'We', collective agency; and the 'You', the singular actor).These are indeed increasingly social but never independent from the properties and powers of people, possessed and exercised in their concrete singularity and in constant relation with the natural and practical orders of reality.

That is why it is important to start in this section with the vexed question of the 'self' – not the Cartesian *cogito*, not the soul, not

[17] M. Emirbayer, 'A Manifesto for a Relational Sociology', *American Journal of Sociology*, 103 (1997), 281–317.

[18] All arguments presented here are developed more fully in Margaret S. Archer, *Being Human: The Problem of Agency*.

	Natural Order	**Practical Order**	**Social Order**
Relationship	Object/Object	Subject/Object	Subject/Subject
Knowledge Type	Embodied	Practical	Discursive
Emergent from	Coordination	Compliance	Commitment
Relations Contributing to	Differentiating bodily envelope from environment	Distinction between subjects and objects	Distinguishing self from other people

Figure 3.1 Three kinds of relations with natural reality and their resultant types of knowledge
Source: Archer, 'Routine, Reflexivity and Realism', *Sociological Theory* 28:3 (2010), 293.

William James' 'self of selves' in its inner citadel, and not the variable social concepts of the self – but how the *sense of self* is formed through our relations with the three orders of reality, many of which are prelinguistic and therefore independent of linguistic mediation. This realist reconceptualization grants humankind significant degrees of (i) temporal priority, (ii) relative autonomy, and (iii) causal efficacy, in relation to the social beings that they become and the powers of transformative reflexivity and action that they bring to their social contexts, or to any other. Nevertheless, the process is relational through and through. Permit me to condense the lengthy argument from *Being Human* into Figure 3.1, summarizing our different relational acquisitions from our unavoidable human involvement in the world that contribute to the *sense of self*.

These are distinct contributions (even though many settings are empirical combinations natural reality's different orders). They are distinct – and not merely analytically so – because our direct encounters with nature are *object/object* ones (in relation to water, our bodies are floatables); with material artefacts they are *subject/object* relations where we, as subjects, encounter their resistances and affordances, acquiring skills in relation to them (children master holding and slowly tipping a full bottle of milk and drinking it at three months). Of course, this bottle was socially given to them, but a much later present of golf clubs never made anyone a golf player; the skill of 'catching on' has to be personally acquired by everyone as does the embodied skill of swimming. If practical knowledge is the source of 'knowing how', the major contribution of linguistically encoded discursive knowledge, involving *subject/subject* relations, is 'knowing that'; theoretical and authoritative statements not reliant upon experience (but by being told that touching the fire will hurt).

What do these forms of knowledge have to do with the formation of the *sense of self*? The differentiation of this *sense* is taken as synonymous with 'self-consciousness',[19] and since this sensing is wordless because it is both prelinguistic and alinguistic – being acquired through touching, moving, manipulating – then it cannot be a socially acquired concept. Its modality is sensual, and the medium of inscription is the body. Differentiation emerges from the use and development of sensory-motor skills in the immediate surrounding environment, where their relationship generates an emergent awareness of the difference between the two.[20] Thus, Merleau-Ponty maintains that the nascent and yet unnamed 'I' can self-consciously manipulate the dialectical relationship between self and otherness and, in this very process, reinforces the distinction between the two.[21]

John O'Neill starts to move the argument to the next stage. So far: the 'phenomenal body is the matrix of human existence . . . Through the phenomenal body we are open to a world of objects as polarities of bodily action. The phenomenal body is a modality of being-in-the-world which is privileged because it is the Archimedean point of action.'[22] But, which actions work to secure the differentiation of subject from objects? Here, Piaget is of huge assistance in presenting practical action as the wordless source of reason, and specifically of referential detachment.[23] His aim was to demonstrate that

[19] Harry G. Frankfurt, *The Importance of What We Care About* (Cambridge: Cambridge University Press, 1988), pp. 161–2.

[20] Even Harré admits that 'touch permits the establishment of a distinction between perceiver and perceived that is wholly within the experiential context of *one perceiver*'. Rom Harré, *Physical Being* (Oxford: Blackwell, 1991), p. 96 (italics added).

[21] M. Merleau-Ponty, *Phenomenology, Language and Society* (London: Heinemann, 1974), pp. 283–284f.

[22] John O'Neill, *Perception, Expression and History* (Evanston, IL: Northwestern University Press, 1970), p. 87.

[23] This is not the Piaget of the educationalists who construed him as presenting some kind of iron law of four cognitive stages of child development, but the patient observer and ethnographer of his own offspring and deviser of experiments fostering logical mastery through hands-on practice.

once we detach objects from ourselves, we simultaneously accept that they are governed by powers independent from our own. Thus 'it is only by achieving belief in the object's permanence that the child succeeds in organizing space, time and causality.' Piaget's research programme began with investigation of the practical activities of pre-linguist children 'which tend to construct the object as such.'[24] Through the visual and auditory tracking of objects by manipulative activities such as reaching and grasping, to the point where the child seeks for hidden objects she shows by her practical action that she attributes permanence to objects, which she conceives of as possessing autonomy and permanence distinct from her own subjectivity.

This acceptance of objects' intransitivity and the separation of their powers from ours is the start of living in the real world. In autumn, I watched my five-month-old granddaughter both mastering and being mastered by her 'bouncy chair'. She already appeared to understand that her movements caused the chair to move up and down as she squirmed. Then, within an afternoon, she discovered that a determined pumping action with her leg produced more bounces. What cured her of believing that the chair was subject to her subjectivity, signalled by a waving leg? Simply, that when she overdid her pumping, the chair tipped over and decanted her. Thereafter her leg pump was more respectfully discreet. Not a bad lesson in 'accommodation' to have acquired in one afternoon.

To grasp the permanence of objects and their distinctive properties and powers, an intransitivity that Piaget termed 'object conservation' and, more broadly 'objectification', is crucially linked in his thought with coming to appreciate the logical principles of identity and non-contradiction.[25] This is because the young learners have to resist appearances (there seems to be less water in a small, fat vessel than a tall, thin one) and learn to do so faster through pouring the liquid back and forth themselves, which instils 'sameness of quantity' and overcomes the seeming visual contradiction. Through practical activity, 'it is the child's own action that encourages the acquisition of

[24] Jean Piaget, *The Construction of Reality in the Child* (London: Routledge and Kegan Paul, 1955), p. 93f.

[25] Jean Piaget, *The Child's Conception of the World* (London: Routledge and Kegan Paul, 1967).

conservation,'[26] and from there, a rudimentary but serviceable grasp of the logical canon.

The import of this is nothing less than supplying the necessary condition for being able to participate in the discursive order of reality. The very possibility of communication is ultimately dependent upon beings who already have some understanding of the law of identity and who are obedient to the law of non-contradiction. Otherwise, no information can be conveyed verbally, including the use of natural language itself, as distinct from mimetic noises.[27] The basic laws of logic are learned through relations with objects; they cannot be taught through language, because the linguistic medium of socialization presupposes them.[28]

In this section, I have completely reversed the Meadian or Vygotskian sequence in order to allow for the impact of our human relations with all three orders of natural reality, rather than endorsing the overwhelming primacy of the social or discursive order. Nonetheless, this remains an entirely relational account. Whatever its shortcomings, it at least serves to show that Relational Sociology and specifically the conceptualization of the Relational Subject does not depend upon asserting the complete, necessary, and exhaustive hegemony of the social domain. In *Being Human* it is held that such an approach would entail 'downwards conflation', where the social impress obliterates all personal properties and powers of the subject.[29] Yet, for instance, I hazard a guess that none of us were taught to incline our body weight forward when going uphill and the reverse for down an incline; we ourselves just found it easier that way.

The preceding paragraph refers to entirely different propositions from one which a 'Relationalist' sociologist maintains, but the social relation is the central entity in Relational Sociology ('entia' implying no substantialism or materialism, but deriving from the Latin verb 'esse' meaning to exist, i.e. to be real). That conceptual and theoretical focus is not contradicted here, providing it is allowed that the relations

26 Jean Piaget, *Experiments in Contradiction* (Chicago: University of Chicago Press, 1974), pp. 185–201.

27 For example, children can repeat nursery rhymes by rote, but to understand 'Baa, baa black sheep' entails that if the wool seller has three sacks (and sells by the sack) there can be only three purchasers or recipients.

28 See Steven Lukes, 'Some Problems about Rationality', in Bryan R. Wilson (ed.), *Rationality* (Oxford: Blackwell, 1979).

29 See Archer, *Culture and Agency*, chapters 2, 3, 4.

of Relational Subjects are not confined to the social order, but are plural and – most importantly – intertwined with one another. Why this caveat is held crucial will be demonstrated in the next section, which outlines the stratified ontology of the Relational Subject. In so doing, it will be essential to introduce very early on the subjects' relationships with their contexts of action because there is no such thing as decontextualized action. (I rather resist the term 'situated action', which may be innocent but could imply 'central conflation'.) No context, such as a subject's natal background, can be reduced to entirely social terms, to something like 'other people' in Watkins' canonical statement of Methodological Individualism.[30] All the same, it is vital to understand and explain their interrelationship.

Generically, this is equally the case for relational encounters with structure and culture, which, contra Emirbayer, are not reifications but are irreducible to what X possesses and believes compared with Y and the indeterminate and interminable 'transactions' that ensue between them. Indeed, one of the strengths of much of Relational Sociology is its endorsement of emergence from relations themselves (relational goods and evils) and the emergent powers deriving from relations between relations. This was a hallmark of the great American pragmatists, such as Peirce and Mead, it is fully acknowledged by Crossley, and it has been most thoroughly developed by my co-author. In short, a Relational Sociology which accepts that all social action is both 'context dependent' and 'concept dependent' cannot merge into 'Actor-Network' theory and follow Latour's injunction to 'keep ontology flat.'

The process of becoming a full person: 'I', 'Me', 'We', and 'You'

The sense of self is nothing more or less than sensing oneself to be one and the same human being over time, occupying the same body and usually denoted by the same given name. This does not mean the 'sense' is constant, because we accumulate new sensed experiences; nor does it imply that the 'self' is unchanging, because it is modified by organic changes over the life-span, cumulative changes because

[30] The canon is taken to be J. W. N. Watkins, 'Methodological Individualism and Social Tendencies', in May Brodbeck (ed.) *Readings in the Philosophy of the Social Sciences* (New York: Macmillan, 1968).

of the life lived and its accompanying life-styles; and circumstantial alterations, deriving from accident, illness, displacement, relocation to the effects of political policy and international relations. The sense is continuous, but there is no essence of the self to detect. When people sometimes say, 'I am not the person I once was', this requires the thread of continuous sensing in order to make the contrast.

Neither is this thread of literal self-awareness possessed of many characteristics that have been claimed for it in philosophy: of infallibility (Descartes), of first-person omniscience (Hume), of indubitability (Hamilton), or of incorrigibility (Ayer). It claims only the self-warrant[31] of being the sole 'insider' account (in the first person), which is not of necessity an 'outsider's interpretation' (in the third person).[32] This is an ontological claim, not an epistemological claim. It rests upon being the one and only occupant of that body who experienced whatever it went through in its life-course to date and has sufficient memory (not perfect recall or epistemic reliability) to know *that* it underwent a sequence of occurrences, which may well be concealed from other people, and *what* was entailed may be known only partially by the subject. (Soldiers recalled suffering in the trenches during the First World War, without necessarily sharing their experiences later on, let alone knowing the main causes of that war.)

This is very different from the standard Meadian account,[33] still proffered in recent works laying claim to 'Relational Sociology'. Thus, Crossley begins correctly enough by writing that 'To acquire a sense of self is to acquire a sense of one's own particularity,'[34] but rapidly reverts to his argument[35] that 'our sense of self is achieved within a narrative mode.' In other words, it is about storytelling, for 'Stories are the means by which we make sense of our self and past

31 I follow William Alston here, defining 'self-warranted' belief as: 'Each person is so related to propositions ascribing current mental states to himself that it is logically impossible both for him to belief that such a proposition is true and not to be justified in holding this belief; while no one else is so related to such propositions.' 'Varieties of Privileged Access', *American Philosophical Quarterly*, 8 (1971), 235.

32 Donald Davidson, 'First-Person Authority', *Dialectica*, 38 (1984), 110.

33 For my critique of Mead, see *Structure, Agency and the Internal Conversation*, pp. 78–90.

34 Nick Crossley, *Towards Relational Sociology*, p. 91.

35 Nick Crossley, *Introducing Narrative Psychology* (Buckinghamshire: Open University Press, 2000).

actions . . . Moreover, stories and storytelling, both individual and collective, furnish the "definition of the situation" that many sociologists deem central'[36] as well as the other actors involved because 'We know others as we know ourselves; by way of stories.'[37] Within four pages, Structure, Culture, and Agency, besides the self, have been severed from reality and have joined the ranks of fiction.

Lack of space restricts me to commenting only that in this swift lurch towards fictional selves, we lose any importance attaching to *internal relations* (including that which Mead himself attached to the 'inner conversation', since he did not reduce reflexivity to one's internal campfire tales). We also sacrifice our *relations to the world* as a whole whose properties and powers become as fictitious as stage scenery; the accumulated skills, artefacts, and science through which the human race has survived to date; and, most bizarrely of all, *we yield up the reality of social relations* (as anything more than narrative exchanges).

Instead, I want to preserve all of these aspects of relationality and how they are intertwined, and will start by returning to the continuous sense of self that is the 'I' and build upwards to our *internal and external relations*. In the process, I wish to defend the proposition that the 'Me' has an objective as well as a subjective face, *precisely because* every 'Me' does undergo a 'situated' development. No decontextualized 'self' has ever been born. Indeed, whether or not it can survive its organic liabilities, can develop any of its potential capacities, and how long it lives may have everything to do with that context and nothing else at all. The same is the case for the 'You', if only because everyone's horizons are circumscribed by the aspirations it is possible to entertain at a particular historical date. Quite properly, sociology accentuates the 'You' that is open to some *subjects* socially and objectively inaccessible to others.[38]

The distinctions among the 'I', the 'Me' and the 'You' are relational and temporal; all three change over time and therefore the respective pronouns, which remain constant, in fact point to changing referents in each case. Today's 'I' is not the same as that of last week, last year, or of our adolescence or childhood. The 'I' alters as it moves along the time-line which is also the 'life-line' of each person. Correspondingly,

36 Crossley, *Towards Relational Sociology*, pp. 94–95.
37 Crossley, *ibid*. p. 97.
38 One that positivism has overdone through its (imperfect) correlations between the situated 'Me' and the future 'You'.

the past-self or 'Me' also changes, if only because it accumulates over the life-course, and the future-self or 'You' changes simultaneously, if only because its potential attenuates. Moreover, as the three alter in synchrony with one another, so do the relations between them.

If the 'I', the 'Me' and the 'You' are quintessentially temporal concepts referring to the real internal relations of the self, then they are not reified entities. Even the constancy of the 'I', in reflexively sensing itself to be the same continuous being over time, does not mean that it is unchanging. Similarly, the 'Me' and the 'You' change accordingly. For example, the past 'Me' of a recent widower is now one to which has been added the experience of losing his wife, the sense of bereavement has accrued to his present 'I', whilst his future 'You' has acquired the potential for re-marriage. Yet, has this created another problem: 'how do we distinguish between aspects of what is in fact continuous?'

This is not problematic because we can make an *analytical* cut[39] at some point in time and for some purpose in hand, so that the activities of the acting 'I', and its dialogue with itself can be examined at a given T1, wherever that is situated historically. It is only by separating them in this way that the influences of the past upon the present can be identified and the effects of the present upon the future can be determined. Project the 'I' forwards and backwards over time and it is continuous. This is easier to grasp if it is thought of over the life-span of a singular subject, as in Figure 3.2.

The 'I' changes over time; partly as the consequences (including the unintended) of its own past life-projects, and partly because of the contingencies of life in an open system. Thus, the 'I' of any particular interval will have a different past self and future self to whom it will refer. During Shakespeare's 'seven ages of man', the arrow representing the 'I' changes because the self is undergoing transformation and so too are the circumstances that it confronts sequentially. But the 'I' takes the 'Me' and the 'You' reflexively into account within its internal

[39] Making *analytical* cuts is something Dépelteau rejects and also misconstrues in relation to 'structure' ('What is the Direction of the "Relational Turn"', in C. Powell and F. Dépelteau, *Conceptualizing Relational Sociology*, New York: Palgrave Macmillan, 2013). In the basic morphogenetic diagram, if drawn correctly, there is never a moment when social life is not structurally conditioned. This is the case when past conditioning (diachronic) is distinguished from current conditioning (synchronic) because the distinction between them is only an analytical one. The *process* of conditioning is continuous although the *form* taken by structure changes over time.

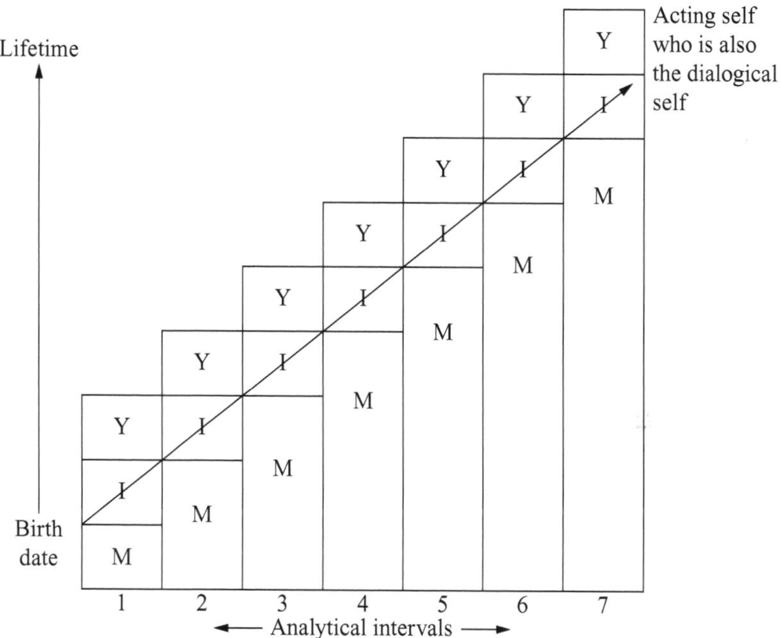

Figure 3.2 Relational phases of the self
Source: Archer, *Structure, Agency and the Internal Conversation*, 2003, p. 114.

conversations – prospectively and retrospectively – thus helping to shape the trajectory of the 'I' across the life-course as we make our way through the world.[40]

The making of full personhood

It is time to get better acquainted with the *external relations* of our subject, because the 'Me', the 'We', and the 'You' are all occupants of a social context, though certainly not the same one. Figure 3.3 illustrates how the full person comes to assume all of these characters. The 'I', as the only speaker in the internal conversation,[41] takes heed of the others who constitute its *internal relations* but retains responsibility for the course of action in the world pursued at any given T1. Therefore, the 'I'

[40] Margaret S. Archer, *Making our Way through the World; Human Reflexivity and Social Mobility*.
[41] See Archer, *Structure, Agency and the Internal Conversation*, p. 93f.

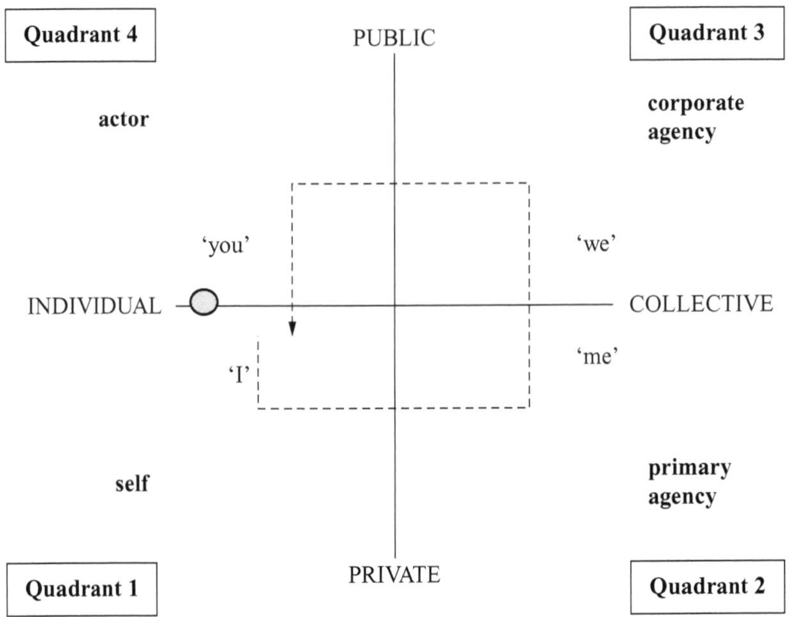

Figure 3.3 A life-long task : the making of a Person
Source: Archer, *Being Human*, 2000, p. 295.

retains its own personal properties and powers: these are not socially untrammelled as is the 'individual' in *Modernity's Man* but neither are they nonexistent or mysterious as in *Society's Being*. The 'I' is always striving for some governance over its own life in the social order.

Figure 3.3[42] represents only the first circuit made by the neonate up to 'maturity'. Probably much more important for most people in late modernity, as morphogenesis intensifies and morphostatic processes decline in significance,[43] is that we all continue to re-circle the square throughout our lives. The last section of this chapter seeks to show that quite literally 'personal development' cannot be captured unless social relations are given due attention in two respects: first, as 'companions', who are acquired on the first circuit and may be hard to shed even if they are not 'good companions'; second, the interrelations between

42 This is the exact reverse of the 'Vygotskian Square' presented by Rom Harré, *Personal Being* (Oxford: Blackwell, 1983), p. 77.

43 See Margaret S. Archer (ed.), *Social Morphogenesis* (Dordrecht: Springer, 2013).

the first and subsequent 'companions', that is, their relationality or the relations between relations, are the stuff of subsequent circuits.

The 'Me' as involuntary social relations

At the start of life (within Quadrant 1), the human subject simultaneously becomes objectively enmeshed in society – involuntarily, but inexorably – because at birth we all acquire positions on society's distributions of scarce resources and become members of a collectivity sharing the same life-chances, that is, part of an aggregate grouping of Primary Agents. Gradually, throughout childhood, the self-conscious human being learns about his or her objective placement and its relationship to the social ordering of qualities conferring *self-worth* and their opposites. 'I' realize *my* privileged or underprivileged position *vis-à-vis* him or her – the objects and opportunities which they have and 'I' do not, or vice versa. Because this is a completely involuntary placement, the Primary Agent is an object to herself. There are many things that 'I' can discover about 'my' objective position, which is only possible because there is a self-conscious 'I' which can make discoveries about 'Me' as a Primary Agent. The 'Me' is thus the object of society (that is, the outcome of previous interaction that has delineated its position along with others like it and different from it). The 'Me' is also an object to the 'I', who has the capacity to learn about it and reflect upon it, subjectively, evaluatively, and, above all, relationally.

What the subject reflects upon is clearly not her sociological status as a Primary Agent, but rather the day-to-day manifestations of objective and externally determined life-chances – as with the child who questions 'Why can't I have more to eat, or a bike?', versus the one who learns that its 'wants list' is always much better satisfied than those of its peers. Both learn that they have a place in the social world which is independent of (and oblivious to) their own merits or clamouring.

Moreover, the notion of 'self-worth', that supremely social concern operative in the discursive order,[44] begins to develop as 'I' discover that there are all sorts of things about 'Me' that are positively or negatively regarded, despite their being involuntary. These are qualities that are objective to the self, and thus belonging to a different category from

[44] Distinguished by being what Charles Taylor calls a 'subject-referring property': *Human Agency and Language* (Cambridge: Cambridge University Press, 1985), p. 54.

those things 'I' can change through acting differently (as in promises of 'good behaviour'). Accompanying these discoveries that the 'I' makes about the 'Me' come various forms of affect. 'I' have concerns about the things 'I' see (whether bikes or birthday parties) and the emotion felt is the commentary passed when 'I' learn that they are not for 'Me' – or, conversely, are 'mine for the asking'. Frustration and gratification are therefore the basic affective responses to different social placements.

The 'I' makes all kinds of discoveries about the 'Me', which are every bit as much of a discovery as those that it makes about self-sufficient objects in the world. Just as the 'I' learns that there are 'dangerous' and 'pleasant' objects, she also learns that she herself has 'desirable' and/or 'undesirable' characteristics. Thus, the 'I' may discover that its 'Me' is considered to speak with the wrong accent, to be of a disfavoured colour or gender, and that nothing 'I' can immediately do will change matters. Alternatively, 'I' may be gratified that there is something about 'Me' which has to be lived up to in order to keep my position ('live up to my good name'). In either case, considerations of self-worth have dawned, along with the realization that both sets of characteristics in question and the evaluations they receive are external in origin. Being a reflexive monitor, the 'I' may show a variety of responses towards the socially favoured or disfavoured 'Me' as it moves through childhood. Which predominates for given subjects appears to be highly dependent upon the relations prevailing in its natal environment and the type of social context in which that is embedded.[45]

The process of socialization today is taken up in detail in my next chapter (see especially Figure 4.2), but the young subjects' responses hinge crucially upon the degree to which relational goods versus evils are experienced within the family through relations with caretakers. The greater these goods (normative consensus among the adults, stability and warmth within the unit, concern for and involvement of the offspring), the more the young subjects will tend to identify with and later seek to reproduce a similar unit themselves. This does indeed mean that, in their case, the dispositionality they develop both reconciles them to and prepares them for the reproduction of the objective 'Me' they have 'inherited'. That course of action is dependent upon two major factors: the absence of countervailing relational influences from peers, and the presence of sufficient 'contextual continuity' in the

[45] Archer, *The Reflexive Imperative*, chapter 3.

social order to render reproduction a feasible project. The extensiveness of contemporary social change makes this decreasingly possible or, at least, increasingly difficult, which is why the majority of today's young are no longer Bourdieu's people because they do not inhabit Bourdieu's largely stable social world.[46]

This is particularly marked among the young recipients of relational evils from their natal backgrounds, whose response is to reject not only their proximate family unit but also its surrounds (neighbourhood, religion, ethnicity, language, etc.). Such a rejection is also a repudiation of the involuntarily assigned 'Me'. The acquisition of a different 'Me' depends upon the affordances of the broader social context and the subjects' determination to make them theirs. Similarly, those brought up within stable but nonconsensual units tend not to take sides (which would spell a further qualitative deterioration in relations), but to inspect the surrounding environment for a relational group (gang, club, sports association, church, cause, social movement, etc.) whose focal concern attracts them. Affiliation with such a 'We' can eventually prove to be the doorway to a different 'Me'.

Thus, there are relational reasons for endorsing the natal 'Me' or rejecting it (as will be examined in the next chapter). The majority of the young who seek to change their involuntary placement for another 'Me' do so because they have encountered a different form of (Corporate) Agency that recommends itself to their concerns and is socially available to them. Such nascent concerns may be ephemeral because the teenagers, as yet, do not know enough about themselves and about the world and are best seen as tentative and localized experiments. The key to the durability and development of the concern and its loosely associated 'Me' is the existence of a complementary 'We'. Membership of an aggregate of 'Me's' sharing the same life-chances alone is not a satisfying or sustainable way of life for almost anybody.

Becoming a 'We' as an act of solidarity

It is the powers of the person in his or her concrete singularity to reflexively monitor the self, others, and relations between them that enables this subject to make *commitments* in a genuine act of solidarity

[46] See Craig Calhoun, 'Habitus, Field and Capital: The Question of Historical Specificity', in Craig Calhoun, Edward LiPuma, and Moishe Postone (eds.), *Bourdieu: Critical Perspectives* (Cambridge: Polity, 1993), p. 82.

from which any 'We' arises. Primary Agents, as collectivities sharing similar life-chances, are mere aggregates and cannot be *strategically* involved in social change. For that, the leverage of a 'We' is required.

'We's' come in all shapes and sizes from the couple, to families, to sporting, cultural, or volunteer groups, up to social movements.[47] Each of these generates its own *sui generis* effects; all are important because of their interrelations with one another. Thus, we should glance briefly at macro-, meso-, and micro-forms of 'We's' to disengage how their emergent properties exert both upwards and downwards causal effects.

Starting at the macro-level, Primary Agents lack a say in structural or cultural modelling: they neither express interests nor organize for their strategic pursuit, unless and until they become related within a form of 'We' that I call Corporate Agency. The typical powers of this relationship are capacities for articulating shared concerns, organizing for collective action, and exercising influence as a group in decision-making. Corporate Agents act together and interact with other Agents, and they do so strategically, that is, in a manner which cannot be construed as the summation of individuals' preferences. To talk of strategic action implies that Corporate Agents are 'active' rather than 'passive',[48] that is they are social subjects with reasons for seeking to bring about certain outcomes. Yet these reasons have to be found good in order for Primary Agents to commit themselves to such a 'We', and their own micro-relations can hinder their mobilization. For example, in the past, workers with dependent families had to weigh providing bread for them today versus jam and justice tomorrow, through becoming involved with unionization and strike action.

The implication is that the 'I' and the satisfactions/dissatisfactions it experiences as it discovers and reflects upon the involuntary 'Me' can only reproduce/transform the macroscopic Socio-Cultural system, which gave the 'Me' its particular object status, by collaborating with a 'We' in collective action. That is a necessary but not sufficient condition for influencing social transformation, which then creates a greater

[47] In the Prologue to Part III, we explain why it is rare and difficult for the Government or State to be a solidary 'We', although this may be the case in the early days of political party formation or even new nationhood.

[48] Martin Hollis, *Models of Man* (Cambridge: Cambridge University Press, 1977).

array of roles (at T4) in which the totality of 'I's' can invest themselves. In sum, the relational activities of Corporate Agents are the linking mechanism that narrows the gap between the 'I' and the 'Me' for increasing sections of the population as they acquire the 'Voice' of a 'We'.

If Corporate Agents are successful in introducing morphogenesis (to some degree) at the macro-level, this also entails the 'double morphogenesis' of Agency itself. In the 'double morphogenesis', the collective action (partially) transforming some part of the social order is inexorably drawn into transforming the categories of Corporate and Primary Agents themselves. The morphogenetic scenario has the following consequences for the 'double morphogenesis' of Agency in late modernity: the progressive expansion of the number of Corporate Agents, of those who are counted among them, and of the divergent concerns represented by them, which intensifies conflict between them. Accompanying this process is a complementary shrinkage of Primary Agents, due in part to their mobilization to join burgeoning promotive groups and in part to the formation of new social movements and defensive associations, as some of them combine to form novel types of Corporate Agency. In shorthand, throughout later modernity the active 'We's' expand proportionately and diversify, whilst the passive 'Me's' diminish accordingly.

Increasingly, within *Relationalism*, the meso-level is represented by networks. Whilst network analysis is useful in establishing *connections*, it is misleading to elide these with *relations*. For example, the distribution list of a given journal can be presented as a network of recipients, with the Editorial Board as the broker, often presumed to exercise influence over the nodes. However, connectivity is not relationality; recipients may discard the journal and have better things to discuss with their colleagues than another dismal publication. Deducing influence from connections is simply empiricist. As far as the *relational* 'We' is concerned, this entails at least a degree of commitment; the 'We' in question may be aspirational at first (the journals we would wish to appear in), but later becomes a working 'We' (journals we actively support through our efforts, demonstrating our commitment through willingness to read, edit, translate, and submit our articles, unprompted by empiricist 'impact factors').

The reciprocity that is definitional of the 'We' relationship is predicated upon some initial involvement of the part of the 'I's' (which may

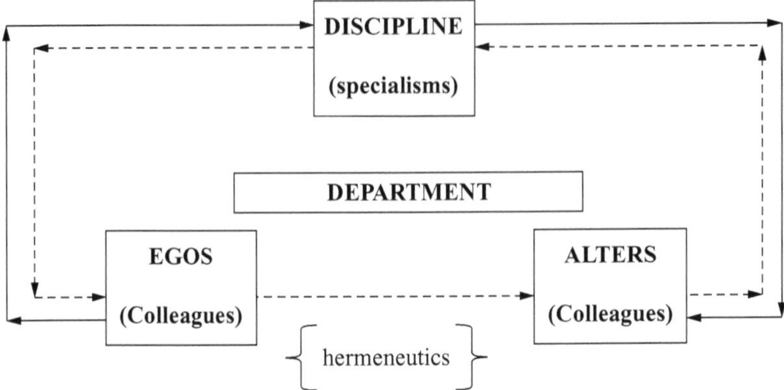

Figure 3.4 Relational Reflexivity entails the Third in the department
Source: Archer, 'Collective Reflexivity: A Relational Case for It', in C. Powell and F. Dépelteau, (eds.), *Conceptualizing Relational Sociology: Ontological and Theoretical Issues* (New York, Palgrave Macmillan, 2013), p. 158.

be stimulated by appropriate social policies).[49] Given it, both relational goods and evils can be generated. On the one hand, concerted work on a small, new journal may speedily refine its school of thought and its qualitative standing as well as enlarging the 'We' itself. On the other hand, the same scale of enterprise might result in preaching to a small chapel of the converted, intensifying their resistance to any synergistic elaboration of their approach, thus branding and stranding this 'We' in the position of 'true believers'.

Similarly, the diverse extramural 'We' affiliations of members of a department with their discipline are essential for understanding what they will and will not do and with whom they will ally and vote at meetings. Collective reflexivity means that all colleagues have their relation to the discipline (or a section of it) in mind as they interact in the department, but they do not have the same thoughts in their heads; their intentionality is not shared, and neither are their commitments to the discipline identical in kind. What is collective is the colleagues' common orientation to their common discipline. What is reflexive is that this orientation is bent back and affects what they do (and decline to do) in the department and how they do it (see Figure 3.4).

[49] Donati gives various examples, including 'family intervention', in his own chapters.

Micro-level relationships serve to illustrate the important point that subjects who belong – as most of us do – to multiple 'We's' may find that these can be both compatible and incompatible (as is also the case at the meso-level). In a longitudinal study of undergraduates,[50] the relationality between 'families', 'home friends', and new 'university friends' was particularly problematic and preoccupying for active young agents. Complementarity and incongruity are lived realities that subjects strive to deal with reflexively. Sustaining complementarity often involved experimenting with mixing their 'We's' or temporization or compartmentalization, but usually confronted subjects with making an unwanted choice between their 'We's'. Commitment is always involved: the minority most closely bonded with their families were ready, though frequently reluctant, to cede their new friends and vice versa. This is discussed further in my next chapter.

The 'You' as social identity and a relational outcome

Over the life course, the different constituents making for full personhood develop sequentially as shown in Figure 3.5.

Human selfhood ⇒⇒⇒ **Social Agent** ⇒⇒⇒ **Social Actor**

(Grandparent) *(Parent)* *(Offspring)*

Figure 3.5 The stratified ontological development of the human Person

Infant Agents have a long way to go before they become mature Actors. Nevertheless, the kind of Primary Agents, the 'Me' that they start out being without any choice, because of parental relations and social life-chances, profoundly influences what type of Actor they become. Certain opportunities and information are open to the privileged and closed to the nonprivileged. Options are not determined for these 'Me's, but the opportunity costs of attaining them are stacked very differently for the two groups. It is the fact that people heed such opportunity costs which produces the well-known regularities in differential attainment of top positions, according to class, gender, and ethnicity. Such differential costs constitute good reasons for initially opting for different sections of the total role array. Initial choice of

[50] Margaret S. Archer, *The Reflexive Imperative in Late Modernity*.

position is corrigible, but big corrections entail increased costs, which are further reasons why not very many will undertake drastic remedial measures (why, for example, so few female, Asian home-workers ever find their way to university).

These initial interests with which Agents are endowed, through their life-chances, provide the leverage upon which reasons (otherwise known as constraints, enablements, and motivations) for different courses of action operate. They do not determine the particular Social Actor an individual chooses to become, but they strongly condition what type of Social Actor the vast majority can and do become. So far, only choice of part of the role array has been made explicable (the part that satisfies empiricists), but explanation can go much further – both over time and down to the level of the singular person – provided the role of the relational 'We' is introduced.

The 'We' forms a series of bridges to the 'You'. At the macro-level, the interaction between Corporate Agents morphogenetically extends the array of roles for occupancy through the changes it introduces, thus modifying the distribution of 'Me's' as part of the 'double morphogenesis'. At the meso-level, the 'We's' that develop are often a direct bridge to career choice, occupational placement, and work experience: young people who become active in Greenpeace will receive information and discouragement about entertaining a future in accountancy, whilst those involved in a sports club will have the opportunity of training and trials that are openings to professionalism for the talented. At the micro-level, an intense 'We' involvement in gang membership can become a relational bond whose bridge leads only to further illegal activities. Conversely, becoming active in a voluntary organization may reveal the extent of unmet needs and furnish role models for those already dedicated to improvement that fosters a desire to contribute full-time to the generation of relational goods on the part of the subject by training to work in that field. For good or ill, the 'We' has potential repercussions for the precise 'You's' developed and how they are 'personified' by the Actor. This is not simply a matter of 'role-taking', because the Actors' personifications are part of role-making that is itself morphogenetic in its consequences. This is because a decade or two later, this will have helped to shape the modified role extended to the next 'generation' of Actors-to-be. These phases are summarized in Figure 3.6.

The conditioned 'Me' – primary agent

T1

The interactive 'We' – corporate agent

T2 **T3**

The elaborated 'You' – P.I. + S.I

T4

Figure 3.6 The morphogenetic elaboration of personal and social identities
Source: Archer, *Being Human: The Problem of Agency* (Cambridge: Cambridge University Press, 1988), p. 296.

A lifetime of circling the square: the developing 'I', 'Me', 'We', and 'You'

This account has sought to give due importance to our personal properties and powers and simultaneously to the properties and powers of our social relations, because the two are intertwined although irreducible to one another. Analytically, the rest of anyone's life can be represented as a ceaseless circling of the square presented in Figure 3.7 with the same two powers constantly and conjointly at play.

As always, the features elaborated at the end of a morphogenetic cycle by T4 then become the new T1′, that is, those features which condition subsequent interaction. Thus, at the end of the first or developmental sequence, we finished with subjects who had achieved strict social identity by finding a role(s) in which they found it worthwhile to invest themselves, and who had also acquired the personal identity which enabled them to personify it in a unique manner, reflective of *who* they themselves were – as defined by their constellation of concerns. Of course, they continue doing this at the new T1′. In living out the initial role(s), which they had found good reason to occupy, they bring their singular manner of personifying it or them, which has consequences over time. What this can do creatively is to introduce a continuous stream of unscripted role performances which, also over time, can cumulatively transform role expectations. These creative acts are thus transformative of society's very normativity, which is often most clearly spelt out in the norms attaching to specific roles. Equally,

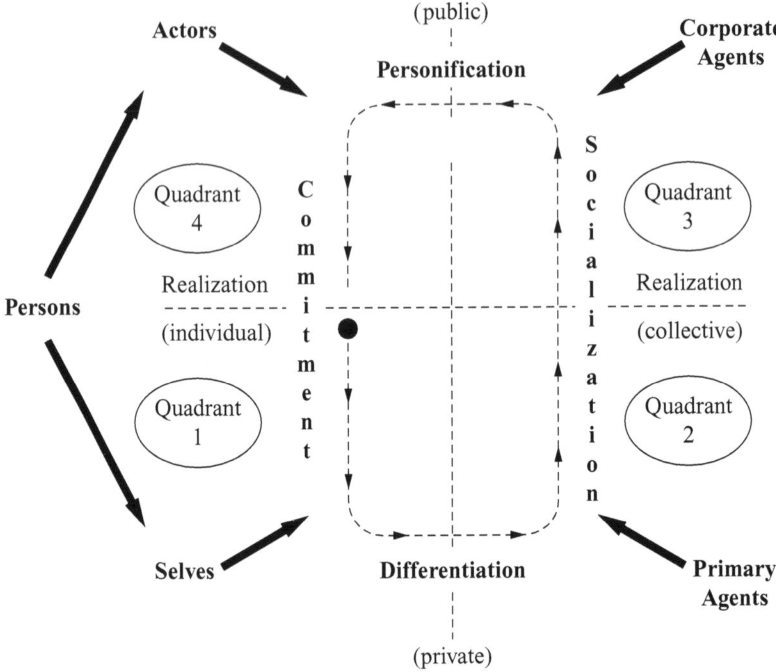

Figure 3.7 The development of the stratified human being
Source: Archer, *Being Human*, p. 260.

the obverse can occur at the new T1′ or at successive T1's, as given Actors continue to circle around the square.

Each successive circuit will find that the Actors have changed experientially, their relationships have altered, and so have their contextual circumstances. In other words, the micro-, the meso-, and the macro-levels continue to interpenetrate and to influence one another. The complexities involved can be reduced by following hypothetical Actors[51] when they revisit each Quadrant in turn, as a continuous 'I,' who fallibly and reflexively attempts to take stock of the developments they have undergone in relation to the 'Me', the 'We', and the 'You', which have been part of each subject's personal morphogenesis.

[51] These are based upon the in-depth interviews conducted for my trilogy on Reflexivity: *Structure, Agency and the Internal Conversation* (2003), *Making our Way through the World* (2007), and *The Reflexive Imperative in Late Modernity* (2012).

Although this is obviously an analytical contrivance, it will allow an illustration of the part played by relational goods or evils in decisively shaping the trajectory taken, which is anything but a lone monadic journey.[52]

Re-entering Quadrant 1 and intrapersonal relations

This is very much the place of personal reflexivity, where our continuous self-consciousness has a new item to address, namely the personal and social self that 'I' have become. The 'I' and 'myself' have the most intimate of all relationships. They have insider information and legitimately engage in insider dealing. Thus they share their uncertainties and self-doubts of which the world may be oblivious. Perhaps some readers will recognize the internal reaction, 'Well, you may have fooled the driving test examiner, but you're not safe to be on the road'. Furthermore, the 'You' has given the 'I' something to live up to (or to live down), but necessarily to live with: and 'I' have to be a collaborator in my own life because 'I' have been there all along, complicit in though not having sole responsibility for shaping what it has become. But 'I' am an active collaborator because the future still has to be made, and these acquired characteristics do not determine its making. The Actor cannot remain fixated on the thought, 'Hasn't she come a long way': the day after graduation or ordination or motherhood. The 'I' has to pick up the baton and take the responsibility for living out the identities it has developed in conjunction with others, who remain part of the Actor's internal life and some of whom continue to people her external social world. The significance of these relations has a different bearing when re-visiting the other three Quadrants.

Re-entering Quadrant 2 and the relations of the 'Me'

The initial involuntary placement of all Primary Agents on society's distribution of scarce resources is not itself deterministic, and the relationality of subjects with their natal environments, especially their

[52] This point has been perversely and repeatedly misunderstood by Anthony King, despite it being clear that *Being Human* was deliberately written to pick out 'the generic transformations which our *powers as persons* can induce' (*ibid.*, p. 299), in opposition to a growing body of literature (endorsing 'Society's Being') that denies personal powers.

families, plays a crucial role in their aims to endorse or to repudiate their original 'Me's and thus their social origins. However, both reflexive aspirations and the receipt of relational goods and evils in early family life have to contend with changes in society's opportunity structure, their unequal distribution, and their increasingly morphogenetic nature.[53]

Generically, what social morphogenesis spells is a reduction of *family and natal bonds* and the maintaining of, at best, *interpersonal relationships* with family members. This means that dense bonding with the natal environment (its predominant socio-economic character, geolocal situation, ethnic or religious affiliation) are replaced by thinner *interpersonal relations*, effectively severed from the surrounding environment – one that should not in any case be construed as a traditional community – in which the parental generation is situated and perhaps embedded.

Such *interpersonal relations* represent an acknowledgement of gifts and care received during their upbringing, some enduring (often rueful) affection for the parent(s), but, nevertheless, they constitute something close to repayment of a debt. These new and distanced 'Me's' regard their original bonds in the light of shackles and endorse the new 'Me' over the original 'Me'. What remains is a sense of interpersonal responsibility for the older generation ('seeing that they are alright'), a duty to their parents that ends abruptly with their deaths. But this involves a family relationship being re-construed as the exchange of (near) equivalents (in extreme form, exchanging receipt of early care for giving late-in-life provisions). It is an interpersonal manner of commodifying familial relations, which may well be accompanied by feelings of guilt, but sometimes entails overcoming reluctance.[54]

The reduction of bonding to *interpersonal relations* has the direct effect of weakening *social integration*, specifically by reducing intergenerational solidarity. These new 'Me's' have effectively substituted exchange for reciprocity. This type of exchange or *quid pro quo* is personalized and carries a date stamp. It has no future, and its influence as a pattern of conduct reinforces this. In both ways, it is the

[53] See Margaret S. Archer (ed.), *Social Morphogenesis* (Dordrecht: Springer, 2013).

[54] On both sides, it can prompt resistance to any notion of cohabitation, which is why the 'three g' family tends to be rare, even compared with relatively recent postwar practices, and is presented in Northern Europe as 'experimental'.

reverse of reciprocal action. Reciprocity both kick-starts and sustains noncommodified social relations. Indeed, part of reciprocal free-giving is precisely that it is far removed from interpersonal exchange, but can be 'passed down the line'; reciprocation can involve generous actions towards others (including distant others, as with adoption at a distance), thus expanding the ripple effect. Its consequence is a reinforcement of social solidarity, whereas the result of the interpersonal exchanges above – ones that terminate when a particularistic duty has been discharged – is to weaken it. This tendency is reinforced by macro-morphogenetic social changes encouraging the new 'Me's' to take jobs anywhere, thus serving to justify nothing more than dutiful behaviour, because geography can be held responsible instead of agential disengagement and separation. In this way, still future 'Me's' can feel it acceptable to distance themselves still further.

Natal relations that are experienced as relational evils prompt flight but can be hard to escape, especially for poorer and less educated subjects.[55] A fairly common resort is to forge a different 'Me' amongst peers in the locality. The 'Me' who had suffered neglect and abuse may escape by gravitating towards a local gang and their 'groupies'. Their changed status can be viewed as promotion unless or until it results in a criminal record when, objectively, the obstacles to extricating themselves constructively are intensified. The parallel can be the single mother, temporarily buoyed up by acquiring 'someone to love' and also social housing, but sometimes resorting to a truce with her family or the serial partnering of desperate loneliness. When such subjects re-circle the square, they may be equally dissatisfied with the natal and the current 'Me', but as passive Agents they look only to contingency (a lottery win or the randomness of popular 'celebrity') for a change in their lot. What they do not hope for, because they have little experience of them, are relational goods. This outlook is reinforced by the diversity of the urban poor, which intensifies during late modernity, whose differences outweigh their commonalities and are barriers to the development of any cohesive and localized 'We'.

[55] An example of successfully quitting an abusive natal environment is examined in *The Reflexive Imperative*, *ibid.*: follow 'Shirin' in chapter 7. The difficulties she overcame were formidable.

Re-entering Quadrant 3 and the vicissitudes of the We

So far, the discussion has focussed upon the effects of subjects receiving and responding to first-order relational goods and evils. However, it is especially with the 'We', the Collective subject, that second-order relations – meaning relations between relations – are confronted in the form of congruities and incongruities, which exercise their own causal powers. This confrontation arises for the simple reason that most of the time most of us belong to more than one 'We'.

Because of their denial of emergence, *Relationists* often reduce the resultant constraints and enablements to, as Emirbayer puts it, network effects, that is, 'the direct and indirect connections among actors. This approach explains certain behaviours or processes through the fact of connectivity itself – as well as through the density, strength, symmetry, range and so on, of the ties that bind.'[56] Instead of resting content with the empiricism of 'connectivity', he advocates a more stratified social ontology, but without explicitly exploring the second-order effects of relationality.

I will begin discussion of this important topic by underlining something else that occurs covertly or overtly as a consequence of subjects revisiting Quadrant 2. Not only do they make a *personalized* assessment of the place that their new 'Me' has upon the social distribution of resources and life-chances, they evaluate these distributions themselves as fair or unfair. Under their own descriptions they will judge that certain people and their activities are not receiving their due *because* such distributions are too steep, too flat, or too skewed. Depending on their evaluations, subjects (who may now have become Collective subjects as part of a couple, generating relational goods), will respond very differently. Contentment with themselves and acceptance of their social positioning will not activate second-order powers; it will prompt affinities with a 'We' who is similarly placed, which is morphostatic in its consequences and thus does not disrupt the continued generation of their domestic relational goods (barring the contingencies of life in an open system).

Conversely, a couple who concludes they should strive to narrow the gap between the 'Me' that they have become and that which they would

[56] Mustafa Emirbayer and Jeff Goodwin, 'Network Analysis, Culture, and the Problem of Agency', *American Journal of Sociology*, 99 (1994), 1411–1454, p. 1419.

be, do embroil themselves in second-order relationality by acting upon their judgement. This nexus is the source of mature students, career changes, late vocations and, perhaps, the decision not to have a family. In many cases, this means that the two partners will be electing to form part of different 'We's' from one another, even if this is regarded as temporary. But these two new elective 'We's' may pull the pair in different directions – new friends, new values, new horizons, and new opportunities. Unless, as a Collective subject, they can synthesise these differences into a joint project for action, one that creatively establishes complementarity,[57] the couple itself suffers *qua relationship* from the incongruities it has activated.

This will be more pronounced if only one of the couple takes this course. To begin with, the pair may deliberate together and determine that this action on the part of one of them is 'for the good of the family', without reflexive awareness that it may well threaten the continued generation of their familial relational goods. Tasks, responsibilities, and the domestic division of labour will all have to be accommodated to the change, which the couple may try to plan in advance. However, what they cannot foresee is how they themselves will change and most importantly in their relationship with each other, as one of them electively forges a new 'We' (e.g. my new friends at university). The unintended consequence will also tend to be that the two partners are coming to occupy different social positions in terms of their 'Me's', although this was intended for their common good and defined as temporary. But, temporary may be too long. It can happen to either of the partners, and it will take time for them to realize that their (now) incongruent 'We's' have gradually transformed their original relational goods into evils: into feelings of unfairness, resentment, embarrassment, unease, and perhaps envy and betrayal. It is not inevitable, but having cut the generative motor producing relational goods as a couple and, at worst, having changed them into relational evils, it is also far from unusual for divorce or re-partnering to ensue. Mature students have been known to 'joke' that they received their degree and their *decree nisi* in the same year.

In discussing couples, I have focussed on the micro- to meso-level effects of incongruent 'We' relationships. A parallel phenomenon

[57] A tense example of this happening successfully is provided by 'Ryan and Vickie' in *The Reflexive Imperative*, chapter 6.

characterizes the relationality between the meso- and the macro-levels. This can be illustrated by a trajectory common to many charities. In late modernity the pattern taken by these voluntary associations is quite similar and utterly different from the Bill and Melinda Gates Foundation with its 8000 employees. First, a 'We', as a small Corporate Agent, would identify a specific unmet need, sometimes through personal experiences or those of family members (for instance, palliative medicine, the hospice movement, care for the autistic, riding for the disabled) or pioneer a novel way of providing services that were unavailable (for example, food banks, micro-credit, charity shops, and free-cycle). Second, it would gain local publicity, attract funds from events in the vicinity, and the 'We' would grow as new volunteers were drawn to it. Finally, it could possibly become national or even international, through attraction and imitation, then acquiring formal organization, registered charity status, accountants, and employees. Up to this latter stage, it would be generating relational goods for those helped and for those helping, with volunteers coming forward on a fairly democratic basis and gaining something nonmaterial from belonging to this 'We'.

However, these collective subjects making up the 'third sector' are vulnerable to both 'colonization' (take over by market and state) and to 'counter-institutionalization' (turning themselves into organizations modelled on market and state practices). Both processes contribute towards a diminished generation of relational goods because of these macro-level influences. Simultaneously, the meaningfulness of being a voluntary member of such a 'We' diminishes as hierarchy, professionalism, and performance regulation increase, all of which spell assaults on the 'We', previously electively embraced and bonded through co-working.

'Colonization'[58] by the market consists in taking over voluntary innovations and simply turning them into for-profit associations, subject to bureaucratic regulation. Many activities that were successfully pioneered by voluntary initiative have been turned into business ventures, floated on the stock market (as in chains of care homes). Pedagogical innovation in private Progressive schools became the state's free research and development agency – one that could be raided *and*

[58] J. Habermas, *The Theory of Communicative Action* (Cambridge: Polity Press, 1989).

ridiculed. Similarly, attempts to create and consolidate the 'cyber commons' through peer-to-peer exchanges were promptly appropriated by *Wikinomics*,[59] as a method for harvesting free technical solutions under what was euphemistically termed 'dispersed production'.

'Counter-institutionalization' works the other way round, prompted by the self-defence of a 'We', which transforms itself in this process. Charities become charitable enterprises, as was already presaged several decades ago by the commercialized 'plate dinner', where the self-promotional photo-call displaced free-giving as a motive. More recently, employing commercial fund-raisers.com has become standard (competitive) practice, as has media promotion, the employment of lobbyists, and 'celebrity' representation.

Necessarily, these 'We's' have their lifetimes, too: their associations, organizations, and movements succeed and become incorporated, they mutate strategically, they fail and amalgamate, regroup, or disband. What this means is that every time Quadrant 3 is revisited, every person brings with them their biography as a relational 'We'. Equally importantly, they have to determine the next episode of it and whether or not they will remain part of it.

Revisiting Quadrant 4 as a review of our commitments

On each visit to Quadrant 3, we re-monitor our commitments to the 'We' and reflexively re-determine *how* we will stand with *whom* in solidarity. This is much the same process as subjects conduct regularly in relation to their personal commitments to a particular role (say, university teacher) and how they have so far been able to personify it (active role-making). Such re-evaluations are unavoidable because we ourselves change – as in Figure 3.2, 'Relational phases of the Self' – as do the 'We's to whom we belong and the 'You's that are most expressive of who we are because they represent our ultimate concerns. In both cases, the question is whether or not to continue our previous dedication to that 'We' or that 'You', *despite* the changes undergone by both. Alternatively, subjects ask themselves whether they should and could *reflexively change* those groupings with whom they feel they can

[59] Don Tapscott and Anthony Williams, *Wikinomics: How Mass Collaboration Changes Everything* (New York: Penguin, 2007).

form a solidary 'We', as a Collective subject, and change those roles through which the 'You' can express its ultimate concerns.

In their internal conversations through which they attempt to accomplish these two tasks, variations in the receipt of relational goods and evils will play a crucial part. Sometimes, although not necessarily, shifts in relational goods/evils will involve one and the same succession of changes for the 'We' and the 'You'. The example on which I will finish is probably recognizable to many readers, at least among those over a certain age.

People who sought to become university teachers, as expressive of their commitment to the discipline and also affording congenial colleagues and students with the same kind of interests, have found these relational goods plummeting over the last twenty-five years. Public accountability, metrification, research evaluation criteria, ranking of 'worthwhile' publication outlets, and the transformation of students into customers or clients have *inter alia* transformed 'science as a vocation' into a form of public administration. In turn, collegiality – and the stimulus of exchanges with one's colleagues – is a crucial relational good that has been transformed into its opposite. We are pitted against one another in marketized competition, ranked according to bureaucratized performance indicators, fearful of student evaluations, hermeneutically suspicious of 'peer review', and waiting in trepidation for the next round of departmental (or course or syllabus) 'rationalization'.

These changes, in response to new economic and governmental practices, are themselves morphogenetic, but it is active Relational Subjects who are responsible for collaborating with them or challenging them. Which response will predominate depends upon the increasing receipt of relational goods or evils and their reflexive reception by the relational 'We' – unless its solidarity is destroyed through these very processes.

4 Socialization as Relational Reflexivity

MARGARET S. ARCHER

Introduction

Often the ability to state a problem is as important as the capacity to solve it. To that extent, Mead's conviction that the processes of socialization and reflexivity (which he called 'inner conversation') were necessarily intertwined was a breakthrough. It promised to provide leverage upon inescapable issues: how were 'individual and society' connected? How did the social order enter into the constitution of the human being? How was the tension between singular impulses and social normativity resolved? In his responses, Mead never relinquished his belief that the process of socialization also entailed processes of reflexive reception and reflexive reasoning on the part of subjects. This I consider to be his great achievement, despite serious doubts that his key linking mechanism between socialization and reflexivity, the 'generalized other', remains responsible today, as he himself came to question after the First World War.[1] Therefore, it seems a squandering of his patrimony that those forming the line of Mead's successors – Parsons, Habermas, and Beck – should all have *abandoned* reflexivity in their accounts of socialization.[2]

There are also two root difficulties in this long tradition of conceptualizing socialization. The first is that *human subjects are cut off from linguistically unmediated relations with the world*, as seen in

[1] Mead accepted that 'the community may in its size transcend the social organization, may go beyond the social organization which makes such identification possible. The most striking illustration of that is the economic community. This includes everybody with whom one can trade in any circumstances, *but it represents a whole in which it would be next to impossible for all to enter into the attitudes of others*.' G. H. Mead, *Mind, Self and Society* (Chicago: University of Chicago Press, 1934), pp. 326–327 (italics added). For a discussion, see Margaret S. Archer, *Structure, Agency and the Internal Conversation* (Cambridge: Cambridge University Press, 2003), pp. 64–78.

[2] This chapter draws upon my *The Reflexive Imperative in Late Modernity* (Cambridge: Cambridge University Press, 2012).

Chapter 3. Habermas, endorsing Mead, encapsulates this when he says that everything the self is emerges because it 'runs through the network of linguistically mediated interactions'.[3] Intentionality, which is quintessential to meaningful action, is required to make a detour through the medium of language and thus linguistic inter-relations: 'the linguistic socialization of consciousness and the intentional relation to the world are mutually constitutive in the circular sense that each presupposes the other conceptually.'[4]

To give such epistemological primacy to language precludes any other mode of relational contact between human subjects and the different orders of natural reality (see Chapter 3). What is real and of efficacy in relation to human consciousness is confined to the communicational order (here termed the 'discursive' order). Whilst this is stretched to include (dubious) communications to and maybe with posterity, it appears to be restricted to the Socio-Cultural level and to exclude reflexive internal conversation with those parts of the Cultural System[5] that do not enjoy social salience at any given time. Obviously, it is also severed from encounters with the natural and practical orders of reality and would deny both the possibility and the significance of these being bodily encoded and themselves exercising a *dispositional* influence upon the shunning and seeking of subsequent experiences, including many within the social order. Yet, reflexivity is broader than language because it can register, record, and respond in terms of visceral and visual messages[6] and, thus, is operative prior to the acquisition of the public linguistic medium.[7] Dispositions are indeed important, but cannot be presumed to have their locus exclusively in the social (i.e. the discursive) order.

[3] Jürgen Habermas, 'Individuation through Socialization: On Mead's Theory of Subjectivity', in his *Post-metaphysical Thinking: Philosophical Essays* (Cambridge: Polity Press, 1992), p. 170. The same assumptions are endorsed by almost all social theorists who have taken the 'linguistic turn'.

[4] Jürgen Habermas, 'The Language Game of Responsible Agency and the Problem of Free Will: How Can Epistemic Dualism Be Reconciled with Ontological Monism?', *Philosophical Explorations*, 10 (2007), 13–50.

[5] For the distinction between the Cultural System and the Socio-Cultural levels see Margaret S. Archer, *Culture and Agency* (Cambridge: Cambridge University Press, 1988).

[6] Norbert Wiley, 'Inner Speech as a Language: A Saussurean Inquiry', *Journal for the Theory of Social Behaviour*, 36 (2006), 319–341.

[7] Neurological support is provided for this view by Jason E. Brown, 'Morphogenesis and mental process', *Development and Psychopathology*, 6 (1994), 551–563.

Our relations with the real world are truncated because they are circumscribed by language, which postpones relations with all else until it can be discursively mediated. As in the neo-Wittgensteinian tradition, epistemology is given priority over ontology. Social realism reverses this relationship, and it does so because it holds that it is our doings in the world which secure meanings, and not *vice versa*. Some of these are forms of engagement with the world that begin before the acquisition of language. Therefore, whilst terming children 'pre-linguistic' is relatively unproblematic, the confidence with which many authors designate a 'pre-reflexive' stage is highly questionable. In fact, doing so simply reflects their assumption that all human reflexivity has to postdate language acquisition by definition. This I have explored in *Being Human*,[8] and I want to suggest that the argument presented there provides the basis for an alternative account of socialization – one of *socialization as an active process of engagement with the world that works through Relational Reflexivity*.

The second root difference from the dominant tradition is that it will be argued that *the development of the socialized subject*, defined as someone who has achieved both personal and social identity, is relational through and through. It is ironic that throughout the whole swathe of that tradition, although the entire responsibility for socialization is vested in and confined to the social order, *relational reality does not feature in it at all*. Whether we consider Mead's 'generalized other', Parsons' 'central value system', or Habermas' 'universal communication community', not one of them deals with human relations and their emergent effects. Instead, socialization derives from either *systemic* influences of the 'whole community' in Mead, from the system's defining normative subsystem in Parsons, or from ideals held to inhere in the 'unlimited communication community' by Habermas. These all pass, as it were, through human relations, treated as fully permeable membranes, to influence young subjects whose passivity and pliability are presumed to be their main characteristics. Real relations are dissolved into agents as *träger*, with the parental generation being mere executors of society's normativity and the next generation becoming its passive absorbers. In this 'blotting paper' account of socialization, the real relations between these generations, taking place within the family and natal background, are totally ignored. This excludes *a priori* any reflexive evaluation on the part of young subjects in actively

[8] Archer, *Being Human*, chapter 4.

selecting or rejecting parental messages and values *according to the family's emergent relations.*

In this chapter, contemporary socialization is not viewed as a passive process. Partly, this is because the messages received from 'socializers' are increasingly 'mixed' rather than those held to stem from normatively consensual families and natal backgrounds in the past. In greater part, the more social morphogenesis outweighs morphostasis today, the greater the 'contextual incongruity' faced by the socialized, regardless of the consensuality of their socializers. The 'reflexive imperative' is confronted in the form of the '*necessity of selection*' among the increasing options becoming available. This requires an active 'socializant' who is a 'strong evaluator' of his or her concerns – that now represent their only compass – and also of the emergent relational goods and evils each has experienced within their natal backgrounds and their later relations. Reflexivity is the process through which most young people attempt to shape their own lives, but its exercise is a relational enterprise through and through. In other words, making the necessary selections and shaping these into a way of life (*modus vivendi*) are relationally reflexive endeavours, often dependent on Relational Reflexivity itself.

In sum, there are three reasons that prompt the reconceptualization of socialization today, compared with the traditional approach inherited from Mead to Habermas:

(a) Traditional conceptions of socialization no longer solve the original problem set by Durkheim, namely how to reconcile increasingly fast social differentiation – which can no longer be described as 'functional' – with the individuation that it not only continues to produce but fosters more rapidly and intensively.
(b) The contextual conditions necessary for the subject's socialization to be governed by the 'generalized other' (i.e. *the receipt of consensual messages, clear and durable role expectations, and normative consistency*) no longer maintain. On the contrary, by the late twentieth century each condition had become the obverse of the above. As nascent morphogenesis increasingly replaced morphostatic processes fostering social reproduction, especially from the 1980s onwards, 'Socio-Cultural' integration declined precipitously; stable functional differentiation ceded the way to novel variety in organizations, roles and occupations; and the

'Cultural System's' integration plummeted as global connectivity increasingly exposed larger tracts of *both* ideational *complementarities and contradictions* to more and more of the world's population.

(c) As social change intensifies, socialization can no longer be credibly conceptualized as a largely passive process of 'internalization' because there is less and less to normalize – that is, to present as *being normal* and *normatively binding*. Correspondingly, the traditional agencies of socialization – the Community (for Mead), the Family (for Parsons), Social Class (for Bourdieu), or the Lifeworld (for Habermas) – can no longer be conceived of as almost exclusively responsible for the process.

Rethinking socialization as relationally reflexive

The aim of the following argument is to retrieve two elements from the preceding theorists and to recombine them in a form appropriate to the contextual transformations that increasingly characterize the social order of the new millennium. On the one hand, reflexivity is retrieved and redoubled in importance because, given the decline of authoritative sources of normativity, young people are increasingly thrown back upon reflexively assessing how to realize their personal concerns in order to make their way through the world. On the other hand, their real relations with others also need retrieving as variable but powerful influences upon the equally variable outcomes that now constitute the lifelong socialization process. Otherwise, the entire concept risks drifting into an unacceptable monadism or slipping into Beck's portrayal of subjects' capricious and serial self-reinvention in a social context reduced to 'institutionalized individualism'.[9]

Instead, what I have termed 'Relational Reflexivity' is a reconceptualization that recombines these elements. In so doing, it provides traction upon how the main tasks confronting young and active agents are tackled, enabling them (i) to make personally meaningful (not instrumentally rational) choices from among the mixed messages they receive and (ii) to achieve some governance over the future trajectory of their own lives.

[9] Ulrich Beck and Elizabeth Beck-Gernsheim, *Individualization* (London: Sage, 2002), p. 51f.

Apart from its 'over-social' nature, a great strength to retain from Mead – one immediately relinquished by Parsons – is that socialization was not conceptualized as a passive process. The very need for reflexive dialogue between the 'impulsive' 'I' and the 'me' (represented by the 'generalized other') allowed the subject her *active inclinations* and to battle internally for them, even if they were usually over-ruled by the 'me', as the 'voice' of community normativity.[10] Returning to view socialization as an active, reflexive, and relational process is a good starting point for reconceptualization, even if the rest of the Meadian scaffolding is set aside.

Necessary selection as the beginning of shaping a life by defining what matters to us

Relationally, each 'invitation' to a new experience produces a response from the subject, via the experiment taking place between them, one registered in terms of satisfaction or dissatisfaction (which may come close to reflex-rejection where fear or repugnance are concerned). Yet, every form of relation may also generate emergent properties that are irreducible to their two components. The one of supreme importance here, even though it may be misjudged, misevaluated, and not be sustained, is the subject's discovery that a previously unknown experience '*matters* to me'. This is the beginning of practical reasoning about how one should live because it furnishes the potential raw materials, which may or may not be mutually compatible and thus have no guarantee of being retained. But what is meant by something 'mattering', as opposed to initial experiences being satisfying enough for someone to welcome their repetition, whilst simultaneously recognizing some of them as trivial (such as regularly enjoying, if not positively seeking, another ice-cream)? What does it mean for a subject to discern that 'this is important to me'?

[10] As Mead puts it, 'We are in possession of selves just in so far as we can and do take the attitudes of others towards ourselves and respond to those attitudes. We pat ourselves upon the back and in blind fury attack ourselves'. 'The Genesis of the Self and Social Control' (1924–5), in Andrew R. Reck, *Selected Writings: George Herbert Mead* (New York: Bobbs-Merrill, 1964), p. 288. Equally strongly, '(s)ocial control is the expression of the "me" over against the expression of the "I". It sets the limits', *Mind, Self and Society*, *ibid.*, p. 210.

In my DDD scheme of reflexive deliberation,[11] to care about something is the same thing as saying that 'something' is of concern or importance to someone, which is why the initial *discernment phase* is about identifying what does and does not matter to a subject. These are the foundation stones for our final ends (or 'ultimate concerns'), which are likely to be the key-stone(s) upon which practical reasoning is based. However, with young subjects, some things will not yet have been encountered or fully experienced – although these can later be incorporated. In short, *discernment* is messy, incomplete, and provisional at first. It does not culminate in *dedication* until near 'maturity', which is another effect of morphogenesis now introducing new options *whilst* the young are still growing up. Nevertheless, what caring means remains constant, even if the 'list' of subjects' concerns undergoes addition and deletion as well as accommodation and subordination.

To care is different from to want or to desire (i.e. from the Humean 'passions',[12] which he held, as do current rational choice theorists,[13] to be what moves us to action). This is because we can know that even some of our strong feelings are inconsequential ('Please may I not have a 6.00 am start') or undesirable ('I could kill for a cigarette'). Nor does expressing our desires as preferences bring us any closer to understanding what it means to have a concern. For example, any student could produce a preference order for the four modules they study each year, but this does not tell us if they care about their course at all. To care is not the same as exercising moral judgement or high-mindedness, because someone can have a deep concern for something that they themselves would not try to justify, at least publicly (for instance, the campus availability of drugs). Consequently, there need be nothing laudable about our engagements.

To have a concern is a challenge to make a commitment, providing circumstances are propitious. If they are, it is an active, willing

11 'DDD' stands for 'Discernment → Deliberation → Dedication'. See Archer, *Being Human*, *ibid.*, pp. 230–249.

12 'Reason alone can never be a motive to any action of the will... reason is and ought only to be the slave of the passions and can never pretend to any other office than to serve and obey them'. David Hume, *A Treatise on Human Nature* [1739–40] (Harmondsworth: Penguin, 1969), book II, part III, section 3.

13 Margaret S. Archer, 'Homo economicus, Homo sociologicus and Homo sentiens', in Archer and Tritter (eds.), *Rational Choice Theory, ibid.*, pp. 36–56.

endorsement of that which moves some people to care; this is of real and (is believed to be) of enduring importance to such subjects. In short, that concern is part of the subject's personal identity. It is also an affirmation of one kind of engagement with the world; things of no concern are the reverse. A student who feels that pursuing an interest in car mechanics is important to him is literally engaged differently with his own vehicle (if competent, he is independent in maintaining it), with the students he knows and some he doesn't (the guy who can fix car problems), with fellow motorists (the helper not the helped), with the garage and car trade (the one you don't rip off), etc. Note that the above instances of engagement are quite distinct from other forms of engaged action that he *may also* elect to join, such as belonging to a car club, taking formal qualifications in mechanics, or participating in the collective action of motoring organizations.

It follows from the above that the mental activities involved in caring – making commitments that build our identities and affirm a particular engagement with the world – are all ones that entail reflexivity. As Frankfurt puts it:

> [b]y its very nature, caring manifests and depends upon our distinctive [human] capacity to have thoughts, desires and attitudes that are *about* our own attitudes, desires and thoughts. In other words, it depends upon the fact that the human mind is *reflexive* . . . Creatures like ourselves are not limited to desires that move them to act. In addition they have the reflexive capacity to form desires regarding their own desires – that is, regarding both what they want to want, and what they want not to want.[14]

In that case, to reconceptualize socialization as first entailing an active selection about what is and is not important for a subject, from the array of experiences that have come his or her way, is to endorse not only the active agent but one whose relations *with* the world also actively shape the kind of agency he or she seeks to exercise *in* the world.

Of course, the young subject, like all subjects, will remain ignorant about many things that do matter to them. But, necessarily, and regardless of its form, further socialization always takes place in at least partial ignorance. One of the effects of nascent morphogenesis is that there is more and more about which we all remain in the dark.

[14] Harry G. Frankfurt, *The Reasons of Love* (Princeton, NJ: Princeton University Press, 2004), pp. 17–18.

Nevertheless, in rigidly stratified societies there was always plenty that the young of any stratum were prevented from knowing.

Moreover, what anyone determines that they care about (or don't) involves a judgement about what they find worthwhile. It makes no sense to say, 'this is very important to me, but it's completely worthless'. However, that is not to maintain that in their internal conversations subjects reach an accurate assessment of the objective worth of their concerns. That would be illegitimately to impose the way the world is upon our knowledge about it and deliberations towards it. It would be one version of the 'ontic fallacy' which subordinates our epistemology to being a reflection of ontology and entails equal and opposite defects from the 'epistemic fallacy':[15] we are no more compelled to see and to know things as they are, when we can, than we are free to make what we will of any state of affairs. That any of us may learn more at some later time does not conflict with the fact that what we commit ourselves to caring about at a given time has to be deemed worthwhile for us to make it part of our identities.

The moment of *discernment* serves to highlight people's concerns without discriminating between them. It can be seen as a logging-in process in which actual and potential items considered worthy of concern are registered for consideration. Sifting of a negative kind is involved because the contingency of experience means that the self reviews a restricted set out of the plenitude of possible concerns available. Only those that have been logged in constitute topics for further *deliberation*. Nevertheless, the 'list' of potential and available concerns remains open, and that is one of the main obstacles to a young subject in speedily designing a *modus vivendi.*

New sources of experience are resources for identity formation or consolidation. One novel experience that almost all those interviewed[16] have in common is being at university for the first time; necessarily all have to assess reflexively the courses they have chosen (which is why a small handful had been at university before but had deemed the institution or the degree to have been a mistaken choice). Beyond that, there is a plethora of potential experiences (joining campus societies; using sports, arts, and social facilities; making new

[15] See Andrew Collier, *Critical Realism* (London: Verso, 1994), pp. 76–85.

[16] This refers to the longitudinal interviews – meaning annually from university entry to exit – conducted by Archer, *The Reflexive Imperative in Late Modernity* (Cambridge: Cambridge University Press, 2012).

friends) which at least require cursory reflexive inspection. However, these young people are not experimental subjects compelled to review them all and record their responses. Certainly, *knowing of* is not the same as *knowing that*, but some young subjects do not want to know about certain things at all. In other words, they will actively select those tracts of new experience to which they will expose themselves.

This is because most already have some emotionally transvalued commitments[17] that filter what new experiences they will reflexively shun or court, and which old ones they continue to repeat, because each is of some concern to them. Where novelty of experience is inescapable (as in the degree course), it should not be surprising that for some, this is already viewed through the lens of *how it will combine* with what is *already important to me*, whilst to others this new potential source of concern may entail a radical reorganization of their nascent but provisional constellation of concerns.

In the *deliberation* phase, further recourse to reflexivity for the task of prioritizing, accommodating, and subordinating a subject's cluster of concerns can be highlighted by comparison with the traditional model of socialization as the passive internalization of a normative order, be it societal, regional, class, engendered, and so forth. Not only could such normative systems, their associated role arrays and rule-sets, be presumed stable by virtue of morphostasis (although the presumption was usually exaggerated) but also as a system that defined how the complex of roles and rules fitted together. Each specified who could do what, the order of priority between role requirements and procedures for avoiding role conflict (for example, until the mid-twentieth century in Britain, women were required to resign from many professional and administrative posts upon marriage). In other words, the tasks of prioritization and accommodation were performed for the subject by the system. Now, this task, which St Augustine called 'loving in due order', has to be shouldered reflexively by the subjects themselves.

[17] Jon Elster refers to the second-order process, as 'transmutation': *Alchemies of the Mind* (Cambridge: Cambridge University Press, 1999); John Greenwood as 'transformation': *Realism, Identity and the Emotions* (London: Sage, 1994); and Charles Taylor as 'transvaluation': *Human Agency and Language* (Cambridge: Cambridge University Press, 1985).

Configuring our concerns in relation with other ones

The biggest problem for many young subjects is *how* or *what* to designate as their 'ultimate concern(s)'. It is not that the accommodation and subordination of other concerns then follows automatically. The process of defining a *modus vivendi* amounts to a (preliminary and corrigible) delineation of those subjects and objects in the world with whom and with which we *willingly* become engaged, and when we do so also represents the final phase of *dedication.* Until this is completed *pro tem*, the active process of socialization is not regarded as complete. Only with the designation of an ultimate concern – or specification of the relationship between them if subjects have more than one final end – can lesser concerns then be accommodated in due order and the *modus vivendi* thus take shape. In turn, the ordering of concerns that is constitutive of this shaping also specifies the precise kinds of engagement with the world that are endorsed by different subjects. In other words, the relative importance of what we care about is the door to that with which we will then become engaged – to greater or lesser degrees.

The prioritization of ultimate concern(s) is extremely difficult for many young subjects because the time at which they are necessarily deliberating about their careers – that will play a significant part in the social identities they assume – many are busy falling in love and are also considering their 'relationship' as a future part of their *modus vivendi.* What they have to resolve reflexively is *whether, how*, and *in what combination* these two kinds of final ends[18] can go forward together and accommodate other concerns, which may be subordinated without being repudiated.

At this point, Frankfurt's counsels on love become too thin for two reasons. First, he suggests that having plural loves (of a person, an institution, an ideal, one's work, etc.) is probable: 'However important to him a beloved [anything in parenthesis above] may be, it is unlikely to be the only thing that is important to him. It is unlikely, indeed to be the only thing that he loves. Thus there is ordinarily a strong possibility that disruptive conflict may arise between the lover's devotion to something that he loves and his concern for his other

[18] This is an empirical statement about a common occurrence. There is no necessity about it. Some may experience no such dilemma, and others may have a different one about their ultimate concern.

interests.'[19] The lover will suffer distress because serving one love will mean neglecting the requirements of the other. Here, Frankfurt gives a warning rather than a solution – love is risky, therefore exercise caution: 'They must try to avoid being caused to love what it would be undesirable for them to love.'[20] Yet this advice is impossible to follow, especially in relation to his two recurrent examples – love of a spouse and love of one's children. Prudential action would entail refraining from reproduction, in the knowledge that this can lead to a conflict of interests, but to do so denies the fact that to one or both partners having children is crucial to *the expression* of their love. In that case, to refrain is contrary to loving wholeheartedly, and it leaves at least one partner in distress.

Second, Frankfurt also accepts that however close the identification of a lover is with any of his loves, nevertheless, this is bound to be 'both inexact and less than totally comprehensive. His interests and those of his beloved can never be entirely the same; and it is improbable that they will even be wholly compatible.'[21] His general line of argument here is that we have no volitional option ('No choice in the matter') but to yield to the claims of love because 'the necessity with which love binds the will puts an end to indecisiveness concerning what to care about.'[22] This is not implausible, except in the case where the 'incompatibility' is *between two 'final ends' themselves;* for example, between the work[23] the two people each believe they (will) love and the couple's belief that they (will continue to) love one another. Where final ends are concerned, resolution cannot consist in repudiating one of them. Couples are left with the unavoidable dilemma of how to combine 'love' and 'work'.

Why a Relational Solution is needed

To establish a *modus vivendi* is initially and deliberatively to design a way of life that the subject reflexively deems worth living and, all being well, subsequently finds can be lived out. So far, however, I

19 Frankfurt, *The Reasons of Love*, *ibid.*, p. 62.
20 *Ibid.* 21 *Ibid.* 22 *Ibid.*, p. 65.
23 Frankfurt admits that for people in general 'useful work is among their final ends. They desire it for its own sake, since without it life is empty and vain', 'On the Usefulness of Final Ends', in his *Necessity, Volition and Love* (Cambridge: Cambridge University Press, 1999), p. 91.

have only dealt with what in prospect (during the *deliberation* phase) powerfully draws a subject because of the satisfactions a particular *modus vivendi* holds out. But this design seems to come to grief if two final ends are incompatible and constitute what some hold to be *incommensurables*,[24] preventing the establishment of even an ordinal preference scale (thus precluding the dilemma being solved by becoming Rational Actors). All the same, we seem to get by without resorting to arbitrary decisions about final ends. How is this possible?

Here, I want to draw upon Charles Taylor's Aristotelian suggestion and to flesh it out by considering what makes for sustainability over time. Taylor works on the intuition that a diversity of goods needs to be balanced with the unity of a life, at least as an aspiration, which is roughly what I have called 'dovetailing'. In other words, 'even if we see a plurality of final ends of equal rank, we still have to *live* them, that is, we have to design a life in which they can be integrated, in some proportions, since any life is finite and cannot admit of unlimited pursuit of any good. This sense of a life – or design or plan, if we want to emphasise our powers of leading here – is necessarily one. If this is our final end, there can only be one.'[25]

This suggests a way out of Frankfurt's gloomy conclusion that to engage in love's volitional commitments from which we cannot withdraw means that some of our concerns must be severely damaged and in a completely arbitrary manner because there can be no reason for selecting between final ends. Taylor's proposal also seems to gel with Lear's argument, which is of especial importance here because he dwells upon the primacy of staying connected to the world. This reflects exactly the same concern with *engagement* that I am pressing as necessary for making our way through the world as active agents: 'From this point of view, what would be centrally important about volitional unity, even to the lover, would not be the unity of the will per se, but the types of connection to the world that that unity permitted.'[26]

The process of Shaping a Life is necessarily a matter of relations, but these are not approached relationally by most philosophers, even

[24] Ruth Chang (ed.), *Incommensurability, Incompatibility and Practical Reason* (Cambridge MA.: Harvard University Press, 1997).

[25] Charles Taylor, 'Leading a Life', in Ruth Chang (ed.), *Incommensurability*, *ibid.*, p. 183.

[26] Jonathan Lear, 'Love's Authority', in Sarah Buss and Lee Overton (eds.), *Contours of Agency* (Cambridge, MA: MIT Press, 2002), p. 281.

when they are dealing with careers or, more blatantly, with friendship, romance, or parenthood. Instead, these are considered unilaterally, from the standpoint of a single lover. My argument will be that the social relations, within which the designation of ultimate concerns is enmeshed, are indispensable to explaining the Life that is Shaped. Taylor's argument will be of considerable help here, but it will need supplementing by relational considerations.

The dilemma Taylor examines is how does our practical reasoning enable us to produce unity out of diversity? How can we define our (ultimate) 'life goods' from the 'constitutive goods' that make it up, if the latter themselves conflict? Specifically, how do we manage to reach non-arbitrary conclusions when deliberating between goods that are very different? This problem is bypassed in Utilitarianism, because right action is that producing the greatest consequent utility, and in Kantianism, where it is action that proceeds from a maxim susceptible of universalization. It is also bypassed in the theories of socialization as 'internalization' because it is presumed to be solved in advance by virtue of the 'pre-packaged' coherence of what is internalized.[27] Taylor's suggestion hinges upon the dilemma being 'not so much a matter of the relative importance of goods but of a sense of how they fit together in a whole life. In the end, what we are called upon to do is not just carry out isolated acts, each one being right, but to live a life, and that means to be and become a certain kind of human being.'[28]

Leading a life is both to have a bent towards moving in some direction and, as an active agent in one's own life, to exercise governance in guiding this movement to a certain degree. Taylor's insight is that 'insofar as we have some sense of our lives, of what we are trying to lead, we will be relating the different goods we seek not just in regard to their differential importance, *but also in the way they fit, or fail to fit, together in the unfolding of our lives.*'[29] What is at stake here is the dilemma – the fact that our concerns may not cohere with one another – but also the source of its solution (albeit fallible and *pro tem*). This lies in 'a sense of the complementarity and of how it may be

[27] Thus Taylor comments: 'Habermas claims to be able to show that the standard of a discourse ethic is binding on us by showing how we are already committed to it in virtue of talking with each other the way we do. We can bypass altogether reflection on the good.' 'Leading a Life', *ibid.*, p. 174.

[28] *Ibid.*, p. 179. [29] *Ibid.*, p. 180 (italics inserted).

threatened at some point by the overwhelming of one side in the name of the other.'[30]

However, this sense of complementarity itself is held to depend upon 'our sense of the shape of our lives, and how different goods fit together within it – their different places and times.'[31]

Yet, this is the problem as far as young subjects are concerned. For them, the completion of the *dedication* stage is the last phase of their socialization, but they have not reached it yet. For all of them it is work in progress. Therefore, Taylor's intuition that the 'diversity of goods needs to be balanced with the unity of life, at least as an inescapable aspiration'[32] is one with which I agree for those who have reached 'maturity', but the difficulty for all young subjects is that they lack precisely this crucial 'sense of unity'. Far from having achieved that meta-good, the 'sense of a life', this is exactly what they are struggling towards. Without it, they cannot have any corresponding 'sense of complementarity' with regard to the relative importance of diverse goods, such as their future 'career' and the future of their 'relationship'. Both are still relatively undefined and yet, as both continue to unfold, they will influence each other's definition. The sense of the life they wish to lead (even in aspiration) is inchoate, if it exists at all. Thus, it cannot arbitrate on their dilemmas, which may not even be perceived as such.

Hence, Taylor's conclusion that, 'this sense of a life – or design or plan . . . is necessarily one. If this is our final end, there can only be one' may ultimately be correct (as I believe it to be), but what is not accounted for is *how this comes about*. In seeking to understand the process involved, it is important not to see it as a lone individual accomplishment. This is the implication of much of the philosophical literature, and something of it may derive from the fact that the end result *must*, indeed, be a personal property in that only one person can have the internal, subjective sense of what gives unity to his or her own life. Nevertheless, the fact that this is *what* people end up with is not the same thing – or to be confused with – *how* they came by it. The achievement of that sense of what makes for unity in each of their lives (upon which the establishment of a *modus vivendi* is based), is *relationally* dependent. *This is necessarily so because to have a concern entails a relationship and to have plural concerns involves*

[30] *Ibid.*, pp. 181–182. [31] *Ibid.*, p. 183. [32] *Ibid.*

plural relations. All the same, we should not relinquish Taylor's insight about 'complementarity', but rather rethink it in relational terms.

This means considering the reflexive and the relational[33] in conjunction. On the one hand, it is her reflexivity that is decisive for *which* relations are relevant because it is the subject who has *discerned* what matters to her (although it has been stressed that she always does this in a particular context that is not of her making or choosing, in this case one of contextual incongruity). Therefore, she is partially responsible for her dilemma – the outcome of her *deliberation* that has concluded two ultimate concerns are of importance to her. On the other hand, it does not follow that she alone – as a lone individual[34] – determines the outcome as far as her final ends are concerned. *On the contrary, it is the relationships accompanying and surrounding her concerns that promote both the subjective sense of compatibility and objectively make concerns compatible, or the opposite.*

Complementarity as actively sought

This section attempts to answer the question: where does Taylor's 'sense of unity' in a life come from along with the 'sense of compatibility' about its constituent concerns? It is important to reply because only when a subject has dovetailed her concerns can she move forward in the context of intensifying morphogenesis and dedicate herself to a particular course of action as her response to the new opportunities available. The difficulty for most students at the point of university entry is that their concerns are fluid and often incomplete. In other words, they provide insufficient guidance for Shaping a Life. Whilst concerns can always be displaced and replaced (without this being prompted by dramatic contingencies), it indicates that the Necessity of Selection is still on-going and thus cannot provide the necessary

33 Much of the following discussion of relations and relationality is indebted to the work of Pierpaolo Donati, *Teoria relazionale della società* (Milan: FrancoAngeli, 1991); 'Conclusioni e prospettive: la sociologia relazionale come paradigma della società dopo-moderna' in his *Teoria relazionale della società: i concetti di base* (Milan: FrancoAngeli, 2009), pp. 357–406; Pierpaolo Donati and Ivo Colozzi (eds.), *Il paradigma relazionale nelle scienze sociali: le prospettive sociologiche* (Bologna: Il Mulino, 2006).

34 This strange and perverse assertion has been attributed to me repeatedly by Anthony King. For his latest repetition of it see, 'The odd couple: Margaret Archer, Anthony Giddens and British social theory', British Journal of Sociology, 60th Anniversary edition, 2010.

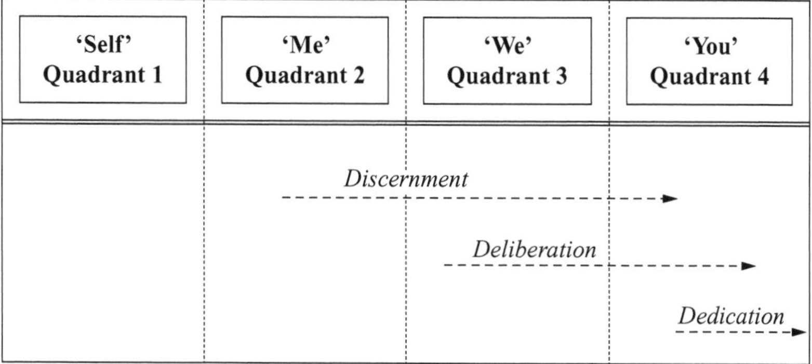

Figure 4.1 Where students stand on the DDD scheme at point of entry[35]

traction for even being preoccupied about coherence amongst the components that the subject has started to flag-up as important to her. That is where the majority of university entrants find themselves.

In terms of the DDD scheme, this is summarized in Figure 4.1, which basically signals 'unfinished business'. No one has completed their reflexive *discernment*, although some have made more progress than others, and no one has finished their reflexive *deliberation* where issues of complementarity begin to arise. Therefore, almost none is in the position to achieve the reflexive *dedication* involved in Shaping a Life.

Those few who do tackle *dedication* by the time of graduating – which is far from all – will have determinate concerns, now consolidated into projects, whose realization they hope can lead to the establishment of a satisfying and sustainable *modus vivendi.* If they are correct, then in one sense it can be said that the active process of socialization is provisionally complete, although subjects will circulate around the issues involved again and again. Especially in the nascent morphogenetic social order, socialization must now be considered as lifelong learning,[36] given the ineluctability of acquiring new skills, of undergoing novel experiences, and encountering brand new opportunities. Of course, lives can be reshaped and sometimes have to be, though

35 Full human personhood, formed by movement through the four quadrants, has been discussed in my last chapter.

36 Consider the age spread of those going online, which is now the case for more than three-quarters of British households and means that Internet skills, experiences, and practices have broken the 'retirement barrier'.

not in the irrational and cavalier sense of serial self-reinvention trivialized by Beck,[37] and not in the sense of merely proffering 'accountable biographies', as suggested by Habermas, both of which, by definition, deny any serious *engagement with the world on the part of the subject.* Each of those accounts merely offers us *provisional* man and *pro tem* woman. They have both thrown in the towel as far as Shaping a Life is concerned.

Yet this is of real concern to young people, who at least want to make lasting commitments and are quite capable, for the most part, of projecting ten years ahead and describing the contours of the life they would then like to be leading. This means that the three years of being an undergraduate will also be the time for many when the Necessity of Selection meets the need to Shape a Life. Why is this described as a 'need'? Because no one can simply continue adding to their list of concerns *ad infinitum* since they have insufficient time to attend to them all and would discover that some conflict, generating dissatisfaction (for example, it is almost impossible to be an avid gardener and to be travelling for six months of the year). Consequently, complementarity between concerns is sought and not as some abstract idea or strain towards consistency, but because it is desirable in itself. It is what ensures – as well as we can ensure anything – that what matters to us most is well served and that matters of less importance to us do not detract from it. This is why subjects actively though fallibly seek to dovetail their concerns.

One part of this process is that there will be a two-way relationship between Selection and Shaping; the inevitability of having multiple concerns[38] is the raw material, as it were, out of which a Life is Shaped (as a satisfying and sustainable *modus vivendi*). But to give shape and to achieve these desiderata often means that concerns have to be modified, as well as subordinated or, in some cases, abandoned. This will prove common amongst those whose concerns are still fluid and imprecisely defined. Equally, the design of the *modus vivendi* may have to undergo modification in order to accommodate a 'stubborn'

[37] Ulrich Beck and Elizabeth Beck Gernsheim, *Individualization* (London: Sage, 2002). For a critique see Archer, *Making our Way*, *ibid.*, pp. 32–37.

[38] In *Being Human* (*ibid.*, chapter 6), I argued that we have three ineluctable concerns: with our 'physical well-being' in the natural order; with our 'performative competence' in the practical order; and with our 'self worth' in the social order.

concern that a subject is unwilling to relinquish even if it is not an ultimate concern. The other part will be the issue already touched upon through Frankfurt and Taylor, namely how is the complementarity sought actually achieved or even achievable when two 'ultimate concerns' are vying for pride of place and wholehearted volitional commitment?

Reflexivity is relationally moulded

Today, the family is the first agency to confront children with the 'necessity of selection'. The large majority of parents or caretakers do not constitute a normatively consensual small group, as presumed in past theories of socialization. Elder-Vass[39] defines a 'norm circle' as one whose exercise of consensual normativity would have the emergent consequence of heightening adherence to the same norms amongst other members of the group, too, in this case children and young people. On the contrary, most parents/caretakers present the young with 'mixed messages' because of their own normative differences.[40] Mixed messages, and especially messages that do not mix, involve a need to choose. In other words, parental injunctions, guidelines, and recommendations about courses of action or attitudes come in *interrogative* form, because countered by something *incongruent*, rather than as taken-for-granted normative sharing. Normative dissensus between parents unavoidably involves the young asking themselves where they stand (or with whom they stand), unless they internally declare a plague on both your houses. Yet these are reflexive responses illustrating how reflexivity has been awakened and pressed into action, compared with how it could once largely slumber on, implying little (or occasional) practical engagement with the social world beyond a domestic environment whose message was 'this is how things are done here and this is what happens next'.

Thus, most millennial families were actively, though unintentionally, fostering the 'reflexive imperative' *within* the home. Generically,

[39] Dave Elder-Vass, *The Causal Power of Social Structures: Emergence, Structure and Agency* (Cambridge: Cambridge University Press, 2010), pp. 122–127f.

[40] All such statements are based upon information volunteered by respondents during interview. Although they are undoubtedly matters of the students' perceptions, what seems crucial is precisely that they had perceived parental normativity in this nonconsensual way.

'contextual incongruity' stands for the inability of the parental generation to supply relevant guidelines to their children for establishing a satisfying and sustainable *modus vivendi* in the society that now confronts the younger generation. 'Contextual incongruity' is first encountered in the domestic setting as mixed messages about the appropriate response and behaviour in the domestic setting. In its importance, such normative incongruity was found to exceed that of disjunctive experiences, such as moving to a different area, parental death or divorce, prolonged ill-heath or being sent to boarding school, in terms of its impact upon the mode of reflexivity practised by those affected. Instead, what mattered was the qualitative dimension of family relations.

Qualitatively family relationships shape the mode of reflexivity developed, which is closely related to the severity of 'contextual incongruity' encountered in today's family 'socialization'. Part of this impact can be attributed to the transmission of mixed messages themselves that confront children with the problem of normatively evaluating and arbitrating upon this mélange before they can crystallize their own personal concerns, which then provide traction in their exercise of reflexivity. In part, it also consists in the widening gap between parental preparation – however consensual – and the more rapidly changing contexts through which the young must navigate.

Relational goods in the family and modes of reflexivity

The direct and crucial implication is that 'social relations' can never be reduced to 'interpersonal relations', which are non-emergent because all that is involved in the latter can be 'personalized'[41] by reduction to the influences of A upon B and vice versa. Instead, 'relations' both are the 'mediation' of prior structural and cultural conditioning and have emergent powers, of causal consequence in their own right and of their own kind. Thus, as my co-author puts it, the relation 'is not merely the product of perceptions, sentiments and inter-subjective mental states of

[41] A central strategy of methodological individualism from the beginning of its canon was to construe 'emergent properties' as the effects of 'other people'; see J. W. N Watkins, 'Methodological Individualism and Social Tendencies', in May Brodbeck (ed.), *Readings in the Philosophy of the Social Sciences* (New York: Macmillan, 1968), p. 271f. For a critique see Archer, *Realist Social Theory: The Morphogenetic Approach*, pp. 33–46.

empathy, but is both a *symbolic* fact, ("a reference to") and a *structural* fact ("a link between"). As such, *it cannot be reduced to the subjects even though it can only "come alive" through these subjects.* It is in them that the relation takes on a peculiar life of its own.'[42]

It follows that the relational approach can *both* conceptualize the emergence of 'relational goods' within any unit of social interaction and point to their opposites, 'relational evils', whose consequences *may* be personally morphogenetic but can also merely increase the quotient of human misery without further outcome. It lends itself to forging the link between the types of 'relational goods' generated by the subjects' families and their intensified reflexivity, as well as the dominant mode tending to characterize their internal conversations (at the point of leaving home).[43] These are:–

Communicative Reflexivity (internal conversations need to be confirmed and completed by others before leading to action);
Autonomous Reflexivity (internal conversations are self-contained, leading directly to action);
Meta-reflexivity (internal conversations critically evaluate previous inner dialogues and are critical about effective action in society);
Fractured Reflexivity (internal conversation cannot lead to purposeful courses of action but only intensify personal distress and disorientation).

Figure 4.2 provides an 'ontological reconstruction' of what *being* in that relationship had constituted in qualitative terms. Nevertheless, this permits the examination of one of the emergent properties of such prior reciprocal action, namely its consequences for the reflexivity of the young subject. It allows hypotheses to be ventured about the interconnections between 'relational goods', the selection of opportunities, and the modes of reflexivity to develop together with the forms of social engagement pursued.[44]

42 Pierpaolo Donati, *Relational Sociology* , p. 130.
43 The dominant modes were established by in-depth interviewing and ICONI (Internal Conversation Indicator). See Margaret S. Archer, *Making our Way Through the World: Human Reflexivity and Social Mobility*, Appendix.
44 Margaret S. Archer, 'The Ontological Status of Subjectivity: The Missing Link between Structure and Agency', in Clive Lawson, John Latsis, and Nuno Martins (eds.), *Contributions to Social Ontology* (London: Routledge, 2007), pp. 17–31.

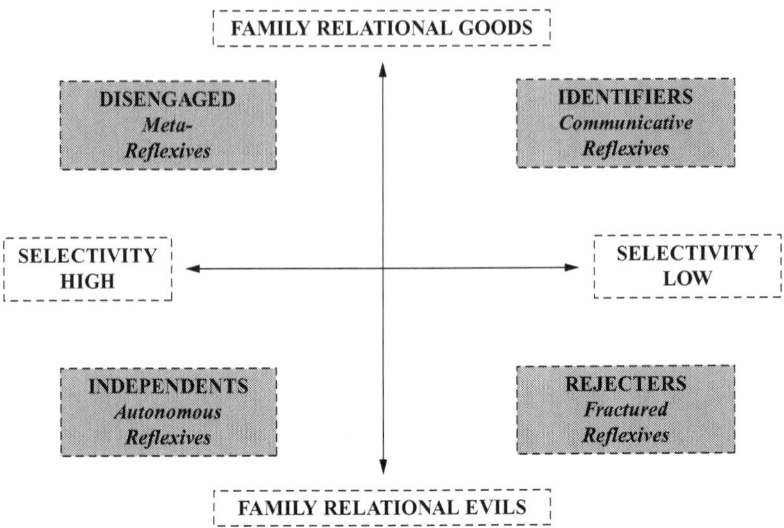

Figure 4.2 Family relational goods and necessary selection

Where positive 'relational goods' are concerned, these have the generative tendency to create bonds and interdependencies at the empirical level amongst the persons involved. They denote more than 'good interpersonal relations' and indicate more than some degree of warmth and some regularity of contact. That 'more' refers to emergent properties, in this case, 'internal goods' (love, caring, trust), which cannot be produced by aggregation and are *also* deemed highly worthwhile in themselves. As 'strong evaluators',[45] the young subjects from such close families recognized the value of what they themselves have helped to generate, which cannot be reduced to the sum of each and every interactive transaction and defies interpersonal substitutions. This recognition means respect, even reverence, for the relational goods produced and a concern for the preservation and prolongation of this worth, which encourages a commitment to fostering a replicatory relationship itself.

It spells endorsement of the family's *modus vivendi*, without preventing the subject from contemplating the odd tweak and reflexively having to work at producing an approximation to it in a changed and

[45] Charles Taylor, 'Self-Interpreting Animals', in his *Human Agency and Language* (Cambridge: Cambridge University Press, 1985), pp. 35–76.

changing context. Only a small subgroup[46] of students were found to be such 'Identifiers' with their parents' domestic way of life and invested much of themselves in reproducing it. Such families were the exceptions to the general transmission of 'mixed messages'. Instead, mother and father were normatively consensual and these subjects uniformly wished their own future families to be 'much the same'. Hence, the 'necessity of selection' had been drastically curtailed for them. Generally, this subgroup were not on the look-out for new items of experiential variety. On the contrary, their high valuation of their familial 'relational goods' acted as a filter, sifting friendships, social activities, and leisure pursuits to ensure congruity with their families' normativity.

Their engagement was intense and a crucial issue was simply 'staying in touch'. These were the students who went home most for weekends and vacations and who also sustained the most continuous contact, phoning home up to three times a day. Their parents were initiated into emailing and free Skype phoning as well as making much more prolific use of mobiles, texting, and sending letters more than any others in different subgroups. In short, they acted as intergenerational variants upon the LAT pattern (living-apart-but-together) and did so through constant communication. Thus, there seems to be a direct connection between membership of a family which generates positive 'relational goods', this intensity of communication, and the practice of Communicative Reflexivity.

Julie exemplifies these 'Identifiers,' and she gave little sense of a biography punctuated with doings, significant changes, or emotionally charged episodes, but rather a constant enveloping in trust and sharing. The family of five – mother (nurse), father (accountant), and two slightly older sisters at university – was described as 'close and united', and it had also integrated Julie's boyfriend. She describes her mother as 'my best friend' and her boyfriend and mother get on extremely well. Her family is integrated but also differentiated because Julie's relations with her two parents are quite different. With her father, she seeks to gain approbation, feeling, as the youngest child, that she must excel in his eyes as her sisters have done.

[46] The percentages for each dominant mode of Reflexivity upon entry to university were: Communicative reflexives = 13.5%; Autonomous reflexives = 19.0%; Meta-reflexives = 38.6%; and Fractured reflexives = 17.4%. N = 126. Archer, *Reflexive Imperative*, p. 293.

This family does appear to work in a normatively consensual manner, one that accentuated the value of familial relational goods on Julie's part because she would like her own to be modelled upon it, with the same mother-daughter relationship being repeated. Relationally, Julie also prefers to be furnished with normative guidelines: 'I like to know what people expect of me and I don't like to get it wrong'. Thus, she found it difficult at university to know what the precise expectations were without having her constant interlocutors to hand.

The receipt of positive 'relational goods' prior to university entry had helped to generate this small group of such 'Identifiers' for whom the 'necessity of selection' was minimized through decreasing the salience of new opportunities to them. In other words, the impact of 'contextual incongruity' was greatly softened *by their turning their backs* upon morphogenetic novelty and variety – though to different degrees – and continuing to practise Communicative Reflexivity.

At the opposite extreme was a subgroup of the same small size whose experience was of 'relational evils' within their home backgrounds. The root causes, as recounted, included excessive maternal domination as well as parental coercion, antagonism, and exploitation. In every case, the response to these relations by the young person upon whom this negativity rebounded was the repudiation of their home background as the source of their personal misery. Yet, equally uniformly, since their priority had been escape, it was accompanied by no clear notion of towards what; getting away was an end in itself. 'Necessary selection' could not be handled purposefully, the need to make choices and to avail themselves of opportunities simply intensified their disorientation and distress, but the situational logic of opportunity did not disappear. The need to survive predominated, meaning for some just trying to hold themselves together and for others taking impulsive courses of action whose consequences intensified their difficulties. Not surprisingly, all 'Rejecters' scored as Fractured reflexives.

Again, a case will be presented to give a feel for 'relational evil' (i.e. sustained mistrust, uncaring, and manipulation), which is the reverse of mutual reciprocity. This was the most brutal instance encountered. Unlike some others in this subgroup, Yasmin did succeed in developing a functioning mode of reflexivity before leaving university. Brought up in a strict Pakistani family in the Midlands, she already had problems as a child with her step-mother, who eventually left taking the three step-brothers with her and leaving Yasmin with all the domestic responsibilities at the age of ten. Somehow her father scapegoated her for his wife's departure (and the loss of his sons) and scarcely spoke to her.

Yasmin says, 'I've always believed that education is so important so you can provide for yourself, you can be self-sufficient and self-reliant.' Yet, how was she to obtain this education – the one option she had selected? Cyberspace supplied the opportunities otherwise closed to her and she learned more from the Internet than anywhere else, given a father who refused her information and a deficient school. She was depressed and wanting to get out, but where was the door? In fact she had found it already. Through the Internet, Yasmin discovered university bursaries and through her largely self-taught computer skills she managed to maintain herself during her first degree as a computing advisor. From her first year at university, she ceased visiting home. Yasmin's critique, as a 'Rejecter', extended to the Pakistani community in the Midlands, its arranged marriages, and its young women with up to fourteen kids who take over the street without recognizing that it is a cul-de-sac.[47]

So far, the extremes of family experience in generating relational goods and evils have been examined for their effects upon responses to 'necessity selectivity' and the mode of reflexivity practised. In fact there is a gradient in domestic relationality with the majority falling between the two poles already examined (see Figure 4.2).

Turning now to the 'Independents', the aim is the same, namely to link the mode of reflexivity they developed to the types of relational goods/evils generated by their family backgrounds. Those starting university as Autonomous reflexives had one family feature in common that was also disproportionately concentrated amongst them: divorced or separated parents, fathers and mothers effectively living apart, and adoption. From their accounts, disruptive family dynamics had induced an early independence amongst these subjects, who

[47] 'It's like they don't know anything, and they want you to be the same... They just dont want you to learn, they dont want you to have a good job. Its seen as immoral and Westernized and un-Islamic and they say, you know, you should just get married and stay at home and be a housewife and then pop out the kids and you're just not meant to achieve anything in your life... And their lives are so narrow, they don't get out of the area and me, I was like I want out of this area please.

recognized the need to take responsibility for themselves and to avoid becoming responsible for the family situation or a particular parent. Nothing tied them to the 'mess other people had made', and the dissention they breathed was met by self-distancing. As 'Independents', with no desire to be bound, they were free both to select certain elements from their background, evaluated as worth retaining, but also to combine them with an unfazed examination of the opportunities on offer in the world beyond. 'Necessary selection' had been their lot so far, but the prospect of making their own independent choices was relished.

Riccardo's biography represents a response to marital disaccord between his parents and an even stronger inducement to consider global opportunities as being well within his grasp. His father is Italian, his mother from New Zealand, and extended family members were spread out over the world. Riccardo shouldered a lot of responsibility at home since dad had gone to develop his company in Africa, when his son was five. Assuming independence was further necessitated when mother contracted cancer and he became accustomed to taking domestic responsibility. Given his parents' 'rocky relationship' and pursuit of their own independent exploits, Riccardo did likewise and used his gap year to extend his own experience and to foster one of his passions – car mechanics. He now refuses to take responsibility for his mother, phones once a week, and could not contemplate returning to live at home after university. Although he visits his father in Africa, 'Dad doesn't understand university', so such trips merely serve to intensify his global citizenship and sense of opportunity. These seem to constitute the patrimony of his socialization.

Finally, there is the largest group – the 'Disengaged' – who, despite not having experienced family breakdown like the 'Independents', manifest a critical detachment from their parents and a dissatisfaction with the *modus vivendi* in which they had been reared, largely because of tense domestic dissention. Reviewing the parental way of life, their evaluation was that 'there must be better than this' and an avowed desire that their own would indeed be different. What distinguished these Meta-reflexives from the previous subgroup was that in their distancing they had, as adolescents, already selected a 'cause' with which to identify. Doing this before they were twenty, it was not that they later withdrew their dedication, but rather fine-tuned their 'vocation', given that some of the new opportunities coming into view were selected for advancing their 'ultimate concern', which was already being drawn into service as an architectonic principle.

There is no need for the parting with parental ways to be a searing or acrimonious experience because disengagement can sometimes be accomplished conventionally and may even leave (distanced) interpersonal relations more or less intact. However, deselecting the family is always costly, although the price may be paid in various currencies. Valerie comes from a rural background and both parents are financial advisors, her loss of economic comfort being a price she still counts for making a radical break with their life-style. She made her commitment at sixteen, which also entailed a shift away from her parents' Anglican Church and towards small charismatic house-groups.

Valerie recounts having realized early that she also sought a *modus vivendi* very different from that of her middle class parents. At the age of nineteen she met and married a fellow evangelical, and the couple soon produced three children. The pair gradually made their peace with the Established Church, culminating in her husband's ordination. Besides the need to raise their own family on very little income, the main cost Valerie incurred for the pursuit of her own values was ten years out of the labour market, coming to university as a mature student in her early thirties, and having to engage intensively in her own reflexive deliberations about her occupational future in relation to her continuing commitments.

To recapitulate, Figure 4.2 summarized the influence of the quality of familial relational goods – a gradient from highly positive to extremely negative – on subjects' experiences of the 'necessity of selection' whilst living at home. From this, three conclusions can be drawn.

1. The small subgroup of 'Identifiers' were the only young people who could be said to approximate to the traditional image of socialization as internalizing the normativity of their parents and identifying with the *modus vivendi* through which this was lived out. In other words, they dealt with the 'necessity of selection' by trying to turn their backs on it and endorsing what had been given them.
2. For very different reasons – linked directly to their positions on the axis of familial relational goods/evils – all of the other subgroups had already encountered the 'necessity of selection'. The descending quality of their family relations and their active responses to them also meant that they displayed very different orientations towards

selection: 'Independents' being open and ready to avail themselves of the situational logic of opportunity; the 'Disengaged' already having made a preliminary identification of what they cared about most within the array of opportunities known to them; and the 'Rejecters' having escaped from negative family relations but being completely unprepared to face the 'necessity of selection' with reflexive purposefulness.

3. These four subgroups had already developed a dominant mode of reflexivity prior to university entry, which the vast majority of them retained throughout their undergraduate years. The question is, how would they make the first move towards Shaping their Lives in the context of new relationships and new opportunities?

Relations between relations

The continuing and effective practice of any mode of reflexivity (obviously excluding the Fractured) is dependent upon the relational matrix within which it is exercised. Unavoidably, subjects' networks of relations expand over time, though they themselves can exert significant governance over their composition. Nevertheless, they cannot evade and often cannot foresee the second-order impact that relations between relations will have upon them and their selections (particularly of careers and partnerships) in their first attempt to forge their own *modus vivendi*. This is because second-order relationality generates its own objective relational goods and evils, which are not reducible to the interpersonal level because those involved (family, old friends and new) may never have met and their congruence or incongruence is mediated through subjects themselves.

This can be illustrated from the three basic options open to student subjects: they can (1) give priority to home friends, (2) seek to maintain their two friendship groups or, (3) opt for their university friends. Option 1 is most propitious to 'Identifiers' remaining as such and succeeding in their aim of replicating their natal context, because the relationality between 'home friends' and 'family background' tends to be positively reinforcing, even though home friends do not remain completely unchanged and, insofar as they do, may be perceived differently by the subject. Option 2 is at the mercy of how the two groups gel, and if they do not, the subject may reluctantly find herself caught between one and the other.

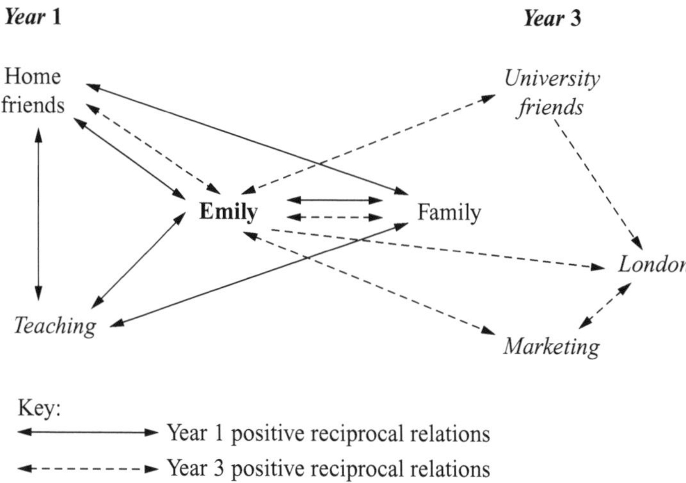

Figure 4.3 Emily's inability to Shape a Life as an undergraduate

To an even greater extent, Option 3 necessarily introduces differences into friendship relations because new friends cannot be 'similars', let alone 'familiars' in the way home friends are: usually with shared biographies, a common fund of local references, some intertwining with significant others from the same background, and a commonwealth of mutual knowledge. Therefore, university friends will invariably be a source of new variety, and it follows that, if 'familiarity' grows between them, the subject's identification with her natal background is likely to diminish, though not be discarded.

This does not mean that she will cease to be a Communicative reflexive, but opting for her university friends (wholly or in part) spells a change of interlocutors, which implies some shift away from or tension with the normativity of her familial background. It is the reason why the 'Identifiers'/'Communicatives' are not only a shrinking group in late modernity – thus substantially reducing social integration – but also why they are *the most likely of all to undergo Fracturing*. This is particularly the case when subjects attempt to put Option 2 into practice and relations between the groups prove incongruent in terms of the future *modus vivendi* they encourage for the subject. Figure 4.3 illustrates this for Emily, who on starting her degree had a typical profile of the Communicative reflexive, had compartmentalized 'home' and 'university' as an undergraduate, but, as exit approached, was unable to select between the competing relational pulls and pressures and was immobilized. As a subject who had Fractured, she had also become a passive agent, unable to make the necessary selection and hence incapable of shaping her own life. She could no longer compartmentalize, so her 'solution' was to temporize: a few years of London living and then a return home.

Conversely, neither Autonomous subjects ('Independents') nor Meta-reflexives ('Disengaged') confronted this problem because the former had been extremely selective about retaining only those from their natal backgrounds with outlooks congruent with their own, and the latter had determinedly distanced themselves from their early relations.[48] However, in neither case could the threat or impact of second-order relationality be avoided, especially when subjects were responding to Taylor's challenge of endorsing plural final ends but yet achieving a 'unity of life' or when encountering 'Frankfurt's "revenge"' and discovering that 'no-one can serve two masters'. The reason is that this is precisely when second-order relational goods and evils come into play. This can be illustrated by young couples seeking to Shape a Life together, but also one that accommodates a satisfying career as an ultimate concern of both. Briefly, I am going to maintain that it is only if the couple can develop collective reflexivity (see our Chapter 2) that Taylor's 'unity of a life' can be realized – perhaps *pro tem* – and that failure to do so will give Frankfurt his 'revenge' because there, indeed, it would be a question of two individual and independent volitions, each of which is vulnerable to the second-order influences of relationality.

Considered interpersonally, Couple A, who met at university and soon married, were bonded by their feelings for one another alone. In terms of priorities, each was equally committed to having a very different but successful and satisfying career. As jobs came up in different places, there was some transaction about when they would be able to live together again, but they had not generated their own relational goods of mutual trust, confidence, and concern. Because of this, they had no bulwark against either their separation itself or against the second-order influence exerted by their segregated networks of friends

[48] In both cases this may have been total rejection or distancing from some, but did not imply that interpersonal relations or a sense of duty could not be sustained, provided they were kept at arm's length.

and the animosity expressed by their respective families towards a marriage neither approved. When the infidelity of one partner became known, this was a signal for the two sets of friends and two families to polarize in overt antagonism; protecting and reclaiming one of the partners whilst vilifying the other and the other 'side'. Couple A made tentative efforts at reconciliation, but their mistrustfulness of the other could not withstand the doubts, suspicions, and cautions fuelled by and between the partisan groups of families and friends. Relational evils intensified at both levels through the positive feedback between them, with this vicious circle ending in divorce.

In the case of Couple B, instead of realizing Frankfurt's expectations of volitional conflict between wholeheartedly meeting the same two final ends as those of Couple A (marriage and careers), the personal relational goods they generated were reinforced by second-order ones to create a stable felicitous circle – a relational vindication of Taylor's 'unity of a life' together. The key difference was that Couple B developed 'collective reflexivity' in their practical reasoning. Instead of careers being a matter of negotiated compromises, they had sketched a plan for a conjoint and reciprocal enterprise before leaving university. It depended upon their mutual trust, for it had no individual insurance clauses. In turn, their project had a better objective chance of success because it was now resourced in various currencies through their co-commitment to it. Simultaneously, their reciprocity subjectively increased the complementarity of their joint concern through their co-endorsement of a plan that shaped their life as a couple by operating as its architectonic principle. As my co-author puts it, such 'Relational Reflexivity' 'consists in orientating the subjects to the reality emergent from their interactions by their taking into consideration how this reality is able (by virtue of its own powers) to feed back onto the subjects . . . since it exceeds their individual as well as their aggregated personal powers'.[49] As their relational good they *both* now have a great deal to lose by damaging it – or their relationship.

Their joint *dedication* to and orientation towards their business project in turn acted as a sieve towards their friends, because only those with some interest in the enterprise were retained, whilst new friends encountered through the project were added to a group that came to constitute *our* friends. Similarly, those family members alone who

[49] Pierpaolo Donati, 'Preface' to his *Relational Sociology*.

could enter into the couple's 'unitary life' remained close to them. Consequently, those retained as 'friends and family' after university were a supply of normatively consensual approbation. Relations between relations were not the source of 'mixed messages' that might have induced second thoughts in Couple B. Correspondingly, their 'we-ness' strengthened as they encountered no challenge to the complementarity of their concerns.

Conclusion

As the world changes and with it the generative mechanism underlying socialization-as-internalization (involving the transmission of consensual messages; the existence of clear and durable role expectations; and the pervasiveness of normative consistency), so too must the conceptualization of the process of socialization within social theory. The latter needs to move from a concept of a passive process to an active one; from assuming an unreflexive acceptance by the young to acknowledging their highly reflexive selectivity; and from stereotyped assumptions about relations and relationality between 'socializers' and 'socializants' to incorporating their variations and varying contributions to different outcomes.

5 Cultural reproaches to Relationist Sociology

MARGARET S. ARCHER

Every theory about the social order necessarily has to incorporate SAC: Structure, Agency, and Culture. The problem in hand will govern which of the three is accorded most attention, so the acronym SAC is *not* a general rank ordering of priority between the three elements. This is a logical point; if something is deemed indispensable to something else, it makes no sense to ask if one element is more indispensable than the others. If all are necessary, then they have to be recognized as playing some role in every social theory. Indispensability means that social life comes in a SAC – always and everywhere.

Without being strict about definitions for a moment, leave out 'Structure' and the contexts people confront then become kaleidoscopically contingent[1]; omit culture and no one has a repertoire of ideas for construing the situations in which they find themselves[2]; without agency we lose activity-dependence as the efficient cause of there being any social order. In consequence, contingency or determinism would have a clear field – one cleared of social theorizing.

During the last quarter of a century, the ranks of SAC deniers have swollen dramatically. As Doug Porpora maintains,[3] the

The arguments in this paper are based upon my *Culture and Agency: The Place of Culture in Social Theory* (1988). See also a very abridged version: Archer, 'Structure, Culture and Agency', in M. D. Jacobs and N. W. Hanrahan (eds.), *The Blackwell Companion to the Sociology of Culture* (Oxford: Blackwell, 2005), chapter 1.

1 The reason for not imposing definitions (yet) is that this statement applies equally to those Individualists for whom 'structure' is generically no more than an aggregate as it does to strong 'Emergentists' such as Critical Realists.

2 Again this statement is impartial between those who define culture in one way or another as 'shared meanings' and those who, like me, do not.

3 D. V. Porpora, 'Morphogenesis and Social Change', in Margaret S. Archer (ed.), *Social Morphogenesis* (Dordrecht: Springer, 2013) and *Restructuring Sociology: The Critical Realist Approach* (Cambridge: Cambridge University Press, 2015, forthcoming).

meta-theoretical stance of denial rests upon conflation.[4] Instead of distinctive properties and powers pertaining to Structure, Culture, and Agency, any pair is conflated with one another, thus ruling out examination of the (changing) interplay between them and its theorization. The guiding metaphor becomes that of 'flows' or 'liquidity' – and it depends upon a prior dissolution of all three components of SAC. Thus, today's leading trope of 'liquid modernity' explicitly depends on an eclectic combination of denials of 'Structure' (replaced, for example, by theoretical assertions about 'destructuration' in the work of Beck[5]), denials of 'Culture' as anything more than what people carry in their heads (endorsed by Elder-Vass[6]), and of 'Agency', rendered fluid by notions of serial self-reinvention, thus severing ties with personal and group 'identities', 'interests', and 'commitments'. In consequence, the picture of the social order being shaped and reshaped by groups seeking to advance their material interests, their ideal interests, and who they are is obliterated by the imagery of fluidity.

In earlier chapters we have already noted the aversion of 'Relationists' to the concept of emergence; indeed, this is how we differentiate between 'relationism' and 'Relational Sociology'[7]. So far in our argument, we have frequently accentuated the 'Relationist' refusal to countenance relational goods and evils as emergent properties exercising causal powers. Equally, the rejection of 'Structure' is marked,[8] even to the point of denying that all action – thus including all relationships – takes place in a pre-existing context that impinges upon agents and actors and influences what they do in them. At most, it is accepted that action is 'situated'. However, the term 'situated action' is not only 'presentist' by implying a covert version of Giddens' instantiation-by-agency-in-the-present, but this simultaneously entails his position of

4 Archer, *Culture and Agency*, summary pp. 97–100.

5 U. Beck and E. Beck-Gernsheim, *Individualization* (London: Sage, 2002).

6 In Margaret S. Archer and D. Elder-Vass, 'Cultural System or Norm Circles? An Exchange', *European Journal of Social Theory*, 52 (2011), 1–23.

7 Pierpaolo Donati defines 'relationism' as approaches 'which reduce social reality to mere processes, without distinguishing the contribution of the individual components from those of their relations as emergent phenomena.' In his *Relational Sociology: A New Paradigm for the Social Sciences* (London: Routledge, 2011), p. 71.

8 A clear example is F. Dépelteau, 'Relational Thinking: A Critique of Co-Determinist Theories of Structure and Agency', *Sociological Theory*, 26 (2008), 51–73.

'central conflation'.[9] However, this chapter will not repeat or rehearse the arguments that have raged over this issue during the last thirty years. Instead, I want to examine the conceptualization of culture within 'relationism' and to present both a critique and an alternative.

Culture is neither fully consistent nor shared

'Culture' has been and remains the poor relation of 'Structure'. This manifests itself in how the properties and the powers of the two have been conceptualized over time. On the one hand, there is no ready fund of analytical units for differentiating components of the cultural realm that correspond to those delineating parts of the structural domain (roles, networks, organizations, institutions, systems, etc.). On the other hand, in relation to causal powers, consistent attention has been given to *how* Structure exercises an influence *vis-à-vis* agents, and considerable progress has been made away from determinism and towards less hydraulic conceptions of 'conditioning'. Conversely, in 'relationism' culture is simply posited as being 'shared' and irresistibly so since it is held socially to shape our cognitive constitution.

Specifically, (i) because culture(s) have conventionally been regarded as homogeneous, meaning that their internal components are always coherently integrated, then (ii) members of 'a culture' are also presumed to share the same ideational homogeneity – a uniformity of beliefs, collective representations, central values, ideology, mythology, form of life, and so on. The two presumptions are canonical. However, they are equally compatible with assigning maximal causal influence to Culture, as society's bandmaster (crude functionalism), or zero efficacy to Culture, as the mirror of class domination (vulgar marxism). Something is clearly amiss because both views cannot be (universally) correct.

Generically, what is wrong is the canon itself – on both counts. *A priori*, there is no reason why, (i) the constituents of Culture should be presumed to be coherently integrated, rather than harbouring ideational contradictions (as well as autonomous elements, alternative sources of variety, etc.). And *a priori* there is also no reason to assume (ii) that all members of a 'community' share a 'common culture'. If both

9 Margaret S. Archer, 'Morphogenesis versus Structuration: on combining structure and action', *British Journal of Sociology*, XXXIII (1982), 455–483.

assumptions are suspended, then it is possible to theorize about *variations* in cultural integration and their relationship to *variations* in social integration. In other words, the interplay *between* Culture and Agency could be examined in the same way as between Structure and Agency. The latter relies, as Lockwood first suggested, upon distinguishing 'system integration' (in this case, the orderly or conflictual nature of parts of the Cultural System) from 'social integration' (in this case, the orderly or conflictual nature of Socio-Cultural relations between people).[10] Then the two levels could be allowed to vary independently of one another, contra the cultural canon, and different combinations of them could be hypothesized to generate cultural reproduction or transformation.[11]

Before proceeding to discuss how to make and use the distinction between properties and powers of the Cultural System (henceforth C.S.) and the independent properties and powers of Socio-Cultural interaction (henceforth S-C), it is important to identify how these two different ontological levels became conflated within the canon. This is not a quest for historical origins *per se*, but an attempt to explain why the conflation between the 'parts' constitutive of culture and the 'people' as cultural agents has, (a) endured *amongst* theoretical adversaries (for example, by many functionalists, marxists, and structuration theorists), and (b) why the evergreen conflation of the C.S. with the S-C continues today in new forms, such as discourse theory and much of 'Relationalist' theory (and its fellow travellers).

The Myth of Cultural Integration: composition and conservation of the canon

The Myth of Cultural Integration[12] is held here to embody 'one of the most deep-seated fallacies in social science . . . the assumption of a high degree of consistency in the interpretations produced by societal units'.[13] Much the same comment is made by Emirbayer: 'There has

[10] David Lockwood, 'Social Integration and System Integration', in G. K. Zollschan and W. Hirsch (eds.), *Explorations in Social Change* (Boston: Houghton Mifflin, 1964).

[11] Margaret S. Archer, *Realist Social Theory*, chapter 5.

[12] Margaret S. Archer, 'The Myth of Cultural Integration', *British Journal of Sociology*, 36 (1985), 333–353.

[13] A. Etzioni, *The Active Society* (London: Free Press, 1968), p. 146.

probably never been but one overarching cultural idiom, narrative, or discourse operative in any given historical context.'[14] The most proximate and powerful origins of this Myth, which bonds the C.S. and the S-C indissolubly together, is the heritage of anthropology. There was substantial concord amongst early anthropologists about the main property of culture, namely its strong and coherent integration. This central notion of culture as an integrated whole was grounded in German *historismus* but still echoes down the decades. Malinowski's conceptualization of 'an individual culture as a coherent whole'[15] reverberates through Ruth Benedict's 'cultural patterns',[16] Meyer Shapiro's 'cultural style',[17] and Kroeber's 'ethos of total cultural patterns',[18] to resurface in Mary Douglas's notion of 'one single, symbolically consistent universe'.[19] This generic approach, based upon the intuitive grasp of cultural phenomena, entailed a crucial prejudgement, namely that coherence was there to be found – and a corresponding mental closure against the discovery of cultural inconsistencies.

From the beginning, this conventional anthropological approach conflated the two distinct levels (the C.S. and S-C), through eliding:

- The notion of *cultural coherence* – or ideational unity and consistency, with
- The notion of *uniform practices* – or a community smoothly integrated into a common way of life.

Running the two together, as 'a community of shared meanings', conflated the 'community' (S-C) with the 'meanings' (C.S.). By so doing, the Myth perpetrated a basic analytical confusion between these two elements, which are both logically and sociologically distinct. What were inextricably confounded in the Myth and continued to be in the canon were:

14 M. Emirbayer and J. Goodwin, 'Network Analysis, Culture, and the Problem of Agency', *American Journal of Sociology*, 99 (1994), 1411–1454, p. 1441.

15 B. Malinowski, *A Scientific Theory of Culture* (Chapel Hill: University of North Carolina Press, 1944), p. 38.

16 Ruth Benedict, *Patterns of Culture* (London: Routledge and Kegan Paul, 1961).

17 Meyer Shapiro, 'Style', in Sol Tax (ed.), *Anthropology Today* (Chicago: University of Chicago Press, 1962), p. 278.

18 A. L. Kroeber, *Anthropology, Culture, Patterns and Processes* (New York: Harcourt Brace, 1963).

19 Mary Douglas, *Purity and Danger* (London: Routledge and Kegan Paul, 1966), p. 69.

- *Logical consistency*, that is, the degree of internal compatibility between the components of culture (C.S.), and
- *Causal consensus*, that is the degree of social uniformity produced by the ideational influence of one set of people on another (an S-C matter).

Logical consistency is a property of the world of ideas, which requires no knowing subject, whilst causal consensus is a property of people and their interaction. The proposition advanced here is that the two are both analytically and empirically distinct, hence they can vary independently of one another. It is a distinction that is also upheld by Emirbayer and Goodwin: 'cultural discourses, narratives, and idioms are also *analytically autonomous* with respect to network patterns of social relationships. These symbolic formations have emergent properties – an internal logic and organization of their own – that require that they be conceptualized as "cultural structures."'[20] Certainly, this distinction was least visible in primitive society (although Gellner maintained that it was neither absent nor invisible)[21] and the constancy of routine practices was readily made part and parcel of ideational consistency.

The intensity of this general anthropological image can be gauged from Evans-Pritchard's conflationary characterization of the Azande. 'In this web of belief every strand depends upon every other strand, and a Zande cannot get out of its meshes because it is the only world he knows. The web is not an external structure in which he is enclosed. It is the texture of his thought and he cannot think that his thought is wrong'.[22]

If this statement is taken as epitomizing the Myth, it is very clear how the resulting canon conflates Culture and Agency, such that neither is granted distinct properties and powers. Therefore, there can be no interplay between the two, and thus there is no source of internal cultural dynamics that could account for change. Consequently it is not an accident that the locus of change was always located *externally* – in cultural contact, clash, conquest, or colonization.

20 Emirbayer and Goodwin, 'Network Analysis, Culture, and the Problem of Agency', *ibid.*, p. 1438.

21 Ernest Gellner, *Legitimation of Belief* (Cambridge: Cambridge University Press, 1974), pp. 143–144.

22 E. E. Evans-Pritchard, *Witchcraft, Oracles and Magic among the Azande* (Oxford: Oxford University Press, 1937), p. 195.

However, there is a special feature to note about the conflation of Culture and Agency in this early anthropological image of cultural coherence. Once culture had been defined as a community of shared meanings, thus eliding the 'community' with the 'meanings', it really did not matter whether the assumption about coherence was attached to the consistency of meanings or to the smooth integration of the community, for the other element was not capable of independent variation. (Azande culture [C.S.] was a tight-mesh web in which Zande agents [S-C] were tightly enmeshed – none of their doings, including their thinking, enabled them to be reflexive about collective beliefs.) The fact that both of these statements were endorsed in relation to 'cold' societies simply rendered one of them redundant and made the resulting cultural integration of early society an overdetermined phenomenon.

Basically, what twentieth-century cultural theorists shed was simply the idea of overdetermination. The notion of a tight bonding between stable and shared cultural *practices* and consistent and common *meanings* was a feature of the old and cold past. It ceased to be appropriate given the social differentiation and ideational diversity, taken as definitive of modernity from Durkheim onwards. However, what proved extraordinarily resilient was the conflation of Culture and Agency itself. Instead, the new features of modernity, and then of late-modernity, were accommodated in diverse schools of thought by the development of *different versions* of conflationary theorizing. Conjointly, they elaborated the Fallacy of Conflation. Fundamentally, what is wrong with conflationary theorizing is that it prevents the *interplay* between Culture and Agency from contributing to cultural reproduction *or* transformation. This is because in every version of the Fallacy, the conflation of the C.S. and the S-C withholds any autonomy or independence from one of them, if not from both, which precludes a two-way interplay between Culture and Agency.

Fallacies of conflation

Conflation of the two levels of analysis always takes place in a particular direction, and there are only three directions possible. The first pair make either Culture or Agency an epiphenomenon of the other. They differ about which is held to be epiphenomenal, but not about the legitimacy of conflation itself. Thus either version renders the dependent element inert, be it the C.S. or the S-C. Consequently, proponents of epiphenomenalism advance rather crude unilateral accounts when explaining cultural stability or change. In downwards conflation, some cultural code or central value system imposes its choreography on cultural life, and agents are reduced to bearers of its properties, usually through (over-) socialization. In upwards conflation, cultural properties are simply formed and transformed by some hegemonic dominant group, which successfully universalizes an ideological conspectus to advance its material interests.

However, the Fallacy of Conflation does not depend upon epiphenomenalism, or on rendering one aspect of cultural reality inert. This is shown by the remaining possibility, namely 'central' conflation, where elision occurs in the 'middle'. Instead, what happens is that autonomy is withheld from *both culture and agents*, which has precisely the same effect of precluding an examination of their interplay. Here the properties of Cultural Systems and the properties of Socio-Cultural interaction are conflated because they are presented as being mutually constitutive. However, this is unlike everyday terms involving mutual constitution, such as 'singing'. There, the song and the singer have separate properties, some of which are irrelevant to the practice – such as the marital status of the singer – and some of whose interplay is vital to the practice – the song's difficulty and the singer's virtuosity. Instead, in central conflation the intimacy of their reciprocal constitution amounts to an actual elision of the two components, which cannot be untied, and thus their influences upon one another cannot be unravelled. Once again, the net effect of conflation is that the possibility of gaining explanatory leverage upon cultural dynamics from the interplay between Culture and Agency is relinquished from the outset.

Contesting and replacing the old canon

When I first began to theorize Culture, it was almost taken for granted to view Culture as 'a community of shared meanings'. It seemed to me then and still does that this wrongly and unhelpfully elides the 'meanings' with their being 'shared'. The roots of this conflation are deeply embedded in early anthropology, but gained philosophical reinforcement when Wittgenstein's 'forms of life' were imported into social theory. This approach holds Culture to be both *shared* and *coherent.* It thus rules out both cultural divisions within a 'community' and cultural contradictions within a conspectus of ideas. Because both are ubiquitous, their denial seemed overdue for revision. This was advanced in my Morphogenetic Approach to Culture (1988), based on the following three propositions:

1. *Ideas are sui generis real.* Where propositions are concerned, these are human products that are either true or false. At any given time, the stock of knowledge contains both, although we are epistemically incapable of knowing which is which for many ideas. (Historically most of science, medicine, etc., was wrong, which is neither to maintain that what is now held is correct, nor that discredited ideas 'die', otherwise we would be incapable of knowing, for example, about 'phlogiston' or the 'homunculus'). The full corpus of ideas, known or available to be known at any time, is termed the 'Cultural System' (C.S.). To refer to the C.S. is to say nothing about the consistency or contradiction of its components.
2. *The sharing of ideas is contingent.* So, too, is whether or not a given idea has salience in the social order – or part of it – at any given time. This contingency depends upon who is promoting (upholding, diffusing, imposing, etc.) particular ideas at that time, how well they do it, and what opposition they encounter or stimulate. These are Socio-Cultural (S-C) matters. Culture cannot be confined to ideas that are currently endorsed by social groups (at any T_1) because these are always *only a portion of the ideas available* for endorsement. Usually, S-C conflict leads to the activation of some of that nonsalient portion, specifically those ideas which challenge whatever is or bids to be hegemonic. Thus, unfashionable ideas can be revived, as appears to be the case for 'paganism' today. Yet, how can ideas be revived, rediscovered, retrieved, or reactivated unless they are credited with ontological status?
3. *The interplay between 'ideas'* (C.S.) *and 'groups'* (S-C) *is dynamic and accounts for cultural elaboration.* An adequate theoretical approach to Culture (like Structure) requires both diachronic analysis of how certain ideas came to be in social currency at any time, of which groups sponsored them, and why they did and may still do so (and against what past or on-going opposition), as well as synchronic analysis of what maintains cultural morphostasis for as long as it lasts.

To treat Culture as a seamless web of 'transactions' does entail a bias towards 'presentism'. This is because it consistently focusses upon the synchronic, given that historical regress is selective and ultimate regress impossible. Above all, the 'Relationists' have no 'toolkit' (or underpinning social ontology) with which to break up the undifferentiated flow of 'transactions'. The implicit assumption is that synchronic accounts can somehow be conducted without serious reference to diachronic processes: who won out and who lost out badly in the previous S-C round of group interaction and how that advantages some groups and disadvantages others (by privileging certain tracts of the C.S.) in the current round of cultural interaction. From my point of view, any 'cultural transaction' had a history and a biography that defined the 'starting positions' of different agential groups at the beginning of any analysis of a particular episode (who was most educated, whose views were institutionalized, who had the best equipped laboratories for what, and who were less culturally privileged?).

In Realism a stratified social ontology is endorsed, with different emergent properties and powers pertaining to different levels of reality and, in this case, cultural reality. Therefore, the fact that I distinguish the Cultural System from Socio-Cultural interaction – which *empirically* are encountered conjointly, although *ontologically* they constitute different strata – will be resisted by 'Relationists' who maintain that this ontological distinction is not warranted and thus cannot be of theoretical or practical use. *Because of their flat ontology, 'Relationists' consider every aspect of culture to be Socio-Cultural in kind.*

The distinction I am making is an everyday one used by lay people, in their own terms. Culture as a whole is defined as referring to all intelligibilia, that is to any 'item'[23] having the dispositional ability to be understood by someone – whether or not anyone does so at a given time. Within this corpus, the C.S. is that subset of items to which the law of contradiction can be applied – that is, society's propositional register at any given time. Contradictions and complementarities are *logical* properties of the world of ideas, or, if preferred, of the contents of the universal library or archive.

[23] Nothing hangs on this term; an 'element' of culture could be substituted. This is an illustration of the comparative poverty of cultural compared with structural concepts.

We use this concept every day when we say that the ideas of X are *consistent* with those of Y, or that theory or belief A *contradicts* theory or belief B.[24] In so doing, we grant that a C.S. has an objective existence because of the autonomous logical relations amongst its component ideas (doctrines, theories, beliefs and individual propositions). These are independent of anyone's claim to know, to believe, to assert, or to assent to them, because this is knowledge independent of a knowing subject –such as any unread book whose author is now dead.

However, the above is quite different from another kind of everyday statement, namely that the ideas of X *were influenced* by those of Y, where we refer to the influence of people on one another – such as teachers on pupils, television on its audience, or earlier thinkers on later ones. These depend upon *causal relations*, that is, the degree of cultural uniformity produced by the imposition of ideas by one group of people on another through the whole gamut of familiar techniques – exhortation, argument, persuasion, manipulation, and mystification – which often entail the use of power.

At any moment, the contents of the C.S. are the product of historical S-C interaction but, once having emerged, *qua* product the C.S. has properties and powers of its own kind. As with Structure, some of its most important causal powers are those of constraints, enablements, and sources of motivation.[25] In the cultural domain these stem from contradictions and complementarities. However, again like Structure, constraints require something to constrain and enablements something to enable. Those 'somethings' are the ideational projects of people – the beliefs they seek to uphold, the theories they wish to vindicate, the propositions they want to be able to deem valid, and the counter ideas or ideologies they seek to promote.

In other words, the *exercise of C.S. causal powers* is dependent upon their activation from the S-C level. At any given time, what ideas are entertained Socio-Culturally result from the properties and powers belonging to that level. It is interaction at the S-C level that explains why particular groups wish to uphold a particular idea – or

[24] Whether or not they are shared by someone or group is irrelevant to the existence of a contradiction. Of course, if they are, then how their holders cope is an interesting question, which Kuhn, for example, regards as important when 'anomalies' to a paradigm begin to accumulate.

[25] D. V. Porpora, 'Four Concepts of Social Structure', *Journal for the Theory of Social Behaviour*, 19 (1989), 195–212.

to undermine one held by another group. However, once they do, then their ideational projects will confront C.S. properties (not of their own making) and unleash these contradictions or complementarities upon themselves, which other groups may seek to realise or to contain.

For example, such logically 'constraining contradictions' exist when there is an internal or necessary relationship between the ideas (A), advanced by a given group, and other ideas (B), which are lodged in the C.S. – and yet (A) and (B) are in logical tension. Durkheim provides a superb historical example of this in his analysis of the logical inconsistencies in which Christianity was embroiled, from earliest times, because its inescapable dependence upon classicism confronted the Church with 'a contradiction against which it has fought for centuries'.[26] Because the relationship between (A) and (B) is a necessary one, their contradiction could not be evaded by the simple renunciation of (B); Christians could not repudiate the classical languages in which the Gospel was written nor the classical philosophical concepts through which it was theologically explicated. Although substantively far removed, the 'constraining contradiction' also confronts any explanatory theory (A), which is advanced in science, but whose observational theory (B) does not provide immediate empirical corroboration – that is, if scientists think they have good reason not to jettison (A).[27]

Equally, the Socio-Cultural level possesses causal powers of its own kind in relation to the C.S.; it can resolve apparent contradictions and respond adaptively to real ones, or explore and exploit the complementarities it confronts, thus modifying the Cultural System in the process. Socio-Cultural relations can set their own cultural agenda, often prompted by a group's structurally based interests, through creatively adding new items to the systemic register. In these ways, the S-C level is responsible for elaborating upon the composition of the C.S. level morphogenetically. Relationships between the two levels are summarized in Figure 5.1.

Thus, even when Socio-Cultural integration is found to be high, this says *nothing* whatsoever about whether the corpus of ideas endorsed

26 Emile Durkheim, *The Evolution of Educational Thought* (London: Routledge and Kegan Paul, 1977), p. 22.

27 Imre Lakatos, 'Falsification and the methodology of scientific research programmes', in I. Lakatos and A. Musgrave (eds.), *Criticism and the Growth of Knowledge* (London: Cambridge University Press, 1970), p. 99f.

Cultural level	Dependent upon	Type of relations
CULTURAL SYSTEM	Other ideas	Logical
SOCIO-CULTURAL	Other people	Causal

Figure 5.1 Logical and causal relations within Culture
Source: Based upon Archer, 1988, Culture and Agency: The Place of Culture in Social Theory, Cambridge, Cambridge University Press, p. 134.

are *logically consistent* (i.e. that ideas X are compatible with ideas Y). They may well not be, in which case the contradiction remains (at the level of the Cultural System) as a permanent fault line that can be split open if and when (some of) the population in question develops articulate interests in doing so and an organization for doing it. Equally, the components of the C.S. making up its corpus of ideas can have high logical consistency, and yet Socio-Cultural dissensus and actual social antagonism may be profound. As Gouldner pointed out,[28] no normative corpus is proof against groups with divergent interests differentially accentuating particular elements and according them particularistic interpretations in order to promote the concerns of one group against others. In other words, Socio-Cultural and Cultural System integration can vary independently from one another: 'sharedness' is variable rather than definitional.

In the morphogenetic approach, Culture's relative stability versus its transformation and the substantive form taken by the development of any corpus of beliefs, theories, or propositions, plus whether or not such ideational changes can be made to stick Socio-Culturally, are all dependent upon sustaining and utilizing the distinction between the C.S. and the S-C levels rather than conflating them. Kuhn's 'normalization' of scientific paradigms and Bourdieu's 'naturalization' of 'cultural arbitraries' should be seen as *attempts at ideational unification*, but ones whose success can never be a foregone conclusion.

[28] Alvin Gouldner, *The Coming Crisis of Western Sociology* (London: Heinemann, 1971).

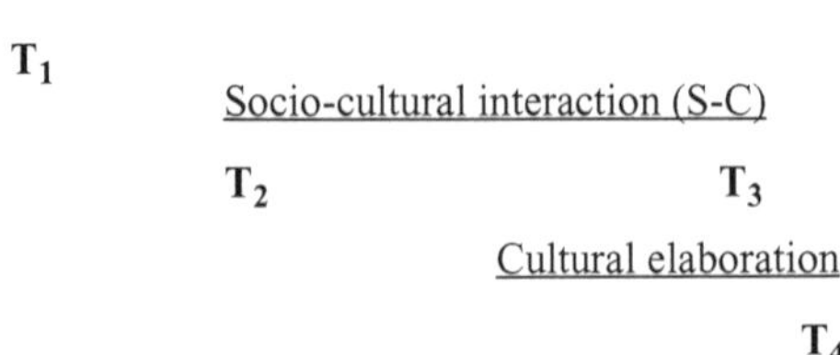

Figure 5.2 Cultural Morphogenesis
Source: Adapted from Archer, Realist Social Theory: The Morphogenetic Approach (Cambridge. Cambridge University Press, 1995) p. 193.

To repeat, when the two levels are allowed to vary independently of one another, their different combinations can be hypothesized to generate cultural reproduction or transformation. Without this, we have no theory about when one or the other will result *ceteris paribus*, and the outcome thus remains a purely empirical matter.

Instead, the relations between the C.S. and the S-C form the three phases of an analytical cycle made up of: ⟨Cultural Conditioning ⇒ Socio-Cultural Interaction ⇒ Cultural Elaboration⟩. In fact, the final phase may culminate at T_4 in either morphogenesis (transformation) or morphostasis (reproduction). In both cases, T_4 constitutes the new T_1', the conditional influences affecting subsequent social relations. This explanatory framework, employing analytical dualism when undertaking practical cultural investigations, depends upon two simple propositions: that the cultural *status quo ante* necessarily pre-dates the actions which transform it; and that cultural elaboration necessarily post-dates those actions (Figure 5.2). It should be noted that *since* T_4 constitutes the new T_1', it derives from nothing but the results of 'relational transactions'.

However, for example, winning a football match or a research contract can be influential outcomes; at T_1' a team starts a new season in the top league and thus plays different teams from if it had lost the last (crucial) game in the previous season. Similarly, it must also be stressed that the 'social interaction' between T_2–T_3 is shorthand for: ⟨agents ↔ agents ↔ agents⟩, all of whom are social actors and groups, who necessarily but temporally have to act in the context defined for them by prior 'transactions' between people. Some of these may be the same persons/groups, the results of whose previous relations (winning the last key match) now confront them with a different (footballing) situation. As part and parcel of bringing about this change, they themselves will also have changed in what I call the process of 'double morphogenesis': they will now be able to command higher transfer fees, to be paid for product sponsorship, and perhaps to acquire celebrity status.

Project all the above lines forward and backwards and they connect with previous or subsequent 'transactions'. It is the investigators' research problem that breaks up the sequence analytically. The phases differentiated will differ in duration for explaining why a team got into the top football league from why research team X succeeds/fails with its grant submissions.

The Relationists' responses considered

Because 'Relationists' confine culture to Socio-Cultural phenomena alone, they have two generic objections to the approach just outlined. (1) They object to 'ideas' being upheld as *sui generis* real and thus contest that there can be such a thing as C.S. logical relations that are ideational rather than interpersonal or intergroup (that is, S-C). (2) It follows that to the 'Relationist', there is no knowledge without a knowing subject. These objections rest in turn on the arguments that (a) the only locus for ideas is within people's heads, because 'books' are merely physical objects (belonging to Popper's World 1).[29] Such 'books', standing for the multimedia archive, are held (b) to depend entirely upon skilled readers, who may differ in their interpretations of them.

(1) Are C.S. ideas real or dependent upon suitable knowing subjects?

My riposte is to doubt that it is necessary for an idea to be in someone's head in order legitimately to accord it ontological status. Sometimes in everyday life an idea migrates from head to paper and back again. Suppose I make a shopping list, then it is misplaced, and I do the shopping without it. I will forget some items that I do need. In that case, my full shopping needs were not in my head but on the list.

[29] Karl Popper, *Objective Knowledge* (Oxford: Clarendon Press, 1979).

Similarly, many of us keep the instructions to domestic appliances, accepting that these are more accurate guides to making them work properly than the rather vague ideas retained in our heads, which we do not trust as being correct. Then again, if uncertain about our mental recall, we reread Durkheim's *Rules*, and I would say we are consulting his published ideas (not his personal thoughts). Certainly, we are not consulting Durkheim himself, are not capable of gaining access to his mind by occult means, and neither do we take our colleagues' views on Durkheim as being authoritative. Anyway, these opinions usually differ. Yet, Elder-Vass,[30] for example, doubts that *Rules* can 'contain ideas as such' because the book only consists of 'marks on paper'. However, when we 'look something up', we are no longer a 'knowing subject' but a subject knowingly in search of knowledge. Thus far, I stand by my claim that saying a book has 'the dispositional capacity to be understood' means the same as saying 'it contains ideas'.

It follows that I think it mistaken to construe books simply as World I physical artefacts. As Bhaskar maintains, 'books are social forms'[31] and thus have the same ontological status as 'structures', 'organizations', 'roles', and so forth. In order to avoid reification he rightly insists that 'the causal power of social forms is mediated through social agency'.[32] Thus, a book requires not only a mind to create it but also another mind(s) to understand it. Mediation is always required,[33] otherwise both structural and cultural properties are held to operate mysteriously but nevertheless as hydraulic forces. It also follows that unread books, whilst retaining their dispositional ability to be understood, can exert no causal powers on anyone. This is a reason why 'properties' and causal 'powers' should not be run together: many properties exist unexercised. Thus, I think Elder-Vass is wrong to maintain that what books and the like 'contain is only a potential to be understood by a skilled reader, and not ideas as such'. What can this potential consist of if it is not ideational? After all, many human

30 Dave Elder-Vass, 'The Emergence of Culture', in G. Albert and S. Sigmund (eds.), *Soziologische Theoriekontrovers* (Wiesbaden: VS Verlag, 2010).

31 Roy Bhaskar, *The Possibility of Naturalism* (London: Routledge, 1989 [1979]), p. 40.

32 *Ibid*, p. 26.

33 Margaret S. Archer, *Structure, Agency and the Internal Conversation* (Cambridge: Cambridge University Press, 2003), chapter 4.

capacities exist only *in potential* (a baby's capacity to walk and talk), but are nonetheless real for not yet being exercised.

His fundamental objection is that 'the archive contains not knowledge as such but only potential knowledge: that as a material resource it contains only marks on paper (or some other medium) and that there is no informational content to such marks in the absence of a reader or other interpreter'.[34] This denial of 'informational content' to our diachronically established archive and its reductive dependency for meaning upon 'knowing subjects' can, I think, be shown to unravel.

First, I have insisted that the items lodged in the 'library' must have the 'dispositional capacity to be understood'. This is what makes them intelligibilia rather than mere markings, such as those made by the legendary monkeys-at-the-keyboard or, in the case of runes, by natural geophysical processes. How, at first, do we know that the marks are intelligible? We don't. But, initially, neither do we know that an unknown language is indeed a language rather than randomly produced sounds. Lack of human epistemic recognition at a given time is no guide to ontological intelligibility.

What then distinguishes between intelligible and random markings? Ultimately, it is their decipherability. Certainly, the jury may not be convened for centuries (as with the Rosetta Stone whilst it was hidden under the sands), its members may disagree for a time (as with the Dead Sea Scrolls), and they are fallible as interpreters (which is why museum exhibits often have to be later relabelled). In addition, although there is certainly a need for 'mediation', there is no *a priori* reason why the intelligible content requires a 'mind' to understand it – this task could be done by a computer and then put to use by mediating agents, as in cryptography from Enigma onwards.

In my view, a 'book's' 'potential to be understood' cannot be ontologically dependent upon 'the capabilities of the reader'. If ideas are made to depend upon our human abilities to understand them, this entails a form of the epistemic fallacy: *what is* becomes reduced to what 'we' can grasp, at any given time. After all, to be misunderstood at first has been the fate of many scientific theories and novel artistic forms. Undoubtedly, for any 'intelligible' to become causally

[34] Dave Elder-Vass, 'The Emergence of Culture', *ibid*, p. 356. See also the exchange between Archer and Elder-Vass, 'Cultural System or Norm Circles? An Exchange', *European Journal of Social Theory*, 52 (2011), 1–23.

efficacious, someone does have (partially) to grasp it, but what they are grasping at is something real. These are ideas, culturally deposited by previous thinkers, which cannot be reduced to their subjective apprehension and appropriation and thus transferred to Popper's World 2.

As Popper himself pointed out, because all of the implications of a single hypothesis cannot be comprehended, knowledge cannot be restricted to the known or to the knower at any point in time. Hence, it cannot be the case that 'cultural content only exists in people's heads'. By recording ideas we pass their 'potential' along the time-line, and they retain their dispositional ability to be understood, activated, used, and abused.

Thus, in my view, it is quite legitimate to conceive of contradictions or complementarities *existing* between two intelligibles, independently of anyone knowing or caring. Idea X *is* incompatible with idea Y, whether or not any of us yet understand this – just as the contents of the next two books we read may turn out to be. To maintain otherwise is again to commit the epistemic fallacy by making the books' understandability depend upon our current understanding, which is both anthropocentric and relativistic.

Why is this important? I have fully agreed that someone/some group needs to 'activate' an idea before it becomes socially salient and influential. The point is that in so doing the group also becomes *embroiled* in that idea's *logical* connections with others. Recall Durkheim's[35] splendid example of how early Christian thinking was dogged by its inescapable connections with incompatible Greek eudaemonistic thought. Because Scripture was written in Greek, it entailed further forays into pagan classical philosophy in order for its concepts to be understood.

In other words, the ideas endorsed by a group have to be upheld within an ideational corpus that was established prior to them (today's Muslims did not write the Koran). This pre-existing cultural conspectus may be 'hostile' (exposing contemporary holders to logical contradictions) or 'friendly' (introducing them to unsuspected compatibilities) – as Weber described respectively for ancient Judaism compared with Confucianism and Hinduism. In turn, this context profoundly affects how the ideas held by a group develop: through corrective 'syncretism' when confronted by 'constraining contradictions' (as with

[35] Emile Durkheim, *The Evolution of Educational Thought*.

Christianity) versus elaborative 'systematization' where 'concomitant complementarities'[36] are encountered (as with Hinduism). These divergent ideational developments remain inexplicable without reference to the logical properties of the field of ideas into which a contemporary group has plunged itself by embracing a particular belief, theory, or set of propositions. The morphogenetic approach to culture was advanced precisely to give a handle to this (i.e. the connection between T_1 and T_2–T_3).

Underlying my disagreement with the 'Relationalists' is that discussion of the Cultural System hinges on other debates, particularly about the ontological status of logic, which there is no space to enter here. Hence, I will simply signal what I see as being the crux of that issue. This concerns the 'Relationist' view – still underdeveloped – that seems to veer towards the Strong Programme of Barnes and Bloor,[37] namely that people's shared understandings of 'logical relations' depend decisively not upon our similar human cognitive capacities but on local conventions of logic. On the contrary, I maintain[38] that fundamental logical principles of identity and noncontradiction are acquired in natural practice and are predicates of both being able to think at all and thus also of verbal communication. The understanding of logical relations is therefore primitive to the expression of logic as ideas. In other words, logical *relations* are not themselves ideas, only *formulations of logic* are such.

(2) The C.S. has no independence from the Conventions of understanding in local Communities, that is, S-C sharedness

'Relationists' hold that the Socio-Cultural level embraces what I have held to be the objective aspects of culture, thus making them exclusively the property of a social group. This is quite different from maintaining, rightly, that the dispositions of individuals to conform to group beliefs, norms, and values is enhanced by their group membership. That is exactly what I hold that social groups try to do through Socio-Cultural

36 See Archer, *Culture and Agency*, pp. 185–226.

37 Barry Barnes and David Bloor, 'Relativism, Rationalism and the Strong Programme', in Martin Hollis and Steven Lukes (eds.), *Rationality and Relativism* (Oxford: Blackwell, 1982).

38 Margaret S. Archer, *Being Human: The Problem of Agency* (Cambridge: Cambridge University Press, 2000), pp. 145–152.

interaction, in which they exercise causal powers of their own kind, thus (potentially) increasing normative conformity.[39] Equally, actions intended to produce cultural unification through, for example, censorship, containment strategies, or ideological manipulation pertain to the S-C level alone. In addition, however, the emergent causal powers of intelligibilia are needed to explain *why* any group would try to restrict access to the archive in the foregoing ways. In so doing, these actors themselves acknowledge the objective (C.S.) capacity of ideas contrary to their own to threaten what they hold ideationally – hence the largely symbolic act of publicly burning books.

Given the ubiquity of social conflict over ideas, this raises a problem about the supposedly shared nature of the S-C level. For many theorists, Culture is *synonymous with* 'a *shared* set of practices and understandings'.[40] To me, such *sharing* is always an *aim* on the part of a particular group *and never a definition*, much less a morphostatic state of affairs 'that tends to produce and sustain shared ways of living'.[41] In order to discuss *sharedness* it will be helpful to introduce an example of a group that *aims* to produce normative conformity amongst its members. I will examine the Roman Catholic Church in greater depth because the existence of its Magisterium (which includes the Catechism and Social Doctrine) shows that it clearly *intends* its norms to be shared by all members of the 'one, holy, catholic and apostolic church'.

However, neither of these two criteria of normative *sharedness* are met, namely, common 'practices' and common 'understandings'. 'Practices' as diverse as the sexual norms advocated in the encyclical *Humanae Vitae* and the liturgical norms endorsed by the Second Vatican Council are, in the first case, widely ignored, and in the second case, hotly contested (by those seeking to re-universalize the Roman Rite). Certainly, many Catholics do share other beliefs (although most of these have been contentious at one time or another), so how much has to be shared? Equally, they draw upon different strands from the long history of catholic thinking, ones that are not fully ideationally compatible, so how consensual does a norm group have to be?

'Understandings' are equally problematic. Every Sunday it is the duty of the faithful to say the Creed but, were it broken down into its

[39] Archer, *Culture and Agency*, *ibid.*, pp. 185–226.
[40] Elder-Vass, 'The Emergence of Culture', *ibid.*, p. 352. [41] *Ibid.*, p. 362.

component propositions, the most diverse array of understood meanings would result. Rather differently, because the Church's Social Doctrine is frequently called its 'best kept secret', what 'proportion' of group norms is required to be Socio-Culturally shared? Members of a group can profess beliefs only if they know them, but if those with such knowledge are a small percentage, then in what sense can it be said to be shared knowledge? The foregoing examples of 'practices' (actions) show that Catholics practising contraception know they are flouting the norm and the examples of 'understandings' show that norms are overtly contested or that many members have no knowledge of them, in which cases they cannot be either shared or consistent.

What are we to make of the Catholic Church, given its intention to generate shared beliefs? Here, it seems those arguing for shared and consistent belief (theory or norms) as *definitive* of any cultural group appear to be caught on the horns of a dilemma. They can respond that the Catholic Church is not what it wants to be *because* it lacks the *sharedness* of practices and understandings, in which case it must be admitted to harbour an *inconsistent set of beliefs*. Or, the alternative response could be to maintain that the Catholic Church is, in fact not 'one' but many groups in various degrees of ideational conflict with one another. However, the fact that the subgroups mentioned earlier remain in the Church raises the question of what holds them together, despite their ideational differences (often drawn from distinct parts of the C.S. and pulling in contrary directions)? It will hardly do to say that they *must* have sufficient in common *because* 'the group' does not fall apart.

In addition, the requirement that a cultural group shares consistency in its set of relevant understandings poses another problem, one encountered in discussions of Wittgenstein's notion of a 'form of life'. If the demand for cultural consensus is stringent, then 'the group' meeting it becomes diminishingly small,[42] perhaps reducing to two people. Yet the normative dyad hardly qualifies as an 'epistemic community' or a paradigm for society. However, if the demand is not fairly stringent, in what sense can it be justifiable to talk about a collectivity being *a cultural* group, rather than *several*, as delineated by their ideational differences?

42 Roger Trigg, *Reason and Commitment* (Cambridge: Cambridge University Press, 1973), pp. 70–71.

Finally, at the Socio-Cultural level, it is important that all who manifestly adhere to some theory or cluster of beliefs are not automatically assumed to be 'true believers'. To slide from observing an overt 'sharing' of ideas into the assumption that this represents a genuine 'community' is always a mistake (as would have been the case in Soviet Eastern Europe). In the attempt to mobilize support for a cause, some will be culturally bamboozled and others will be calculative in deploying ideas to resist or undermine those of their opponents. Still others will become disillusioned and be preparing a bid for normative breakaway. To do so, their leaders will scrutinize the supposed conspectus for loose ends and contradictory threads.

They will also do as we do when stuck over an idea – go and raid the library for some new material. The archive that is the Cultural System is also their reclamation yard from which inert ideas can be given new social salience, be retooled into sources of critique, of self-legitimation, or of counter-ideologies. Because their S-C opponents do not usually feel secure enough to remain speechless, they will do likewise. From their subsequent clash, the elaboration of ideas develops. Thus, it is rarely adequate for explaining the outcome of S-C conflict (or quiescence) to remain at the level of group hostility or hegemony; cultural dynamics also involve the C.S. and how agents actively mediate and deploy the ideational resources deposited there.

Three concluding points

First, my concern as a 'relational realist' is to develop and refine an analytical framework that is useful for conducting substantive analyses of why the cultural order – or part of it – is, in Max Weber's words, 'so rather than otherwise'. That is why I call the morphogenetic approach an 'explanatory framework', in other words, a practical toolkit.[43] This means attempting to provide guidelines for producing particular explanations of cultural phenomena in different times and places, the most important being, as was summarily presented in Figure 5.2:

– How the prior context in which cultural interrelations develop influences the form they take

[43] John Parker, *Structuration* (Buckingham: Open University Press, 2000), pp. 69–85.

- Which relations between agents respond most closely to these influences and which tend to cross-cut or nullify them
- Most generally, under what conditions do cultural interrelationships result in morphostasis rather than morphogenesis

None of these distinctions can be employed by 'Relationists' to render the endless sequence of cultural 'transactions' manageable in concrete analyses.

Second, 'Relationists', in their denial of emergence, often seem to take pride in being impregnable to the change of reification (still regularly levelled against Realism, for example by Dépelteau)[44] and also to criticisms of the misattribution of causal powers to entities that cannot be powerful particulars (Manicas[45]; Varela[46]). This invulnerability is because they make a seemingly more minimalist claim that – in both the structural and cultural domains – 'groups influence their members'. (It should be noted that this effect may or may not be construed as an emergent property and power: to Elder-Vass it is; to Dépelteau it is not.) In turn, such minimalism carries a heavy price in terms of its reduced explanatory power. Effectively, its advocates place a Big Etcetera after the term 'transactions'. Because the latter often attracts the adjective 'myriad',[47] it becomes hard to see how 'Relationism' constitutes a toolkit (explanatory programme) for conducting concrete research.

Minimalism does enable ecumenical collaboration with many more sociological approaches, and it is unsurprising that network theory appears to offer a means for making a 'myriad transactions' methodologically tractable (see Crossley).[48] However, network theory is no longer one and unitary. In the able hands of a neo-structuralist such as Lazega,[49] who has predominantly studied cultural issues (prestige

44 See Dépelteau, 'Relational Thinking', *ibid.*

45 Peter T. Manicas, *A Realist Philosophy of Social Science* (Cambridge: Cambridge University Press, 2006).

46 Charles R. Varela, 'Elder-Vass's Move and Giddens's Call', *Journal for the Theory of Social Behaviour*, 37 (2007), 201–210.

47 See Mustafa Emirbayer, 'Manifesto for a Relational Sociology', *American Journal of Sociology*, 103 (1997), 281–317.

48 Nick Crossley, *Towards Relational Sociology* (London: Routledge, 2011), chapters 9 and 10.

49 E. Lazega, M. Jourda, L. Mounier and R. Stofer, 'Des poissons et des mares: l'analyse de réseaux multi-niveaux', *Revue française de sociologie*, 48 (2007), 93–131, and E. Lazega, M. Jourda, L. Mounier and R. Stofer, 'Catching up

in and among research groups and the differential quest for advice from commercial court judges), 'transactions' do not retain their flat ontology but pose some of the same issues about structured culture and agential competition as discussed in this chapter.

Moreover, it seems to me that there is both a price to minimalism's openness and a question about its sustainability. The price is a slide towards 'central conflation'. Few will balk at 'group influence'; does anyone seriously challenge those social psychologists of the 1950s who pioneered experiments such as the auto-kinetic effect? Yet, because 'Relationism' is *defined* by its denial of emergence, others will have little difficulty in incorporating it into the agenda of structuration theory, under their own descriptions. The way to avoid this happening links directly to the issue I have called sustainability. It seems insufficient to remain content with the designation of cultural groups (a more complex sociological task than it appears at first glance, as we have seen when discussing the case of the Roman Catholic Church) and their potential effect upon their members. The exercise of this influence is a matter of relations within the group and its relationality with other groupings (or relations between relations). Donati's development of Relational Sociology[50] shows that a growing cluster of emergent properties require acknowledgement, even if the aim is limited to explaining reciprocal exchanges between Ego and Alter. This is why he regards his theoretical approach in Relational Sociology as being Realist[51] and of the non-minimalist kind.

Third, it is well worth noting that we have returned to exactly the same issue raised in my first chapter. Given the way that human beings are constituted, the way the world is, and the ineluctability of their interaction, it is unavoidable that human relations are with all orders of natural reality: nature, practice, and the social. Although when taxed to define the distinctive subject matter of sociology it is perfectly valid to designate our social relations with one another, that does not dispense us from giving due weight to other forms of relationality because

with big fish in the big pond ? Multi-level network analysis through linked design', *Social Networks*, 30 (2008), 157–176.

[50] P. Donati, *Introduzione alla sociologia relazionale* (Milan: FrancoAngeli, 1983), chapter 1. See also P. Donati and I. Colozzi (eds.), *Il Paradigma relazionale nelle scienze sociali: le prospettive sociologiche* (Bologna: Mulino, 2006).

[51] P. Donati, *Relational Sociology*, chapter 3.

they are necessarily intertwined with them. John Donne's famous line does not simply refer to our human reliance upon others; the bell will also toll in the absence of drinkable water, of artefacts providing shelter, and certainly if some Robinson Crusoe had insufficient practical mastery of the logical canon in which reflexively to think out, criticize, and correct his ideas about meeting his human needs. Thus, theoretical assertions that social *relations* are the subject matter of sociology is not the same as maintaining that all relations relevant to given sociological explanations are *social in kind.* Denial of the Cultural System is the heavy price paid for this remorseless exorbitation of our sociality.

PART III

Prologue: The range of Relational Subjects: where and how they emerge

The range of Relational Subjects

Examples of 'social subjects' can be organized in a framework based on the level, type, and degree of mediation of their relations. The *degree* of mediation runs from a minimum (face-to-face, direct relationships) to a maximum (hyper-mediated, indirect relations, as in social mass movements).[1] We will distinguish between three *levels*; micro-, meso-, and macro,[2] where the *type* of mediation varies with the specific qualities of the social relations in play. Of course, various other typologies are often used; the most simple differentiates four types of spheres:

[1] Obviously, other classifications of social relations also exist. For example, Rachid Bagaoui proposes a typology that differentiates between: (i) the level of interactions between actors (three types: *effects of the interaction* = Elias; *interplay between actors* = Crozier; *stakes between actors* = Touraine and the marxists); (ii) the type of relations between agents and structures (three types: *non-separability between agents and structures*, that is, the relation as co-determined between agent and structure = Giddens; *relation covered in the media* = Bourdieu; relation as *separable* = Archer); (iii) the systemic level (three types: *system/environment relations* = Luhmann; *totality-parts relations* = Morin; *exchange relations* = Laflamme). Rachid Bagaoui, 'Un paradigme systémique relationnel est-il possible? Proposition d'une typologie relationnelle', *Nouvelles perspectives en sciences sociales: revue internationale de systémique complexe et d'études relationnelles*, 3 (2007), 151–175. However, it seems that this typology groups together many things that are very different from one another, and above all, that it confuses relations in a logical or analytical sense and empirical social relations. Moreover, some of these types are not properly social relations (for example, Luhmann's system/environment relations entail a binary distinction that is a complete separation, not a relation properly (cf. Donati, *Teoria relazionale della società*, 1991, chapter 4). Bagaoui, in effect, does not consider social relations as such, but rather as ways in which various scholars have used the linguistic term *relation*. He does not deal with social relation itself, does not analyze it in its structure and dynamics, but remains outside, limiting himself to cataloguing the different uses of the word.

[2] The micro-, meso-, and macro-levels can be defined on the *analytical* level or the *empirical* level. For reasons of space, we will address them only on the empirical level.

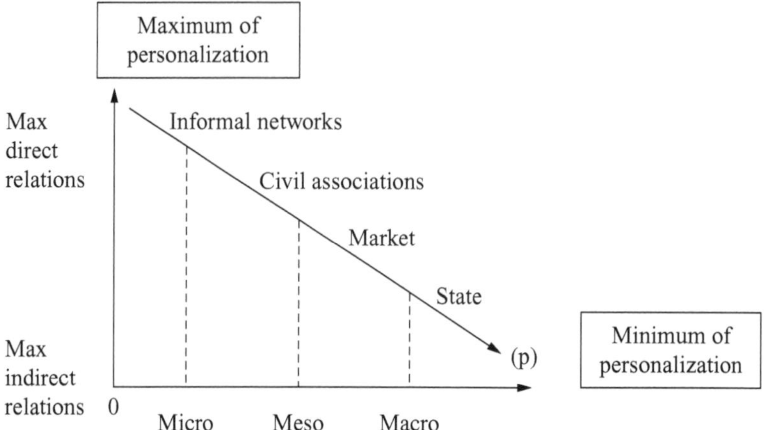

Figure P.1 A map of Relational Subjects: the probability (p) of there being Relational Subjects.

mediations in the life world sphere – in the family, kinship, friendship, acquaintances; mediations in the sphere of civil society – in voluntary associations and organizations; mediations in the economic market; and mediations in the political-administrative system and its apparatuses. The three criteria of level, type and degree are intercorrelated but are not identical and are mapped in Figure P.1.

Instances of Relational Subjects at the micro-, meso-, and macro-levels

At the micro-level: the couple and informal relations

The couple – as a stable relation between two partners – is a Relational Subject if and to the extent to which the two partners act with reference to their relation (to its structure, its needs, and its conditions), being oriented to it rather than considering the relation as a function of the Selves involved. The same holds for informal relations (kinship, neighbours, friendship, etc.).

Each partner is increasingly a Relational Subject the more his/her concerns and actions are 'centered' on the relation with the Other. The couple *as such* is a relational *social* subject if and to the extent to which their relation as partners *emerges* as a reality distinct from the two individual subjects and, in turn, influences each of them.

The existence of this Relational Subject (the couple) requires that:

(i) Ego must 'be aware of the relation' with Alter and vice versa, where 'awareness' means considering the relation as a reality that is distinct from the Self;
(ii) In turn, this means that the Ego-Alter relation must not be considered simply as a projection of Ego onto Alter and vice versa (as is the case with Husserl's notion of 'appresentation'),[3] nor as Ego and Alter sharing thoughts, as in Plural Subject theory.
(iii) The relation must be defined as a 'We' by the parties concerned;
(iv) The 'We' must be 'symbolized' (by Ego and Alter avowing to being 'a couple' in some way), even if the symbol employed is interpreted through different thoughts and meanings by Ego and by Alter. The symbol *indicates* the reality of the relation (We, not-Them),[4] such that whatever the We does (for example, eating

[3] What makes the constitution and apprehension of the Other possible at all? Husserl writes: '*A certain mediacy of intentionality* must be present here, going out from the substratum, "primordial world", (which, in any case, is the incessantly underlying basis) and making present to the consciousness a "there too", which nevertheless is not itself there and can never become an "itself there". We have here, accordingly, a kind of *making "co-present"*, a kind of "appresentation."' E. Husserl, *Cartesian Meditations* (The Hague: Martinus Nijhoff, 1973), p. 139.

[4] Note that the words 'we' and 'them' can have two meanings, i.e. as an interpersonal entity or as an objectified entity. This difference is captured by Martin Buber's (1923) distinction between the *I-You* and *I-It* relationships. The *Ich-Es* ("I-It") relationship is nearly the opposite of *Ich-Du*. Whereas in *Ich-Du* the two beings encounter one another, in an *Ich-Es* relationship the beings do not actually meet. Instead, the 'I' confronts an idea, or concept, of the being in its presence and treats that being as an object. All such objects are considered to be merely mental representations, created and sustained by the individual mind. This is based partly on Kant's theory of phenomenon, in that these objects reside in the cognitive agent's mind, existing only as thoughts. Therefore, the *Ich-Es* relationship is in fact a relationship with oneself; it is not a dialogue, but a monologue. In the *Ich-Es* relationship, an individual treats other things, people, etc., as objects to be used and experienced. Essentially, this form of objectification means relating to the world in terms of the self – with the other as an object serving the individual's interest. Buber argued that human life consists of an oscillation between *Ich-Du* and *Ich-Es*, and that in fact *Ich-Du* experiences are rather few and far between. In diagnosing the various perceived ills of modernity (e.g. isolation, dehumanization), Buber believed that the expansion of a purely analytic, material view of existence was at heart an advocacy of *Ich-Es* relations – even between human beings. Buber argued that this paradigm devalued not only existents, but the meaning of all existence.

a meal together, spending a holiday together) is defined and lived as a relation (reciprocal action);

(v) The emergent 'We' arises from interactions between Ego and Alter and becomes part of their personal and social identities, which then conditions their actions, as was illustrated in Figure 2.1, for David and Helen.[5]

In the couple, to say that the Ego (David) and Alter (Helen) are *personal* Relational Subjects meant seeing them as singular actors (in Figure 2.1, while the *social* Relational Subject, which we call 'couple', is the We-relation that emerges from their relations.

It is worth emphasizing the differences among ways of defining social relations. There is a radical difference between Relational Sociology, which is based on Critical Realism, and those sociologies that, although they call themselves relational, are based on flat, unstratified ontologies; for instance, those that see the relation as essentially a 'transaction' in the interactions between individuals (Emirbayer) or as 'communicative exchange' that generates emotions (Laflamme).[6] For us, the relation implies an exchange, and therefore a communication, but is not reducible to either exchange or mere communication. The social relation, such as that of the couple, is a reality that emerges from interactions but has its own reality (life) because it exists even when the exchange is interrupted or the communication falls silent, thus having a reality that goes beyond the contents of exchange and communication. If one partner goes to work far away from the other partner and does not exchange or communicate anything for some time, the couple relation continues to exist. Certainly, during that period of time, the couple relation ceases to exert some of its effects, but it persists as a relational structure that places specific requirements and conditions on the partners and continues to furnish relational goods (security, future prospects and even 'togetherness'). Indeed, the couple relation can exist even if communication and exchange between the partners

[5] For a more extensive discussion see the text with the original figure: P. Donati, 'Engagement as a Social Relation: A Leap into Trans-Modernity', in Margaret S. Archer and A. M. Maccarini (eds.), *Engaging with the World. Agency, Institutions, Historical Formations* (London: Routledge, 2013), pp. 129–161.

[6] M. Emirbayer, 'Manifesto for a relational sociology', *American Journal of Sociology*, 103 (1997), 281–317; S. Laflamme, *Communication et emotions. Essai de microsociologie relationelle* (Paris: L'Harmattan, 1995).

are not satisfying, or if they do not give them what they individually expect or hope for at some given point in time.

The following vignette provides an example of how the process of desisting from offending occurs within and between people who share social and familial networks.[7] In part of London, a gang of young men grow up together and offend together. They become close friends over the years, but these gang members also form intimate/marital relationships, which gradually assume paramount importance among the constellation of their concerns. When a feud erupts between them, dividing the gang into two, Mike, the original gang leader, moves to another area, where he starts work. He remains close to certain members and suggests that they too move to his new area and make a fresh start. He helps them to move and gain work training, thus providing them with an opportunity to give up crime, which some do. Obviously, very different reflexive deliberations will have taken place among those accepting Mike's offer.

The question is, could this scenario be described as an example of Relational Reflexivity? It seems so, because: (1) Mike has realized that he should break his links with the old gang (leaving his previous social network); (2) he felt that a new social context (network) was needed (in a sense, he realized that the gang network was a relational evil); and (3) he undertook the reestablishment of relations with and among those gang members who joined him. We argue that this is an instance of collective reflexivity because Mike's orientation was consistently towards relational goods and evils. (However, we are making the unsubstantiated assumption that this was also the case for those who joined him.) Mike's concern was to build up a new Relational Subject (the new network) which could produce relational goods.

In case the foregoing example of collective reflexivity is considered to be unduly speculative, let's consider the university department in which many of us work. It is not possible either to understand or explain what our colleagues do (their contributions, reactions, motivations etc.) on an intradepartmental basis by hermeneutically examining every permutation of relations between these Egos and Alters. For many, everything they do in the department (in terms of teaching,

[7] This example has been inspired by reading an article on how the relational context matters in preventing people from offending: see Beth Weaver, 'The Relational Context of Desistance: Some Implications and Opportunities for Social Policy', *Social Policy & Administration*, 46 (2012), 395–412.

administration, and research) is mediated through an intangible relational good, generated by them and countless unknown others – their academic discipline. For a person or a research group, the discipline might mean a section of it or specialism within it to which they are oriented. (See Figure 3.4.)

Collective reflexivity means that all colleagues have their relation to the discipline (or a section of it) in mind as they interact in the department, but they do not have the same thoughts in their heads; their intentionality is not shared, and neither are their commitments to the discipline identical in kind. What is collective is the colleagues' common orientation to their common discipline. What is reflexive is that this orientation is bent back and affects what they do (and decline to do) in the department and how they do it.

So far, 'the discipline' has been assumed to be a relational good; orientation towards it and working for it (reviewing, editing, organizing events, etc.) contribute incrementally to its development and diffusion.[8] However, there are circumstances under which the discipline as generated becomes a relational evil. Currently, in most developed countries, political power relations[9] (expressed through funding, reward, and recognition for departments and academics) seek to enforce particular manifestations of 'appropriate' orientations towards each discipline (via various performance indicators and associated sanctions for noncompliance). The results are relationally negative: collaboration become competition; informal esteem becomes a formal hierarchy with the 'non–research active' at the bottom; concern for students becomes keeping 'office hours'; journals are selected for their 'impact factor', articles written with a weather eye to citation indices, and so forth as we know too well. Departmental relations themselves only deteriorate under the dehumanization inherent in this induced instrumental rationality.

At the meso-level: voluntary associations

Let us take the case of the voluntary associations in civil society. At first glance, the meso-level can appear to be only an extension

[8] This is not the place to enter a philosophical discussion about the definition and dynamics of the growth of knowledge.

[9] Their advent requires a morphogenetic analysis in itself.

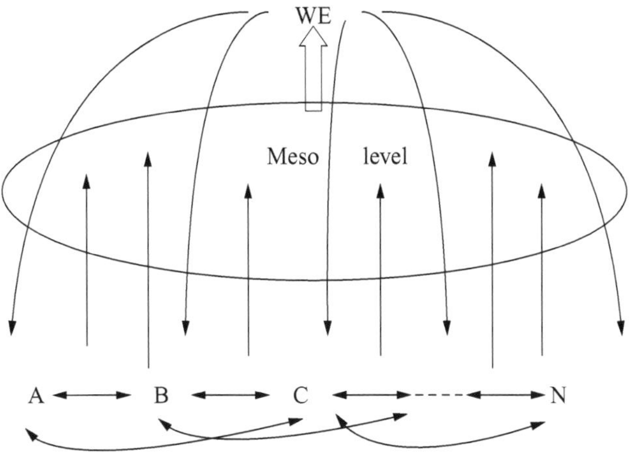

Figure P.2 The Relational Subject at the meso-level

of the micro-level, but this is not the case, for many reasons (see Figure P.2).

The first difference consists in the fact that interactions between the N members are multiplied out of all proportion. Consequently, the sheer number of relations that emerge from single interactions among the N members create problems in defining the We at the meso-level. There is a relational social subject if and only if the N members of the association have the same We that is emergent from their interactions. In other words, the voluntary association is a network of nodes (the N members) with certain relations among them, which must converge toward the same We. Thus, whether or not a relational social subject exists, constituted by the association's N members, depends on how their network of relations (internal, but clearly related to the exterior) works. Shared goals are needed to unite the We, and the more diffuse or disputed the goal is, the less likely it becomes that a Relational Subject will be created (for example, peace movements are very divided among themselves because their goal has different meanings, according to members' ideologies or political positions).

All of this means that a relational social subject comes into existence on the meso-level when at least two conditions are met; these involve joint action and joint commitment without entailing 'we thinking'. First, the goal of the We must be held 'in common,' not in the sense of being understood and interpreted in an identical way by the N members, but rather in being perceived as a common task (*co-munus*) that can only be accomplished by their being in a We-relation, which means carrying out the *munus together*, that is, relationally. Second, in interactions among the N members, whether on an interpersonal level or on the level of emergent meso-relations, the We must be *recognized* as a commitment that binds and connects the N members in the shared enterprise.

If these two conditions are not satisfied, a relational social subject does not emerge. The fact that a 'joint commitment' exists[10] does not guarantee that there will be a 'genuine' social subject, because a joint commitment does not guarantee any authentic relation among the members (that is, a relation that can effectively generate the existence of a social subject, since the sharing of a commitment may only indicate the existence of mechanical solidarity between individuals and not solidarity of a relational type).[11]

Relational goods can be produced only by means of that *specific* type of solidary relation that connects the various members of the association. Achieving and maintaining the We relation is the problem of all voluntary associations. Often when the association is founded, the We seems clear at the start (the falling in love phase described by Alberoni).[12] However, over time, relations evolve among the members, including those that result in the weakening or disappearance of the Relational Subject – when, for example, some members come to dominate others (in keeping with Robert Michels' 'iron law of oligarchy'). Generically in these cases, the meso-level has become insulated from and unresponsive to the primary relations at micro-level.

The case of companies (corporations) is quite different from voluntary associations, because in entrepreneurial enterprises the

[10] Margaret Gilbert, *On Social Facts* (Princeton, NJ: Princeton University Press, 1989); M. Gilbert, 'Walking Together. A paradigmatic Social Phenomenon', *Midwest Studies in Philosophy*, 15 (1990), 1–14; M. Gilbert, 'Shared Intention and Personal Intention', *Philosophical Studies*, 144 (2009), 167–187.

[11] P. Donati, 'Morphogenic Society and the Structure of Social Relations', in Margaret S. Archer (ed.), *Late Modernity. Trajectories towards Morphogenic Society* (Dordrecht: Springer, 2014), pp. 143–172.

[12] F. Alberoni, *Statu nascenti. Studi sui processi collettivi* (Bologna: il Mulino, 1968); Alberoni, *Movimento e istituzione. Teoria generale* (Bologna: il Mulino, 1981).

'constitutive relation' making for the social subject is missing.[13] On the other hand, enterprises of a cooperative type, such as the Italian cooperatives of social solidarity (established by national Law n. 318/1991), have an associational constitution according to their statutes. Nevertheless, in these latter cases, it is always necessary to ascertain if and how the association actually produces the relational networks that make a We (as in Figure P.2). A further example that deserves separate analysis is that of *social networks* and the creation of a *commons* on the Internet, such as *peer-to-peer* production.[14]

At the macro-level: public institutions

The macro level is represented by public institutions, such as the State and its apparatuses (public administration), local authorities, the churches, international organizations (such as the U.N.) or supranational ones (such as the European Union). These institutions differ from 'meso-subjects', which are intermediate Corporate Agents operating between individuals and macro-systems. The question is: in what sense can we say that macro-institutional entities – for example, a State or a country's judicial system – are (or can be) relational social subjects? Characteristically, they are constituted by relations that are highly impersonal, because such institutions are normatively obliged to act according to formal, public criteria and involve individuals whose personal qualities, ideas, cultures and social origins differ greatly from one another. Given these characteristics, it is highly improbable that the N macro-institutional members (the citizens of a State, the members of a Church, etc.) can give rise to (animate) a social Relational Subject. The gap between micro- (interpersonal) relations and the membership of a public macro-institution becomes so wide as to render the constitution of a We improbable.

[13] L. R. Baker, *Persons and Bodies. A Constitution View* (Cambridge: Cambridge University Press, 2000); R. Prandini, 'Soggettività sociali riflessive: la costituzione di un 'noi' riflessivo', *Sociologia e Politiche Sociali*, 13 (2010), 81–113.

[14] M. Bauwens, 'Par cum pari. Notes on the horizontality of peer to peer relationships in the context of the verticality of a hierarchy of values', in Margaret S. Archer and P. Donati (eds.), *Pursuing the Common Good: How Solidarity and Subsidiarity Can Work Together* (Rome: Vatican Press, 2008), pp. 247–262.

Yet these macro-institutions are considered 'moral persons'[15] because they seem to operate as a We. In everyday language, we say that the State, the E.U., the public administration, the Church, the local authorities all act – they take decisions, formulate goals, behave in a certain way, and so forth. Whether or not the attribution of a We to such bodies is only a fiction, as nominalists would claim,[16] or if, instead, it identifies a structural reality, as critical realists assert,[17] is a question that cannot be discussed here, although we lean towards the second view.

It seems to us that a public macro-institution can be a relational social subject only in rare and exceptional cases, under very special conditions. These conditions are most frequently associated with an institution in *statu nascendi*, in Max Weber's sense, as opposed to one working by routine action. From the theoretical standpoint, these conditions are ones that promote *interpenetration* between the institution's systemic integration and social integration. This means that the systemic mechanisms are subjectively endorsed by the participants interacting with them and do not operate as mere systemic functions or as automatic devices.

For example, we know that a social network's holes create dependencies on the part of certain nodes (the more isolated ones) upon other nodes called brokers (the more connected ones).[18] *Interpenetration* begins to be generated as soon as a broker in the structural network, instead of operating as a 'mechanical' mediator between the nodes that it connects, seeks to foster 'subsidiary mediation' between the more isolated agents and actors by putting them into relational contact with one another. In such a case, the broker does not simply leave the nodes as he/she finds them, but seeks to empower them, giving them more space and voice by fostering direct contact between them, in turn reducing the influential powers of the brokers

[15] On the notion of *persona moralis*, see R. Hittinger, 'Social Pluralism and Subsidiarity in Catholic Social Doctrine', *Annales Teologici*, 16 (2002), 385–408.

[16] P. Winch, *The Idea of a Social Science* (London: Routledge and Kegan Paul, 1958).

[17] D. V. Porpora, 'Four Concepts of Social Structure', *Journal for the Theory of Social Behaviour*, 19 (1989), 195–211.

[18] B. Wellman and S. D. Berkowitz (eds.), *Social Structures. A Network Approach* (Cambridge: Cambridge University Press, 1988).

themselves. Thus, *interpenetration* consists in the redistribution of power by the empowerment of the weakest nodes.

This rarely happens, although much depends on the type of social sphere in question. It is highly improbable, if not impossible, in the political sphere because the quest for power entails the strengthening of structural mechanisms rather than their weakening. The same is the case in the 'for-profit' economic sphere, although it is not quintessential to markets *per se*. Civil society relations in third sector organizations and its networks are different, and it is more probable to find subsidiarity and solidarity in operation, oriented toward empowering the weak and marginalized. In the family sphere and in informal relations, because the level of collective reflexivity is normally low, this renders explicit intertwining between processes of social and systemic integration relatively uncommon, although a spontaneous intertwining, under subjects' own descriptions, is more frequent.

Public services (statutory welfare services, municipalities, health centres, churches, etc.) can be 'moral persons' if and only if they act through a We-relation as 'Relational Subjects'. They are not such by virtue simply of being public services, and they become Relational Subjects if and only if their institutional roles open themselves to external conversation with subjects in their lifeworlds. That is, when they work together with the latter to build a network of relations among themselves, leading to the creation or regeneration of the common good (a good constituted by their relations – the common good as a relational good).[19]

Summarizing Relational Reflexivity

In all the cases considered, from the micro-level (couple, family), to the meso-level (voluntary associations), to the macro-level (public institutions), social subjects can be relational and, therefore, fully 'moral persons' if we can attribute *Relational Reflexivity* to them,[20] which is to say, a reflexivity that is practised by means of internal and external conversation about the relations between the agents and actors that

[19] P. Donati and R. Solci, *I beni relazionali. Che cosa sono e quali effetti producono* (Turin: Bollati Boringhieri, 2011).

[20] P. Donati, *Sociologia della riflessività. Come si entra nel dopo-moderno* (Bologna: il Mulino, 2011), chapter 2.

take part in the decisions and practical initiatives. A couple, a family, a company, a union, an institutional welfare service, all become 'relational social subjects' if and only if the persons involved share a We-relation that arises from their reflexive interactions.

At this point, it may be useful to summarize the necessary conditions for Relational Reflexivity to exist. Their core consists in the various agents and actors: (a) *believing* that the social relation that connects them is *desirable and attractive*; (b) *aspiring to create a relational effect among themselves that is an emergent good and not purely aggregative*; (c) *expecting that this effect (inherent in the We-relation) will be good for them (a relational good)*; (d) being aware that *they will exist as a relational social subject only as long as and in so far as their relational processes continue to have the above characteristics.*

Putting relational analysis on the right track

Relational social subjects cannot be the work of individuals, either singly or as the result of aggregation, or of systems that operate as impersonal institutions. The relational social subject exists only when social and cultural structures are reproduced or transformed by agents and actors during the temporal phases of the morphostatic/morphogenetic sequence [conditioning structure → interaction → structural elaboration]. In this framework, the crucially important players in the pivotal phase of 'interaction' are relational social subjects in their We-relationship, exercising their collective reflexivity through their orientation to relational goods. As we have signalled, they are not the only players and have to contend with both powerful individuals and naked exercises of power.

Relational subjects are emergent from relations between agents and actors in a structural context and acquire different characteristics depending on the type and degree of constraints and enablements that the social structures exert *on* them and *between* them, as mediated through their reflexive deliberations.

Different social structures can be more formal or informal, more direct (in a network of interpersonal relationships) or indirect (impersonal), and so on, depending on the type (quality and strengths) of the relations and resources that become morphostatic over time as structures.[21] In all cases, however, the social structures that impinge upon agents and actors operate as specific contextual constraints and opportunities but remain continuously activity-dependent. In turn, 'interactions' create relations that alter the structures themselves. They may simply reproduce the initial systems, reiterate them or, by freeing up new relations (which are creative), may transform the initial structure, thus introducing new opportunities for the subsequent elaboration of new Relational Subjects. This explanatory framework can be applied to the structure of a family, a corporation, a voluntary association, or a public welfare service, over different tracts of time.

However, in the conceptual framework of the morphostatic/morphogenetic approach, social structures are real – they have their own social ontology, their own *reality*. Social structures are not merely *patterns of transactions with no causal power of their own*, as Emirbayer and Dépelteau[22] hold, but have causal powers and their own effects on the actions of singular actors and primary and Corporate Agents, and on their interactions in that they condition their relations and, in turn, are re-elaborated by the emergent relations among agents and actors.

The substantial differences between *Relational Sociology*, based on Critical Realism, and *transactional* sociology, based on the pragmatics of communication and interaction, reside in the fact that, in the former, structures have emergent properties and powers (as Archer and Donati believe), while in the latter, they are merely empirical patterns with no power of their own (as Emirbayer, Dépelteau and Powell believe).

We hope that this brief Prologue and Chapters 6–8 that follow will clarify that in order to understand and explain what the Relational Subjects are and how they work, it is necessary to adopt relational realism. If flat social ontologies that deny emergence and emergents are endorsed, they cannot succeed in apprehending the Relational Subject – who remains at the mercy of individuals or systems or their elision.

21 P. Donati, *Relational Sociology. A New Paradigm for the Social Sciences* (London: Routledge, 2011).

22 M. Emirbayer, *Manifesto for a relational sociology*, *ibid*.; F. Dépelteau, 'Relational Thinking: A Critique of Co-Deterministic Theories of Structure and Agency', *Sociological Theory*, 26 (2008), 51–73.

Relational Subjects at the meso-macro levels

Part III addresses the theme of the Relational Subject on a meso-macro level by attempting to answer the following questions: why and how do Relational Subjects emerge in present-day societies, and with what consequences? The aim is to identify the Relational Subjects who now occupy centre stage in late modernity.

Chapter 6 clarifies the scope of the new Relational Subjects by highlighting the goods that they produce. For some years now, the social sciences have been demonstrating the existence of a type of goods that are neither material things, nor ideas, nor functional performances but consist, instead, of social relations and for this reason are called relational goods. This chapter proposes, first of all, to clarify this concept and, subsequently, to show that such goods can be produced only by those social subjects that we call 'Relational Subjects'. We shall then examine in what sense and in which way Relational Subjects, and the goods they generate, can contribute to the making of a new civil society, no longer the typically modern civil society – the bourgeois society of the market – but an 'associational' society able to sustain a mature democracy as a form of governance best suited to pursing the well-being of all citizens.

Chapter 7 starts from the recognition that the world system is based on the financialization of the economy and, we could well say, of all social relations, and is undergoing a chronic crisis. How might this be overcome? The basic thesis is that, as a response to this crisis, new ways of operating within and reconstituting society are arising, which may prefigure a new civil society that is not subordinate to the compromise between state and market (the *lib/lab* configuration of society that produced the crisis). Relational subjects constitute the innovating agents of this new civil society.

It is possible to apply a notion of 'reconversion' to the advent of this new civil society by analogy with what happened to the market when it shifted from an economy based on large industrial concerns to the information and knowledge economy. It can be defined as a reconversion of civil society if we think of it as a 'bottom up' promotion of networks of social relations that are not responsive to functional imperatives imposed by state laws or to monetary equivalence criteria but, rather, meet the need to create relational goods. The reconfiguration of civil society according to this scenario would also redefine the State and Market themselves.

Chapter 8 deals with the rise of 'relational ethics' as an expression of the needs of new Relational Subjects in the economic market. Since Aristotle, traditional ethics has imputed the morality of action to the 'acting subject' on the basis of a principle of linear causality. Over time and, in particular, with the advent of modern social sciences, the social, economic, and cultural conditioning weighing on the subject has been highlighted. The result has been to attribute moral responsibility to a 'conditioned subject', one that is constrained by existing societal structures (including 'unjust laws'). However, with globalization, the importance of systems of interdependence increases at the expense of functional systems. Structural and cultural conditioning do not disappear, but interdependency is the source of a novel challenge to the pursuit of vested interests and to the clash of cultural systems alike – though not preventing either from perpetrating their atrocities.

Nevertheless, moral responsibility encounters a process of morphogenesis such that, as a result, it is extended to refer to the obligations of 'Relational Subjects' constituted by the network of participants. The subject acting in a societal network is required to know and configure this network 'relationally'. Ethics need to become relational in the sense that the attribution of responsibility for acting for good or ill cannot be limited to a single act, but invokes the reflexivity of subjects and of social processes that take place in networks of relations. The morality of action must make reference to the reflexive awareness that subjects have of how good and evil are produced by social relations and consist of social relations within increasingly complex causal networks. The ethics of intention is no longer sufficient. It must be integrated with an ethics of responsibility that is not restricted to the direct consequences of individual acts, but also takes into account the indirect consequences of relational networks. As it does so, the ultimate social concern for global eudemonia begins to be voiced and enacted by Relational Subjects.

6 *When Relational Subjects generate relational goods*

PIERPAOLO DONATI

In search of 'other goods' that confer solidity on a robust democratic civil society

For some years now the social sciences have highlighted the existence of a type of goods that are neither material things, nor ideas, nor functional performances but consist, instead, of social relations and, for this reason, are called relational goods.

This chapter proposes, first of all, to clarify this concept and, subsequently, to show that such goods can be produced only by specific social subjects, which we call 'Relational Subjects'. We shall then see in which sense and in which way Relational Subjects, and the goods they generate, can contribute to making civil society more robust: that is, no longer the typically modern civil society – the bourgeois society of the market – but an 'associational' society able to sustain a mature democracy as a welfare society's form of governance.

It is important to emphasize from the beginning that the type of goods that we call relational cannot be traced back to traditional or premodern forms of social organization, because they require conditions that only modernity has created by making individuals more free and guaranteeing a considerable amount of social mobility. For a long time these goods have been dismissed or even repressed by capitalistic society as well as by societies dominated by dictatorships. Today they are emerging as the yeast of an advanced democracy. They are created precisely where relations between consociates are tendentially symmetrical (not hierarchical), free, and responsible (not constrained by authoritative norms or powers), not mercantile, in the sense of being dictated by the pursuit of individual profit.

Empirical studies show how widespread they really are. These are goods that are invisible to the naked eye (they are *intangible goods*) and are continually sought by people, but they come into existence only under particular conditions. As examples we could think of goods such as the following: trust between people; cooperation between families in difficulty who help one another; a collaborative and congenial climate in a company; the feeling of safety among the residents of a neighbourhood; a social or health service able to improve the quality of relations between parents and offspring; the spirit of collaboration in a sports team; a good harmonization between the musicians in an orchestra; an Internet site that receives and gives useful information to a network of people interested in that service; coproduction of local services, peer-to-peer production, and so on. Our life is a continual search for relational goods, but people have a very limited awareness of what they are and how they can be generated and regenerated.

Some might ask whether it is possible to draw up a list of relational goods. From our point of view, this request does not make much sense, because they are innumerable and ubiquitous. As will be explained later, *they can be found anywhere that a certain good can be enjoyed only through being engaged in particular relations with others*. Indeed, they consist of this very relationality (sociability), because these goods can be produced and obtained only through positive reciprocal actions. Of course, a list of relational goods can (and should) foresee the possibility that their opposites, that is, the relational evils, can be produced in their place. So, for instance, the relational goods of trusting people and cooperating in a team have their opposites in distrusting people and obstructing the teamwork. The relational good mentioned earlier as a 'collaborative workplace climate' has its opposite in a 'bad (highly competitive and aggressive) workplace climate', and so on.

An interesting question is whether relational goods necessarily imply interpersonal relations or not. In response, I suggest distinguishing between *primary* relational goods (such as friendship, family, small informal groups, which have a deep intersubjective character) and *collective or secondary* relational goods (which have an associative character and could be generated through more impersonal relations, for instance the relational goods produced by a voluntary association).[1]

We encounter a relational good when the participating individuals themselves produce and enjoy it together. An example is the collaboration in a scientific research team. The participants can be individuals, but also groups or social networks. In the latter case, the relational goods take on a more complex organizational character. For instance,

[1] P. Donati, *Teoria relazionale della società* (Milan: FrancoAngeli, 1991), pp. 156–161.

we could think of small associations of families constituting a second-level network or association with goals of reciprocal mutuality; another example is volunteering in particular local associations. Or we could think of a second-level network among social cooperatives that create a fabric of strong cohesion and social solidarity in a certain territory. The relational good, in other words, primarily concerns people and their relations (primary goods). But it can also be found at the level of secondary relations among people who do not know one another directly, as a result of their sharing an associative affiliation (in these cases, relational goods are said to be secondary because they do not involve face-to-face relations).

In essence, relational goods have the following properties: they are not 'things' but consist of social relations that have a *sui generis* reality; they are produced and enjoyed *together* by those who participate in them; and the good that they entail is an *emergent effect* which redounds to the benefit of participants as well as of those who share in its positive repercussions from the outside, without any single subject's having the ability to appropriate it for him/herself. Relational goods have an intrinsically democratic character in that they distinguish themselves from bureaucratic organizations (such as public administration) that act by command and generate goods that redound to their surrounding community's benefit (whether territorial or not). They are not particularistic and 'closed' goods, such as those sought by groups connected to lobbyists or the mafia. Perhaps the best way to understand them is to refer to Alexis de Tocqueville's key concept when he showed that the fundamental source of nourishment for a modern liberal-democratic society is 'the art of association'. He gave an essentially civic version of this concept. For Tocqueville, in fact, democratic associations are those that gather together citizens in order to solve the problems of a political community (such as creating a public garden or placing a fountain in a square). Today we have at our disposal a more extensive and refined theory of those goods that pertain to the art of associating for civic ends.

Relational goods are a reality that escapes the public/private dichotomy

The concept of the relational good arises primarily from dissatisfaction with a dichotomy, introduced during modernity, between public and private, which separates and classifies every type of good into one or another domain. That which is public is understood to be accessible to everyone and impersonal. That which is private is understood to be available only to autonomous subjects who are its owners. Consequently, society is differentiated into a public sphere, in which sociality is neutral and open, and a private sphere, in which sociality is particularistic and closed. It is obvious to ask: is there nothing in between? Furthermore, if by chance there were something in between, would this possible 'third' not be such as to redefine the two poles of public and private?

Once modernity constrains social organization to divide social goods into public as opposed to private goods, it generated evident gaps and vacuums (most importantly in trust, needed in both but specific to neither, yet vital to new ventures). Where can we then seek those goods in which the sociability of human persons and their social networks is expressed without such forms having necessarily to be ascribed to the public or private arena?

With the term 'sociability',[2] I am referring to *social relationality*, which can be interpersonal (face-to-face) but also more impersonal (as in organizations or social movements in which it becomes synonymous with a sense of belonging) on condition that the latter is active and consists of reciprocal actions (even if at a distance) that generate emergent effects of a prosocial nature.

The concept of *emergence* here means the coming into existence of new *entia* (including social forms, structures, concepts) that are generated out of pre-existing entities, from which they could have been neither induced nor deduced. The pre-existing entities, through cycles of reciprocal interactions and relations, lead to the constitution of a new entity that possesses *sui generis* qualities and properties.[3] Emergent phenomena in the physical world and those in the social world have a fundamental difference. *Physical emergence* is a reaction of a deterministic type that leads to the emergence of a relational structure (a whole) that does not depend on interactions similar to social ones; for

[2] G. Simmel, 'La sociabilité', in *Sociologie et épistémologie* (Paris: Puf, 1981), pp. 121–136.

[3] For more details see J. Morgan, *Emergence*, in M. Hartwig (ed.), *Dictionary of Critical Realism* (London: Routledge, 2007), pp. 166–167; C. Smith, *What Is a Person? Rethinking Humanity, Social Life, and the Moral Good from the Person Up* (Chicago: The University of Chicago Press, 2010), pp. 25–42.

example, the chemical reaction [$2H + O \rightarrow H_2O$]. *Social emergence* is the result of an interactive process in which absolute determinism does not exist; causality operates on certain conditions that are not subject to mere physical determinism. In the realm of social phenomena, this process implies the relative autonomy of both individual actions and conditional effects of the social structure, and the continuous cycle of interaction between them. A given (conditioning) structure pre-dates the action(s) which transform it, and the structural elaboration necessarily post-dates those actions. Actions and structure are two related levels of organization that co-evolve over time through the formation of social networks that have a generative character. The social emergent is a relational structure in which the whole does not explain its parts. For example, a social emergent is the couple as Relational Subject [Ann + Tom → couple]; the social emergent does not constitute a whole as in the physical world because the couple is a We-relation endowed with variability in the elements that constitute it (the actions that make the emergent social form called the 'couple relation').

Just to give a few examples of social emergents, we could think of friendship and neighbourhood networks, self-help and mutual aid networks, and small groups that carry out many initiatives to help the weakest and least fortunate members of society; or, at another level, there are social movements (whether local, global, or glocal) that actively intervene in civic problems and peer-to-peer social networks that produce shared goods on the Internet. In all of these cases, it would be difficult to ascribe the initiatives to the strictly private or public arena. There is an 'intermediate' social space that remains little explored.

The concept of relational goods fills in the gap between private and public goods. It points to a reality in which certain aspects of what is private are intertwined with some aspects of what is public, without being either one or the other. Such relational goods are essential in order to make many aspects of society less impoverished, risky, insecure, mistrustful, and pathological. It is important to emphasize that these realities could not exist before modernity transformed the intermediate social sphere between public and private into a desert. Those who think of relational goods as a revival of things from the past that were typical of premodern society (such as the confraternities or charitable organizations) would be committing a serious error of perspective.

More precisely, the typically modern polarization between the public sphere (identified by the State) and the private sphere (identified by the capitalistic market) entails the advent of social forms that have a sociability whose quality is different from that of those forms present in traditional societies, such as the medieval religious confraternities, the *monte di pieta* (pawnbrokers), the charitable establishments for the poor and sick, and other similar institutions. The reason for the difference lies in the processes of multiplication of the intersecting circles that produce a new individualization[4] and, consequently, a different type of sociability. In premodern societies the forms of sociability that create relational goods are generally of an ascriptive and asymmetrical type as regards power relationships: the positions of those who participate are not egalitarian but reflect stratification by rank or class. Instead, in modernized societies, they are of an acquisitive and tendentially symmetrical type as regards the power relationships among participants in as much as the old forms of social stratification diminish and a principle of equality is asserted.

The notion of the relational good emerges when one becomes aware of the existence of other goods that are neither available on the basis of private ownership nor accessible to everyone indiscriminately. They are goods that do not have an owner, nor do they belong to the collectivity as generically understood. They are the goods of human sociability, goods that are crucial for the very existence of society, which could not survive without them. If these goods are ignored, dismissed, or repressed, the entire social order is impoverished, mutilated, and deprived of lifeblood with serious harm caused to people and the overall social organization alike. Those who do not understand this point or seek to trace relational goods to either the public or private arena fail completely to understand relational goods' meaning, mode of being, functions, and social value. Let us consider a few examples of relational goods.

A group of parents decides to constitute an association for organizing educational services for their own children, which will also be

[4] We owe to Georg Simmel the idea that the individualization of people is increasingly enhanced the greater the number of 'social circles' (associations, groups, communication and exchange networks) in which individuals participate. D. Levine (ed.), *Georg Simmel on Individuality and Social Forms: Selected Writings* (Chicago: The Chicago University Press, 1972); G. Simmel, *Sociologia* (Milan: Edizioni di Comunità, 1989), pp. 347–348.

available to other children in the community, and they obtain premises and payment for utilities from the municipality while they themselves manage the actual service (for example, a nursery, preschool, or primary school): is this initiative public or private? To modern eyes it would be private because the parents manage it, but the agreement with the municipality complicates things because the nursery takes place on public property, and, moreover, the agreement with the municipality stipulates accountability and inspection, or supervision at the very least. It is evident here that the public/private categories do not grasp the initiative's more truly *social* nature.

A group of families that share a given problem (they have a disabled child, a non-autonomous elderly relative, an alcoholic or dependent family member, etc.) create an association to help one another in turn (mutual aid) and to take actions of *advocacy* (demanding rights), for themselves as well as for the other families facing the same situation: is this association private or public? There is no doubt that it is private, but does it correspond to modernity's definition of the private (according to which the private is such because it lacks public responsibilities)? I think not.

More generally, we can think of the social goods produced by third sector (nonprofit) organizations that deliver care services to people, not only to disabled persons or those with serious pathologies, but also to healthy people who have need of support in terms of educational services, social and health care assistance, sport and cultural services, and so on. It is obvious to point out that the grounds for activity of an associative and network type that we call 'the domain of the social', to use the social term for that which exists between the public and the private,[5] not only generates good things (relational goods) but also their opposites (relational evils). For example, if we ask people who participate in an association whether, in recent years, trust toward other members of the association has grown or decreased, we can find cases in which trust has grown and other cases in which it has diminished. In the case of a relational evil, their answer will be of the following type: 'The more I participated in the association, the more I saw that one cannot trust the other members'. Social relations can thus generate negative instead of positive effects. Therefore, it is of

[5] H. Arendt, *The Human Condition* (Chicago: University of Chicago Press, 1958).

the greatest importance to identify the (cultural, structural, agential) conditions in which relational goods, rather than evils, are generated.

Can we make a list of these goods? The type of good in question is not a category that can be inventoried, as one does for material goods. This does not mean that we are dealing with a purely ideal good, that is, a value in an abstract or symbolic sense. It is an intangible good in which energy and resources can be invested and from which energy and resources are drawn. If it is not *cared for*, the relational good deteriorates and can disappear. In essence, the relational good cannot be catalogued as a functionally specific good but, rather, is *a way to generate goods* – which can be material or not, such as children's education, the production of consumer goods, a sports team's or an orchestra's performance, a scientific research group's results, or the services offered by a volunteer group. These goods would be devalued, commodified, or bureaucratized if they were not produced in this relational way. We could say that what is important in relational goods is their 'mode of production' because relational goods are thus regarded from the generative point of view (in terms of how they are generated and work together to generate other goods). This mode of production requires particular kinds of social subjects. Precisely for this reason, both the relational goods and the subjects that produce them are fragile. In any case, the type of good that we call relational is not on the same plane as the public-private axis conceived of in the modern sense. It exists on another level of reality, a level that is obscured by the public-private axis. How do we manage to detect it?

How did the theory of relational goods arise?

The theory of relational goods did not arise out of nothing but germinated in a terrain that had been previously tilled and sowed. This terrain is the one in which, given that social goods cannot be traced back or reduced to the modern categories of public and private, the concept of *social private* was elaborated. The term 'social private' indicates every sphere that is private as regards property and management but which has pro-social ends, and not ends of instrumental expediency for the participants.[6] Expediency for the participants is not excluded

[6] P. Donati, 'The Emergent Third Sector in Europe: Actors, Relations and Social Capital', in H. K. Anheier, G. Rossi, and L. Boccacin (eds.), *The Social*

but cannot be the associative end, which must be social solidarity both internally and toward the exterior. The conceptual category of the social private is incomprehensible for modern political and economic thought in which private actors are necessarily self-interested; otherwise, they must be impersonal (public) actors, and so on. For the modern economy, a private subject can only be one who pursues interests that are primarily to his/her own advantage. Nonprofit or private charitable entities, which do not act out of private interests, are indeed considered as positive initiatives, particularly in order to remedy social ills, but are not regarded as agencies that produce socially and economically significant goods.

At the time that the concept of the social private was first proposed,[7] there was still no relational theory of the social sphere available that could have underpinned a redefinition of the social private as a possible space for the emergence of relational goods.

The notion of the social private, in any case, involved a conceptual framework that was completely new with respect to the sociological approaches then in existence; in particular, it aimed to overcome the dualisms peculiar to modernity. In 1989 I defined the relational good in the following terms: 'Saying that human life is a "relational good" means to say that it is a type of shared good that depends on the relations of subjects toward one another and that can be enjoyed only if they orient themselves accordingly. Human life is the object of enjoyment (and thus of rights) not as an "individual" (in the sense of individualistic) good, nor a "public" (in the modern technical sense) good, but precisely as a *common* good of the subjects that are in relation. Such a good must be defined not as a function of individual activities taken singularly (privately) or collectively, but as a function of their relations.'[8]

In 1989 an American scholar, Carole Jean Uhlaner, used the term relational goods to indicate local public goods produced by the sharing of political objectives of people who encounter one another

Generative Action of the Third Sector. Comparing International Experiences (Milan: Vita e Pensiero, 2008), pp. 13–47.

[7] P. Donati, *Pubblico e privato: fine di una alternativa?* [*Public and Private: End of an Alternative?*] (Bologna: Cappelli, 1978), pp. 112–114.

[8] P. Donati, 'Nuove istanze sociali e dignità umana', in P. Donati (ed.), *La cultura della vita. Dalla società tradizionale a quella post-moderna* [*The Culture of Life. From Traditional Society to Post-Modern Society*] (Milan: FrancoAngeli, 1989), pp. 161–182.

repeatedly.[9] For her, relational goods are goods that cannot be enjoyed alone. Examples would include participation in a choir, soccer team, or some voluntary group activity. There is some relation between this idea and the model of joint production or the concept of 'crowding in'. The definition of relational good that Uhlaner gives is the following: 'Assuming that people are restricted to such ends [optimization of individually possessed goods] is neither necessary nor useful. People also pursue relational goods which cannot be acquired by an isolated individual. Instead, these goods arise as a function of a relationship with others. The relational goods can only be possessed by mutual agreement that they exist after appropriate joint actions have been taken by a person and non-arbitrary others'.[10] These are thus goods (also things) produced by the consensus achieved among a certain number of subjects having interpersonal relations: an example could be deciding together to vote for a certain candidate in political elections.

The concept of relational good helped Uhlaner to explain political participation in democratic states. Uhlaner wanted to understand why and in what way individuals actively participate in political life, notwithstanding the feeling that the individual vote has little influence on an election's outcome. She found the answer in a model centred on individual rationality. In her view, relational goods are the product of rational individuals who together mobilize themselves for political elections in the same way that groups are organized to make political demands in everyday life. Relying on the *rational choice* approach, Uhlaner treated relational goods as public goods, an understanding of them that is completely within modernity's frame of reference and completely American. Because Uhlaner uses a *rational choice* approach (even if it is revised on the basis of a wider spectrum of strictly utilitarian motivations), her concept of the relational good has had broad repercussions and has been widely used by economists.

[9] C. J. Uhlaner, '"Relational goods" and participation. Incorporating sociability into a theory of rational action', *Public Choice*, 62 (1989), 253–285.

[10] *Ibid.*, p. 254. In an attempt at identifying their nature, she adds: 'Relational goods can only be shared with some others. They are thus unlike private goods, which are enjoyed alone, and standard public goods, which can be enjoyed by any number. Relational goods are a subset of local public goods, as they enter into two or more persons' utility function' (*ibid.*, p. 254).

Those who have followed in Uhlaner's footsteps, such as the economists Antoci, Sabatini, and Sodini,[11] have treated relational goods as 'things' chosen by individuals in cooperative games. Social relations are considered as the means for obtaining material goods: hence the thesis according to which relational goods are interchangeable with material things for the purpose of promoting people's well-being. These are clear distortions of the concept of relational goods because the relational good is not fungible (it is not interchangeable) with material goods. It does not consist in the well-being that it procures for individuals but, rather, in the relations among them upon which this well-being depends.

In the past two decades economists have used the concept of relational good in various ways, but they have done so without having a suitable theory of social relations. In fact, for mainstream economists, social relations result from individuals' intentional projects and strategic choices. Relational goods are considered to be social relations that take on a particular affective quality and foster cooperative rather than competitive games.

For example, Benedetto Gui defines relational good as a special 'encounter' between persons who exchange goods with a particular reciprocal fellow-feeling for each other; for him, relational goods are interpersonal relations that people value and invest in for expressive reasons, namely that these make transactions more sympathetic and friendly.[12] Following Gui, Robert Sugden defines relational goods as the affective and sentimental components (the latter understood as *fellow-feeling*) that support norms of cooperation.[13] These goods are the added value created by doing something together as opposed to doing it alone. This added value consists in the people's affective states that assist individual cooperative action. Here we are straddling economy and psychology within methodological individualism. For these authors, relational goods are found in markets for caregiving services but also where the interaction is minimal, as in a walk in

[11] A. Antoci, F. Sabatini, and M. Sodini, 'The Solaria syndrome: Social capital in a growing hyper-technological economy', *Journal of Economic Behavior & Organization*, 81 (2012), 802–814.

[12] B. Gui, 'On "relational goods": strategic implications of investment in relationships', *International Journal of Social Economics*, 23 (1996), 260–278.

[13] B. Gui and R. Sugden, *Economics and Social Interaction: Accounting for Interpersonal Relations* (Cambridge: Cambridge University Press, 2005).

the mountains with a fellow hiker, for example. They are a source of direct value because they procure pleasure and individual well-being but are also of indirect value since they support the motivations necessary for generating the trust and reciprocity that serve economic growth. The tradition upon which this thinking draws is that of Adam Smith, and their analysis remains firmly anchored in economic debate.

In synthesis, for Uhlaner, Gui, and Sugden, as for mainstream economists in general, relational goods do not coincide with relations as such because the relation is assessed from the point of view of individual feelings and individual action. For these authors, for example, friendship is a relational good in that, because it is constituted by interactions repeated with some affectivity, it gives a certain empathy and congeniality to relations among people. The relational good is a quality of interactions that are repeated, leading to the sharing of something. In this way, the fact that the relational good is a relation that has its own reality (the relation's order of reality) is totally misunderstood. The fact that such a relation emerges because of *reciprocity* among participants is obscured. This is the reciprocity of the We-relation, which confers the quality and powers peculiar to the relational good. Moreover, in relational goods the 'why', that is, the motivation that propels one to act toward the other, is an essential element that cannot be reduced to convenience, even to an affective feeling of ease and, more generally, to the sense of well-being that individuals derive from the relation.[14]

A conception of relational good built on these bases cannot grasp the relational sense of the goods of which we are speaking.

The turning point

A turning point in the definition of relational goods came about with the classification of social goods on the basis of two axes, depending on whether the consumer is sovereign/non-sovereign and consumption is competitive/non-competitive (see Figure 6.1). In this way, private goods are conceptualized as those characterized by a sovereign consumer and competitive consumption (cell 4), and public goods are those characterized by a non-sovereign consumer and non-competitive

[14] As Aristotle already reminded us, the highest friendship, which contributes to *eudaimonia*/happiness, can never be instrumental because it is a virtue.

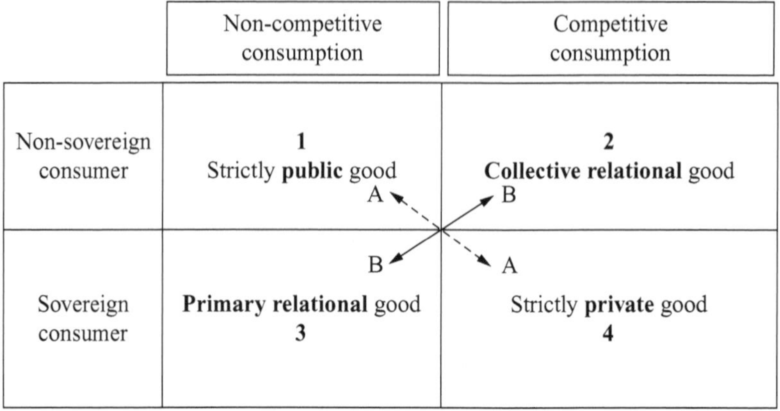

Figure 6.1 The four fundamental types of goods produced in society
Source: P. Donati, *La cittadinanza societaria* [*Societal Citizenship*] (Rome-Bari: Laterza, 2000 [1993]), chapter 2.

consumption (cell 1). In the second cell (non-sovereign consumer and competitive consumption) we find another type of goods, that is, secondary (i.e. associative) relational goods. In the third cell, we find goods with a sovereign consumer and non-competitive consumption (as in a lending library).

Arrow A in Figure 6.1 (between cells 1 and 4) indicates that private goods (*lib*) and public goods (*lab*) *can* be converted one into the other (the line is broken because this is a possibility). For example, if a set of private subjects that produce goods (such as electricity, transport, or health services) are nationalized, private goods become public. *Vice versa*, if a good produced in a monopolistic system (such as telephone service, rail transport, or the management of a water network) is entrusted to the competition of private subjects, we have the privatization of public goods. The user still receives the same functional service (even if at different prices). The nature of the good or service produced does not change.

Unlike private and public goods, relational goods are not interchangeable. They can indeed become private or public goods, but with this they perish because they lose the qualities and powers that are peculiar to them: they lose their peculiar relationality – which does not transpire when there is the privatization of public goods or when private goods become public (these goods can certainly change in certain ways, but without altering their functionality with respect to the service provided).

Arrow B in Figure 6.1 (between cells 2 and 3) indicates that interchanges between primary relational goods and collective relational goods always exist (for this reason, the line is solid). Empirical research demonstrates that there is continuity, and not discontinuity, between the relational goods produced in primary groups and the relational goods of larger and more formal organizations.[15] Primary relational goods contribute to reinforcing secondary relational goods, and *vice versa*.

This scheme has had various subsequent empirical confirmations of its validity, in particular, the connections between a community's or association's social capital and the production in it of relational goods.[16] At this point, I would like to synthesize what we know today about the requirements, qualities, and properties of relational goods.

(A) *Requirements*. In order to come into existence, the relational good *requires*:

 (i) *a personal and social identity* of the participants; no relational good exists between anonymous subjects because the relational good implies that the actions of subjects refer to each other's identity as a personal and social being;

[15] P. Donati and R. Prandini, 'The family in the light of a new relational theory of primary, secondary and generalized social capital', *International Review of Sociology*, 17 (2007), 209–223; P. Donati and L. Tronca, *Il capitale sociale degli italiani. Le radici familiari, comunitarie e associative del civismo* [*The Social Capital of Italians. Civism's Familial, Communitarian, and Associative Roots*] (Milan: FrancoAngeli, 2008).

[16] V. Pelligra (ed.), 'Fiducia, capitale sociale e beni relazionali' [Trust, social capital, and relational goods], *Impresa sociale*, 17 (2007), 45–74; M. Pendenza, *Teorie del capitale sociale* [*Theories of Social Capital*] (Soveria Mannelli: Rubbettino, 2008); on the case of the school, see P. Donati, 'Tre forme di capitale sociale tra famiglia e scuola: chi e come genera beni relazionali nei processi di socializzazione delle nuove generazioni' [Three forms of social capital between family and school: who generates, and how to generate, relational goods in processes of socialization of the new generations], in P. Donati and I. Colozzi (eds.), *Terzo settore e valorizzazione del capitale sociale in Italia: luoghi e attori* [*The Third Sector and the Valorization of Social Capital in Italy: Places and Actors*] (Milan: FrancoAngeli, 2006); I. Colozzi (ed.), *Scuola e capitale sociale. Un' indagine nelle scuole secondarie di secondo grado della Provincia di Trento* [*School and Social Capital. An Investigation into Second Level Secondary Schools in the Province of Trento*] (Trento: Edizioni Erickson, 2011).

(ii) *a non-instrumental motivation* of each subject in his/her involvement with the other: interest toward the other must be characterized by caring; it must be about taking care of the other and not using him/her for some purpose other than the good that is intrinsic to the reciprocal relation as a good in itself, notwithstanding that it could also yield other outcomes (that is, positive externalities and added social value);

(iii) that *conduct is inspired by the rule of reciprocity*: where reciprocity signifies symbolic exchange and not a *do ut des*; reciprocity implies that *Ego* gives to *Alter* that which *Alter* needs or could give him/her pleasure, knowing that *Alter* will do the same for *Ego* when *Ego* has need of it;

(iv) *total sharing*: the relational good can only be produced and used together by those who participate in it, that is, it comes into existence if and only if the participants generate and enjoy it together; no one can produce it alone or can ask others to produce it without him/her, even temporarily;

(v) in general, *it requires elaboration over time* (the relation's temporal history) and a simple interaction at a given moment is not sufficient, such as, for example, an act of kindness or reciprocal empathy in a purchase or in an exchange of objects; in short, the temporal register must be historical-relational and not interactional;[17]

(vi) *a reflexivity that operates relationally*, thus, not a reflexivity of an autonomous type or one that is blocked or fractured; Relational Reflexivity is required in order for identity, reciprocity, and sharing to be undertaken with reference to the good of the relation *as such*, which must be produced and enjoyed together by the participants.

(B) *Qualities and properties*. The relational good has the following qualities and properties:

(i) it is an emergent effect, cannot exist or be acquired otherwise, and is a way of satisfying primary needs. Saying that it is an *emergent effect* means that it requires a certain combination (not a simple aggregation) of factors, elements, or components

[17] For the three registers of *social* time (interactional, relational, and symbolic): P. Donati, *Relational Sociology. A New Paradigm for the Social Sciences* (London: Routledge, 2011), pp. 179–181.

as discussed earlier; its emergent character accentuates the fact that any relational good is a 'third' entity that exceeds the contributions of the subjects involved and that, in certain cases, may not have been foreseen or thought of with the initial intention of producing it;

(ii) it can be produced and benefited from only by means of the relations that make that good, and it *cannot be exchanged or replaced by anything else*; in particular, it cannot be bought with money and cannot be produced by command or by law;

(iii) it is a good in that it *corresponds to the fundamental primary needs of the human person and social groups*, needs that have to do with sociability without which individuals would be monads unable to realize themselves and experience happiness.

On the other hand, relational evils are the product of relations that do not have these constituents and qualities. In relational evils, we observe the lack of or deficit in one or more of the necessary elements (identity, non-instrumental motivations, reciprocity, sharing, temporal duration, reflexivity) or a lack of coherence or harmony among them. Above all, the relational evil is today connected with those pathological forms of reflexivity that are designated as blocked, hindered, or Fractured Reflexivity.[18]

In essence, *relational goods are those immaterial entities (intangible goods) that consist of social relations that emerge from subjects' reflexivity that is oriented toward producing and enjoying together, in a shared manner, a good that they could not obtain otherwise.*

We could ask what the role of relational goods is in relations, even dialectical relations, between the State and civil society. To put it synthetically, relational goods are the new common goods, no longer understood as public things or public properties, but as goods co-produced by networks of persons and social formations (the Relational Subjects) that generate them and benefit from them continuously without their having an 'owner'. In the following sections we explore this theme more deeply.

[18] Margaret S. Archer, *Structure, Agency and the Internal Conversation* (Cambridge: Cambridge University Press, 2003). However, it may be the fractured subject who suffers most from this.

The concept of relational good redefines the map of common goods

The common good is often identified with the public good. Relational theory, instead, posits a distinction between these types of goods. The *common* good should not be confused either with the private good or with the public good. What characterizes the common good is the fact that the advantage each person derives from belonging to a certain association or community cannot be severed from the advantage that others also derive from it. This means that each person's interest is realized *together* with that of others, not *in opposition* to it (as happens with the private good) nor *apart* from others' interest (as happens with the public good).

In this sense, the term 'common' (*communis*) is opposed to 'proper' (*proprium* in the sense of 'one's own'), as 'public' is opposed to 'private'. That which is not one's own (private) nor belongs to everyone indiscriminately (public) is common. The common good is the space of that which not only belongs to some people or even to everyone indifferently. It is not a collective good in the modern sense of a 'state' good (belonging to the State). It derives from the privileged space of social relations when subjects are oriented toward promoting the good of the relations existing among them and thus, also, toward caring for the entities that represent these goods (that is, common goods): for example, a shared house or a *commons* on the Internet (such as Wikipedia).[19]

The common good, in its relational version, is not a concerted idea either, as some understand it to be. It is not the derivative of political programs typical of neo-corporate democratic government.[20] In the latter arrangement, actors hold specific interests and lay claim to them by taking a seat at a table from which they hope to rise seeing them satisfied, at least in large part, after a conflict characterized by bargaining. The relational good is not of this type. It puts the good of

[19] M. Bauwens, 'Par cum pari. Notes on the horizontality of peer to peer relationships in the context of the verticality of a hierarchy of values', in Margaret S. Archer and P. Donati (eds.), *Pursuing the Common Good: How Solidarity and Subsidiarity Can Work Together* (Rome: Vatican Press, 2008), pp. 247–262.

[20] H. L. Wilensky, *The New Corporatism. Centralization and the Welfare State* (London: Sage, 1976).

relations before that of individual, group, or categorical interests. The relations alluded to by this good are those of subjects' common needs that also pertain to the surrounding societal community.

The criterion for identifying those particular common goods that are relational *is based on the principle of positive reciprocity*,[21] and not on that of equality of individual opportunities (or of outcome), which is peculiar to individualism. Let us think about what this means for the relationships between the sexes, between men and women, in families and in the public sphere. Today, the common good between men and women is generally understood as the sum of individual goods acquired through individual opportunities. This happens in the couple, for example, as well as in the job market where men and women face one another. The so-called 'pure relation' theorized by Giddens[22] is a relation in which each partner negotiates the maximum individual satisfaction; it is not a relational good. Equal opportunity programs in the work place try to equalize access to jobs and remuneration between men and women as individuals; they do not have as their objective the pursuit of a relational good. Instead, the relational good is a relation of reciprocity (or 'symbolic exchange') between individuals whose aim is to build relational goods for and between them, such as the balance between work and family life. Relational goods come from being in a relation of full reciprocity. They are neither an aggregation of individual goods nor a collective good that must be distributed among the participants. Relational goods are sensitive to intersubjective relations and cannot be the result of individual advantages (they do not guarantee that each person can pursue his/her own particular interest if this is incompatible with the common good).

Relational goods are the subset of common goods that can only be generated together: no one who takes part in this generation can be excluded from them; they cannot be subdivided and are not the sum of individual goods. *Saying that a common good is relational means that*

[21] The term *reciprocity* here indicates relations in which the subjects give to one another and exchange things or services or, in any case, help one another in turn in a social network that acknowledges itself to be a circle of subjects cooperating among themselves. Although it is useful, reciprocity is not activated and maintained for instrumental reasons but for reasons of identity in belonging to a community of reciprocal assistance. For this reason, sometimes the term 'reciprocity' is interchangeable with that of 'symbolic exchange'.

[22] A. Giddens, *The Transformation of Intimacy. Sexuality, Love and Eroticism in Modern Societies* (Cambridge: Polity Press, 1992).

it is a type of good that depends on the relations of the subjects toward one another and can be enjoyed only if the subjects orient themselves accordingly. In this sense, we say that human life is a common good in that it is the object of enjoyment and therefore of rights, not as a private, individual good in an individualistic sense, nor as a public good in the modern technical sense of a state good, but precisely as a relational good of subjects who are in relation with one another.

Present-day society expresses the need for new common goods in a very precise phenomenological sense: *common* goods are those that only communities of people, only primary and associative groups, can develop, express, and safeguard. This is a new generation of rights: precisely, the generation of *human* rights, beyond civil and political rights and those of socio-economic welfare. When we appeal today, for example, to the child's right to have a family that cares for him/her, we are appealing to a right that is human, not civil in the modern sense of the term[23] or political or socio-economic. What category of rights is this? The answer cannot but be: a human right that is intrinsically relational.

The legal system has only recently begun to understand the need to introduce this category of rights. We are referring to the type of rights that we can call relational because they involve a relational good (not a public or collective good). Beyond the grand assertions contained in international and national documents on civil rights emanating from a liberal-individualistic matrix, it is necessary to develop a specific reflection on people's rights to common goods and on the rights of common goods as such, in as much as they are relational goods. The latter are rights pertaining to those relational goods that enjoy the status of a legal subject (for example, a social cooperative: these are the rights *of* the cooperative and not only the rights of the individuals *in* the cooperative). This is a new area for reflection and social practices that is beginning to mature and come to the fore today.

The proof that today's public ethics does not involve a common good in a relational sense is found in the case in which, for example, the problems of peace, development, the environment, and also

[23] I remind the reader that the term 'civil rights' refers to the individual rights promoted by market liberalism starting in the 1700s (such as the right of the individual to practice religion, to hold and voice opinions, and to associate with others, and also the right of the person to physical integrity, due process in court proceedings, etc.).

of new forms of poverty are not confronted as problems of concrete human relations between co-present subjects but are simply treated as 'things' to eliminate by marginalizing violent persons, punishing those who do not succeed in competing, banning polluters, and helping the poor with measures that promote passivity. Problems are confronted by putting people where they cannot cause trouble. These are false solutions to problems because they are not inspired by the common good in that they leave aside completely the necessity of involving poor and marginalized people, deviants, and even those prone to violence in seeking to solve problems as common, shared problems. In the arena of social policies, it is now very clear that these modalities for confronting distress, poverty, and social marginalization are completely unsatisfactory. Peace, development, a clean and safe environment, a decent life for everyone – these are all goods that correspond to the relational character of these objectives: this is to say that they can only be achieved together; they are not a sum of individual preferences but a function of the relational system that connects subjects with one another – a function of their comprehensive internal and external relations.

Relational goods are the key for moving from the *welfare state* to the *welfare society*. It is important to underscore that the common good takes on the form of a relational good in all the areas of welfare in which relations among human subjects are in play.

Figure 6.2 synthesizes the various areas in which socially significant goods are produced. Relational goods are found in the areas defined by cells 2 and 3. Outside these areas of welfare, we find non-relational goods (and subjects). On the one hand (cell 1), we find public goods in a strict sense, which can and must be pursued through systemic or technological, redistributive apparatuses (such as the State's fiscal revenues, public pensions, the State's monetary transfers, services in which people's participation is bound and constrained by legal requirements). On the other hand (cell 4), we find those strictly private goods (of the Darwinian market) that, in order to be obtained, do not necessarily require a relation involving cooperation and reciprocity between buyer and seller.

It is nonetheless necessary to clarify that collective relational goods (secondary, associational), while peculiar to the social private and third sectors, can also be generated in the State and Market on condition that actors comply with the requirements that are specific to relational goods (which were discussed in the section entitled 'The turning point')

	Non-competitive goods	Competitive goods
Agent/ Actor is *constrained*	**1** With strictly public goods, relations are binding apart from individual interests (constricted sharing) [whoever does not adapt is considered to be a deviant or a free rider]	**2** With secondary relational goods, relations are bound to prosocial ends, which means that individual interest depends on the relations that make up the common good, which has positive externalities for unknown others [whoever does not adapt weakens the common good or generates relational evils]
Agent/ Actor is *free*	**3** With primary relational goods, relations are characterized by the symbolic exchange among those who belong to a primary group (face-to-face group) [whoever does not adapt weakens the group or generates relational evils]	**4** With strictly private goods, relations are purely instrumental or irrelevant [whoever does not adapt decreases his/her ability to compete]

Figure 6.2 Four areas of social relations differentiated on the basis of degrees of actors' freedom and the type of good produced (public goods, primary and secondary relational goods, and private goods in a strict sense)

because *where* they are produced is not important but rather *how* they are produced. They can be pursued *within* each of these spheres and *between* them. The fact that in the *lib/lab* arrangement they are weakened and marginalized depends on the non-relational way in which the *lib/lab* system has until now configured the State and market and their relationships.

Who are the subjects generating relational goods and under what conditions?

Generally speaking, relational goods are the product of processes of association among individual agents/actors. The agents/actors can also be collective. But in that case the conditions for generating relational goods are much more complex and onerous. For this reason, it is quite rare that relational goods are able to emerge among collective subjects. It is necessary that the social context be non-competitive (that is, not combative). Relational goods can be and, indeed, are competitive goods, but in terms of solidarity in the sense of competition (*cum-petere*) as in the search for the best solutions in a contest which is not detrimental to the other participants but stimulates each participant to contribute his/her best effort toward achieving the same common goal.

For example, players in the same sports team can create the relational good of their team. But a game played between two football teams, as in every competitive activity that must lead to a victor or, at least, to a ranking of winners and losers, cannot create a relational good. The combative context and its rules prohibit this. Conversely, a second-level organization that unites two or more mutual aid associations for the purposes of reciprocal cooperation can, under certain conditions, create relational goods and therefore can be a Relational Subject that creates relational goods among participating associations.

Relational goods are produced by those Relational Subjects that operate according to the characteristics highlighted in the preceding sections ('The turning point' and 'The concept of relational good redefines the map of common goods'). Figure 6.3 synthesizes the placement of Relational Subjects in the societal arena.

We can find them in lifeworld spheres as primary groups and in the spheres of civil society as Third sector organizations and volunteer associations. Collective Relational Subjects do not necessarily have to be bound to any particular territory because means of communication can also create associative forms at a distance. However, the distance must allow for a minimum of intersubjective relations. Figure 6.3 tells us that Relational Subjects cannot arise and exist either in the bureaucratic organizations of states (state apparatuses, such as public administration) (cell 1) or in the capitalistic market, Darwinian in type (cell 4).

Primary Relational Subjects are those characterized by intersubjective, face-to-face relations (in cell 3 of Figure 6.3). *Secondary Relational Subjects* (in cell 2) are created in the social networks that weave together formal (professional) relationships and informal (non-professional) relationships on condition that the organizational relations are not purely functional but leave space to superfunctional

	The goods produced are non-competitive	The goods produced are competitive
Agents/ Actors are constrained	**1** State apparatuses (Public Administration)	**2** Collective relational subjects constituted by organizations of the social private sphere, third sector, civil associations, and NGOs
Agents/ Actors are free	**3** Primary relational subjects constituted by primary groups (families, informal networks)	**4** Capitalistic market enterprises (Darwinian)

Figure 6.3 The placement of Relational Subjects among the four fundamental types of social subjects (distinguished on the basis of degrees of agents/actors' freedom and the type of goods produced)

action.[24] The specificity of these networks resides in the fact of being institutions of social solidarity that produce positive externalities for third subjects and operate as training grounds for substantial, that is, civil democracy.

Relational subjects can be distinguished at three levels: micro, meso, and macro.

(i) On a *micro*-level we find families, small groups, and informal networks that practice internal inter-subjective relations by means of Relational Reflexivity. Emblematic examples are many self- and mutual-help groups that present the characteristics discussed in the sections entitled 'The turning point' and 'The concept of relational good redefines the map of common goods'.

(ii) On a *meso*-level we find organizations that are broader and have a certain formalization of their structures and activities. These are

[24] By the term 'superfunctional,' I mean an individual or organizational action that is not oriented toward the specialization of roles (that is, it is not guided by functional differentiation), but is oriented toward the exercise of a plurality of functions that cannot be enumerated – and can also be latent – in that it operates with relations, on relations, and through relations. In order to understand the superfunctional reality of the social sphere, it is necessary to abandon modernity's functionalistic approach as was theorized by Talcott Parsons and Niklas Luhmann.

the organizations of the social private sphere, the third sector, and civic associations such as associations for social promotion, volunteer organizations, social solidarity cooperatives, and certain social networks on the Internet. These can also be for-profit economic enterprises on condition that they practice corporate social responsibility, that is, they have as an objective the production of positive externalities (relational goods) in favour of the surrounding community and that this objective is not instrumental to making a profit for the company but is envisaged as an ethical criterion of entrepreneurial activity. This is the civil economy.

(iii) On a *macro*-level we find second- and third-level organizations that organize lower level Relational Subjects in an associative manner. We can think of those international non-governmental organizations that, unlike organizations that lobby States or international institutions, create a network of local associative units that operate on a micro scale. Once again, it is necessary here to see whether there exist or not the conditions peculiar to a Relational Subject's action.

We might wonder whether certain international organizations can be or become Relational Subjects. These could be the UN, the European Union, or the Mercosur. The probability that organizations of this type can be Relational Subjects is practically zero owing to the fact that they never have the conditions of intersubjectivity and reflexivity that are necessary for producing relational goods. These are, generally speaking, instrumental organizations that conceive of the common good in aggregative and combinatory terms, and never in relational terms. Nevertheless, in the abstract, it could be imagined that in the future it would be possible to create macro-level organizations that adopt a relational culture and realize at least some of the conditions peculiar to Relational Subjects.

The new civil democracy

Civil democracy (as distinct from economic, political, and social democracy) is the form of *societal governance* that pursues the common good not as a state of affairs, nor as a sum or aggregation of single goods, nor as a super-ordinate reality, but as the totality of those *conditions* of social life that allow groups, as well as their individual members, to achieve their own improvement more fully and quickly through the creation of relational goods.

Over the course of the twentieth century this vision was translated into the idea that ensuring the conditions for the development of people and their social formations meant providing assistance and state-sponsored redistribution using resources coming from the market. This way of thinking and acting was a legacy of the Enlightenment State inspired by concern for the population's well-being and managed from above as a form of 'good government' (*politeia*). It materialized from the absolutist and later constitutional States established in Europe between the seventeenth and nineteenth centuries.

Today we find ourselves facing a distinct historical discontinuity. With respect to the past, generating the common good presupposes the relational participation of all those interested in such a good (which cannot be abstract entities but concrete personal and associative subjects in specific situations) and presupposes the nexus between each actor's freedom and responsibility in producing the common good. Those who make reference to the classical political conception continue to identify the common good in the State, as its function and chief task. But there is a clear shift, even if it is gradual and tempered, of the concept of common good toward non-state political communities. The new 'welfare' cannot be produced only from below (from individuals), or only from above (by an increasingly interventionist State), or from a mixture of the two, but rather from a suitable relation – involving both subsidiarity and solidarity – among the members of a political community (understood precisely as the totality who must decide on their common good).

To arrive at a concrete definition of this vision, social theory must clarify the reality of the relational order, that is, the reality of the relations that substantiate the common good, and must see its autonomous potentialities in what we could call the 'subject of society', which means seeing it in the capacity of civil society (defined as the totality of subjects – both individual and collective – who do not have roles in public institutions) to express themselves as social subjects (we should say 'societarian' subjects) who generate relational goods.

To this end, it becomes essential that there be integration between three visions of the common good which imply different perspectives on what is called the principle of subsidiarity: the common good which only a political authority can guarantee from above (vertical subsidiarity), the common good which is peculiar to the relations between the state and civil subjects (horizontal subsidiarity), and the common good as defined in the relations among the subjects of civil society (lateral subsidiarity).[25]

Implications for the future political organization of society

To the degree that the limitations and structural defects of the current model of the social (welfare) state can be recognized, the alternative idea of a *society based upon a sound combination of subsidiarity and solidarity* gains ground, a society that is pursued through the expansion of relational goods. This goes beyond a *neo-lib/lab vision* of the social state and of well-being because it emphasizes three fundamental things.

First, it redefines well-being starting from subjects, who are simultaneously its recipients and architects. Second, it confers on the state the political role of guarantor of the common good, in as much as it decides the general rules but does not produce civil society but, even worse, often represents a power system that interprets civil society as a function of political hegemony. Third, it abandons the aim of including people in a single institutional order they must embrace but, rather, promotes different institutions in a plural order which rewards the best results obtained through the adoption of the principles of subsidiarity and solidarity.

It is evident that civil society produces relational goods if and to the extent to which it makes use of its own resources: in the first place, its moral resources (i.e. values and virtues), which involve relying on a first-person, rather than a third-person, ethics.[26] The failures of the

[25] H. Willke, 'Governance complessa e modello europeo di sussidiarietà', in P. Donati (ed.), *Verso una società sussidiaria. Teorie e pratiche della sussidiarietà in Europa* (Bologna: Bononia University Press, 2011), pp. 77–95; H. Willke, *Smart Governance. Governing the Global Knowledge Society* (Frankfurt and New York: Campus, 2007); P. Donati, '"Pacem in Terris" and the Principle of Subsidiarity: Beyond the Misunderstandings', in M. A. Glendon, R. Hittinger, and M. Sanchez Sorondo (eds.), *The Global Quest for Tranquillitas Ordinis* (Rome: Vatican Press, 2013), pp. 436–471.

[26] Let us clarify the terms. *First-person ethics* (also "virtue ethics") holds that ethics is a search for the global good of man, that is, the good of human life taken as a totality. It looks to the acting subject, that is, to the person who, by means of his/her free action rooted in reason, moves toward the ultimate good. The question arises: what is the truly good life that deserves to be lived? How can we become better and live the better life, individually and together? The

lib/lab configuration of society are due to the fact of having extolled third-person ethics, and abandoning, indeed destroying, first-person ethics.

We could ask: why is the *societal vision* of the common good as a relational good, *inflected in terms of a subsidiarity characterized by solidarity*, more human? This is basically for three reasons. First, because it not only respects negative freedom (freedom from constraints) but also nourishes positive freedom (freedom *for* – i.e. in favour of – social finalities) of people and social subjects. Second, it does not forcibly impose solidarity but produces it by incentivizing and rewarding whoever adopts courses of action that produce relational goods. Third, it does not privilege exit solutions or those of mercantile competition but, rather, those that strive toward the construction of social autonomies able to combine universalism and particularity.

The superseding of the twentieth-century social state by a political system that promotes a civil society capable of responding to the challenges posed by a globalizing world that generates ever new crises is not a simple operation. Certainly, it cannot be achieved within the framework of negotiations and compromises between market and political democracy, merely conceding token acknowledgements to the third sector, which remains residual and dependent on the first two sectors. The passage to a new social order is happening today under the aegis of a social morphogenesis[27] that is enfranchising an 'other' civil society

answer must be constructed by considering human agency from the point of view of the person who acts, the person in action; considering conduct not in and of itself, as in abstraction from its author, but in as much as it is practiced by the subject. *Third person ethics* (also "normativist ethics"), on the other hand, does not accord centrality to the consideration of the person with a view to achieving a good life by exercising the virtues. The acting subject is rejected as a central category. Here the ethical problem consists in identifying and following the norms that regulate social relationships among subjects who seek their own legitimate ends. The construction of a liveable society must be irrespective of the acting subject in that each one has his/her own conception of the good and his/her own life project that is incommensurate with that of others, because no truth exists regarding the good in which each rational subject can recognize him/herself (it is assumed that the consociates are morally estranged). The solution of this ethical problem (that is, the construction of social relations among affectively asocial subjects) consists in the production of a complex of norms, of a legal system originating from human convention or extrapolated from instrumental reason according to the purely formal needs of coherence, functionality, and universality.

27 Margaret S. Archer (ed.), *Social Morphogenesis* (Dordrecht: Springer, 2013).

whose forms of sociality are different from those of current political institutions and the capitalistic market.[28]

Should the social state constitute all or only a part of society? It has oscillated, in its ideologies and practices, from one pole to the other, configuring the State as the synthesis of everything (polarization of a *lab* type) or, *vice versa*, as a residual subsystem (polarization of a *lib* type). We risk remaining stuck in this game. To the question inherited from modernity, namely, 'Must the state still be everything or only a part?', the twenty-first century could answer by completely shifting perspective and configuring the State as a differentiated function of the political body, specialized in ensuring that social processes do not create poverty and exclusion but, rather, wealth and social cohesion through the production of relational goods. It addresses everyone (not only the poor), but as to this 'everyone', it is concerned with their conditions of participation, seen as the result of a triangulation among risks undertaken, responsibilities assumed, and opportunities enjoyed. This means seeing the state as the specific subsystem that must politically govern society but must not replace it, nor colonize it, nor produce it. The state must come to a halt when faced by that which does not pertain to it, that which is not available to it, such as the ethical sphere. It must be a means through which the community takes on the collective responsibility of including in social life those who cannot or have not succeeded in becoming part of it.

The society of subsidiary solidarity has its political form in what I call the 'relational social State.'[29] What is a relational state? In my opinion, it is characterized by the following modalities:

(1) The relational State is no longer conceived as the centre of society but as a functionally differentiated politico-administrative subsystem for the governance of a society regarded as a network of social (public, private, and mixed) subjects and institutions. In its aspect as an institution, the State becomes an ensemble of apparatuses having specific political and administrative functions that must operate in a subsidiary manner – relatively symmetrical in

[28] P. Donati, 'Alla ricerca di una società civile. Che cosa dobbiamo fare per aumentare le capacità di civilizzazione del Paese?', in P. Donati (ed.), *La società civile in Italia* (Milan: Mondadori, 1997), pp. 21–80.

[29] P. Donati, 'Are we witnessing the emergence of a new "relational state"?', in P. Donati and L. Martignani (eds.), *Towards a New Local Welfare. Best Practices and Networks of Social Inclusion* (Bononia University Press, 2015), chapter 9.

terms of power – with respect to other fundamental subsystems of society, that is, the market, civil society, and the subsystem of the family and informal networks.

(2) The relational state is configured as a legal and social system that must realize *complex citizenship*. Citizenship is said to be complex for three types of reasons:
   (i) because it recognizes not only civil, political, and economic-social rights (as theorized by T. H. Marshall and others)[30] but also *human* rights, which are the rights of the human person in relation to the social formations in which he/she develops and conducts his/her activities; these refer to over four generations of rights, the last of which is still being defined;
   (ii) because it interweaves citizenship in a state (traditional citizenship, defined as the individual's belonging to a national state) and societal citizenship (defined as persons' belonging to associative forms of civil society that are recognized as collective subjects – that are public but not pertaining to the state – acting with politically significant functions in the local, regional, national, or super-national sphere); and, with this, makes possible *differentiated and multiple* forms of citizenship;
   (iii) because complex citizenship refers not only to individuals but also to the social formations of civil society (which constitutes a reason for a sharp discontinuity with modernity); in effect, from a sociological point of view, the relational social State arises when typically modern *political constitutions* (from the nineteenth and twentieth centuries) are reformed through processes of *constitutionalizing private spheres*, that is, by attributing a political value (authorizing binding collective decisions for the common good) and connecting public functions, to organizations of a non-state type.[31]

The relational state is de/centred and articulated in an associational (or federal) manner, whether upward (for example, the European Union)

[30] T. H. Marshall, *Citizenship and Social Class* (Cambridge: Cambridge University Press, 1950); T. Bottomore and T. H. Marshall, *Citizenship and Social Class* (London: Pluto, 1992).

[31] Gunther Teubner, *Constitutional Fragments: Societal Constitutionalism and Globalization* (Oxford: Oxford University Press, 2012).

or downward (local communities and organizations of civil society). The consequences for social policies are of enormous import. The passage from the traditional welfare state to the relational social State entails, in fact, at least three great structural changes.

In the first place, the symbolic code that presides over social inclusion (or cohesion) policies changes: the prevailing symbolic code is no longer that of the state (by which the common good is by definition that of the state) but becomes what we can call a *relational symbolic code* (by which the common good is the relational one). In the second place, social policies become a widespread function of society, that is, a function pursued by a plurality of actors, who are public and private, combined and intertwined (in relation) in various ways with one another (plural welfare, societal conceptions, multi-stakeholders in welfare organizations, and still others). In the third place, the social policies, which until now have been upheld primarily by the two pillars of freedom (the *lib* side or that of the market) and equality (the *lab* side or that of the redistributive State), should institutionalize a third pillar, that of solidarity, as autonomous and distinct and that cannot be derived from the other two. This pillar represents *ad hoc* societal, plural, and subsidiary welfare institutions as they arise. Until now, social policies have treated solidarity as a by-product of other policies pursued primarily through combinations of individual freedom and equality of opportunity in welfare systems, conceived of as a compromise between state and market. It is not by chance that solidarity still does not appear as a value and end in itself alongside the other two values of the European Union's master plan.

The relational social state expresses the need for a qualitative leap towards a new configuration of freedom, equality, and solidarity that does not make social solidarity residual because it does not understand the latter to be charity or compensation for the weakest or marginalized members of society but places it on the same level as freedom and equality of opportunity. It also does so in terms of the elaboration of rights (new relational rights) and the production of goods and services (new relational goods) of welfare.

To synthesize: the relational social state conceives the common good to be a good that valorizes relations of reciprocal enrichment on the part of free and responsible actors who create welfare. It brings about a complex citizenship that operates by valorizing the principle of relationality as applied to all of society's spheres. Social policies are not understood as sectorial or residual policies for the poor or needy but as a general form of reflective action of society on itself in terms of the production and distribution of social goods (in a broad sense), without separating normal conditions from particular conditions (those that indicate risk or are deviant or pathological). The relationality that connotes complex citizenship operates at all territorial levels and in every sector of intervention because citizenship must be extended to all potential actors (not as passive beneficiaries but, rather, as active subjects that choose it and put it into practice) (inclusive citizenship) and must be deepened, that is, made to be concrete and situated (deep citizenship). Relational modalities substantially alter the hierarchical, bureaucratic, and disciplinary characteristics, as well as those regarding assistance and workfare, that have been typical of the traditional twentieth-century welfare state.

The contribution of Relational Subjects to substantial democracy consists in promoting the birth and development of civil welfare institutions that create relational goods by acting with Relational Reflexivity. Sociological analysis must be able to grasp those phenomena that indicate how morphogenic society can evolve toward a structural and cultural complex able to promote the specific reflexivity that generates common goods as relational goods.

7 The emergence of collective Relational Subjects and their societal impact: beyond the market/state binary code

PIERPAOLO DONATI

Why the recurrent worldwide economic crises?

Do the recurrent worldwide economic crises have a sociological explanation?

The world crisis of the financial economy that broke out in September 2008 – first in the USA and then in Europe – has been interpreted in many different ways, though mostly from a strictly economic point of view. Basically, the crisis has been attributed to a 'malfunctioning' of financial markets, obviously widely resorting in the process to moral considerations concerning economic actors failing to behave ethically. Solutions have been seeking to identify new rules capable of moralizing markets.

Politics has been assigned the task of finding practical solutions, that is, measures to be implemented by national States and formulated by international agreements among States. International monetary authorities have been called upon by governments to act as fire brigades (i.e. to bail out banks and financial agencies from bankruptcy). Governments have adopted measures to limit the crisis's effects on unemployment as well as increases in national poverty rates.

We still lack a sociological interpretation of the crisis *per se*, differing from interpretations centred upon economic, political, and moral factors. Certainly many sociologists have provided sound analyses of the crisis, but their explanations have focussed mainly upon the interplay between the economic and political systems, without comprehending the very social features of the crisis.[1] Other sociologists, for instance

[1] By the phrase 'the very social features' I mean the full content of social relations, not only their economic and political dimensions, but also their underlying values and norms (as it will be clarified later).

the supporters of the so-called theory of 'reflexive modernization', have dealt with the crisis in an abstract way, that is, as a historical stage in which modernization radicalizes itself, turns onto itself, and becomes a problem to itself.

Sociological analyses have often been confused with moral ones. Take, for instance, the proposals regarding a new economy with a 'human face', drawing economic behaviour from philosophical anthropology (in particular from a 'personalistic' anthropology rooted in both Catholic and Islamic thought).[2] Such philosophical proposals, although they are worthy of attention,[3] fall short of making the link between anthropology and economics by not considering the specifically social factors that are the subject matter of sociology.

In fact, these interpretations that have tried to show how the crisis was determined by a lack of ethics in the economy have also shown that ethics alone – that is, seen as a call upon economic actors to act more morally – can do very little, if not to say nothing. It has been observed that only political coercion can introduce rules into the economy, whose ethical quality is always debatable. Instances of ethical self-regulation on the part of economic actors and financial markets have been rare in for-profit sectors. This in turn has highlighted to an even greater extent the weakness of the marriage between ethics and economics as a remedy for the crisis.

In my view, we need a sociological analysis to show how the crisis stemmed from a certain organization of the so-called 'global society'. Such a setup is the product of a long historical development, which pre-dates the outbreak of the financial crisis in 2008.

The question we ask is the following: from a sociological standpoint, why did this crisis occur and what remedies can be found? Luhmann's sociological analysis turns out to be very useful in understanding the situation in question. Luhmann holds that highly modernized societies act as a *world system* (a *world society*) of a functional kind, in which

[2] It is certainly remarkable that Catholic anthropology has been associated with the Islamic Ummah on the grounds that Islamic finance is reported to use money only as a means and not as a goal, which would explain why Islamic financial institutions were able to avoid crashing with the world crisis of September 2008.

[3] See for instance João César das Neves, 'Market and Common Good', in M. Schlag and J. A. Mercado (eds.), *Free Markets and the Culture of Common Good* (Dordrecht: Springer, 2012), pp. 53–59.

each subsystem, for instance the economic one, is self-referential and autopoietic.[4] It is precisely from there that the financialization of the economy has emerged.[5] This means that in Western societal systems, representing the paradigmatic model of modernization processes for the rest of the world, political power can enforce some limitations upon economic systems. These limitations, however, are only contingent, merely functional, and they cannot meet normative imperatives that lie beyond economic and political action. Ethics is turned into an *exaggerated steering mania*, which proves itself to be practically ineffective when challenged by real incidents.[6]

In other words, it is clear that modernized societies cannot make resort to solid moral values, least of all to *business ethics*, simply because this goes against the idea of modernization itself. Modernized societies are constructed in such a way as to be immune to ethics. As Luhmann put it bluntly and brutally, man is no longer the yardstick of society.

I am not going to expound Luhmann's theory here, but take it as well known. I will get straight to the point: the point being that sociological theory nowadays converges on the idea that world society is bound to face a future bristling with risks, uncertainties, disorientation, and even chaos (in the technical sense of the word). A future which, as Luhmann put it, *cannot* even *begin*. 'Reflexive modernization' theory, though with different emphases, has in essence legitimized such an analysis of the current situation and of future prospects.[7]

What, then, is/lies behind the world financial crisis that started in 2008? It is certainly a very different crisis from that of 1929. The historical circumstances are totally different. At that time capitalism was scarcely regulated and lacked a substantial welfare state structure. Nowadays markets are far more regulated and benefit from of more developed social security systems.

As nation states play a much larger part than in the 1930s, the measures that are now put in place to solve the crisis amount to three kinds

[4] N. Luhmann, *Social Systems* (Palo Alto, CA: Stanford University Press, 1995).

[5] N. Luhmann, 'Politics and Economy', *Thesis Eleven*, 53 (1998), 1–10.

[6] N. Luhmann, 'Limits of Steering', *Theory, Culture and Society*, 14 (1997), 41–57.

[7] U. Beck, A. Giddens, and S. Lash, *Reflexive Modernization* (Cambridge: Polity Press, 1994).

of action: (i) incentives to, and enforcement of market best practices by political-administrative systems; (ii) the ban on 'dirty' financial products and on fiscal havens; and (iii) greater public commitment in terms of social expenditure, to nurture the real economy's virtuous cycles (by supporting family expenses, by limiting the damages of unemployment, by protecting poorer segments of the population).

And yet are they the solution? It is reasonable to have doubts about it.

The crisis of *lib/lab* systems

The measures adopted today cannot solve the crisis, and for various reasons they can at most provide temporary pauses and remedies.

First of all, all these remedies remain within the 'economic-political system', which would confirm Luhmann's arguments by which the ⟨market + state system⟩ will continue to dominate even during an endemic crisis. I call it the '*lib/lab*' configuration. My argument, then, is that if we want to avoid a permanent crisis – more or less 'under control' as the case may be – then remedies have to break away from the self-referential logic of economic-political systems. In Luhmann's conceptual framework this is not possible. We then have to accept the challenge posed by having to prove that an alternative societal set-up not only is abstractly possible, but also is necessary and realistic, if we really want to escape from a system producing a chronic crisis.

Second, the ethics that is called upon to correct the markets' malfunctioning has no credible sociological foundations, because the ethical principles endorsed by *lib/lab*, and that it would like to uphold, have nowhere from which to be generated or regenerated in this societal configuration, since neither the market nor the state are sources of ethical standards. If ethical corrections are to work, one needs to think of a different way of organizing society. Such a new set-up: (i) has to be capable of allowing for the emergence of social subjects (operating as 'social environments' for the economic and political system) that can generate and adopt certain ethical standards of conduct and uphold them in economic-political systems, and (ii) has to meet such a condition in a structural manner and not by way of occasional voluntary commitment. Luhmann would say that this is not possible, because – in his view – society's multiple spheres cannot in any way influence one another, least of all by exchanging ethical services. I propose to meet the challenge of showing that this is not only possible, but – as a matter of fact – really happening through the emergence of new Relational Subjects who escape the logic of modernity.

My argument, sociological in kind, is that *the configuration of world society is as such an unstable set-up that it is impossible to escape except by reforming its own lib/lab basic structure*. Let me explain this.

Societies that have been or are in the process of modernization are based on a structural (systemic) compromise between Market (*lib*) and State (*lab*). By 'Market' I mean free competition and capitalistic production theories and practices based on liberalism as an economic doctrine (this is the *lib* side, on which we find, for instance, the Chicago school). By 'State', I mean the state intervention theories and practices, aimed at guaranteeing equal opportunities and a bare welfare minimum as a right of citizenship, which is generally supported by socialist-oriented political doctrines (this is the *lab* side, on which we find, for instance, the doctrines going back to Keynes, Lord Beveridge, and Richard Titmuss).

In brief, modernized systems are a mix of *lib* and *lab*, that is, *lib/lab* systems. Whenever the market (*lib*) is insolvent, resort is made to the state (*lab*); whenever the state (*lab*) is insolvent, resort is made to the market (*lib*). This is the game of the modern economy, which attained its most sophisticated form in the second half of the twentieth century.

Our societies are still working on the basis of this framework, looking to stabilize economic cycles and a fairer resource distribution through *lib/lab* regulations.

What is wrong with this societal configuration? On the one hand, it is said that the *lib/lab* set-up has so far offered remarkable advantages, in as much as it has guaranteed freedom and more extensive political and social citizenship rights. In fact, the same can be said about this set-up as about liberal democracies, that is, that although this system is full of defects, it is the best human history has so far produced. On the other hand, its structural faults are not insignificant, and they entail certain mechanisms that intrinsically and inevitably produce recurrent crises. In other words, *lib/lab systems are not sustainable as long-term systems*.

What are the mechanisms that make for this social order? I would like to analyze the problematic aspects of *lib/lab* systems and establish whether or not there can be a societal configuration able to overcome these limitations.

Let us examine the intrinsic defects of the *lib/lab* configuration.[8]

(a) According to the *lib/lab* approach, society is merely an intertwining of economics and politics against which all else is seen as insignificant for the common good and for citizenship. In particular, life worlds are conceived of as merely a 'private' sphere. Instead, from a sociological point of view, what lies outside the State-Market pair is not insignificant for the achievement of the common good, for citizenship, and for the workings of both Market and State. If life worlds are conceived as 'leftovers', the *lib/lab* system succumbs to a chronic crisis it cannot remedy.

(b) For the *lib/lab* system, *there is no alternative to the combination of liberalism and socialism.*[9] Such a societal configuration is essentially considered as a problem of *balancing* between (anti-systemic) freedom and equality (provoked by extending individual freedoms), and refrains from tackling the *social integration* problems[10] posed by such an approach. Even though one may agree that systemic social planning is not a workable regulatory response, it is still clear that the *lib/lab* combination has almost nothing to say about social integration problems in contemporary social systems. To put it another way, *lib/lab* systems generate

[8] For a more detailed analysis see P. Donati, 'Freedom vs. Control in Post-Modern Society: A Relational Approach', in E. K. Scheuch and D. Sciulli (eds.), *Societies, Corporations and the Nation State* (Leiden: Brill, 2000), pp. 47–76; P. Donati, *La cittadinanza societaria* (Rome-Bari: Laterza, 2000), pp. 229–260; P. Donati, *Il lavoro che emerge. Prospettive del lavoro come relazione sociale in una economia dopo-moderna* (Turin: Bollati Boringhieri, 2001), pp. 202–227.

[9] A champion of this approach, Ralph Dahrendorf sees citizenship as a gift granted (*octroyée*) by an enlightened political élite, including entitlements guaranteed by the state versus other provisions offered by the free market: R. Dahrendorf, 'The Changing Quality of Citizenship', in B. van Steenberger (ed.), *The Condition of Citizenship* (London: Sage, 1994), pp. 10–19.

[10] I am using the phrase 'social integration' here to distinguish it from 'systemic integration'. D. Lockwood, 'Social Integration and System Integration', in D. Lockwood, *Solidarity and Schism. 'The Problem of Disorder' in Durkheimian and Marxist Sociology* (Oxford: Clarendon Press, 1992), pp. 399–412; *id.*, 'Civic Integration and Social Cohesion', in I. Gough and G. Olofsson (eds.), *Capitalism and Social Cohesion: Essays on Exclusion and Integration* (Basingstoke, UK: Macmillan, 1999), pp. 63–84.

increasing deficits in social integration (the so-called 'pathologies of modernity')[11] for which they provide no remedies.

(c) The *lib/lab* set-up seeks to tame the 'competition-profit versus solidarity-social redistribution' conflict without providing alternatives to the permanent opposition between these two contradictory needs. The conflict is seen and dealt with as an insoluble opposition, which may only be kept under control through political democracy, especially in the form of neo-corporativist democracy. However, these contradictions bring about a structural imbalance. In the USA, the competition-profit side has the upper hand over social citizenship rights, which entails serious social inequality and poverty in Third World contexts. In Europe the solidarity-redistribution side prevails on the basis of a citizenship principle that seeks to be unconditional without actually succeeding in that aim.

The *world system* (or globalization), marked by the economy's financialization, is the outcome of this current worldwide societal *lib/lab* structure.

The recurrent crises are not those predicted by Karl Marx. The polarization process setting the leading world imperialist bourgeoisie against the proletarian masses does not occur on a worldwide scale, but in limited geo-political-economic areas, where it is restrained by *lib/lab* systems, which seek, despite all their shortcomings, to reduce social inequalities. Furthermore, globalization gives rise to many other intermediary economic actors between the two poles envisaged by Marx.

What determines the crises occurring in systems based on the *lib/lab* compromise between state and market is the very 'economic logic',[12] which is not purely capitalistic, but is based on the intertwining of market and state, and thus embraces society as a whole (starting with the market). Such an economic logic has unexpected side effects and negative externalities that erode the civil society on which the *lib/lab* system is based.

[11] This well-known expression was first proposed by Jürgen Habermas, who deals with such pathologies in terms of communicative forms and not as a more complex problem. J. Habermas, *Theorie des Kommunikativen Handelns* (Frankfurt a.M.: Suhrkamp, 1981). At the cultural level it has been employed by Charles Taylor.

[12] The term 'economic' here is used in an analytical generalized sense.

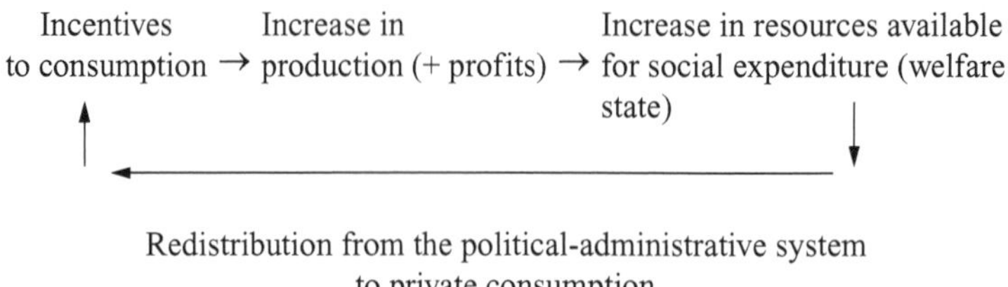

Figure 7.1 *Lib/lab* systems' economic logic (an evolutionary model, supposedly bringing 'progress')

Let me summarize this logic in Figure 7.1. The economic logic in question consists in using political power to increase consumption, which in turn fosters productivity and profits, so as to be able to draw on fiscal revenues for the financial resources needed to stimulate consumption. The rest is irrelevant. Banks and financial systems serve this logic.

Such a systemic logic, with all its internal mechanisms, cannot be extended beyond certain thresholds, because serious social problems arise once particular economic growth levels are exceeded. The present societal model proves functional in breaking away from poverty and under development, whereas it becomes dysfunctional for a welfare society. In particular:

(a) consumerism generates a broad range of problematic or pathological human conditions because consumption needs are artificially induced and technologies, especially the media, are misused;
(b) the social inclusion model that is supported by this logic (founded on a simple extension of the typical twentieth-century welfare state) makes beneficiaries ever more passive and produces distorted effects: for instance, it creates various 'traps' (the poverty trap, the 'crystal ceiling' limiting women's social mobility and distorting equal opportunities on the basis of sex, etc.), and above all it immunizes individuals from social relations.

Many will point out that there are no alternatives to the systemic logic I am talking about (Figure 7.1) because: (i) if you curb consumption, you also stop economic growth; (ii) if you cut social expenditure (the welfare state), you create poverty.

What, then, is to be done?

The proposals put forward today are centred on introducing two kinds of correcting tools:

(1) putting '*more ethics into the market*', as proposed by many, in the hope of making actors more responsible: two examples of this are 'business ethics' at the production stage and 'fairness ethics' in the distribution of goods – such proposals are especially aimed at correcting the *lib* side of this set-up;
(2) extending citizenship is proposed by others, to make it 'more inclusive' to embrace the weakest social segments, in order to reduce poverty and social problems – such proposals are especially aimed at correcting the *lab* side of this set-up.

I note that such corrective measures do not modify the systemic logic of *lib/lab* systems. As generous as the foregoing proposals may be, they do not stand much chance of succeeding because it is the *lib/lab* system itself which makes them ineffective. The system continues to work in such a way as to be functional to a moral order centred upon individual, instrumental, and utilitarian values and criteria. Though sensitive to the need for personal honesty and greater social justice (in the form of equal opportunities), these values and criteria fail to meet the need to create a civil society capable of supporting honest and fair behaviour. On the whole, it is a self-contradictory model, because the economy drives morality without taking it seriously (i.e. without relating to it as an autonomous reality). It is necessary to modify the *lib/lab* logic. I shall now attempt to present these arguments in more detail.

Should we yield to evolutionary laws?

The *lib/lab* view of the *world system* urges us to let society run in accordance with its own evolutionary tendencies. Such an approach is implemented through a so-called 'reflexive' modernization model, which in essence chronically questions itself. As Beck, Bonss, and Lau[13] put it, '"Reflexive" does *not* mean that people today lead a more conscious life. On the contrary, "reflexive" does not signify an "increase in mastery and consciousness, but a heightened awareness that mastery

[13] U. Beck, W. Bonss and C. Lau, 'The Theory of Reflexive Modernization. Problematic, Hypotheses and Research Program', *Theory, Culture & Society*, 20 (2003), 1–33, p. 3.

is impossible." Simple modernity becomes "reflexive modernization" to the extent that it disenchants and then dissolves its own taken-for-granted premises'. This leaves the referent, the purpose, and the point of 'reflexivity' highly ambiguous.

The society envisaged by the *lib/lab* way of thinking is a society which suffers from a permanent identity crisis, pervaded as it is by insoluble social and personal risks. Reflexive modernization is seen as a radical uncertainty affecting every sphere of social life.[14]

According to my argument, on the basis of modernity's own assumptions, the just-mentioned corrective measures (i.e. [a] ethical injections into the market and [b] extension of citizenship rights and their beneficiaries) do not work because: (i) the *lib/lab* logic is relativistic from an ethical point of view and neutralizes any attempt to replace economic criteria by 'non-negotiable' ethical criteria; and (ii) the extension of citizenship rights (in terms of more rights and more beneficiaries) is always unstable and problematic, and, at any rate, if viewed in relation to the typical twentieth-century *lib/lab* welfare state model, faces increasing failures (fiscal crises, inclusions generating exclusions, etc.).

In short, the present modernization processes do not tolerate any restrictive, external regulation of the *lib/lab* logic (at any of the three stages summarized in Figure 7.1: consumption, for-profit production, and redistribution through the welfare state). The only regulations this logic can entertain are functional ones, that is, functional to its own reproduction.

However, neo-functionalism does not ensure any society capable of avoiding the dilemmas and social pathologies produced by such a societal model. It cannot produce any stable social system; it can only induce the same problems again and again. *Neo-functionalism turns out to be just 'another way', and merely an outwardly non-ideological one, of describing the commodification of the world and an evolutionary adaptation of the whole society to such commodification processes.*

Basically, the *lib/lab* model proposes that we live in a society which adapts to Darwin's evolutionary laws, and lacks any finalism to the process of being pushed by its competitive and survival skills. This is globalization's own *world system*.

[14] On a critique of the reflexive modernization theory: see Margaret S. Archer, *Making Our Way through the World: Human Reflexivity and Social Mobility* (Cambridge: Cambridge University Press, 2007) and *The Reflexive Imperative in Late Modernity* (Cambridge: Cambridge University Press, 2012).

There seem to be no alternatives to this state of affairs. Utopias have failed and fallen. Yet, perhaps, a careful analysis of the situation may reveal on-going societal morphogenetic processes which place a question mark over the functionalist view of economic rationality as configured in the *lib/lab* model (Figure 7.1). Sociology has consecrated this model first by means of Talcott Parsons' theory and later, when faced with its failure, with Niklas Luhmann's variant. We now see a new version in place, which we had better examine briefly: it is a version of functionalism proposing an interpretation of markets, particularly financial ones, through key 'reflexive truths'.

George Soros, the international magnate, has pointed out that the working of financial markets follows their own 'reflexivity' (or reflexive rationality) marked by evolutionary mechanisms, which are self-referential and have uncertain outcomes.[15] These 'mechanisms' are rooted in the particular reflexivity of economic actors who 'discount' the future. They shape reality (what actually happens in society, not only in markets) through investments that anticipate the future and pre-empt future reality according to the shape desired by financial operators. Reality is transformed through the financial operators' own 'reflexive truth'.

However, our question is: to what extent can society – interpreted as daily life's social texture – be configured in the same way as financial markets and their 'reflexive' logic promoting an evolution without finalism? The point is that society – if we see it properly as a network of social relationships – is not a *stock exchange*. There are other types of reflexivity to shape society.[16] The argument I would like to advance is that it is these 'other' forms of reflexivity that can extricate us from the crisis that started in 2008 and lead beyond the *lib/lab* systems' own chronic crisis.

Looking for an alternative to an evolution without finalism

Can we conceive of an alternative to the functionalist and evolutionist model I have been discussing? I think that the world needs a

[15] G. Soros, 'Reflexivity in Financial Markets', in *id.*, *Open Society. Reforming Global Capitalism* (New York: Public Affairs, 2000), pp. 58–90.

[16] Margaret S. Archer (ed.), *Conversations about Reflexivity* (London: Routledge, 2010); P. Donati, 'Reflexivity after Modernity: From the Viewpoint of Relational Sociology', in P. Donati, *Relational Sociology. A New Paradigm for the Social Sciences* (London: Routledge, 2011), pp. 192–210.

post-functionalist, indeed an *after*-modern development model, one based on the assumption of definitively abandoning functionalism – theoretical and empirical – as its intellectual infrastructure.[17]

However, a word of caution is needed here. Functionalism cannot be overcome by a backward-looking humanistic view, unable to match the competitive skills of functionalism. It has to be a humanism capable of taking functionalism into account while overcoming its limitations.

Such a post-functionalist development configuration or logic needs to be able to do two things:

(a) at a macro-level, to reduce systemic determinisms, in favour of organizational networks capable of self-steering;
(b) at a micro-level (i.e. of individual action), to modify life-styles, that is, consumption habits, according to more austere value guidelines, to avoid functionalist commercialization mechanisms. Life worlds – meaning primary (face-to-face) relations and interactions, taking place within families, small groups, networks of associations based on interpersonal relations have to be given a chance to speak. One has to take into account the decisive role of *personal* reflexivity, seen as internal conversation and the role of *collective* reflexivity as a quality of relational networks.

It is clear that such changes are not possible within a consumption economy whose only ruling principle is the imperative of GDP growth (as it is in Figure 7.1). They become possible, though, as soon as one takes on board the fact that GDP has been a useful parameter of well-being when used for developing countries with quite a low average income and with widespread poverty, but it is inappropriate for societies that have reached a certain threshold of well-being, such as post-industrial countries. In these countries, GDP has to be replaced by other units of measurement, such as Gross Domestic Well-Being (GDWB), which should be adopted not only by developed countries, but also by developing countries.[18]

[17] I take it that modernity corresponds to a societal spirit and model of a functional type (as was clarified very well by Niklas Luhmann's own theory). I see functionalism as the root of the scientific-technological approach typical of the west and of western modernity, as Davis described it. K. Davis,' The Myth of Functional Analysis as a Special Method in Sociology and Anthropology', *American Sociological Review*, 24 (1959), 757–772.

[18] See the *Report by the Commission on the Measurement of Economic Performance and Social Progress*, 2009, by J. E. Stiglitz, A. Sen, and J.-P. Fitoussi: www.stiglitz-sen-fitoussi.fr

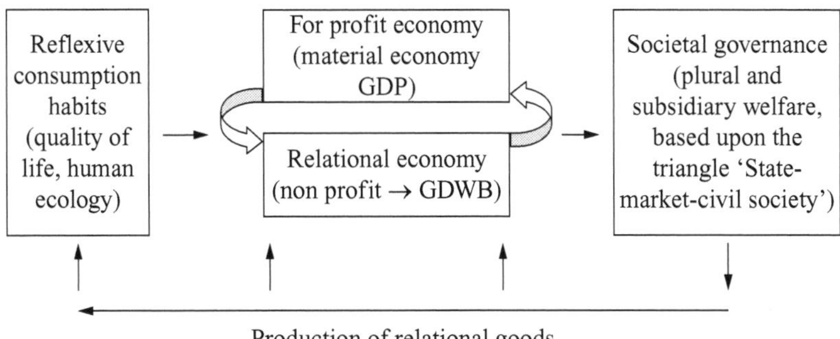

Figure 7.2 The economic logic of a relational society

An austere life-style does not mean a 'poor' economy that reduces aspirations for greater well-being. It does not mean, for instance, mere de-industrialization or the demise of medical services or schooling as proposed in the past, nor does it mean rejecting technology. It does not mean going back to a naively 'naturalistic' way of life. These are utopias without any hope or sense. A different economy is made possible by a different notion, relational and not merely materialistic, of well-being and of happiness.[19] We need another economic logic, if we realize the relational character of society which follows from the 'happiness paradox' (according to which the well-being in the advanced countries does not increase over time, but even declines, in spite of their rising trend in incomes, whilst ever people continue to strive only for money).

We have to ask ourselves if and how it is possible to envisage an economy centred upon the human quality of individuals and social life and focussed on humanizing social relations.

The crisis that emerged in 2008 has effectively stimulated the following novelties (see Figure 7.2):

- consumption habits are becoming (and will become) more reflexive;
- we are seeing an expansion of an economy that may be called relational because it envisages the economic stages of production-distribution-consumption of goods and services in terms of social relations and aims at producing a synergy between profit and non-profit;

[19] R. Diwan, 'Relational wealth and the quality of life', *Journal of Socio-Economics*, 29 (2000), 305–340; P. Donati, 'Welfare e globalizzazione: fra mercificazione e demercificazione', *Studi di Sociologia*, 47 (2009), 3–31.

- the role of the welfare state is gradually being replaced by a societal governance (plural and subsidiary welfare, featuring a market-state-third sector triangle);
- societal governance begins to operate reflectively, both on consumption and on market differentiation (for profit, non-profit, civil economy, etc.) in order to produce relational goods.

Such changes point to the rise of another type of societal configuration, as outlined in Figure 7.2.

It is important to emphasize the role of the social spheres commonly called the 'third sector'. Not only does the influence of their economic role increase (in terms of turnover and workforce), but above all such spheres operate as an 'engine of a civil society' that is as an alternative to the market underpinning the *lib/lab* set-up (as described in my Figure 7.1).

It is the vast world of co-operation (social co-operation, social enterprises), of voluntary associations, of ethical banks and of various forms of microcredit, of fair trade, of NGOs, of multiple forms of enterprises which we call 'civil'. Such bodies create their own financial markets, such as the *Bolsa de Valores Sociales y Ambietais* (BVS&A) in Brazil, SASIX (*South African Social Investment Exchange*) in South Africa, the KIVA project in the USA, the Asian *Impact Investment Exchange (IIX)* managed by the *Social Stock Exchange Asia* (*SSXA*) in Singapore, GEXSI (*Global Exchange For Social Investment*) in the UK, MYC4 in Denmark and *Social Stock Exchange Ltd.* in the UK, involving the Rockefeller Foundation, and finally the *Faccia per Faccia* [Face for Face] event at the *Falacosagiusta* fair in Milan. Others have proposed creating a 'social stock exchange', aimed at managing '*social and welfare business*', which would become an integral part of a horizontal subsidiary organization that a state could not ignore. And this might happen by setting up a sort of AIM (*Alternative Investment Market*), whose financial instruments would be shares (issued by low profit enterprises and non-profit social enterprises) and debt bonds (also issued by for-profit and non-profit bodies).

Such new enterprises as *low profit limited liability companies* and *community interest companies*, as well as new financial markets, can produce a different response to the world economic crisis, not merely by adapting themselves but by giving moral standards priority in economic and social action and by being able to modify life, work, and consumption styles. Compared with traditional capitalist enterprises, such enterprises have a number of distinctive features: for instance, they produce relational goods (and more generally *intangible goods*), they show greater flexibility, and they value lateral social mobility rather than upward or downward job mobility.

These new economic entities do convey a new model of society, but to implement it they have to overcome a number of obstacles: (i) internally, they have to develop their own Relational Reflexivity (which means a reflexivity on social relations)[20]; (ii) externally, they have to get rid of their structural dependence on the state (above all in Europe) and on the for-profit market (above all in the USA).[21]

The argument is that these new initiatives are indicative of a widespread search for the creation of Relational Subjects. Or, at least, they indicate that societies can successfully overcome the failures of the *lib/lab* configuration to the extent that they adopt a relational perspective on the way societal organizations are developed. Practical exemplars reflect the emergence of a new culture focussed upon the 'inter-being', relational living systems, contextuality, connectedness, co-creativity, social co-operation, with a peculiar sensitivity to ecological and human rights issues. Beneath these practices, there are significant shifts: from a logic of achievement, domination and control to a logic of concern, coordination and coproduction; from 'tier upon tier' to 'peer to peer'. The Relational Subject *creates* her network and manages it through a morphogenetic dynamics, whereas the simple modern subject *interprets* her network within pre-given boundaries.

[20] On the concept of 'Relational Reflexivity' see P. Donati, *Sociologia della riflessività. Come si entra nel dopo-moderno* (Bologna: il Mulino, 2011). I maintain that the concept of 'Relational Reflexivity' is strictly linked to the concept of 'relational feedbacks': P. Donati, 'Morphogenesis and Social Networks: Relational Steering Not Mechanical Feedback', in Margaret S. Archer (ed.), *Social Morphogenesis* (Dordrecht: Springer, 2013), pp. 205–231, and P. Donati, 'Social mechanisms and Their Feedbacks: Mechanical vs Relational Emergence of New Social Formations', in Margaret S. Archer (ed.), *Generative Mechanisms Transforming the Social Order* (Dordrecht: Springer, 2015), chapter 4. To be epigraphic: *human reflexivity cannot flourish where the logic of distinction* (or symbolic code in Luhmann's language) *is 'I like/I dislike' as on Facebook*, it needs a relational logic.

[21] An indicator that a *lib/lab* configuration is prevailing in the USA too (and not only in Europe) is that 97% of private debt in the States passes through the State. H. W. Sinn, *Casino Capitalism* (Oxford: Oxford University Press, 2010), chapter 11.

A new civil society generating Relational Subjects

The problem with modernity having reached the globalization stage is that civil society is still seen within a capitalist economy tending to financialize the real economy. The 2008 crisis has revealed this way of regarding civil society and, at the same time, has started to elaborate a new way of interpreting civil society. In other words, the 2008 crisis has highlighted the difference (a real *split*) between the old and the new civil society. We may have reached a turning-point between the one and the other.

On the one hand, the old civil society is still with us, tending to subject every good to the sequence by which money is invested in goods which in turn are used to make more money [Money-Goods-Money (M-G-M)]. That is, actors invest money in a good they have no need for, which is only instrumental to making more money. At first, they attribute a monetary (functional) value to goods and then trade them to make more money. It is important to understand that this mechanism presides over the whole *lib/lab* system. The state also deploys it in its relationship with the market: the state uses the market to get the money to pay for public welfare, which in turn is the source of votes, the political system's own currency. In this context, civil society works hand in hand with the market.

On the other hand, a new civil society has emerged, which is identified with the real economy. In a real economy, in contrast with the previous case, any good is evaluated in itself, and money (also in different forms of currency) is only used by actors as a tool to acquire the goods they need [according to the sequence: Goods-Money-Goods (G-M-G)]. A good is translated into the money needed to obtain another necessary good (for instance: work provides the money used by actors to buy the goods they want).

Rethinking civil society means understanding if and how, it is necessary and possible to shift from the M-G-M sequence to the G-M-G sequence. This shift requires a more complex view of society than modernity's own view. At the core of this view lies the relational nature of goods. Indeed, if it is true that the distinctive feature of a modernizing economy is to erase the relational nature of goods and economic processes, the building blocks of a new economy will be precisely the new need for individual and social relationships. It is not by accident that we see gifts coming back into so many social spheres and in many

Analytic dimensions	**In a 'Modern' society**	**In a 'After-modern' society**
I) instrumental dimension (means)	Money = sole currency	Money > currency (money takes many different forms, monetary and non-monetary)
P) political dimension (collective binding decisions on goals)	The only constraint set by money is for it to produce more money	Functional constraints are set for the use of money (in its various monetary and non-monetary forms), i.e. money is embedded within social contexts
N) normative dimension (social responsibility)	Enterprises only have an internal social responsibility to their employees	Enterprises also have an external responsibility (to the community's stakeholders)
E) evaluative dimension (values)	Value motives are individualistic, instrumental, acquisitive	Value motives are relational (inspired by subsidiarity and solidarity to produce goods seen as relational goods)

Figure 7.3 Two paradigmatic forms of economy

different forms[22]: from a sociological point of view, gifts point to the pursuit of social bonds and to the need for social relations to be forged to cement the sense of community.

Let me explain the distinction I have been drawing between the two societies: the modern one and the one I call after-modern, in more detail (Figure 7.3).

The key element of this distinction is the fact that after-modern society is confronted with the need to produce a 'variety pool' of options (in goods, consumption and production, in life-styles, in welfare measures) which cannot be 'accidental' or amount merely to functional monetary equivalence (as Luhmann holds), but has to be endowed with meaning, permitting the creation of common goods, by which I mean relational goods.[23]

22 See P. Donati, 'Giving and Social Relations: The Culture of Free Giving and Its Differentiation Today', *International Review of Sociology*, 13 (2003), 243–272.

23 P. Donati, 'Discovering the Relational Character of the Common Good', in Margaret S. Archer and P. Donati (eds.), *Pursuing the Common Good: How Solidarity and Subsidiarity Can Work Together* (Rome: Vatican Press, 2008), pp. 659–683.

This results in the rise of a new *Zeitgeist*. Whenever we say that future society will have to be inspired by the ethical criterion of 'sustainability', we have many different things in mind, the first being that instruments, such as finance, technology, etc., must match human needs and not vice versa. In turn, this implies that means have to be used only as means and not as ends or goals in themselves.

I summarize the distinction between modern and after-modern configurations in a table (Figure 7.3).

(i) In modern society:
   I) The financialized economy is based on the equation: money = currency
   P) Money is an end in itself, because of the functional culture which makes all goods and services subject to monetary equivalence;
   N) Enterprises have no broader social responsibility than those strictly associated with their own employees;
   E) the motives of economic action are individual, instrumental, acquisitive.

(ii) *In after-modern society*, on the other hand:
   I) The economy does not assume that money alone amounts to the sole currency, but that there can be other forms of money, meaning by money an entitlement to access goods and services [money > currency, or money = currency plus other forms of entitlements].[24] This economy, therefore, draws a distinction between monetary and non-monetary forms of currency, by connecting them to the 'real economy' (in which many goods and services do not allow for monetary equivalents). Hence, there arises an observable multiplication of forms of money, labour, and capital (not only financial capital, but also political, social, and human) and also a multiplication of contracts, in brief, for all the goods needed to pursue an economic objective;
   P) Money is embedded in social contexts, and therefore subjected to political decisions on social constraints, which may be restrictions on usage or functional constraints (as, for instance, is the case of vouchers, which are bounded forms of money for providing services);

[24] On the different forms of money (different from 'currency'), see Donati, *Il lavoro che emerge* (Turin: Bollati Boringhieri, 2001), pp. 189–197.

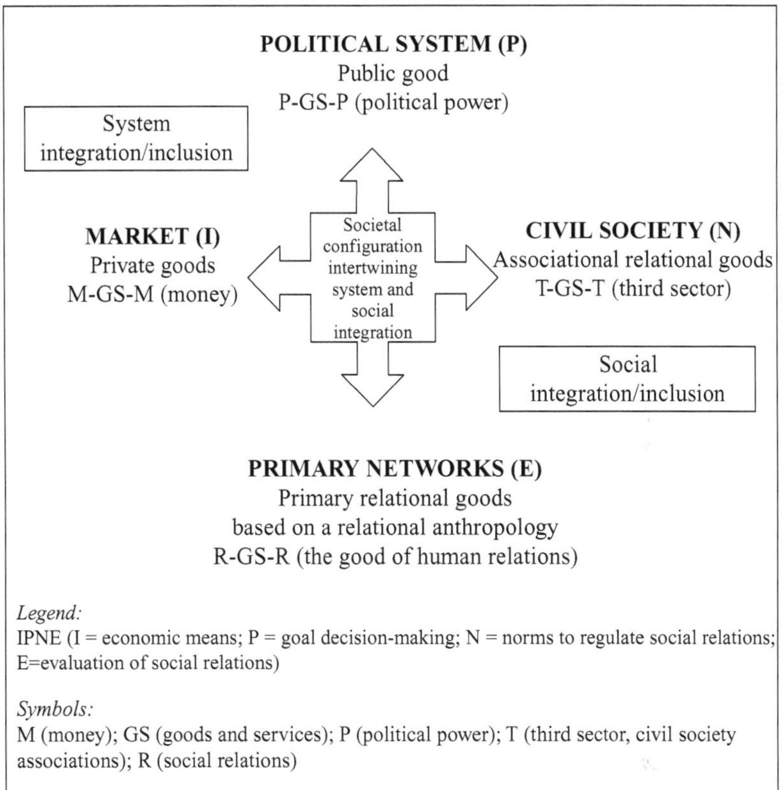

Figure 7.4 The new configuration of after-modern society

N) Corporate social responsibility is extended outside the company to the surrounding community and to stakeholders (profits do not go only or entirely to shareholders, but must be shared with the stakeholders); social responsibility is also broadened with regard to employees with forms of reconciliation between work and family, with relational contracts, as well as corporate citizenship;

E) The motives of economic action relate individual interests to principles of subsidiarity and solidarity that are necessary to produce common goods, which will be relational goods.

The new societal configuration (as outlined in Figure 7.4) does not erase modernity, but sees the modern *lib/lab* set-up as only a particular case, that is, as a way of operating (of organizing economy, politics, etc.), which is no longer general and which cannot be generalized throughout all social spheres and to all actors, but is only applicable to ever more limited areas of action. Earlier on, modernization was seen as potentially extendable throughout all spheres of society. This in turn legitimized the fact that the compromise between state and market was able to turn life worlds into commodities. The new set-up that I call after-modern is not characterized by a logic of dominance of one pole (market or state) over the other or by commercial negotiation logics between sub-systems or social spheres, but by a *network-like logic* which is forced to make the different societal spheres more co-operative, or at least to follow a restrained, mutually non-destructive competitive logic, within a world-systemic sustainability project.

To implement such changes, one needs a relational configuration that modernity was unable to tolerate, because overwhelmed by a general cultural conspectus conceiving of modernity as a way to immunize people against sociality.[25]

The qualities and properties of the 'third' (the Relational Subjects) beyond the Market/State compromise

What is internationally called the 'third sector' indicates a 'third' which is defined not only by the relationships with the first two sectors (State and Market). In fact the third sector comes into being with an autonomous identity, established on the basis of its own guiding distinctions (its own normative-symbolic code and symbolic and generalized means of interchange, linked to social solidarity), even if it must be responsive to its environment (and particularly to the State and the Market). In this sense, the third sector is the privileged sphere of Relational Subjects, though not the only one in which they develop.

The identity of the third sector organizations consists in specifying, for each of the concrete social forms it takes, a particular way of 'being' and 'making' society. The third sector organizations are associative

[25] J. J. Rousseau's works, for instance, provide a paradigmatic example of this position, which has justified an apolitical individualism and at the same time State dictatorships within modernity. See R. Spaemann, *Rousseau. Mensch oder Bürger. Das Dilemma der Moderne* (Stuttgart: Klett-Cotta, 2009).

entities which, far from defining themselves in relation to the State (also negatively, as 'non-state owned') and with the Market (as 'non-profit'), are structured according to their own project and their own charter, on the basis of processes which I call relational rather than functional differentiation.[26]

In order to understand how this can take place, I start by observing that there are four paradigmatic types of orientation which characterize social action (even though the empirical motivations for action can be extremely varied. The four types of orientation are: *action for utility or profit, action for command or obligation, action for reciprocity, action for free giving*. The first two types do not need clarification. The latter two types are difficult to define and practice in the today's world, but they characterize Relational Subjects.

Acting for reciprocity creates *an exchange where the value is intrinsic and not extrinsic to the social relationship*. That is, it creates (activates and reactivates, generates and regenerates) a social relationship as such, for the super-functional value that it has. The prime motive is not the actor's profit, nor conformity to regulations imposed by some – even if legitimate – power or authority. The actor places her/himself in a relationship where s/he knows that by giving something s/he will receive something: this is the structure of the *symbolic exchange*. There is an exchange, but the exchange is not aimed at obtaining a direct and immediate result, nor is it made for convenience or economic advantage; rather it is *indirect* and *deferred* over time. It draws its value from the fact that those involved act in this way because they are placed, and want to remain, in the circle of the subjects who believe that the value of their social relationship is superior to the results (single services) that the relationship itself offers or produces. Although the relationship is not intrinsically utilitarian, it can have a (derived) utility. Although it is not ruled by public regulation, it can (and almost always must) make allowance for it. Because of this, we say that the actor acts voluntarily: it is within his discretion to enter and exit the relationship, even if it is expected that once he has accepted membership, he will

[26] The *relational* differentiation is a fourth type of social differentiation, different from the three forms usually theorized in sociology (segmented, stratified, and functional differentiation). It refers to a social differentiation based upon the qualities and properties of relations, instead of the criteria used by other forms of distinction: P. Donati, 'Doing Sociology in the Age of Globalization', *World Futures*, 68 (2012), 225–247.

act in a way that will regenerate the bond. This is the world of 'civil associations', which primarily arises to enhance the value of social ties, and only secondarily to realize an instrumental goal (economic utility, power, various types of compensation), as in the case of the economic and political associations.

Free giving action is different. It consists in recognizing the otherness of the *alter*, whose 'existence' as a subject is endowed with his or her own dignity. At the same time, it consists in reporting to this *alter* while contributing something (material or not) for his own good, without asking for anything in a utilitarian (*do ut des*) exchange from him. As distinct from reciprocity, there is not an underlying relational structure between the actors (who gives and who receives), which connects them in terms of reciprocal belonging. Where there is no expectation of (direct or indirect, immediate or delayed) reciprocation, there you have a gift relationship. It is a '*bene facere*' (from which the word 'benefaction' derives) and it consists in making gratuitous gifts (in fact, gifts are not always gratuitous). As a matter of fact a real free gift is rare. More often, it is found inside the (limited or expanded) circuits of reciprocity. There it takes on the role of the 'motor' (initiator, activator) for exchange and social binding. On the empirical level, when we observe a giving action we can identify the type of gift by analyzing the type of relationship that the actor is establishing, or intending to establish, in terms of belonging: that is, whether the act of free giving is made while waiting for a 'return' or not.

Reciprocity and free giving are two ways of acting united by the fact that they share a certain anti-individualism, a certain anti-utilitarianism, and a certain orientation to horizontality (that is, to a non-hierarchical reticular action). For them the problem of identity comes *first*, before the question of interests, even if identity and interest cannot be completely separated.

It follows that the third sector is a way of *combining* these two ways of acting. Taken singularly, reciprocity and giving identify 'pure' forms of action which are rarely found in practice. In general, these two types of action are combined together. They derive their meaning from the fact that they have to distinguish themselves from the other two (obedience to an authority and for-profit reasons). Their identity depends on their being able to continuously re-distinguish themselves from the other spheres (political and mercantile) and from the other actors, by re-affirming the guiding principle that prompted the formation of the Third Sector.[27] For example, when an association whose aim is to spread ecological good practice organizes a public activity, it must continuously reflect whether it is pursuing this objective or other objectives. Similarly, a social foundation that distributes monetary donations must examine whether it really operates to serve the social objectives for which it was founded or is using its mission for the service of an economic or political interest. Finally, a family association which advocates a certain care service (benefits for children, assistance for the elderly, housing for young couples) must reflect on whether or not it is applying the distinction between familiar and non-familiar in what is sought and done.

Given these characteristics, it is not difficult to see both the strengths and the weaknesses of the collective Relational Subjects as third sector social forms. Strength and weakness reside both in their internal structure and in their external relations.

(A) Let us try to understand something more about the dynamics of strength and weakness of these collective Relational Subjects in their internal relationality, as social private associational spheres. Their self-originating character consists in the fact that these subjects uphold their own *ethos*, which flows out, and spreads into

[27] The operation of *re-entry* refers to the logics of George Spencer Brown and has been introduced into sociology by Niklas Luhmann, *Theories of distinction: Redescribing the Descriptions of Modernity* (Stanford, CA: Stanford University Press, 2002). Re-entering a distinction is an operation of reflexive revisitation of what has been established in a previous operation by using the same guiding distinction: for instance, if I ask myself what is my '(true) Self' (by using the distinction myself/not-myself), I start by saying 'I am not this' (I discard this particular identity), then I repeat the same distinction to what has remained of myself and say 'I am not that' (I discard another identity), and so on, until I stop by identifying with what I feel to be the 'real myself'. In the case of a third sector organization, the agent/actor starts by asking her/himself 'what am I?', and in subsequent revisitations s/he will reply by saying 'I am not a commercial entity', 'I am not a state agency', 'I am not something I depend on', 'I am not this and that', etc., etc., until s/he finds the 'core/original identity' in which s/he identifies her/his own 'true Self' as a third sector agent/actor. My criticism of Luhmann's use of the notion of re-entry concerns his dualistic (binary) understanding of the distinction to be made, while I maintain that the distinction is a relation and not a sharp separation between the terms that are distinguished: P. Donati, 'Welche soziale Inklusion? 'Lib/lab'sches Neo-Panopticon und sozietale Staatsbürgerschaft: zwei verschiedene sozialpolitische Strategien', *Soziologisches Jahrbuch*, 16 (2002/2003), 392–426; Donati, *Teoria relazionale della società*, chapter 4.

inter-subjective relationships. This is the factor that distinguishes them from the ethos of the political system, of the market, and of the family. To understand these distinctions, it is helpful to focus upon the *ethos* of a social sphere as a social relationship which becomes distinctive depending on where the 'third part', responsible for animating the morality of the action (by motivating the agency of the individuals), is found. The 'third part' can be placed in one of the four fundamental sub-systems: the political system, the economic, the third sector, or the informal networks (including families).

(i) *In the political system, the relationship of two parts (actors) is ethically underwritten by recourse to a third part*, which is the authority or power of the law (usually identified with the State). In the political sphere, this third part is necessarily external to the inter-subjective relationship, particularly since politics has the task of resolving the intrinsic conflicts between the multiplicity and diversity of the identities and interests, through the means of collectively binding decisions are made that must respect criteria of social equality. It is in this sphere that, according to some thinkers,[28] the gift appears as a 'poisoned gift'. Using the words of Relational Sociology, morality guaranteed by political power often contains poison because (if and when) it treats the third sector with *indifference*, it does not recognize its constitutive ethical difference. If one endorses the idea that the morality of civil society can be guaranteed only by a third 'political' part, then the social private confronts an alternative: it can entrust its ethicality to the political-state power or place it in the individual who, as such, orients himself towards the 'face of the other', according to an inter-subjective relationship outside social rules (this is, in fact, Bauman's solution, which follows Lévinas).

(ii) *In the ideal and atomistic market of perfect competition, like that conceived by abstract political economics, the third part is excluded*, because the market is regulated according to the ethics of supply and demand between contracting individuals (the third part enters only in case of conflict in economic

[28] For example Bauman: see the critique by M. Junge, 'Zygmunt Bauman's poisoned gift of morality', *British Journal of Sociology*, 52 (2001), 105–119.

transactions, because only then can the implicit contracts, rules or customs, legal regulations, or other mechanisms – which are behind the scenes of Adam Smith's 'invisible hand' – become operational). It also becomes clear why, while politics renders the ethos of the third sector indifferent, the market neutralizes it, in that it erases the ethical values of the third sector (seen as incompatible with the principle of monetary and functional equivalence).

(iii) *In the informal networks including families, the third part lies in the well-being of the primary group as a community: these spheres are regulated by the ethics of the gift*, which are placed in the giving-receiving-reciprocating circuits (symbolic exchange) without calculability or individual economic profit. They uphold a principle, redolent of Marx, ('from each according to his/her abilities, to each according to his/her needs'). In this case, the third part which guarantees morality is the ethos of the family or the communitarian group/network, which has a particularistic-affective character. Social relations are valued within this symbolic code, and the sociability which is generated inside it primarily serves the informal group/network itself.

(iv) *In the social private domain, the third part lies in the relationship itself; we could better say that it is the relationship itself.* In terms of expectations, the relationship proper to this sphere is not relationally 'communitarian' as it is in the family or small primary groups. Instead, here social relationality is structurally open to people outside the family and the small group. The social private sphere has permeable borders because it shares certain characteristics with the public sphere, such as the possibility of including people who are not family or may even be strangers, at their request. Ethicality is located in the relationships between the subjects (not the family) who must produce and enjoy a relational benefit together. This benefit does not have the characteristics of a primary relationship as in the family or a closed social group, but has a secondary quality, because it is produced by people who do not have family (or closed group) bonds linking them. In order to produce civil benefits the relationship among members of this social form must have an intrinsic ethicality; it cannot and

> it must not resort to a third part external to the associational sphere. If it regularly resorts to a third part (such as a court or a civic tutor), then the third sector enters into the sphere of 'politics' and entrusts its ethicality to something other than itself. In contrast, if the third part is regularly eliminated it becomes mercantile. Inside the social private sphere of collective Relational Subjects, the gift of morality must not be poisoned, because it constitutes its true identity and its basic reason for existing. When this reason no longer holds, the Relational Subject ceases to exist.

The *ethos* of the Relational Subject is *relational* precisely because it places the 'third part' in the relation itself, in the benefits of the relationship as such, when it is lived in full inter-human reciprocity. If its ethicality were entrusted to the political power, the Relational Subject would make its constitutive social relationship indifferent, and therefore it would become dependent on the political-administrative institutions. If its ethicality were entrusted to the market, it would make its constitutive relationship ethically neutral. If its ethicality were entrusted only to the family, it would build 'family type' relationships, instead of being open to enlarged circuits of reciprocity with strangers and anonymous and distant individuals.

The originality of the social private sphere, which constitutes the collective Relational Subject, refers to the fact that it is a sphere of *sui generis* relationships, which, while carrying its own ethicality, expresses and requires its own normative regulation. To understand this point, we must think in terms of the emergent social effects (as opposed to aggregate effects), that is, we must think of the collective Relational Subject (and the third sector) as an emergent phenomenon.[29] The social relationships peculiar to the Relational

[29] The scientific concept of 'emergent' has a long history. The philosopher George Henry Lewes used the term for the first time in 1875, with regard to the criticism of David Hume's theory of causality. Lewes observed that it is necessary to distinguish between two types of effects: *resulting* and *emergent* (with which the concepts of *output* and *input* respectively correspond). The resulting effect is additive, predictable, and decomposable in its components. In contrast, the emergent effect is not additive, is not predictable from the knowledge of its components, and is not decomposable into its components. The classic Lewes' example is that of the formation of a chemical substance's molecules, starting from the atoms which make it up (for example, hydrogen

Subjects are super-individual realities whose properties are not deducible from those of the individuals who make them work, but are emergents.

We propose a relational understanding, according to which emergent phenomena are the product of a morphogenetic process: the interaction between the individuals occurs in a structural context and modifies it. Once established by individuals, the associative sphere establishing a collective Relational Subject has its own reality, not reducible to the properties of the individuals who compose it, or to something holistic and above it.

The originating elements which characterize collective Relational Subjects are cultural (ethical origin) and normative (the criteria of reciprocity according to which it is organized).[30] These elements represent its strength. The problematic aspects come from the need to find the resources and the situated goals (the operative mission) that are sufficient for and coherent with the originating and original elements. It is here that the major internal weaknesses are found.

In fact, although the collective Relational Subjects use money and power, they cannot resort to these instruments as their primary means: they must search for primary resources of another kind (material and symbolic, human and physical), only then combining them with money and power. The mission itself must continuously be redefined on the operational level. In order to determine the situated goals, the statutory ends are definitely not enough (supposing there is a charter), nor are the ideals that generated the collective Relational Subject as a third sector organization. There must be an internal reflexive activity that continuously re-projects and re-assesses the concrete objectives pursued over time. Furthermore, it must find means appropriate for its objectives. Otherwise, the situated goals become prey to instrumentalism and

and oxygen in the formation of water). The properties of water are emergent effects of the chemical combination of the hydrogen and oxygen atoms under certain conditions. Since then, the concept of emergence has been re-discussed and articulated in various ways by a number of scholars. 'Emergentism' recognizes that the social sphere is an emergent phenomenon in that relations (the social molecules) have different properties from the sum of the qualities of the component elements (unit acts).

30 Culture and norms as acted by agents, according to the distinction between the cultural system and the sociocultural interactions: Margaret S. Archer, *Culture and Agency* (Cambridge: Cambridge University Press, 1988). See Chapter 5 in this volume.

contingency, with the consequence that the collective Relational Subject goes adrift or undergoes a heterogenesis in its objectives.

(B) We shall now take a look at the external relationships (in relation to the State, Market, and families/informal networks). In this connection, the collective Relational Subjects find their strength in the fact that society needs specific forms to produce a particular type of goods, called secondary relational goods.[31] These goods are not the product of a simple aggregation and have a series of connected effects, the first of which is the production of a type of sociability which cannot be found elsewhere. Unlike the State and the Market, the consequences of the actions undertaken by the collective subjects of the third sector are not just 'outputs' (functional, linear, and standardized services), but emergent outcomes (super-functional, non-linear, and non-standardizable relations). These emergent effects can be generated only from the social private sphere which is the growing medium of collective Relational Subjects.

The social private sphere is weak precisely because its intrinsic characteristics make the management of relationships with the external environment difficult. The social private acts on the basis of associational, autonomist and cooperative competition, which has no match elsewhere. The communications are often like a dialogue between the deaf, since they take place between the functional systems of the State and of the Market (reducible to functions) and the super-functional systems of the social private (irreducible to functions). Difficulties emerge along various dimensions: first in terms of functional relations of autonomy and dependence in relation to the external actors; second in terms of the time needed to produce the relational goods (the time of the social private is not the same time of the Market and the State); and finally in terms of the qualities of the goods produced by the social private actors, which are expressive-selfless instead of

[31] Claiming that the collective Relational Subjects have their strength in the fact that society needs relational goods does not mean that these goods are functionalist in nature. On the contrary, my formulation has always been super-functional. The functions of relational goods are not only those required by the 'system', fungible and limited to a discrete number, as they have exactly opposite characteristics. They are non-fungible, non-discrete, and super-allocative.

being instrumental-utilitarian as in the Market-State complex of transactions. As in every social relationship, the theorem about the double contingency of the expectations is valid: the fact that the collective Relational Subjects find difficulties in their dialogue with the State and the Market should not surprise us; it would be strange if the contrary were the case.

As a whole, the strength of the collective Relational Subjects lies in the internal factors from which they originated and in the uses (needs) that the society makes of these social forms. In a word, their strength derives from their peculiarity of being non-fungible and irreducible social subjects. They do not have functional replacements and their properties cannot be explained by the properties of single parts or constitutive elements. However, the strength of these subjects is also the basis for their weaknesses (which are their companions). Their intentions and ties are fragile because of their relatively (relational!) indeterminate qualities. Difficulties are increased, not diminished, by the fact that these subjects emphasize their ideal motivations, their being social private, by subordinating instrumental and operative considerations. However, their originating motives cannot withstand the impact of the external environment, because the social private sphere is disadvantaged when it competes with power or profit-based actions in producing goods or allocating services also supplied by the State and Market. At this macro-societal level the collective Relational Subject is weak and marginal.

Taken as a whole, the sector that includes the collective Relational Subjects can appear to be in continuous 'emergence'. It is constantly suspended between the stimulus towards innovation and the recognition of not being able to attain the desired degrees of effectiveness, efficiency, and equity. Because of this, the third sector fluctuates between the effervescence of novelty, encounter, human warmth, shining ideals, and the relapse into the colder, bureaucratic, instrumental and routine forms of action. Yet, this is exactly the way of existing and of 'making society' characteristic of the third sector.

The new relational scenario

Highly modernized societies are shifting from a *non-relational* culture to a way of thinking which is centred on *relationality* as a central category to interpret the human condition and the ways to achieve a full, genuine flourishing of the person and of humanity. Thinking of this kind requires a *deeper evaluation of the category of social relations*. This is what is changing the meaning (historical, cultural, and contextual) of what 'being human' signifies.

Late modernity produces widespread degradations of social life. It generates many emergencies in education, unemployment, and denial of fundamental human rights in so many parts of the globe. Since the social question has become a radically anthropological question, a new society needs an adequate anthropology, that is, an anthropology capable of casting light on all humankind's social relations.

The way out of modernity's failures can be called 'relational', given the fact that it is in the realm of relations that a solution is to be sought. As a spiritual being, the human creature is defined through interpersonal relations. The more authentically he or she lives out these relations, the more his or her own personal identity matures. It is not in isolation that any human being establishes his/her worth, but by placing him/herself in relation with others and the whole world. Relationality becomes an essential element in defining what is human.

The quality of social relations is identified with what people love most, the ultimate concerns they express in their social relations. These concerns are not synonymous with 'nice feelings', but rather they are *certain relations* with oneself, with neighbours and with those who are influenced by our own deeds. Human beings have to care for networks of social relationality. Society is promoted not merely by relationships of rights and duties, but to an even greater and more fundamental extent by relationships of reciprocity, solidarity, cooperation, that is, by a new meaning of what is 'civil'.

In sum: the idea that the social relations in which civil relations are made concrete, can and must turn from being marginal and marginalized occurrences in modern society into principles occupying a primary place in most practical matters, such as the ways of organizing and managing economic enterprises, consumer associations, unions, social service networks, the welfare state, the relations among different groups of people, and so forth. This needs to extend all the way up to the macro-level underwriting the articulation of society, the way of 'setting up societies' (associations in the broad sense of the word), based on a *governance* of a societal and plural type, which realizes the common good through a combination of solidarity and subsidiarity between all society's parts. This holds true from a small organization right up to international relations.

What, though, can induce men and women to take this path, given that the present globalization process is led by rampant capitalism, by ever more pervasive individualism, by clear signs of separation and fragmentation of the social fabric?

Here again emerges the importance of the relational key as a novelty. In fact, beyond well-known issues (the call for integral human development, to fight old and new forms of poverty, etc.), relationality can supply the blueprint and the *unbreakable link* that characterizes what is human.

From this perspective the common good is reinterpreted as a relational good, which can only be achieved by making an appropriate and combined use of the solidarity and subsidiarity principles, on the basis of a relational anthropology and a relational view of society as a whole. In order to go beyond the present domination of the binomial Market-State (*lib/lab* in my language), which destroys sociality, we need much more than good, honest, and altruistic individuals: we need a societal configuration able to generate *relational goods*. The relational good is the name of the common good in a highly differentiated and globalized society. Its bearer is what we can call 'the Relational Subject'.

In a sociological perspective, this means: (i) that we have to see social inclusion as *relational inclusion*,[32] that is, a form of social inclusion achieved not through the State or the Market, but through the joint work of subsidiarity and solidarity among the different social subjects of society; and (ii) that we have to see social differentiation as not merely functional but as *relational differentiation*, that is both auto- and hetero-poietic in respect to the super-functional needs which are to be met in every social sphere.

This means that twenty-first century society has to make a new departure where civil society is concerned. Nowadays, this entails the fact that a New Deal no longer depends on the State alone or on the Market alone, or on a combination of the two, but on the network between State, Market, and civil society (the last being identified in particular, but not exclusively, with third sector organizations). Such

[32] P. Donati, 'Oltre la crisi dello Stato sociale: dal codice inclusione/esclusione al codice relazionale/non relazionale', *Sociologia e Politiche Sociali*, 2 (1999), 195–220: P. Donati, *Relational Sociology. A New Paradigm for the Social Sciences* (London: Routledge, 2011), p. 231.

a network needs to be implemented as a relational network, not as a knot structure (Figure 7.4). A decisive role is assigned to the relational economy, with its prototypical though not exclusive expression in the third sector, capable of providing ethical inputs into state and market. Yet, as demonstrated by empirical sociological research,[33] the third sector in turn needs inputs from which to devise a culture capable of upholding goods and services as social relations, rather than as the means to make money. Such inputs come from the primary networks of families and of interpersonal relations.

Prospects for a new 'way of making society'

The *world system* based on the financialization not only of economy, but of all social relations, experiences a chronic crisis and has to be reconverted. But how? In the present chapter, I have argued that we do not have to resort to an abstract societal 'model', but rather to facilitate some ways of life (forms of *modus vivendi*), that is, ways of operating and making society, which trace out the basic practices of a civil society that is not subordinate to the compromise between State and Market.

It is possible to apply a notion of 'reconversion' to the new civil society by analogy with what happened to market reconversion, when we shifted from an economy based on large industrial concerns to the information and knowledge economy. It can be defined as a reconversion of *civil* society if we think of it as a 'bottom up' promotion of networks of social relations which do not respond to functional imperatives imposed by state laws and with monetary equivalence criteria, but meet the need to create relational goods. These are the new Relational Subjects working to lead society beyond the *lib/lab* configuration. The reconfiguration of civil society according to the scenario just outlined will redefine the State and Market as well.

Certainly, present societal configurations are characterized by great disparities between countries. The gap between the two sides of the Atlantic is well known. In the USA the market is typically *lib* and is celebrated as such. Conversely, in Europe (in the EU), the market

[33] P. Donati and I. Colozzi (eds.), *Generare 'il civile'* (Bologna: il Mulino, 2001); H. K. Anheier, G. Rossi, and L. Boccacin (eds.), *The Social Generative Action of the Third Sector. Comparing International Experiences* (Milano: Vita e Pensiero, 2008).

proclaims itself as 'social' and is celebrated as such. In actual fact, though, in both cases the societal model pursued is the *lib/lab* one, as evidenced by the continuing state and federal intervention in the USA and by the increasing practice of resorting to market privatization (disguised as applications of the subsidiarity principle) in Europe. In the end, not only Europe and North America, but every continent seems to need the new development model that has been outlined here.

The argument that has been put forward is that, as globalization proceeds, a latent social sphere emerges where *sui generis* social relations are established. These relations give life to associative networks that are privately established and managed and guided by pro-social values and action orientations. Being 'private' means that these types of social relations can discretionally select their own openings and closures towards the public sphere, because they are not dependent *ex ante* on a political administrative power. Being 'pro-social' means that they do not act for the profit of their singular members. The possibility of these associational actors achieving useful practical results (including economic profit) is not excluded, as these positive outcomes are necessary for their survival. The point is that these results are considered as instrumental requirements which are subordinated to the not-for-profit ends.

These latent social spheres *become* what we call 'third sector' when they project themselves into the public sphere and connect with the state and the market, that is, when the social private spheres need to be recognized and legitimized by the other public and private actors and must establish reciprocal expectations (therefore also agreements, contracts, etc.) with them. What we call Relational Subjects are networks of relationships where trust, cooperation, and reciprocity are generated. In the sociological sense they represent a 'common world', which is neither private nor public in the modern meaning of these two terms.[34] These 'social private' spheres become what is called the 'third sector' when they assume the part of a social institution that needs to be recognized by the State and the Market, namely when the third

[34] It is interesting to observe that, echoing back to a sociological tradition that goes from H. Arendt to J. Habermas, the term '*social*' indicates a sphere which is neither private nor public in the strict sense, nor a mix between the two, as it *remains on another level* by referring to dialogic relations.

sector must negotiate and have formal relations with the political and economic actors.

Collective Relational Subjects can be recognized in the public sphere in many different ways, ones that correspond more or less to their original impulses, but can also change over time. The processes that ensue can take different directions and bring about different results, which in part were intended and in part were not. The corporate Relational Subject then becomes either a *de facto* or a legally recognized associational formation. It can become a volunteer organization or a social solidarity cooperative; it can become a pro-social association, or, more generally a non-profit organization, or still another kind of organization (civil committees, groups of mutual assistance, peer production, social streets, etc.). This outcome depends on the modalities and the opportunities available and the motivations which the network of relationships among the members can configure between them.

8 *Relational Subjects and the ravages of globalized markets: the need for subjects with relational ethics*

PIERPAOLO DONATI

The problem: the moral responsibility for market outcomes 'at a distance'

Let us start by identifying the problem. A huge literature has demonstrated that the globalization of economic markets is producing widespread ravages all over the world, in terms of the appearance of new inequalities, pauperization processes, and attacks on human rights in many parts of the globe.[1] We ask ourselves: who is responsible for the harm that one or more market agents/actors[2] bring to bear on distant others in an impersonal and unintentional way? The 'others' can be single individuals, vast social groups, and even entire populations.

A question like this becomes more and more relevant in so far as the capitalist economy becomes fully globalized. The issues of agents/actors' morality in the era of globalization cannot be dealt with by traditional ethical norms.

Traditional ethics claims that moral responsibility can be direct, indirect, or adiaphoric.[3]

[1] S. Walby, *Globalization and Inequalities. Complexity and Contested Modernities* (London: Sage, 2009).

[2] With the term *agent,* reference is made to the subject's freedom; with the term *actor,* reference is made to the social role occupied by the subject. *Actors* are subjects who act in the roles of *functional* systems. *Agents* are subjects who act in systems of *interdependence*, both interactive and structural. The harm that market agents/actors cause to 'distant' others can come from functional systems as well as from systems of interdependence, but their moral responsibility is different.

[3] Adiaphoric responsibility is 'technical' responsibility which cannot be judged in the strictly moral terms of good/evil – for example, when a manager says: 'Oh, the dismissal of these workers was decided by the market laws, not by me!'. *Adiaphoron* (plural: *adiaphora* from the Greek ἀδιάφορα 'indifferent things') is a concept of Stoic philosophy that indicates things outside moral law, that is, actions that morality neither mandates nor forbids. In Christianity *adiaphora*

It seems relatively easy to identify direct moral responsibility when, for example, a financial trader directly sells tainted financial products without informing clients of the elevated risk of loss, or when the owner of a sweat shop exploits underage or female workers, violating basic human rights. In these cases, *Ego* inflicts direct harm on *Alter,* who is a proximal (near) person, which does not exclude the possibility of harm done to third parties as well.

But what can we say when economic action is undertaken with the intention of harming no one, yet causes negative effects? Take the example of the decision to move investments in order to create work and wealth in one location when this decision involuntarily causes unemployment and poverty in other locations.

Traditional moral theory usually applies the principle of *double effect* (or the principle of the *indirect volunteer*). As commonly formulated, this principle establishes that it is possible legitimately to allow or tolerate a bad effect that comes about through an act of choice if four conditions are met: (1) the action in itself, apart from the harm caused, is good or at least indifferent; (2) the good effect of the action is what the agent directly intends, only thereby allowing the bad effect to occur; (3) the good effect must not be obtained by means of the bad effect; and (4) the path must be the only one possible or, at least, there must be a proportionately grave reason to allow the negative effect to happen.[4]

refer to matters not regarded as essential to faith, but nevertheless as permissible for Christians or allowed by the church. This concept was resuscitated by the Catholic canonists (Canon Law) in the Middle Ages, and later on it became very important in the Christian world. In practice, all the denominations (Calvinists, Anglicans, etc.) developed an 'ethics' of adiaphoric responsibility. So, many scholars understand and use it in ethics today. What is specifically considered *adiaphora* depends on the specific theology/ethics in question. Here I am referring to the 'adiaphoric society' spoken of by Z. Bauman, *Postmodern Ethics* (Oxford: Blackwell, 1993) and to the 'adiaphoric company' addressed by T. Jensen, 'Beyond Good and Evil: The Adiaphoric Company', *Journal of Business Ethics*, 96 (2010), 425–434. This is surely the dominant ethics today in the Western world. But from the standpoint of Relational Sociology, to maintain that there is an ethics of *adiaphora* – an ethics of that falling outside the moral realm (indifferent actions) – is highly disputable because it presupposes that there are actions – and therefore social relations – without any moral dimension, i.e. actions and relations that are morally 'neutral'.

4 W. May, 'Double Effect', in W. T. Reich (ed.), *Encyclopedia of Bioethics* (New York: MacMillan Library Reference U.S.A., 1978), p. 316; J. L. A. Garçia, 'Double Effect', in *Encyclopedia of Bioethics* (*ibid.*, revised edition, 1995), p. 637.

If these criteria are met, the honest individual investor can feel at ease. But is this really how things are? Is it enough to have honest individuals in order to achieve an equitable and fair market?

The moral criterion of the 'indirect volunteer' presupposes a 'linear' society where the intentionality and causality of social action can be established with certainty. However, in a society in which interactions and relations are increasing and are marked by circularities and long causal chains, this principle goes haywire.

A society in the process of globalization increases the cases in which the morality of action is problematic because action has a multiplicity of effects that, for the most part, are not grasped by the individual subject of the action.[5] The reason for this resides in the fact that the reticularity of society is increasing significantly, that is, the production of effects that are the outcome of complex social networks is increasing.

There was a time when people wondered whether the moral responsibility for poverty should be imputed to the fact that the poor are lazy, incapable, or maladapted or, instead, to certain economic and social structures. Put in these terms, the question today appears disingenuous and simplistic. The social sciences have demonstrated that a reciprocal

[5] In my view, 'subject' (Latin: *subiectus* "lying beneath") refers to a human agent/actor who causes an action, and therefore is causally and, under certain conditions, morally responsible for that action, whatever kind of action (internal or external to the agent/actor) it may be. The subject can be an *individual person* or a social group having in common a social identity, and therefore called a '*collective agent/actor*'. The latter is constituted by a network of people collaborating for some publicly relevant reason and having joint liability towards external agents/actors (i.e. a 'moral person', as defined by Thomas Aquinas; e.g. a family or a corporation). Both the single person and collective agents/actors are 'Relational Subjects': I call the former a 'primary Relational Subject' ('primary' refers to first-order agency), and the latter a 'secondary Relational Subject' ('secondary' refers to the secondary-level agency, in its associational form). Sociologically, the notion of a subject is necessary in order to attribute actions, which may be individual or collective, to a social (i.e. relational, not physical) cause. As a relational and critical realist, I assume that behind (or, if you prefer, 'beneath') an action – be it individual or joint – there should be a human agent/actor, single or collective (properly speaking, animals do not 'act', nor have social relations). I am against the constructionists (like Luhmann) who maintain that the notion of the 'subject' is 'mystical', so that they reduce the 'subject' to nothing but a reference point for communication, and only for communication (to them, 'communication' does not mean to make a thing common – *co-munus*, as in classical philosophy – but only a transfer of information).

influence exists between structure and agency: indeed, there is a real and complex interplay between these factors,[6] so that the problem of knowing who/what is responsible for the condition of poverty of certain individuals and social groups becomes one of knowing how the acting subjects and social structures influence one another. The social sciences have demonstrated for some time now that agents/actors' (direct, indirect, or adiaphoric) moral responsibility can never be separated from the societal structures[7] within which they operate.

Who bears the moral responsibility for the fact that broad strata of society do not have equal life chances as compared with those who enjoy more favourable positions? It is easy to impute the cause of this social fact to societal structures that were produced in the past, for which no one in the present is responsible. Yet the fact is that structures do not think or act by themselves. They are not imposed on the human mind, as some assert (for example, Mary Douglas). Structures' causality is always mediated by agency. Nevertheless, structures do count for at least two broad orders of reasons: (i) because they define the field of immediately accessible opportunities, and (ii) because they place constraints on agents in terms of incentives and sanctions.

This is our problem: given that the responsibility of agents is proportional to their freedom, it is a matter of understanding what freedom agents enjoy *vis-à-vis* market structures in order to prevent the harm that their actions bring to bear on distant others as a result of the causal mechanisms inherent in the market. Obviously, it is presumed that the agents are not immoral or amoral subjects, in which case they would have a direct moral responsibility.

Ostensibly, phenomena such as unemployment, poverty, and undeserved inequalities in life and work opportunities are phenomena that individuals reproduce, but for which they cannot be imputed direct moral responsibility because these are effects that do not depend on their intentions and individual wills. But is it really so? To whom or what should we impute the moral responsibility for harm caused to 'distant others' by actions that the agents/actors carry out in a licit and rational way from the point of view of the market?

[6] Margaret S. Archer, *Realist Social Theory: The Morphogenetic Approach* (Cambridge: Cambridge University Press, 1995).

[7] The term 'societal structures' will indicate from now on the structures of society in its various economic, political, cultural, and social articulations.

The prevailing answers on offer

The answers generally offered by economists consist in claiming that we are dealing with the unintended consequences of free market 'laws'. Harm is conceptualized as a 'side effect' or 'negative externality'. Harm caused to distant others is held to be the inevitable consequence of freedom as the guiding value of the social institution of the market and, thus, a contingency that is intrinsic to it. Redress can be thought of only *ex post* once rock-bottom has been reached.[8]

In democratic regimes one expects that *ex post* consequences will be tempered and countered by political systems. This is what the *master plan* of Western nations says, in effect: on the one hand, it is necessary to stimulate interaction between forces of the free market and of competition while, on the other hand, equality of opportunity must be guaranteed to all citizens.[9] The State is assigned the task of redressing the free market's failures by means of legislation that regulates economic transactions and compensates those who are harmed through public welfare interventions (in a collective and impersonal way). This is the societal arrangement that I call *lib/lab*.[10]

The social sciences, however, point out that the market is a structure (or system) endowed with an ontological reality which, in a necessary and intrinsic manner, unintentionally harms distant others in a variety of ways, whether within single nations or in the relationship between developed and developing countries. These effects are called '*unintentional structural* effects', precisely to indicate that they depend on mechanisms that elude the power of individuals. When

[8] This is the logic clarified by G. Teubner, 'A Constitutional Moment. The Logics of 'Hit the Bottom', in P. Kjaer and G. Teubner (eds.), *The Financial Crisis in Constitutional Perspective: The Dark Side of Functional Differentiation* (Oxford: Hart, 2011), pp. 3–42.

[9] In this way the *master plan* of the new European construction was formulated, based on the *lib/lab* ideology. But the statement also holds for almost all Western countries.

[10] P. Donati, 'The End of Classical Liberalism in the Lib/lab Interplay: What After', in E. Banús and A. Llano (eds.), *Present and Future of Liberalism* (Pamplona: Eunsa, 2004), pp. 169–212. In brief, the *lib/lab* configuration of society is a compromise between the liberal (*lib*) side of capitalist markets (free economy) and the socialist (*lab*) side of the welfare entitlements and equal opportunities guaranteed by the state (political system).

they deviate from the actors' intentions, they are called '*perverse* effects'.[11]

Yet we wonder: is it really true that these mechanisms are inevitable and the effects unexpected? If it is true that these structures do not depend on the power of individuals, can we assert, for this reason, that harm to distant others does not have to do with the moral responsibilities of the agents/actors?

The prevailing answers on offer (direct, indirect, and adiaphoric) attribute responsibility to the structures that condition the agents/actors. Western societies, in as much as they are founded on the compromise between individualistic liberalism and social-democratic holism (the *lib/lab* configuration), abundantly legitimate these answers. In these societies, the welfare state arose and developed precisely in order to render individuals' responsibility collective and impersonal. Liberal culture and socialist culture ended up converging as they relieved agents/actors of their moral responsibility. How and why did this strange convergence come about?

My explanation is that, although they have different conceptions of the social, liberals (individualists) and socialists (holists) end up attributing the moral responsibility for the harm we are discussing to structures and not to agents, due to the fact that both standpoints lack a relational view of society.

On the one hand, the holists understand the social realm in a positivistic way, that is, as a structure that overshadows relations and interactions among human beings and conditions them as if it were a physical or biological law. For this reason, they believe that single agents/actors do not have moral responsibility – whether direct or indirect. The preferred solution is to consider agents' action as morally adiaphoric. As to the harm inflicted, one can only exclaim: *c'est la vie!* This explanation is a form of *downward conflation* from structures to agents.[12]

On the other hand, individualists understand the social realm as an arbitrary and conventional construction. Social causality, societal

[11] R. Boudon, *Effets perverse et ordre social* (Paris: Puf, 1989). The fact that Boudon designates these effects as 'unexpected' evidently depends on the fact that he is not able to give an explanation for them. In point of fact, Boudon assimilates the unintentional, aggregate, and emergent effects, without distinguishing them in an analytical way.

[12] On the three forms of conflation (downward, upward, central conflation), see Archer, *Realist Social Theory*.

structures, and moral responsibility are considered to be merely contingent notions[13] and, thus, always susceptible of modification. Harm to distant others is conceived of as a pure 'possibility' that goes beyond the subjective responsibility of agents. The explanation for societal structures that generate harm (such as poverty, unemployment, unjust inequalities) takes on the form of an *unintentional upward conflation.* According to this view, the answer regarding the role of social structures becomes purely nominalistic. No single agent/actor can assume responsibility for the final outcome.

Hard (holistic) conceptions and weak (individualistic) conceptions of the social structure both end up nullifying the moral responsibility of agents/actors. Systems theorists shift responsibility on to societal structures (defined as adiaphoric). The theorists of individualism undermine the concepts of structure and agents' moral responsibility relative to social facts.

A different viewpoint

I do not share either of these two explanatory modalities. My thesis is another one. I would like to argue for the following point of view.

The social mechanisms or devices that cause certain effects (such as harm to strangers) are not a structure (either strong or weak) that determines agents/actors' behaviour in a compulsive or nominalistic way. Social mechanisms are relational, in the sense that they are made of social relations that are generated by individuals and by the superindividual social subjects that they create. Societal structures are institutionalized social relations, which are the product of networks of relations.[14] For this reason, there exists a moral responsibility on

[13] Contingency understood not as 'dependence on' but rather as 'being able not to be' and thus as 'being always able to be otherwise' (different, in another way).

[14] There are many and diverse conceptions of social structure. D. V. Porpora, 'Four Concepts of Social Structure', *Journal for the Theory of Social Behaviour*, 19 (1989), 195–211. I find interesting the essay by D. Elder-Vass ('Searching for Realism, Structure and Agency in Actor Network Theory', *British Journal of Sociology*, 59 (2008), 455–473), in which he defines social structures through four dimensions: the dimension incorporated in the agents/actors (embodied structure), the institutional dimension (institutional structure), the relational dimension (relational structure), and the emergent dimension (emergent structure). I think that these four faces of social structure are necessary, complementary, and interactive among themselves. In my opinion, they can be understood as the four dimensions that make up the structure according to the AGIL scheme, understood in a relational and not a

the part of individual and collective subjects for outcomes, even for the unwanted outcomes produced in the processes of morphostasis/ morphogenesis of social structures.[15] However, in order to see what is at stake, it is necessary to understand what is meant by the fact that social structures are made *by* individuals, but are not made *of* individuals in as much as they are *made of relations*, and it is here – in the relational dynamic – that the problem of moral responsibility is to be found.

For example, poverty, unemployment, and inequality brought about involuntarily are the product of networks of social relations: indeed, they are themselves social relations for which all actors, whether close at hand or distant, share, in different forms and degrees, some moral responsibility.

Yet we must be careful. If we adopt a relational perspective, there is the risk of falling into a position of circular relativism. The risk is that of locating moral responsibility in a sort of hermeneutic circle in which subjects' and structures' responsibilities alternatively chase after each other and merge (*central conflation*).[16] George Soros[17] offers an example of this when he says that economic structures are produced *by* the expectations ('reflexive rationality') of financial operatives (on the stock exchange, in particular) and, at the same time, consist *of* such expectations, which discount the future. In short, it is assumed that the structures of the financial markets are made by the reflexive truths

functionalist sense (P. Donati, *Relational Sociology. A New Paradigm for the Social Sciences* (London: Routledge, 2011), pp. 147–154).

[15] Morphostasis here refers to a simple reproduction of social forms (structures), whereas morphogenesis indicates the generation of new forms (Archer, *Realist Social Theory*).

[16] Examples of theories that commit the fallacy of central conflation are those of A. Giddens and U. Beck.

[17] In the view of G. Soros ('Reflexivity in Financial Markets' in his *Open Society. Reforming Global Capitalism*, New York: Public Affairs, 2000, pp. 58–90), we are destined to live increasingly in a world in which there are not only true or false statements (i.e. in which there is or there is not correspondence between knowledge and reality), but where a third type of truth exists, 'reflexive truth', i.e. the truth of historical facts (especially economic and political facts) in which it is the expectations of participating agents that modify reality and, therefore, also the knowledge of reality that we define as true or false. A student of Popper, Soros understands reflexivity as the capacity of markets to amplify tendencies to the point that the equilibriums of the economy are mutated. He maintains that investors use a 'reflexive rationality' even if they must acknowledge the fact that the outcomes of this 'rationality' are irrational.

of financial agents, who reproduce them in terms of expectations, so that market outcomes can be completely irrational without it being possible to clearly attribute the causes to structures or agents.[18] In a rather more refined way, Luhmann speaks of reflexive systems that are based on learning to learn, without any finalism.[19]

This is the danger of '*relationism*', that is, of adopting a view that locates responsibility in the pure circularity of relations among market subjects, who create the economic structures by which they are defined as market agents/actors. In order to avoid relationism, it is necessary to adopt an *authentically relational* perspective (I shall say later in what sense), which consists in identifying the specific responsibility of each term of the relations and, at the same time, the causality imputable to the subjects' relations as emergent effects.

Who or what causes impersonal harm to distant others? An analytical scheme regarding the role of social structures

Prevailing explanations of causality imputable to social structures

Emergent structural effects can have various sociological and economic explanations. The comparison almost always takes place between holistic explanations and individualistic explanations, although for years now theories have been proposed that reject this alternative in favour of 'relational' explanations. However, a great deal of confusion reigns in the camp of relational theories.[20]

18 If it were so, social reality would simply be constructed by agents' expectations, which anticipate the future. This statement denies objective reality and presupposes that the market is constituted by amoral agents (I do not say 'immoral'). In other words, he makes improper use of Thomas' theorem (according to which, if Ego believes a thing to be true, such a belief is not necessarily true in itself, but it is true in its consequences) because he considers agents' expectations as if they were the truth of things.

19 N. Luhmann, *Reflexionsprobleme im Erziehungssysteme* (Stuttgart: Ernst Klett, 1979).

20 Many claim to be in favour of a relational approach, but very few focus on the social relation as such. As just one example, Bottero affirms: 'Bourdieu's approach is *relational* but does not focus on *social relationships*, understood as social networks or as an interactional order.' (W. Bottero, 'Relationality and Social Interaction', *British Journal of Sociology*, 60 (2009), 399–420, quotation p. 399). Personally, I have analyzed the different conceptions of the

Holistic explanations prevail in the field of sociology.[21] The most widely held version explains and justifies structural effects as expressions (products) of system requirements in that unintentional effects fulfil certain functions that are necessary to the social system.[22] The paradigmatic theory in this regard is the functionalist one (in its various versions). In this view, there is no responsibility of single social actors, whether individual or collective. If the law of competition demands that the prices of merchandise be kept low, the individual entrepreneur has no choice but to pay lower wages and resort to lay-offs – and cannot worry about the consequences for workers' families. It is noteworthy that functional systems give primacy to the adaptive function.[23]

The possible impersonal social harm brought to bear on distant persons ('distant others') is seen as inevitable, and even morally indifferent, because it is essential to the good functioning of social systems. A certain number of unemployed and poor workers is considered to be an inevitable systemic fact for which market agents/actors do not bear responsibility because the economic system functions only if there is the mechanism constituted by a certain quota of the workforce that is always available to enter or exit the labour market, as warranted by

social relation in the principle sociological approaches (Donati, 'Society as a Relation', in *Relational Sociology. A New Paradigm for the Social Sciences*, London: Routledge, 2011, chapter 2) and have reached the conclusion that almost no approach has a truly relational view of the social relation.

21 Holistic explanations derive to a great extent from the mechanistic interpretations contained in the theories of Karl Marx, Emile Durkheim, and Vilfredo Pareto.

22 We are reminded of the famous polemic between Kingsley Davis and Wilbert Moore, on one side, and Melvin Tumin, on the other. Davis and Moore's thesis was that 'social inequality is . . . an unconsciously evolved device by which societies ensure that the most important positions are conscientiously filled by the most qualified persons.' (K. Davis and W. E. Moore, 'Some principles of stratification', *American Sociological Review*, 10: 2, 1945, 242–249, p. 243). Tumin criticized this functionalist explanation of inequality, maintaining instead that 'social stratification systems function to provide the elite with the political power necessary to procure acceptance and dominance of an ideology which rationalizes the *status quo*, whatever it may be, as "logical," "natural," and "morally right." In this manner social stratification systems function as essentially conservative influences in the societies in which they are found." (M. M. Tumin, 'Some Principles of Stratification: A Critical Analysis', *American Sociological Review*, 18, 1953, 387–393, quotation p. 393).

23 That is, to the A function of AGIL in the version of Luhmann. An extensive analysis of this subject can be found in P. Donati, *Teoria relazionale della società* (Milano: FrancoAngeli, 1991), pp. 214–237.

contingencies.[24] Is this holistic point of view acceptable on the scientific level? In my opinion, it is not acceptable once the so-called 'functional imperatives' (or the alleged 'laws') of the system are demonstrated to be neither necessary nor inevitable.

In the field of economic theory, the opposite point of view prevails, inspired by some version of methodological individualism. A great many mainstream economists hold that structural effects are 'perverse' effects (unexpected and unintentional) due (i) to deviations from market mechanisms' optimal functional mode (which is when there is perfect competition), and (ii) to potential and concomitant defects in the regulation that should be guaranteed by political systems (with legislation on the labour market and redistribution effected by the welfare state). According to prevailing economic policy, the perfect market should not produce negative structural effects – such as poverty, for example – but only positive structural effects – such as legitimate or deserved inequality, for example. Harm to distant others is considered an effect of deviation from norms. The recipe for avoiding social harm thus consists in: (i) correcting those market mechanisms that do not correspond to perfect competition; (ii) correcting welfare state mechanisms that do not guarantee equality of opportunity for individuals in the market and that, on the contrary, generate poverty traps and other similar forms of harm.

In short: a great deal of social thought holds that impersonal harm brought to bear on distant others is the product of long chains of exchanges in which single exchanges can be rational and legitimate, in keeping with market rules.[25] The 'responsibility' for such phenomena is imputed to 'mechanisms' or 'devices' that produce an allocation of resources that is not efficient and/or equitable. If the market system

[24] It is well known that Marx called it capitalism's 'reserve army' and explained it as being the product of dominant economic laws. But this theory today appears simplistic and unacceptable.

[25] If we observe attentively holistic and individualistic explanations of structural effects, we notice that they often become synergic and end up converging when the market is treated as a social system. Examples come from illustrious names, such as Raymond Boudon, Ralph Dahrendorf, Pierre Bourdieu, James Coleman, and many others. These authors converge in giving a system explanation for the perverse effects within the model of society that I have called *lib/lab*. P. Donati, *Il lavoro che emerge. Prospettive del lavoro come relazione sociale in una economia dopo-moderna* (Turin: Bollati Boringhieri, 2001), pp. 202–227. This model of society is built on the presupposition that individuals are relieved as much as possible of their personal responsibilities.

functioned correctly ('perfectly') in accordance with Adam Smith's mercantile ethics,[26] inequality would be only what is deserved by the individual, and poverty would be caused by factors (such as illness, handicaps, or old age) that could be countered solely by means of policy, that is, by assigning the responsibility to redress these problems to the State (the welfare state), and to private charity (such as charitable organizations of the Church). This is also what the Catholic Church's traditional social doctrine recommends.[27]

What I want to underscore here is the fact that negative outcomes (poverty, unemployment, unjust inequality) are imputed to ethically wrong behaviours and to unjust rules while it is assumed that, if agents are 'ethical' and rules just, ethically good outcomes will automatically be produced – which is not true. From this stems the fact that redress for the social harm produced by actions that are licit and rational in themselves *is sought in a different distribution of resources (output), rather than in a change in the network of relations that produces the harm at a distance.* The actors ask for compensation for those who are harmed from a more generous welfare state, that is, through redistributive measures by public means. The responsibility for harm brought to bear on distant others, caused by behaviours that are ethically legitimate in themselves, is considered *ex post* and shifted on to impersonal mechanisms of public welfare rather than influencing the mechanisms that produce negative outcomes from actions that are ethically valid in themselves.

The outcome of this logic is always to resort once again to compromise between State and Market (the *lib/lab* arrangement). According to this reading of the processes, individuals do not bear either direct or indirect responsibility for the impersonal harm inflicted on distant others. The responsibility for social evils falls to the political collectivity, which should provide redress through impersonal measures (*l'État-Providence* as a safeguarding principle that lightens the burden of individuals' personal responsibility, or completely relieves them of it).

This solution is not satisfactory for many reasons. First, it risks making single agents unaccountable. Single agents do not have to change

[26] C. L. Griswold, Jr., *Adam Smith and the Virtues of Enlightenment* (Cambridge: Cambridge University Press, 1999).

[27] Not only in the encyclical *Rerum Novarum* (1891) of Leo XIII, but also recently. See, for example, the second part of the encyclical of Benedict XVI, *Deus Caritas Est* (2005), sections 22–39.

their preferences and can shift their personal responsibility onto the collectivity. Second, it is not satisfactory because, as the history of the welfare state demonstrates, the solution that proposes to redress social evils by socializing harm through a continuous broadening of social citizenship of a *lib/lab* type[28] multiplies the State's pervasive powers without civilizing the Market, given that it reinforces these same Market mechanisms.

Do alternatives exist? In my opinion, we need to begin by acknowledging that markets have become complex systems that no longer answer to linear logics.[29] Systems develop networks that are black boxes in which each social relation is a system that is refractory to its environment, so that the quality of that relation is regulated inside the system without it being possible to see the consequences from the outside.[30]

Traditional ethics finds itself in a position of difficulty precisely because it is still anchored to linear thinking, that is, to finalistic principles and to principles of linear causality, while market systems have expunged finalism and operate via functions and without a principle of linear causality.[31]

[28] See Ralph Dahrendorf's theory of citizenship: 'The Changing Quality of Citizenship', in B. van Steenberger (ed.), *The Condition of Citizenship* (London: Sage, 1994), pp. 10–19.

[29] From *Stanford Encyclopedia of Philosophy*: 'Linear logic is a refinement of classical and intuitionistic logic. Instead of emphasizing *truth*, as in classical logic, or *proof*, as in intuitionistic logic, linear logic emphasizes the role of formulas as *resources*. To achieve this focus, linear logic does not allow the usual structural rules of contraction and weakening to apply to all formulas but only those formulas marked with certain modals. Linear logic contains a fully involutive negation while maintaining a strong constructive interpretation. Linear logic also provides new insights into the nature of proofs in both classical and intuitionistic logic. Given its focus on resources, linear logic has found many applications in Computer Science.'

[30] According to Luhmann (*Social Systems*, Palo Alto, CA: Stanford University Press, 1995): 'systems develop forms of access to complexity that are not available to scientific analysis and simulation . . . <black boxes>' (*ibid.*, p. 14); '*every social contact is understood as a system*' (*ibid.*, p. 15); 'As soon as one goes beyond quantitative theory toward qualification, one can no longer forgo considering that and how systems qualify as elements of the elements that compose them' (*ibid.*, p. 20f).

[31] As Luhmann points out (*ibid.*, p. 302): 'We can seek points of departure for increasing orientation to function, up to what is relatively improbable, in a stronger differentiation between action and observation . . . that at the same time does not question the communicative execution of self-observation. We

Confronted with the functionalistic behaviour of globalized markets, one cannot but wonder whether there still exists the possibility of affirming a humanistic point of view that vindicates the active role of the human person and his/her capacity for modifying purely functional systems on the basis of ideal finalities. It is easy to see the conflict between the neo-functionalist perspective (which holds that all that which is possible for agents/actors is ethically licit, without it being possible to guide the system ethically)[32] and the humanistic perspective (according to which, because social structures are the product of human persons, the latter can change them, giving them an ethical finality).[33] From the sociological point of view, the latter perspective seems to be losing ground and is impossible to maintain, not only because it presupposes an ethics that goes against the utilitarian primacy of the market, but also because it does not take into account the market's perverse effects when agents/actors are honest and the market's rules respect ethical constraints.

What hope does the humanistic perspective have? Or put another way: is it possible to alter market rules by introducing ethics as an independent variable that functions as a constraint on economic activity, considered not only in the single act, but in the causal chain at a distance?

In my view, the answer is negative if we conceive of the markets as functional systems, even if guided by an ethics. This can be the ethics of

thereby avoid teleological explanations, and also causal explanations . . . the hypothesis is that . . . it becomes probable that relatively improbable (more demanding, e.g. more specialized) functional orientations will take place and select corresponding structures.'

32 The most exemplary theory is that of Luhmann.

33 Here are situated the theories of Archer, Donati, and Smith. Cf. Margaret S. Archer, *Being Human. The Problem of Agency* (Cambridge: Cambridge University Press, 2000), P. Donati, *La società dell' umano* (Genova-Milan: Marietti, 2009); C. Smith, *What Is a Person? Rethinking Humanity, Social Life, and the Moral Good from the Person Up* (Chicago: University of Chicago Press, 2010). Smith has attempted to show that social institutions emerge as human products on the basis of an emergent vision of the human person and of social relations. The correspondence between the human characteristics of the person and of social institutions remains quite problematic, however, because society in the process of globalization tends to separate the human from the social (P. Donati, 'The Changing Meaning of Work (Secularized versus Humanistic) and Its Implications for the "New" Society', in M. Archer (ed.), *Towards Reducing Unemployment* (Rome: Vatican Press, 1999), pp. 287–324).

business (see the regulations introduced in national and international financial systems after the crisis of September, 2008) or an organic ethics of a traditional type (such as that of the Catholic Church). In both cases, because they are functional in nature, they make no difference. The answer can become affirmative if we realize that markets can no longer be regarded as functional systems (which are in crisis), but as systems of interdependence, characterized by a growing interaction and relationality. This is what the relational paradigm proposes.[34]

In which direction should research be taken?

Let us start over again with the question: who bears moral responsibility for causing impersonal harm to others?

The ontological answer given by Critical Realism is: the interactions among market agents/actors.[35] I agree. But exactly how do we define these interactions and their outcomes?

We must first reflect on the fact that the points of view of methodological holism and methodological individualism lack relationality.

As regards the holistic position, it should be pointed out that the functionalist theory of social systems encounters insurmountable limits and no longer functions beyond its own restricted operative domain because human persons are not an irrelevant environment for systems' autopoietic mechanisms. People assess and judge these mechanisms and can react reflexively on their *modus operandi* (voice and exit). Agents/actors feel responsibility for the devices that run systems despite (or perhaps because of) the fact that system mechanisms operate 'impersonally', that is, by giving priority to adaptive requirements (the A or adaptation function of the AGIL scheme)[36] as a function of

[34] This was explained on the basis of empirical investigations in two volumes that present the relational paradigm: (a) in sociology, P. Donati and I. Colozzi, *Il paradigma relazionale nelle scienze sociali: le prospettive sociologiche* (Bologna: il Mulino, 2006), and (b) in economics, P. L. Sacco and S. Zamagni, *Teoria economica e relazioni interpersonali* (Bologna: il Mulino, 2006).

[35] D. Elder-Vass, *Towards a Social Ontology of Market Systems* (Cresi, University of Essex: Working Paper number 2009–06, 2009) and *The Causal Power of Social Structures: Emergence, Structure and Agency* (Cambridge: Cambridge University Press, 2010).

[36] The functional AGIL scheme describes an action system which, in order to exist, must face four functional prerequisites: the adaption of means to pursued goals (A), the goal-attainment (G), the need for internal norms that integrate the action system (I), and the value pattern maintenance which is

preset goals (G of AGIL), with no concern for problems of legitimation and of social integration (the dimensions of latency and relationality, the L-I axis of AGIL).

As regards the individualistic position, I point out that the *Coleman boat* that determines market results[37] is not made of individuals who can act according to their wishes, and even less according to the thinking of *rational choice* theory. The network that connects them is not a reality that they can alter to their liking on the basis of individual preferences and tastes. It is not a matter of pointing out only that the network always contains constraints, but that the network cannot be configured on the basis of a purely internal reflexivity of participants because it has to do with social relations as such.[38] A reflexivity that is not merely individual and one that is not only of a rational-acquisitive type is already effectively operating in the face of the endemic crisis of the capitalistic economy. It consists in activating an awareness that reflects on the outcomes of social networks as products of relations rather than of individual acts.

called latency (L). The *relational* version is substantially different in that it conceives AGIL as a relational complex of these dimensions needed to bring about both intentional actions and reflexive social relations without a cybernetic hierarchy among the four dimensions and given the fact that relations are understood as emergent realities from reciprocal actions between agents/actors: see Donati, 'Morphogenic Society and the Structure of Social Relations', in Margaret S. Archer (ed.), *Late Modernity: Trajectories towards Morphogenic Society* (Dordrecht: Springer, 2014), chapter 7.

37 J. Coleman, *Foundations of Social Theory* (Cambridge, MA: The Belknap Press of Harvard University Press, 1990). The *Coleman boat* provides a link between macrosociological phenomena and individual behavior. A macro-level phenomenon is described as instigating particular actions by individuals, which results in a subsequent macro-level phenomenon. In this way, individual action is taken with reference to a macrosociological structure, and that action (by many individuals) results in change to that macro structure.

38 I am here referring to Archer's definition of reflexivity as 'the regular exercise of the mental ability, shared by all normal people, to consider themselves in relation to their (social) contexts and vice versa': Archer, *Making Our Way Through the World: Human Reflexivity and Social Mobility* (Cambridge: Cambridge University Press, 2007), p. 4. I call it *personal reflexivity*. The concept of reflexivity can be extended to a social group (in this case it is called *social* or *Relational Reflexivity*) and – under very restrictive and dissimilar conditions – to social systems (*system reflectivity*): for details see Donati, *Sociologia della riflessività. Come si entra nel dopo-moderno* (Bologna: il Mulino, 2011) and Archer, 'Collective Reflexivity: A Relational Case for It', in C. Powell and F. Dépelteau, *Conceptualizing Relational Sociology* (New York: Palgrave Macmillan, 2013), pp. 145–161.

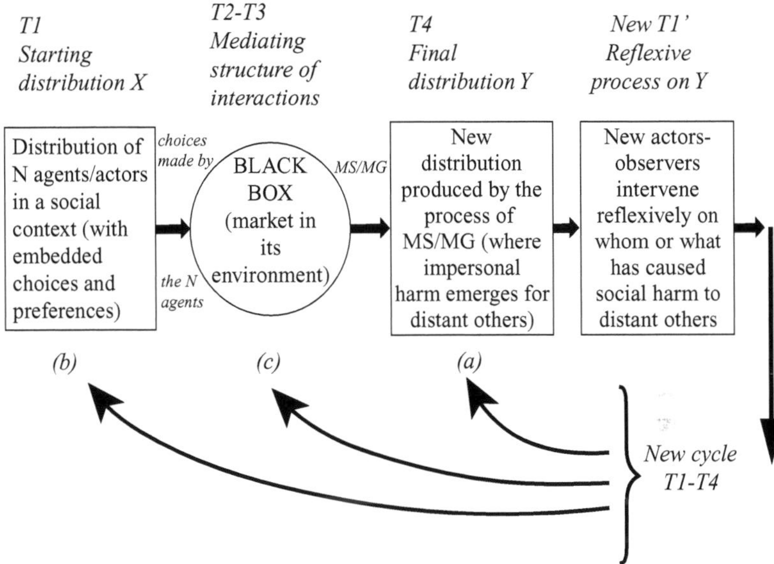

Figure 8.1 A sociological framework for the issue

This awareness is that of second-order reasoning about relations in terms of reciprocity and, because of this, is able to identify agents' responsibility in building certain networks rather than others. In short, the moral responsibility of agents for the impersonal harm brought to bear on strangers becomes visible when the former are not considered as atoms, but as 'parts of a Relational Subject'.

In such a case, it becomes plausible to understand that there exists a moral responsibility of agents if and to the degree that (i) agents consider the effects of their social relations, in as much as they are distinct from technical relations, and (ii) they adopt a vision of the market that makes manifest the ethical value (criterion) that is used latently (unspoken) as the argument for the function-goal of economic activity.

The market as a black box

In order to understand this perspective of sociological analysis, I propose the following scheme of the social processes that we shall address (Figure 8.1).

My comment on Figure 8.1 is as follows. At the beginning of the process (time T1), we observe N agents/actors. They are embedded in a social context that influences their opportunities and action preferences.[39] The context is a structure produced by previous morphostatic/morphogenetic cycles. This structure defines the positions and resources of the N agents/actors in the initial distribution (X). The N agents/actors make individual and reciprocal choices in the interval of time T2-T3. The choices combine with one another in a network of relations between the N agents/actors. This network is a black box that mediates between the initial distribution X and the new distribution Y (which emerges at time T4). It is a matter of knowing this network and understanding its structural, cultural, and agential dynamics. From this network arises the new configuration Y of opportunities and preferences. In distribution Y we can find both relational goods and evils that the black box (the market) produces, both among the agents/actors under consideration as well as between the latter and 'distant others'.

In order to see the harm generated by the market and to whom/what the responsibility should be attributed, new reflexive actors (who are also 'observers')[40] intervene by interacting with the 'old' actors (those who are present in the cycle T1-T4). Old and new actors act in time after the emergence of distribution Y (new T1').[41] Only under certain conditions do these actors/observers have some hope of explaining, understanding, and reflexively assessing the outcomes of the morphostatic/morphogenetic cycle, and start a new cycle T1-T4 aiming at avoiding the relational evils.

The problem that we must confront has four aspects. It is a matter of understanding the following things (with reference to Figure 8.1):

(i) What the acting subjects' autonomy is in pursuing their preferences with respect to the context (the conditioning structure).

39 There exists what Sunstein calls 'endogeneity of embedded preferences': C. Sunstein, *Free Markets and Social Justice* (Oxford: Oxford University Press, 1997).

40 The need to distinguish between 'agent/actor' and 'observer' lies in the fact that the same Self can make observations which are not complementary in themselves and with his/her roles and/or actions.

41 These observers are necessary because: (i) the morphogenetic process cannot be 'finalized' *ex ante* (it is an emergent effect); (ii) the black box is not trivial; and (iii) the individual moral behaviors of actors in the process T1-T4 are not sufficient to produce an 'ethical outcome' (i.e. a relational good).

(ii) How the relations and interactions between the N agents/actors generate the black box, which is the market. In particular, this is a matter of understanding whether and to what extent the agents, with their intentional choices, can determine the structure of mediation (the black box) in a finalistic way or not; and, again, it is a matter of understanding what role material interests and ideal concerns play in configuring the black box and its outcomes.

(iii) Who the agent/actor, aware of the harmful effects caused to distant others, is, and how they can react to the harm with moral conscience (line a).

(iv) Whether it is possible to alter the black box in two ways: by influencing agents/actors' choices in such a way as to retroactively alter the processes that produce distribution Y (line b) or by acting directly on the black box (line c).

Today's prevailing economic ethics provides answers in the following way:

(iv) It considers the N agents/actors as autonomous and rational – and generally hypo-socialized – subjects that are ethical in as much as they respect the regulations in economic transactions (*lex mercatoria*). It forgets that subjects are not truly autonomous because they have social relations that they must take into account (leaving aside market regulations), that their rationality is quite limited by the system's complexity, and that there are many non-rational factors at play.

(v) It assumes that, on condition that the N agents/actors are honest and sympathetic, the black box operates as a eufunctional system (an 'invisible hand') that produces well-being for all participants. As a consequence, it holds that the N agents/actors do not have any moral responsibility for the harm brought to bear on distant others because it thinks that the emergent effects are uncontrollable by the agents/actors (a mechanistic conception of the emergent effects) or, at least, that they do not depend on their choices. This assumption is mistaken because it ignores the emergent effects that are produced in the black box. Economic ethics sees agents' responsibility at the moment of their choice (*ex ante*), but not their responsibility for the effects of their actions (*ex post*).

(vi) The actor-observer who knows the harm inflicted on distant others and is able to react with moral conscience can only be outside the market, which implies that the economy cannot observe and correct itself from the inside; ethics is considered as a constraint of a purely constrictive nature, and not as a (moral and social) resource.

(vii) In this reading of things, the black box cannot be altered *ex ante* by intentional means because it is considered a system with its own deterministic mechanisms. The N agents/actors have only an individual moral responsibility. Redress for the damages caused by the market to distant others must be found elsewhere, generally in the intervention of the State and of political systems in general, which must alter mechanisms of the black box (the Market) with other regulations, devices, constraints, incentives, and sanctions.

In short, those who base their theory on methodological individualism end up embracing a holistic position in the sense that, once it is established that individuals cannot determine harmful outcomes, it considers that harm can be corrected only by the environment outside the market system. In contrast, the holists, after having maintained that individuals are victims of the system, end up appealing to creativity, reflexivity, or other characteristics of individuals in order to change society.

In order to find a solution to the problem, it is necessary to avoid seeing causes only in individuals or only in (social, cultural, economic) structures. Theories of exchange on the free market and theories of hierarchical structuring are losing their explanatory capacity. This reflects the fact that harm to distant others is increasingly caused by impersonal, remote networks in which agents/actors' moral responsibility takes on an indirect or adiaphoric connotation. The question is: if, on one side, free inter-individual exchanges and, on the other side, organizational hierarchies give way to 'social networks', what will be the fate of moral responsibility?

Reflexivity and relational ethics

Let us return to Figure 8.1 in order to understand the causal connections between an average market agent's action and its effects. We have to ascertain the moral responsibility for action, and the criteria for imputing responsibility, by looking at the role played by reflexivity and the Relational Subject.

In the case of *lib/lab* theories, things are quite clear. Agents make their choices from among the opportunities offered by structures and within the degrees of freedom allowed by the structures. This theory emphasizes the pressure of structures on individual actions.[42] The black box works in such a way that harmful outcomes are imputed to structures, not to agents.

In reality, the average agent who participates in the market does not only have the degrees of freedom allowed by the social structure. Economic ethics limits itself to seeing responses to structural conditioning in terms of conformity or deviance. But there exist 'reflexive responses' of another type.

The solutions of *voice* and *exit* emerge from those who discern that distribution Y of the opportunities that emerged at time T4 is not morally (and in certain cases, not politically) acceptable (time T1′). At this point, to whom is responsibility to be imputed?

The ethics of traditional cultures judges results in a deductive manner, *ex post*, with retrospection that does not see the *social* causes of the process; it limits itself to judging a state of affairs as negative and asks to remedy it (line *a* in Figure 8.1). But how can responsibility be imputed if the causes of the harm to distant others are not clear? Asking to compensate those who have been harmed by means of public intervention or with an appeal for private charity does not alter the black box.

If ethics is to fulfil its task of altering the black box, it must thus be made *reflexive*. Reflexive ethics means that it has to 'turn back' and identify the responsibility of who and/or what operated in the black box to produce the social evils.

Then, two paths open up:

(a) Imputing responsibility *only* to the single agents/actors N at the beginning of the process (time T1, line *b* in Figure 8.1). This path is correct in the case of direct harm. In the case of indirect harm, instead, it is necessary to see whether at time T1 there

[42] According to this theory, agents act in a certain way even if they are aware of the harm that they cause because the environmental pressure is so strong that they would otherwise be labelled as deviant and thus would be marginalized from their social group of belonging.

existed different opportunities with respect to behaviours based upon (Autonomous) Communicative or Meta-reflexivity.[43] These forms of reflexivity are encountered when agents act with honest intentions (for example, saving the company by locating a part of it in countries where wages are lower) or, in any case, when agents are 'Smithian'. For these forms of (first-order) reflexivity, not entering the black box would mean leaving the market. However, at the level of a second-order Meta-reflexivity, the agents could have chosen other behaviours and created an 'other' market, 'other economies'. For example, they could have chosen cooperative rather than competitive strategies, which, however, is not achievable by individuals. As evidence of this is the fact that Meta-reflexivity is qualitatively different from other forms of reflexivity because it entails relating to relations. (The Communicative mode entails direct relations with others or the forms of harm with which all can empathize, such as humanitarian disasters.)

(b) The other path consists in imputing responsibility to social relations among agents/actors in the black box (line *c*). In fact, it is the play of relations that led agents to reproduce the same processes (that is, morphostasis = MS in Figure 8.1) or to generate morphogenesis (MG in Figure 8.1).

In order to understand how structures can be changed, it is necessary to understand how they are causally generated (for this, Figure 8.2 is needed).

Structures are made of relations, and relations are made of reciprocal actions (with their intentions, norms, means, and values). What we call 'market rules' are relational structures. Precisely because of their relational character, they generate an 'other' reality with respect to the individuals and structures that we find in a given space-time. This 'third' is constituted by emergent effects, which traditional ethics does not cover because it judges only individuals and structures. It is here that ethics become reflexive or, rather, meta-reflexive, in the sense that it must be capable of judging the morality of actions in light of how they configure relations, leaving aside agents' intentions and existing structures.

[43] On modes of reflexivity, I make reference to the modalities delineated by Archer, *Structure, Agency and the Internal Conversation* (Cambridge: Cambridge University Press, 2003).

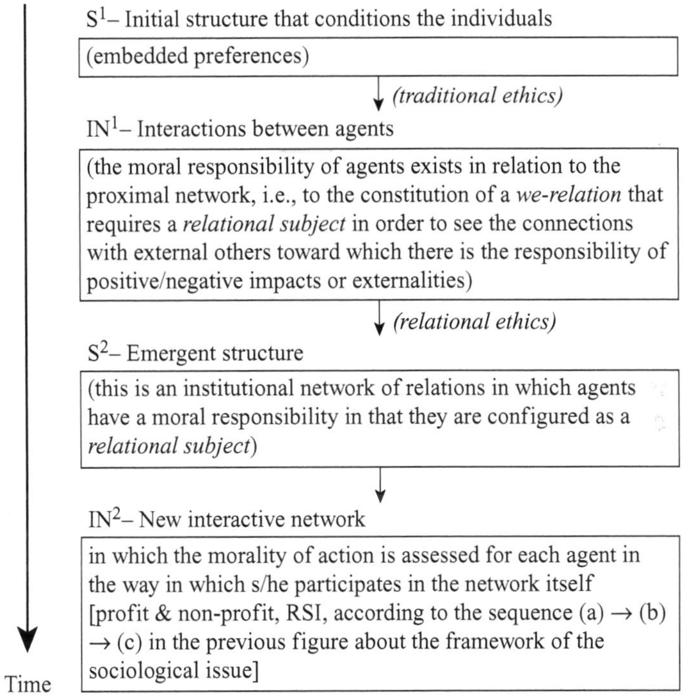

S[1]– Initial structure that conditions the individuals

(embedded preferences)

↓ *(traditional ethics)*

IN[1]– Interactions between agents

(the moral responsibility of agents exists in relation to the proximal network, i.e., to the constitution of a *we-relation* that requires a *relational subject* in order to see the connections with external others toward which there is the responsibility of positive/negative impacts or externalities)

↓ *(relational ethics)*

S[2]– Emergent structure

(this is an institutional network of relations in which agents have a moral responsibility in that they are configured as a *relational subject*)

↓

IN[2]– New interactive network

in which the morality of action is assessed for each agent in the way in which s/he participates in the network itself [profit & non-profit, RSI, according to the sequence (a) → (b) → (c) in the previous figure about the framework of the sociological issue]

Time

Figure 8.2 The morphogenetic cycle of moral responsibility (S = social and cultural structure; IN = interactive network)

This means that the ethical criteria that assess market functioning and its products must make reference to social relations[44] rather than to impersonal system mechanisms or individual preferences, possibly encouraged by incentives to carry out cooperative games.[45] In any

[44] It is important to be aware that social relations always contain explicit or implicit normative components and can never be ethically neutral or adiaphoric.

[45] Many social evils could be avoided if agents, rather than being pushed into more or less cut-throat competition, were pushed to cooperation. Raub and Voss have analyzed the various modalities for promoting cooperation (by means of an authority, by means of iterated attempts to solve together problematic situations, by means of external incentives to cooperate) and have proposed using a model of endogenous change of preferences in which morality is 'a matter of choice motivated entirely by (perhaps even purely selfish) individual interest.' W. Raub and T. Voss, 'Individual Interests and Moral Institutions: An Endogenous Approach to the Modification of Preferences', in M. Hechter, K. D. Opp, and R. Wippler (eds.), *Social*

case, causal imputations can no longer be of a deductive and conditional type, of the type whereby, 'if event X happens, judgment Y then applies.'

It is necessary that the ethical criteria for imputing moral responsibility concern agents not only as regards their individual subjectivity (internal conversation or personal reflexivity), but also as regards their social relations. Agents must reflect on the relations that condition them and on the relations that they generate. They must assess the relation's good (the relation as a good) or the relation's evil (the relation as an evil).[46] Relational good can transform itself into a relational evil if a suitable social (i.e., relational) reflexivity and a certain systemic reflectivity are not activated. Ethics need to become relational. What does this mean?

It means seeing good and evil in relations themselves, and not only in the individual as such or in the conditioning structure. To understand the significance of this statement, one should think about the following examples. Traditional ethics considers poverty as a condition of lacking resources that should be given by the collectivity to those who are most unfortunate. Relational ethics, instead, sees poverty as the product of relations that, even if enacted with good intentions, have objectively deprived some people of opportunities to which they had a right for reasons of reciprocity. Likewise, unemployment is seen as the product of a policy that considers work as a commodity rather than as a social relation.[47] It is certainly true that, a few years ago, the UN learned to conceive of poverty as a lack of *capabilities* which leads to exclusion from the circuits of productivity. Amartya Sen, whose thinking has contributed to this new view, has proposed that the conception of poverty as a pure and simple lack of income be superseded.[48] Nevertheless, concepts such as a 'lack of capabilities' or a 'lack of flexibility in the job market' usually make reference to individuals as such, that

Institutions: Their Emergence, Maintenance, and Effects (New York: Aldine de Gruyter, 1990), pp. 81–117, quotation p. 82.

46 On relational goods and evils, see P. Donati, 'Capitale sociale e beni relazionali: una lettura sociologica delle reti associative a carattere cooperativo', in Vittorio Pelligra (ed.), *Imprese sociali. Scelte individuali e interessi comuni* (Milan: Bruno Mondadori, 2008), pp. 135–153, and P. Donati and R. Solci, *I beni relazionali. Che cosa sono e quali effetti producono* (Turin: Bollati Boringhieri, 2011).

47 Donati, *Il lavoro che emerge*, pp. 170–201.

48 A. Sen, *On Ethics and Economics* (Oxford: Basil Blackwell, 1987).

is, they reflect an individualistic point of view, or they reflect a collective point of view, making reference to impersonal structures, rather than being expressed as forms of social relations. This is due to the fact that the common good is defined as a 'total good' (a product of aggregation) rather than as a 'relational good' (emergent effect).

In general, what I want to claim is that involuntary, but illegitimate, inequalities must be seen as the product of a relationality among actors that lacks reflexivity about the mechanisms that distribute life chances, even if those who participate in the exchanges are individually honest.

At this point a clarification of the concept of ethical good that I am proposing is called for. I assume that ethical good consists in the flourishing of the human person in happiness and, therefore, in virtue, for the development of which ethical norms are needed that become the rules of the happy life. The human person's relationality is seen as part of this concept of ethical good because it presumes that it is in the relation that the person's virtues are expressed which, if positive, generate a positive relation (the social relation is assumed to be configured in a certain way because it was *internally* desired by the person in that way, as Elisabeth Anscombe maintains).[49] What I add to this conceptualization is the thesis according to which the morality of the action requires a richer and more complex view of relationality. The social dimension of the morality of action does not only consist in the fact that the person is morally obliged to relate to others in a virtuous way in terms of his/her own intentionality (necessary condition), but it also includes the person's responsibility for the moral goodness of the relation as such (sufficient condition) and, therefore, the fact of considering the effects of one's own action on others. In this consists the *social* nature of virtue.[50] Briefly, what I want to emphasize is the fact that the morality of an action does not consist only in the person's intentionality, but also in the responsibility that the person has toward the relation that the action supports, considering the relation as a good in itself and as a structure that conditions the people involved.

For this reason, we can say that relational ethics *joins* together *intentionality* toward a good and *responsibility toward the relational value*

49 G. E. M. Anscombe, *Intention* (Cambridge, MA: Harvard University Press, 2000 [1957]).

50 P. Donati, 'Does Relationality Make Sense on a Global Level? Is There a Global Society?', in J. A. G. Sison (ed.), *Handbook of Virtue Ethics in Business and Management* (Dordrecht: Springer, 2016 forthcoming).

of the good. The ethics of intentionality and the ethics of responsibility cannot be separated, precisely because of the relational character of the good. From the ethical point of view, the good which every and any entity possesses in itself[51] is not the same as the good that the entity in question has within the context of social relations. For example, the good that a building has in and of itself (as a thing that is there) is not the good considered from the market viewpoint or from the point of view of particular social groups, the local authorities, etc. The building becomes a social good in as much as it becomes relevant (actually or potentially) to the people who use it in different ways. It can have a use value, an exchange value, a 'bond value' (the value attached to being an entity which bonds people together), and so on. It is the peculiar (*sui generis*) kind of social relation that people have with it, in a situated context that makes it a social good and, therefore, a moral good having a certain value.

The thesis that imputes the moral responsibility for harm inflicted on 'distant others' to a *relational deficit* can seem vague and untenable. It is so from the standpoint of traditional ethics, which considers the concept of relation as a morally indifferent entity of reason and, as regards concrete social relations, imputes the responsibility for their configuration and effects to acting subjects as such.

We are indebted to the modern social sciences for attributing a responsibility increasingly clearly to subjects, not for what they think or do individually, but in as much as they generate social relations that have a *sui generis* reality. This means conferring an ontological status on the concept of relation when it is applied to the social realm. The morality of an action does not reside only in the conscience of the subject acting with an eye to a good in itself, but also to the fact that the subject does or does not respond to the relational nature of the sought-after good.

The Relational Subject

The modern 'discovery' of the reality of the social relation is a moral fact that requires new ethical reflection. Postmodern society and the globalized markets certainly have left the classic ontological paradigm

[51] A. Collier, *Being and Worth* (London: Routledge, 1999).

behind.[52] Nevertheless, they have also opened the way for the emergence of an ontology of the social relation based on a new critical realism as an alternative to a constructivist relationalism that manipulates responsibility, just as it manipulates social relations.

In Figure 8.1 we saw that relational good/evil is created in the interactive network (black box) in the interval between times T2 and T3. Let us now look at what happens inside the black box with the help of Archer's[53] morphogenetic framework (Figure 8.2).

Figure 8.2 is entitled 'The morphogenetic cycle of moral responsibility' to underscore that moral responsibility changes relationally over time. It is not given, once and for all, in the initial decision. It does not only concern single acts in time, but has to do with these acts in as much as they produce relational effects over the course of time.

At the initial time T1, individuals find themselves in a structure that conditions them, and they make their choices (S^1). These choices, at time T2, enter into relationship with the choices of other agents. A network is constituted among 'proximal' individuals (proximity network). In this phase, moral responsibility concerns each agent because of the contribution that he/she makes to the network, that is, with respect to the constitution of a *We-relation.* But this network is not isolated; it has effects that go beyond it towards the outside (distant others).

Decisions in the proximity network affect the outside, even in an unintentional way, because there exist structural (unintended) connections. For example, when white workers in the USA prevented blacks from joining labour unions, they did not do this to prevent them from working – or even due to racism – but because they believed that blacks would not be loyal to the union and, therefore, they thought that they were defending their legitimate interests. They had 'good reasons' for their actions. Nevertheless, the emergent structural effect was to produce unemployment and poverty among blacks, as Merton has shown.[54]

52 Spoken of by N. Luhmann, *Paradigm Lost. Über die Etische Reflexion der Moral* (Frankfurt a.M.: Suhrkamp, 1990).

53 I mean the framework developed since the research on the educational systems by Margaret S. Archer, *Social Origins of Educational Systems* (London: Sage, 1979, third edition 2013) up to now.

54 R. K. Merton, *Social Theory and Social Structure* (New York: The Free Press, 1968), chapter 2. Boudon also offered many examples of this type, but he did not see their relational character and, for this reason, confused emergent, aggregate, compositional, and perverse effects with one another as if they were

From the standpoint of relational ethics, moral responsibility implies knowledge of the relational connections of the networks in which the agent is integrated (IN in Figure 8.2). Yet studies to this effect are quite rare because the issue of knowledge *vis-à-vis* relations and their effects is fairly recent in social research. Nevertheless, it is possible to make several assertions that are validated by network analysis (of a relational, not structuralist, type).

For example, we can say that moral responsibility is proportional to the degree of the Ego's *centrality* in the network. For instance, whoever occupies the position of broker[55] has a supplementary responsibility, because the broker's responsibility is not only toward the network's individual nodes (each Alter), but also toward the network overall in as much as what the network generates depends on the way in which brokers manage the structural roles in which they are located.[56]

Ignorance is not an excuse for refusing to take responsibility. Undoubtedly, some connections are known and certain, while others are not known, or are uncertain. In general, causal connections have a certain degree of probability. The morality of action in a network shares the problems of moral responsibility in facing risks.

It should be noted that the relational interpretation of the principle of responsibility is quite different from the one formulated by Hans Jonas,[57] not only because Jonas has addressed this principle mainly as it relates to phenomena of the natural environment (ecological and bioethical issues), but above all because he has applied it to individual action in the spirit of Kant ('Act in such a way that the effects of your action are compatible with the continuation of an authentically human life'). It is considerably more difficult to address social phenomena and to speak of a relational ethics in social networks. What distinguishes

all similar concepts. R. Boudon, *The Logic of Social Action: An Introduction to Sociological Analysis* (London: Francis & Taylor, 1981).

[55] In network analysis, the broker is an intermediary agent/actor between other agents/actors, so much so that the latter cannot communicate between them without passing through the broker.

[56] I must here direct the reader to the numerous studies on network analysis, beginning with P. Marsden and N. Lin (eds.), *Social Structure and Network Analysis* (Beverly Hills, CA: Sage, 1982) until H. C. White, *Markets from Networks: Socioeconomic Models of Production* (Princeton, NJ: Princeton University Press, 2002) and *Identity and Control: How Social Formations Emerge* (Princeton, NJ: Princeton University Press, 2008).

[57] Hans Jonas, *The Imperative of Responsibility* (Chicago: The University of Chicago Press, 1984).

the latter is the fact that actors must act reflexively on the results of their actions combined (related) with others' actions, and not only on the consequences of their own individual actions. In order for this to happen, it is necessary that a moral Relational Subject, to which moral criteria are applied, be constituted. The morality of *social* action requires that agents be considered as parts of what can be called a *Relational Subject.*

In many cases, the 'remote' causality of the market's economic phenomena is identifiable only if we presuppose the existence of a Relational Subject with respect to which agents are responsible. This is because it is with respect to this Relational Subject that an observer can assess the morality of their actions, whether *ex ante* or *ex post,* in producing those causal chains from which harm brought to bear on distant others is derived.

For example: a company that hires women with no concern for their relations with their children is potentially responsible for the harm suffered by the latter due to a lack of maternal care, which lies outside the company's organizational network (of course, the same holds true for men, because harm to children is an issue of 'parental' care, not only attributable to women). The company did not have these intentions but can produce harm in this respect, as in others, in the human environment of the territory in which it operates. Relational Reflexivity on the process requires one to see the company, the employees, and their families as a Relational Subject.

If we say that a company has social responsibility *vis-à-vis* the inhabitants of its territory, we can say it in as much as we see a network that connects all of the stakeholders and constitutes a Relational Subject. In the same way, we say that employers have a responsibility toward their employees' families, which requires measures for family-work reconciliation that lie outside the so-called contractual synallagma in which a simple equivalence is assumed between services rendered and remuneration of the individual employee's work.

When conceived in a relational sense, moral responsibility is intrinsically reflexive. It is what leads from a simple moral judgment on harm (line *a* of Figure 8.1) to an alteration of the relational configuration acting on subjects (line *b*) and on the structure of market relations (i.e., on the black box, line *c*).

The relational perspective is not wishful thinking but has empirical corroboration in a number of new ways of running the market that follow relational ethics. For example, many companies prevent harm to distant others by building networks in which for-profit and non-profit subjects cooperate, and for this are called 'socially responsible'.

We are witnessing the birth of markets in which agents' behaviours and rules are being redefined from the point of view of the Relational Subject constituted by a broad spectrum of stakeholders (business ownership and management + workers + consumers). New forms of relational economy are being born, integrating for-profit and non-profit sectors and holding as a value the social responsibility of business (corporate social responsibility – CSR, shared responsibilities) and the production of *commons*. More recent than the concept of CSR is that of '*shared value,*' used by Michael Porter, Mark Kramer, and others, which has the advantage of using economic language in the sense that it underscores that the goal of business is value and not only profit. Social and positive ecological effects are included in value. Running through all of these innovations is the observation that the company that pursues only monetary profit is destined to fail.[58]

These configurations are characterized by the fact that they introduce what I call 'Relational Reflexivity'[59] into the black box and, in this way, *civilize* the market, while the typically capitalistic configuration – which is based on an acquisitive Autonomous Reflexivity – commodifies it. An example of innovation in this sense are the relational contracts between employer and employee in which not only services rendered and remuneration received are considered, but so, too, are relations with the employee's family and the services that the latter may need, precisely in order not to harm those who are at a distance from the company. These contracts are not a form of philanthropy, charity, or a gift from the company, but are another

[58] The basic idea is that companies must take the lead in bringing business and society back together. What is proposed is an overall framework for guiding these efforts, going beyond the 'social responsibility' mind-set in which societal issues are at the periphery, not the core. The solution lies in the principle of shared value, which involves creating economic value in a way that *also* creates value for society by addressing its needs and challenges. Businesses must reconnect company success with social progress. Shared value is not social responsibility, philanthropy, or even sustainability, but a new way to achieve economic success. It is not on the margin of what companies do but at the centre: M. Porter and M. Kramer, 'Creating Shared Value', *Harvard Business Review*, 89 (2011), 62–77.

[59] P. Donati, 'Modernization and Relational Reflexivity', *International Review of Sociology*, 21 (2011), 21–39.

way to increase its social and human capital. In any case, they have a positive impact, both within the company as well as on the network outside of it.

Some examples

If market participants do not understand harm brought to bear on distant others as a product of their actions, it is because they do not see, or refuse to acknowledge, the relations that connect them. The prevailing political economy today immunizes them against these relations.[60] How can one respond to someone who refuses to consider relations? How can we address someone who wants to have to do with us only for the things exchanged and not for the relations entailed by the exchange?

Let us look at some examples.

Social dumping

Social dumping[61] is a practice considered in the economic world to be unfair. But in point of fact, in the USA it is a normal praxis backed up by the laws on competition, and in the EU it is a *politics* backed by European Commission policy directives meant to foster market competition among member states. The *lib/lab* system imposes a market structure (S^1) based on social dumping. And so one wonders: what responsibility does the individual business person who practices social dumping have in generating harm in those countries or areas where it causes unemployment and endangers workers' social rights?

[60] On the concept of 'immunization' from social relations: see R. Esposito, *Immunitas. Protezione e negazione della vita* (Turin: Einaudi, 2002).

[61] Social dumping is a term used to describe the fact that an employer moves his enterprise from a country or area where work is more costly to a country or area in which work is less costly and in this way can save money and increase his/her profits. In general, it is a practice involving the export of goods from a country with weak or poorly enforced labour standards, where the exporter's costs are artificially lower than its competitors in countries with higher standards, hence representing an unfair advantage in international trade. It results from differences in direct and indirect labour costs, which constitute a significant competitive advantage for enterprises in one country, with possible negative consequences for social and labour standards in other countries. In particular, it has to do with the unemployment caused in richer nations because of the transfer of jobs with low qualifications (the shift of low skilled jobs) from regions with high salaries to regions of the world that are poor and have lower salaries.

From the perspective of Relational Sociology, conformity to starting structures (S^1) does not absorb all of the entrepreneur's moral responsibility because the latter has degrees of freedom in seeking alternative solutions if and when he/she wants to avoid unintentionally causing harm. Entrepreneurs can adopt cooperative strategies between the workers of the two countries or areas involved, but for this, they must promote the establishment of a Relational Subject that includes both of the participants in their market strategy. The agent's morality can and must come to terms with a plurality of criteria for justice. This is not only the commutative justice of the Market but also the redistributive justice of the State, and that based on solidarity in the third sector. At the basis of everything there is distributive justice as an ontological foundation, which consists in the recognition of the human person's rights. It is in this way that a civil economy arises that respects the ethical criterion of reciprocity as the moral rule of relations. In contrast to other theoreticians of the civil economy, I would like to emphasize the fact that, in order to avoid harm to strangers, it is not a matter of introducing an ethics that lies outside the market, such as one based on fraternity or love,[62] but a matter of configuring relational networks in accordance with their inner virtues.

Acquisition of merchandise produced in violation of human rights

What moral responsibility does the consumer have when he/she buys merchandise produced by the exploitation of child labour or with the low-paid work of women operating in 'sweat shops' in developing countries?

The answer lies in the reflexive awareness of consumers. If they have no knowledge of the fact, we cannot impute moral responsibility to them. But if the network of Corporate Agents (R^1) makes this reality public, and a consumer comes to know about it, he/she has the freedom to choose what to do. And so the knowledge of exploitation is an element in the imputation of responsibility because the consumer has the possibility of not buying sweatshop products.

62 As suggested, for example, by L. Bruni and R. Sugden, 'Fraternity. Why the market need not to be a morally free zone', *Economics and Philosophy*, 24 (2008), 35–64.

The rejection of risks that entails fostering the bankruptcy of countries in financial crisis

Let us take the case of a financial agent who withdraws his/her financial investments from a country in which there are risks of fiscal and financial instability. By acting in this way, the agent contributes to causing unemployment and economic recession in that country. Such an agent is generally perfectly aware of what he/she causes, but imputes harm to the laws of the market. Something analogous happens when bank depositors, hearing a rumour that their bank is going to fail, rush to withdraw their deposits and, thus, effectively cause the bank's failure where it was never a real danger. In these cases, in order to assess agents' responsibility, we can follow one of two paths: appealing to an ethics of risk or else acting in such a way that the feared result does not come about. It is clear that the calculation of risk in these cases is quite difficult and often impossible. Moral responsibility lies above all in the refusal to alter the network of interactions (R^1), which can produce the bankruptcies and, consequently, the harm to distant others. The responsibility is thus proportional to the degrees of freedom available for altering the network of financial actions in such a way as to avoid one's own losses as well as harm to others. Surely, we cannot criticize a person who tries to save his/her modest savings. On the other hand, from a moral standpoint one must reserve a negative judgment for rating agencies which, with their evaluations, contribute to increasing the difficulties experienced by those countries that already have weak economies and, thus, instead of helping these countries to get back on their feet, favour dynamics that lead these economies toward situations of even deeper crisis (they are examples of *self-fulfilling prophecies*).

The involuntary creation of poverty

From the standpoint of sociological analysis, the condition of poverty is not a condition that is caused solely by certain individual characteristics, but is above all the product of a relational system. It arises from a chain of social relations. In order to understand the phenomenon, one could draw an analogy with the more generalized concept of 'economic capital', which is usually employed as a synonym for the means of production and finance. For Relational Sociology, economic capital is not the possession of a sum of money, a company, or real estate but, rather, is a network of social relations that make possible the possession and use of those goods. *Vice versa*, poverty is a context that hinders control of needed goods. Addressing poverty as an emergent effect of networks of relations completely changes the perspective as compared to an essentialist point of view that considers poverty as a condition caused by material (economic or physical) factors which have determined a certain outcome, that is, the lack of means.

If we apply the framework of Figure 8.2, we have the following sequence:

- S^1: there is a given social structure that stratifies agents/actors' opportunities;
- IN^1: agents/actors interact with one another, reproducing or altering the initial stratification;
- S^2: a new structure may or may not arise as a Relational Subject in which each person's expectations are altered based on how the latter, combined with those of other people, create relational goods or evils; poverty is the product of a failed view that it is the result of a deficient relational structure (deficits in a relational structure);
- IN^2: the struggle against poverty in the market – without intervention by the political system – consists in creating a new interactive network of a cooperative type.

'Social causality' is relational causality. Life conditions and opportunities are the outcome of a relational context that not only conditions individuals' choices, but also has its own logic of (systemic or reticular) interdependence.

The category of interdependence is a moral category, not only in that it appeals to the moral obligation of solidarity, but in that it is inherent in the causality of social relations on the empirical level.

The moral responsibility for the creation of poverty does not have to do with the individual behaviour of single persons, but with the consequences of the relations that they activate. They are responsible for the outcomes because they are responsible for the relations that generate them, even if these are emergent effects that come about without their direct intentions.

The poverty of the homeless man on the street or of the illegal immigrant is the result of a long chain of actions that could have been individually legal and honest, but which did not take into account either aggregate or emergent effects. When I see an old lady collect her pension at the post office, she does not know that this money comes from me and from those who are currently active in the workforce. But I know it, and I am responsible for it. If I do not pay my taxes and other contributions to the collectivity, if I do not share in the *We-relation* and the Relational Subject that supports it, I am responsible for the failure of the collectivity to pay this lady's pension.

Civilizing the market: what does this mean?

The idea that the market is a system of exchanges where the golden rule is 'pure' competition, that is, with no premises beyond the mere capacities of individuals,[63] is like the phoenix of mythology. A model of market economy that is based on *this* type of competition is not a model with some defects: it is an intrinsically erroneous model. It is *a pure illusion due to the simple fact that it erases the relations* between market participants. Competition is a social virtue if it means *cum-petere,* that is, *to strive together* toward a good, vying to see who can reach it first, who is best, on condition that this does not entail actions that voluntarily cause harm to those who are competing and, moreover, seeking to reduce involuntary harm.

The modern political economy that originated in the eighteenth century, which in general terms theorizes the market as 'formally free' and, as far as possible, 'deregulated', is based on the removal of social relations because it has a Protestant theological matrix behind it.[64] This model has historically triumphed over the *civil economy* with a relational matrix, which was elaborated by the Italian humanists from the thirteenth century (such as Albertano da Brescia)[65] up to Antonio Genovesi in the eighteenth century.[66] They proposed an interesting

63 What is more, considering individuals as over-socialized agents, as rightly pointed out by Archer (*Structure, Agency and the Internal Conversation*, pp. 117–129).

64 P. Donati, *La matrice teologica della società* (Soveria Mannelli: Rubbettino, 2010).

65 Albertano da Brescia, *Alle radici della grande Europa, del razionalismo economico, dell' umanesimo civile* (Brescia: Industrie Grafiche Bresciane, 1994), 3 vols. In his famed *Essay on the History of Civil Society* (1767), Adam Ferguson completely dismissed this cultural heritage and marked the victory of the utilitarian conception.

66 A. Genovesi, *Lezioni di commercio ossia di economia civile (1765-67)* (Milan: Silvestri, 1820), 2 vols. The reinterpretation of Genovesi's thought recently given by some scholars, such as L. Bruni and S. Zamagni, *Civil Economy* (Oxford: Peter Lang, 2007) is, to a great extent, filtered through the recent Relational Sociology developed in the last three decades.

relational paradigm in the socioeconomic context, because they noted that people spontaneously desired to cultivate a connection with others. In their opinion, people get more pleasure when others participate in their satisfactions, so that people are completely themselves only when they live in free sharing and communion with others. In this sense, their vision of economy was that the commons are the condition for the fulfilment of every single person and that the quality and level of sociality thus constitutes a basic dimension of public happiness. Although Adam Smith spoke of sympathy among market actors, it is quite true that all political economy from Ricardo onwards is pervaded by an ethics of 'immunization' of market agents *against* social relations, viewed as constraints on free exchanges.

Because the economy is effectively relational, its ethics must also be relational. Redistributive economies (based on a central authority) and the so-called social market economies (which are a form of State regulation of the Market) do not have a relational character and, for this reason, fail in combating the harm brought to bear by the Market on distant others. At most, they can bring some relief.

In any case, in order to avoid harm caused by the Market to distant others, recourse to the State is neither sufficient nor appropriate. Rather, mechanisms of civil society are needed, if and in as much as they are relational. An economy is relational not because it entrusts itself to the regulations of some political system, but because it invests in solutions based on the social governance of civil society's networks.

With this we have reached the crux of the problem: the morality of actions in the market is essentially a problem of civilizing the market, considered as a system of interdependences and interactions.

Ethics can operate as an independent variable or a functional-objective of economic activity if it is conceived according to reflexive criteria, and no longer according to unidirectional criteria (that is, the conditional criteria such that, if X happens, then the norm Y is applied).

In a society that entails intensified use of agents' subjectivity and creates ever new relations via the channels of globalization, it is no longer enough to say that the morality of action depends on the conscious intention to pursue something good in itself. Unfortunately, social evils do not derive only from behaviours that are dishonest, corrupt, driven by greed for money or power – which are clearly visible.

The perverse processes are invisible and can be detected only with a suitable instrument – that of reflexive discernment.

The four fundamental principles of a good society (the human person's dignity, the common good, solidarity, and subsidiarity) are not four pillars that stand separately from one another. They must be understood and must operate in a relational and reflexive manner. Each is defined *through* the others. But this presupposes having a relational view of social reality. In this consists the civilization of the market.

From the time of Aristotle, traditional ethics has imputed the morality of action to the 'acting subject'. Over time and, in particular, with the advent of the modern social sciences, the social, economic, and cultural conditioning weighing on the subject have been evidenced. The result has been to attribute moral responsibility to a 'conditioned subject', that is, one who is constrained by existing societal structures (among which figure so-called 'unjust laws'). The increased importance of systems of interdependence, at the expense of functional systems, changes the epistemological framework in what we call global social order.[67] Moral responsibility encounters a process of morphogenesis such that, as a result, the morality of action must make reference to a 'Relational Subject', one that acts in a societal network and is required to know and configure 'relationally'. Ethics is required to make itself relational, in the sense that the attribution of responsibility for acting for good or ill cannot be limited to a single act, but invokes the reflexivity inherent in social processes. The morality of action must therefore make reference to the reflexive awareness that subjects have of how good and evil are produced by social relations and consist of social relations (relational goods/evils), within increasingly complex

[67] Globalization (understood as a process that introduces social issues at world level) and interdependence (as an emergent structural feature of social systems, both within and between them) are distinct phenomena which operate synergistically: the more actors increase in interdependence, the more globalization intensifies, and vice versa. To my mind, only a relational ontological and epistemological matrix can conceptualize and theorize this process. See P. Donati, 'Different cultures, different citizenships? The challenge of a universal citizenship in a multicultural postmodern society', The Annals of the International Institute of Sociology, New Series Volume V (1996), pp. 245–263; 'Beyond the dilemmas of multiculturalism: recognition through "relational reason"', International Review of Sociology, 19 (2009), 55–82; *La matrice teologica della società*, *ibid.*

causal networks. The ethics of intention is no longer sufficient. It must be integrated with an ethics of responsibility that is not restricted to the consequences of individual acts and is not purely instrumental in means-ends terms, but takes into account the effects of relational networks. In a complex society, morality cannot be limited to the intrinsic goodness of aims, but rather must make reference to an integrally relational view of human action.

The initial question, 'Why should Ego be held responsible for the harm inflicted on distant others due to impersonal market mechanisms?' thus has the following answer: because Ego did not exercise his/her freedom, for which he/she is responsible in the first person. This freedom is not that of one's purely internal conscience nor is it freedom *from* external constraints. It is the freedom *to* act for the goods that can only be produced and enjoyed together by all the participants in the market.

9 *Conclusions: Collective subjects and the added value of social relations*

PIERPAOLO DONATI AND
MARGARET S. ARCHER

What are the drivers of Relational Subjects? Evaluating social relations

The Relational Subject is not only s/he who acts reflexively taking into account her/his relations with significant others, but is s/he who operates *on/with/through* social relations. Therefore, it becomes essential to understand how operations happen and are configured. We can translate this issue into the question: what is the role played by social relations in fostering that particular kind of sociability which constitutes the ground on which Relational Subjects can emerge?

Sociability can be defined as trust and cooperation among people who act in terms of reciprocal symbolic references and connections. Empirical research reveals that sociability is a complex factor that creates and enhances collective subjects, but social scientists are divided into two strands of thought.

According to the first strand, the enhancement of collective subjects does not need any network of social relations, or at least takes place without depending upon social networks, because what is necessary and sufficient is held to be the sharing of a common culture (e.g. civic or civil culture) among individual people. That is why collective subjects are quite often assimilated to social movements (such as the Greens or the Anti-Global movement). This simplistic assimilation should be questioned, because in many cases it could be incorrect and misleading. Social theory needs to distinguish between different kinds of social movements. On one hand, there are those movements that commence and consist in a protest and end with it (for instance, movements against the war in Vietnam or Iraq) or consist in reclaiming a right or seeking a vindication that, once obtained, is enjoyed by the individuals in their private lives (for instance, a movement that seeks the abolition of a tax or defends the existence of a public park and its use by individual citizens). On the other hand, there are social movements that create social networks in so far as participation involves collective mobilization and gives rise to structured groups, organizations, or voluntary associations in which a new form of sociability is expressed (for instance, those ecological movements giving birth to local associations, cooperatives, or other agencies, which work steadily for the improvement of a local area and a healthy environment).

According to the first strand, the enhancement of collective goods requires a common target but does not need any network of social relations, or, at least, takes place independently of social networks, while, according to the second, the promotion of collective goods depends on the existence and good functioning of relational networks, to the point that it leads to the creation of social networks (endowed with certain properties and causal powers). Which one is correct?

Behind this division lie two different and opposite conceptions of the social relation. For the first group of theorists, the social relation does not give any added social value because sociability consists, in their opinion, in a cultural legacy (civic-mindedness or the like) which supports the production of collective goods in so far as it is internalized and acted upon by individuals in a given geographical context with no need for specific relations among them. Conversely, for the second group it is precisely in social relations that sociability consists, generating the added social value that constitutes (or, perhaps, 'institutes') collective goods. Thus, it is necessary to ask: does the added social value of social relations exist or not? If so, what is it and how can it be assessed? Answering these questions is crucial to our ability to differentiate between the different kinds of sociability which can lead to the creation and/or enhancement of social subjects and, within them, those peculiar subjects that we call 'relational'.

The sociological approach that we maintain affirms that sociability generates and valorizes collective goods through the mediation of social subjects who grow due to the added social value of social relations. Sociability and Relational Subjects are two realities that are generated and regenerated, or elided, in turn. We must abandon circular and recursive frameworks and conceive of the relationships between sociability and collective goods, mediated by Relational Subjects, as morphogenetic processes occurring over time.

When we adopt this perspective, we can disclose the added social value (henceforth ASV) of primary (interpersonal) relations and secondary relations (associative rather than those based upon personal acquaintance).

In our view, ASV is the emergent effect of the agential and social (interactive) reflexivity, within social bonds when (if and in so far as) they are considered and practiced as opportunities and resources (therefore, as a source of enhancement) rather than as constraints and constrictions that inhibit social actors.

Those who deny that sociability has a relational nature can only note its presence or absence, its greater or lesser efficacy, but cannot explain how and why it is generated or is absent. On the other hand, those who adopt the relational perspective can account for the generative processes of sociability and the different benefits that it can produce, depending on what the added social value of the relations constituting it is.

Sociability and the production of collective goods: a debate replete with aporias

Are primary social networks an obstacle or an aid to the valorization of collective goods?

Many authors who have studied sociability[1] have reached the conclusion, whether explicitly or implicitly, that informal societal networks (primary or of proximity) and formal societal networks (secondary, that is, of organized associations) tend to foster individuals' closure, their particularism and attachment to personal or community interests. Attitudes of openness that are less particularistic (voting, granting generalized interpersonal trust, donating blood, etc.), would, instead, appear to encourage the production on the part of civil society of positive externalities for the entire social context, that is, by producing public benefits.

The most significant consequence of this way of regarding sociability is the circumvention or, at least, the underestimation of the importance

[1] E. C. Banfield, *The moral basis of a backward society* (Glencoe, IL: Research Center in Economic Development and Cultural Change, 1958); P. Bourdieu, 'The Forms of Capital', in J. G. Richardson (ed.), *Handbook of Theory and Research for the Sociology of Education* (New York: Greenwood Press, 1985), pp. 241–258; R. D. Putnam, *Making Democracy Work: Civic Traditions in Modern Italy* (Princeton, NJ: Princeton University Press, 1993); R. Cartocci, *Mappe del tesoro. Atlante del capitale sociale in Italia* (Bologna: il Mulino, 2007).

of social relations because social interaction networks are excluded from the study of collective goods produced by it. In short, it seems that the valorization of collective goods through sociability does not need social relations having specific properties and their own causal powers.

Some writers maintain that: (1) sociability does not have connections with the concept of the social grid/net; (2) networks of proximity establish negative relations with sociability and with individuals' civic-mindedness.

These theses have been called into question by a series of theoretical and empirical investigations that have shown the exact opposite. The first thesis leads one to disregard a vast number of sociological studies that underscore the deep and ineluctable connection between the concept of social network and that of sociability.[2] The second thesis was found to be erroneous by numerous theoretical and empirical studies that shed light on the conditions under which relations of proximity turn out to be efficacious in augmenting pro-sociality and individuals' orientations toward significant others.[3] There are abundant studies that show the existence of a continuity between primary, secondary, and generalized sociability.[4] The definition of these different types of

[2] J. Coleman, 'Social Capital in the Creation of Human Capital', *American Journal of Sociology*, 94 (Supplement 1988), 95–120; E. M. Uslaner, *The Moral Foundations of Trust* (Cambridge: Cambridge University Press, 2002); R. S. Burt, *Brokerage and Closure. An Introduction to Social Capital* (Oxford: Oxford University Press, 2005); S. W. Kwon, C. Heflin, and M. Ruef, 'Community Social Capital and Entrepreneurship', *American Sociological Review*, 78 (2013), 980–1008.

[3] R. D. Putnam, *Bowling Alone. The Collapse and Revival of American Community* (New York: Simon & Schuster, 2000); L. Becchetti, A. Pelloni, and F. Rossetti, 'Relational Goods, Sociability, and Happiness', *Kyklos*, 6 (2008), 343–363; G. Degli Antoni and F. Sabatini, 'Disentangling the Relationship between Nonprofit and Social Capital: The Role of Social Cooperatives and Social Welfare Associations in the Development of Networks of Strong and Weak Ties', *EconomEtica working paper*, 48 (2013) (http://www.econometica.it/wp/wp48.pdf).

[4] P. Dekker and A. van den Broek, 'Involvement in voluntary associations in North America and Western Europe: Trends and correlates 1981–2000', *Journal of Civil Society*, 1 (2005), 45–59; R. S. Burt, 'The Network Structure of Social Capital', in R. I. Sutton and B. M. Staw (eds.), *Research in Organizational Behavior* (Greenwich, CT: JAI Press, 2000), pp. 345–423; P. Dekker and E. M. Uslaner (eds.), *Social Capital and Participation in Everyday Life* (London: Routledge, 2001); D. Wollebaeck and P. Selle, 'Does Participation in Voluntary Associations Contribute to Social Capital? The

sociability (SY) is contained in Figure 9.1. Many surveys have found that familial and communitarian sociability turns out to be positively correlated with voluntary associative and generalized sociability, and that they work together to valorize collective goods. The relative continuity of the different forms of sociability indicates that significant interdependencies and reciprocal synergies exist. But this is seen only if one adopts a relational perspective of sociological analysis.

We can read the balance of power between primary sociability and secondary sociability (as defined in Figure 9.1) from a historical standpoint (in terms of its extent and importance) in the various types of societies that have existed throughout the centuries. In segmentary societies (those that are primitive or simple), primary SY is high and secondary SY is low because a social sphere in an associative sense does not exist outside of the realm of family and kinship (there is no – or a very low – distinction between the private and the public spheres). In stratified societies, the power of primary SY persists but in a manner that is diversified by social class (hence the high-medium gradation) while SY begins to develop outside the family and kinship networks. During early modernization, primary SY is weakened in conjunction with the privatization of the bourgeois family and the large-scale spread of the proletarian family while secondary SY grows (bourgeois civil society). In societies with higher modernization in comparison to prior configurations, we notice a decrease of both primary and secondary SY owing to their growing fragmentation, isolation, and social anomie.

What was gained in terms of an increase in secondary SY as one moves toward the first period of modernization is later lost because if capitalism at first fosters secondary SY, it subsequently erodes it together with family and kinship networks.

In Europe the weakening of SY can be connected to the fact that the modern State-Market complex has colonized the spheres of social

Impact of Intensity, Scope, and Type', *Nonprofit and Voluntary Sector Quarterly*, 31 (2002), 32–61; L. Prouteau and F. C. Wolff, 'Relational Goods and Associational Participation', *Annals of Public and Cooperative Economics*, 75 (2004), 431–463; P. Donati and L. Tronca, *Il capitale sociale degli italiani. Le radici familiari, comunitarie e associative del civismo* (Milano: FrancoAngeli, 2008); E. J. van Ingen and P. Dekker, 'Dissolution of associational Life? Testing the individualization and informalization hypotheses on leisure activities in the Netherlands between 1975 and 2005', *Social Indicators Research*, 100 (2011), 209–224.

Different types of SY:	Social sphere (or subject):	What SY consists in (its dimensions):	Specific SY of that sphere as a factor of:
Primary sociability (SY)	a) Familial SY b) Parental SY c) Communitarian SY of informal networks (of neighbours, friends, co-workers)	1. Primary trust (face- to-face and intersubjective) 2. Interpersonal reciprocity as symbolic exchange, or gift as in a circuit or reciprocal exchanges of giving-receiving-reciprocating without monetary equivalents	Civility: SY produces relations that are civil in that they consist of good manners and positive consideration for the *other*, which are the terms of reference for cooperation and reciprocal solidarity in interpersonal relations
Secondary sociability (SY)	Associative SY of organized social networks in associations of civil society	1. Secondary trust (toward individuals who have in common belonging to a civil or political association or community) 2. Expanded social reciprocity (extension of the symbolic exchange to those who belong to the same civil or political association or community)	Associative democracy: SY generates associative forms for promoting goals that cannot be achieved by individuals but require trust and collaboration between persons or social groups that recognize one another as members of the same social network, association, or organization
Generalized sociability (SY)	SY in the sphere of the public space, or the impersonal arena of a territory considered as political (multicultural, multiethnic, etc.) community	1. Generic (generalized) trust in the Other, that is, the stranger that one encounters in the public sphere 2. Willingness to collaborate in order to produce a collective good (cooperation is demonstrated by electoral participation, donation to organizations with prosocial goals, support of petitions that promote a collective good, advocacy of collective rights, etc.)	Civic culture (or civic mindedness) in a local, national, or global context: SY generates civic mindedness (or civic culture) that consists in the exercise of the virtues of the "good citizen" who is committed to and responsible for collective goods, with trust and collaboration, in places and spheres of impersonal relations among fellow citizens who recognize one another as members of the same political community

Figure 9.1 The distinction among the various forms of sociability (SY): primary, secondary, and generalized

autonomy that were typical of pre-modern civil society (for example, the associative aggregations that arose during the Middle Ages and then in the Renaissance and with the Enlightenment). In addition, the same State-Market complex weakened its primary networks' bases and, therefore, undermined the input of primary SY to secondary SY little by little. The differentials in SY between highly modernized geographical areas (for example, the central and north European countries) and the modernized areas that maintain strong traditional elements (parts of the Mediterranean countries) can be explained on the basis of these configurations' differential trends.

Is it possible to envisage the re-establishment of sociability, in its different forms, in those areas where it has been eroded? In abstract, this is possible, but only on certain conditions. In order to understand this, we can draw upon research which explored not only the relationships between primary SY and secondary SY, but also between these two types of SY and other spheres such as the political sphere and its democratic institutions and the market economy. The results of these investigations show how collective goods are valorized by fostering primary, secondary, and generalized SY.

However, in these studies, it is not clear whether and when SY is an independent or dependent variable.[5] In this way, one ends up with a 'circular' vision of the factors at play, generating suspicion and confusion about the reality of SY as an autonomous factor endowed with its own properties and powers. It is not clear whether SY generates collective goods or whether things proceed in the opposite direction in which it is the existence of collective goods that generates SY. As a property of communities and nations rather than of individuals, sociability is at the same time a cause and an effect. It leads to positive results, such as economic growth and a decrease in crime, but its existence is deduced from these same results. Cities that are well governed and are growing

[5] For instance A. Portes, 'Social Capital: Its Origins and Applications in Modern Sociology', *Annual Review of Sociology*, 24 (1998), 1–24; B. Gui, 'On "relational goods": strategic implications of investment in relationships', *International Journal of Social Economics*, 23 (1996), 260–278; C. J. Uhlaner, 'Relational Goods and Participation. Incorporating Sociability into a Theory of Rational Action', *Public Choice*, 62 (1989), 253–285; F. Comunello, *Networked sociability. Riflessioni e analisi sulle relazioni sociali (anche) mediate dalle tecnologie* (Milan: Guerini, 2010); B. Weaver, 'The Relational Context of Desistance: Some Implications and Opportunities for Social Policy', *Social Policy & Administration*, 46 (2012), 395–412.

economically are in this situation because they have a considerable amount of sociability; poorer cities have a lesser quantity of this civic virtue.

In order to find a way out of these difficulties, we propose an approach to sociability that, from a distinctively sociological point of view: (i) avoids persistent misunderstandings by tracing them back to the partialities and distortions of individualistic and holistic approaches; (ii) allows one to see collective goods – in as much as they are generated in a relational manner – so as to avoid reductionism, in particular, psychological reductionism (thinking of the relational good as affectivity, expressivity, etc. of the relation) and economistic reductionism (thinking of the relational good as the human quality of economic transactions that offers the best competitive advantages and the greatest utility and satisfaction of economic preferences).

In order to find a way of avoiding conflation in understanding and explaining sociability, it is useful to avail oneself of the notion of 'relational goods' as a co-related way in which sociability exists when it takes the form of 'collective' good, where 'collective' means here that it is accessible to anyone who wants to take part in it, observing the norms and conditions that it imposes so that it can be generated and enjoyed together with others. The concept of relational good can be used as an *explanans* and an *explanandum* of sociability. This indicates that some kind of deep connection exists between the two concepts and that the solution to the problem of how they intertwine is to be found in examining these connections.

Our perspective

Our approach enables the relations between sociability and relational goods to be explained avoiding the ambiguities of thinkers who sometimes consider them as an *explanans* and sometimes as an *explanandum*. The solution lies in seeing them as part of a sequence that is not circular but, instead, is morphogenetic.

To clarify this point, we propose a scheme (Figure 9.2) that synthesizes our underlying theses according to which sociability is a product of relational goods and, in turn, is a regenerator of relational goods. The recursiveness between sociability (SY) and relational goods (RG) is only apparent in the sense that it can be resolved by introducing the morphogenetic scheme, which takes into account the temporal phases

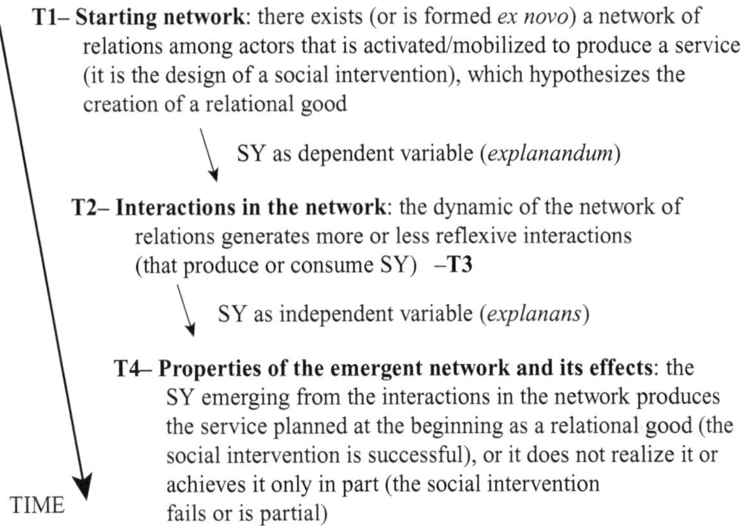

T1– Starting network: there exists (or is formed ex novo) a network of relations among actors that is activated/mobilized to produce a service (it is the design of a social intervention), which hypothesizes the creation of a relational good
SY as dependent variable (explanandum)
T2– Interactions in the network: the dynamic of the network of relations generates more or less reflexive interactions (that produce or consume SY) –T3
SY as independent variable (explanans)
T4– Properties of the emergent network and its effects: the SY emerging from the interactions in the network produces the service planned at the beginning as a relational good (the social intervention is successful), or it does not realize it or achieves it only in part (the social intervention fails or is partial)
TIME

Figure 9.2 Added social value of sociability (SY) as the re-generation of relational goods (RG) over time (cycle T1–T4), that is, as alteration of the order of relations through the order of interactions

and the autonomous ('stratified') input of every element in the process's particular phases.

In this scheme (Figure 9.2), the relationships between SY and RG are clearly seen (having been simplified as much as possible). Whether it is SY that generates RG or *vice versa* depends on the phase in which we observe the social process.

Let us look at an example.

Time T1: The beginning of the process starts when a project (an intervention among different subjects) is organized that entails activating/mobilizing the relation(s) among the actors as a good to be pursued, as a good in itself, that is, as a relational good. For example, when there is a need to organize a care intervention (a day care service for children or home care for the elderly), it is designed and implemented by mobilizing the relations among the individuals to be assisted and the actors belonging to their primary and secondary networks. This generates a situation from which more or less, or even no, SY may emerge in terms of trust, cooperation, and reciprocity among the actors. It should be noticed that trust is an emergent relation in itself, not only a prerequisite of other relations, for example a precondition of fair transactions. The same holds true for the relations of cooperation and reciprocity, which are emergent relations endowed with their distinctive properties and powers, although when they are co-present and reinforce each other, this can be difficult to discern.

Time T2–T3: Whether more or less SY is generated depends on the actors and the network that is created and mobilized. Here the actors' and their networks' reflexivity comes into play.

Time T4: If in the second phase, the dynamic of network interactions generated SY, then the initial relational good is regenerated or even increased. Alternatively, if in the second phase SY was only weakened or destroyed, relational goods are not produced, and even the initial relational good disappears.

From Time T4 another morphogenetic cycle will begin: the existing network of relations at Time T4 will have to deal with the interactions among the subjects so that SY will be put into play once again, from which it could emerge either strengthened or weakened.

It is important to underscore that, in the interactive phase, the actors' personal reflexivity and the Relational Reflexivity of their networks play a decisive role, while the structural context has an impact in fostering a certain type of reflexivity rather than another.

This framework avoids conflations between relational goods (RG) and sociability (SY), keeping them distinct but also in relation with each other.

Let us give an example. It refers to a kind of social project that aims at helping families who have children in difficulty. This type of intervention has been adopted in many countries, although with different names, methodologies, and outcomes.[6] We can call it

[6] It is generally known under the label 'Family Group Conference' (FGC). These are used to make plans for children in a number of different contexts: Child Welfare, Youth Offending, Education Welfare, Domestic Violence, Children as Young Carers, Foster Breakdown, Adoption, etc. In the United States, they are known as Family-Guided Decision Making. In the Netherlands and Flanders, they are known as Eigen Kracht Conferenties (Own Power Conferences). Ireland introduced the process into legislation in 2000 under the Children's and Families Act. The 1989 Children Act (England & Wales) like the New Zealand Children, Young Persons and Their Families Act 1989 has some similar principles which underpin and inform the development of how social workers interact and work with children and families. The challenge for social services was how to achieve a safe balance of partnership and parental responsibility whilst protecting the child from possible or further risk. In 2007 Germany introduced Family Group Conferences for juveniles in Elmshorn,

'building networks of families to help families in dealing with children in need, distress, risk of abuse, deviance, and many other troubles'. It is a structured decision-making meeting made up of 'family' members. Originally (in New Zealand) it was meant for one single family, but recently it has evolved into a kind of intervention that consists in bringing together a plurality of 'families' to form a wide social network.[7] 'Family' is defined broadly, to include the child/ren, parents, extended family, and even significant friends and neighbours of the family who may not actually be blood related. The intervention proceeds in the following way. One or many families sharing a common issue are brought together in a certain initial network composed by families and 'facilitators' (trained professionals) (T1). The aim is to produce a reflexive sociability that can generate a relational good (*explanandum*) among them, so that each family can rely upon the positive effects of the relational good in trying to solve its own troubles. The facilitators stimulate the dialogue (personal and Relational Reflexivity) among all the network's participants in several subsequent meetings in which the families expose and exchange in a simple and spontaneous way their experiences, difficulties, and attempts to cope with their children's problems. Through this phase of interactions and exchanges (T2–T3), the network develops a new sociability (*explanans*) in an elaborated structure (T4) which explains the fact that families are enabled and empowered to decide what they should do on the basis of trust, cooperation and reciprocity with the other participants in the network (including social workers who can provide public resources from outside).

Thus, we can speak of an 'added social value' (ASV) of SY that:

(i) consists in (re)generating (rather than diminishing, annihilating, etc.) relational goods; (ii) can be assessed in terms of the associative network's capacity to produce internal and external relations that act in a reflexive manner in such a way that the shared relations are made more efficacious in that they increase the network's operative efficacy.

Schleswig-Holstein, called 'Gemeinschaftskonferenzen' (GMK). The successful outcomes in many countries demonstrates that this radical approach has great potential.

7 F. Folgheraiter, *Relational Social Work. Toward Networking and Societal Practices* (London: J. Kingsley, 2004); Jaakko Seikkula, Tom Erik Arnkil, *Open Dialogues in Relational Practices. Respecting Otherness in the Present Moment* (manuscript 29.3.2012), Italian translation Metodi dialogici nel lavoro di rete (Trento: Edizioni Erickson, 2013).

This is, therefore, the ASV of relations that we call sociability, namely the capacity to generate relational collective goods, starting from an organized context, with a view to producing such goods. In a social intervention that functions well (because it truly produces collective goods), there is no confusing circularity between sociability and relational goods; rather, a morphogenetic process occurs that follows a precise temporal sequence.

ASV is the difference between the initial situation at Time T1 and the situation at the conclusion of the morphogenetic cycle considered at Time T4 (it can be positive or negative). ASV assesses an associative network's capacity to be efficacious *qua talis* (therefore, not being subject to anything but itself) in that it measures a network's capacity to produce sociability as an added value (that is, as the increase of its relational parameters: for example, the degree of reciprocity, cooperation, trust, affinity, etc.). In other words, it measures whether and to what degree the network succeeds in putting its (internal) relational good in synergy with sociability (in all of its dimensions: bonding, bridging, linking) because the one needs the other in order to produce the fruits of pro-sociality.

An example could be that of the *Tagesmütter* (the so-called 'day mother'). Once this role is created by a contract according to which a mother of a young child (0–3 years old) takes on the task of caring for other (two or three) children of the same age, a relation is created among the parents involved, who had set themselves a common goal or task (the care of their children, entrusted to the *Tagesmütter*). In this action of trust and reciprocal cooperation, there is the premise and the promise of a relational good. It depends on the second phase (how the interactions among parents take place) to ensure that interactions among them operate to generate, and not erode, sociability: in other words, if a relational context is created that fosters trust, cooperation, and reciprocity among the children's parents (who, owing to the type of relation that is established, come to know and spend time with one another and develop properties and powers that a public or private nursery organized in a bureaucratic or commercial fashion would not have produced). In this case, sociability generates a network of families in which relational goods flourish; otherwise, the social intervention should take a different path.

More generally, the so-called third sector and the social private sector are really 'third' in respect to the State and the Market when they are configured as social spheres that produce relational social inclusion through a virtuous interaction between a relational good and sociability. The interaction is virtuous both because it increases them, in turn, and because it operates with pro-social, civic, or civil ends.

The conceptualization presented here (Figure 9.2) resolves the aporias that hold studies on collective subjects captive to conflation between sociability and relational goods in as much as it shows that sociability is a variable that is dependent as well as independent, context-dependent as well as activity-dependent, in respect to relational goods. Sociability includes cultural factors (actors' norms, values, and attitudes) as well as structural factors (made of networks, organizations, and linkages), without conflating any of these elements and dimensions. An entire book would be needed to discuss all of this in depth.

However, given that the theoretical kernel of the issue is clear enough, the conceptual framework just delineated can highlight the added value of social relations that is at stake in the emergence of Relational Subjects and relational goods.

Understanding the added social value of social relations

In short, saying 'added value' means making reference to an increase of the value of something/someone. The increase is produced by something/someone that has acted/operated on something/someone which – due to a causal effect – has augmented its value.

When added value accrues *through* the social relation, we have the added social value *of* the social relation. It is the social relation that valorizes something/someone. If what it valorizes is a relation, then we are on the way to producing a relational good, which will be collective if and in so far as it provides for access for all who have a potential interest in sharing it as a form of relational service.

An associative network or a Private Social or a Third Sector organization creates ASV because, in producing goods or services (for example, a service to care for children, the disabled, the elderly, etc.), it uses a greater quantity and better quality of social relations compared to those that are used by the market or a bureaucratic organization (in the market, the buyer and the seller of a good usually have no interest in developing a particular relation between one another; the same holds true for bureaucratic performances, for instance when a certificate is duly handed by a public administrator to a citizen; in these cases, relations are impersonal and normally standardized). If more numerous and better relations are targeted as such among the subjects involved in a service, then the service itself becomes a relational good. It becomes a *relational service* in a strict sense.

To say that a social relation has an ASV means taking note of the fact that putting something/someone into a relationship with another something/someone produces an entity that goes beyond the properties and powers of the elements/subjects that were put into relation with one another. The phrase 'to put two entities into relation' means both that each entity makes symbolic reference to the other and that a bond or structural connection between them is created at the same time.

The combination of these two dimensions (symbolic and structural) that has been effected also generates an added value because it increases the value of whatever was put into relation through the social relation itself. This is an emergent effect and an effect that emerges precisely from the relation's qualities and causal powers.

In order to understand this process of valorization, it is necessary to conceptualize the 'relation that valorizes', given that not all relations have this emergent effect (to produce relational goods). At times, the emergent effect is negative in the sense that a relational evil (RE) is produced rather than a relational good (RG).

Thus, how is the relation configured that confers added value?

This is illustrated in Figure 9.3. Something/someone's Value can be defined according to four dimensions, which are themselves interrelated: as exchange value (E), as use value (U), as relational value or the value of the bond (R), and as the value of dignity (W).

(E) Something/someone is valorized in terms of exchange value when, through the relation with something/someone other than itself/oneself, their economic value (*Worth* in English, *Wert* in German) is increased with reference to a pricing system (added value in terms of utility); this is the principle upon which the capitalist market works;

(U) Something/someone is valorized in terms of use value when, through the relation with something/someone other than itself/oneself, they meet the super-functional needs of something/someone and this adds value in terms of the latter's ability to

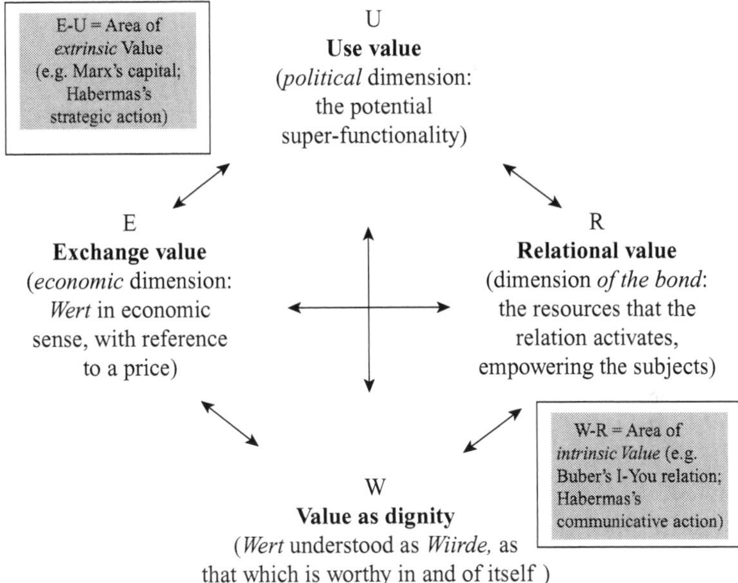

Figure 9.3 The analytical dimensions of something/someone's 'Value'

realize their goals; this is the way in which normal family relations are conducted in domestic life;

(R) Relational Value is the added value of something/someone owing to the relations that it makes available or activates, thus improving the qualities and powers of whatever it was combined with relationally. The relations that we call sociability optimize this criterion; as in the most basic case of friendship;

(W) Something/someone is valorized in its/his/her value of dignity when, through the relation with something/someone other, the sense of dignity one has in and of oneself is acknowledged and amplified, in a manner that cannot be attained through negotiation (added value in terms of acknowledgement – *Würde* in German); as an example we can cite the right of an abandoned child to have a family caring for him/her as a matter of human dignity.

These are the analytical dimensions of 'Value' in the phrase 'added social value'. In social processes, something/someone's value can be increased or simply reproduced as it is, or else diminished or annihilated.

When we mobilize a network of relations in order to enhance someone's value – for example, in the area of human services – we are more or less consciously trying to produce an added social value. We achieve this if and in so far as we use the relational criterion, which does not refer to economic utility or to functional contribution but rather to the capacity of social relations to mobilize resources – including the relations themselves – that empower the subjects who are the service's producers and users (prosumers). This is a clear example of collective Relational Subjects.

This type of operation is, in theory, specific to those Private-social and Third sector spheres when they actually give priority to valorization criteria that refer to relational dimensions and to dignity.

In order for this to happen, it is necessary that the social relation that gives added social value to something/someone (X) be made available. This means that there must be the potential for a certain amount of sociability (that is, a certain amount of willingness to have relations of trust, cooperation, and reciprocity with others). These relations pertain to the area of dignity and relationality (area W-R) of Value, that is, to the area of relations that confer an intrinsic value upon something/someone (X). If this works well, it is possible to produce a relational good that, in turn, feeds sociability in a sequence that is not circular but has a linear character of succession over time (as we saw in Figure 9.2). In this way, the relationality that unfolds in the interaction among actors can increase or decrease the parameters (trust, etc.) of sociability upon which collective Relational Subjects depend. If these parameters dip below a certain threshold, or are even reset to zero, not only can no collective Relational Subject emerge, but also relational goods are not produced and sociability is diminished. This is what usually happens when the process of valorizing something/someone remains confined within the area of exchange (utilitarian) value and use value (area E-U), that is, the area of interactions that privilege the social relation's extrinsic value. Prime instances include the capitalist relationship (expropriation of surplus value) and the evaluation of family relations in terms of the utilitarian advantages gained from them, for example, the exploitation of the use value of domestic labour.

All of this happens on the macro-, meso-, and micro-levels, as has been illustrated in this book. At these levels, we observe the emergence of diverse Relational Subjects. However, there is a final point to make with reference to Figure 9.3. In principle, the area of *extrinsic* value (area E-U: for example, Marx's capital and Habermas's strategic action) and the area of *intrinsic* value (area W-R, for example, Buber's I-You relation and Habermas's communicative action) are at opposite poles from one another. Nevertheless, in real processes of valorization their outcomes are on-going and often co-terminous or overlap in time, so it is advisable not to dichotomize the forms of valorization. Nor should it be assumed, for instance, that added relational value, having in and of itself an intrinsically qualitative character, is necessarily incompatible with, say, added exchange value, which is extrinsic. On the contrary, current tendencies to encourage cooperation between profit and non-profit organizations, by establishing new entities (for instance civil foundations) as Relational Subjects that associate with them in order to produce relational goods, are moving precisely in the direction of a 'composite' process of valorization in which all four of the criteria of worth (in Figure 9.3) work together to create an 'overall' added social value, which fosters new and more powerful Relational Subjects.

Relational evils and reduced social value (RSV)

In the previous section, it was argued that relationality unfolds between subjects and may *increase* or *decrease* the collective goods generated by sociability (especially trust, cooperation, and reciprocity) upon which Relational Subjects depend. This proposition emphasizes that the relations between subjects over time (and at different levels of the social order) are ultimately responsible for augmenting or diminishing the generation of relational goods. In turn, it follows from the arguments presented earlier that added social value (ASV) and its opposite reduced social value (RSV) will rise and fall accordingly. As outcomes, this does indeed appear to be the case. However, that leaves open the question as to whether or not the *interactional processes* accountable for 'relational evils' are *simply the reverse* of those that account for the production of 'relational goods'. The answer given is a qualified affirmative.

The qualifications are twofold. They arise from the fact that the generation of relational goods and also evils are both *context-dependent* and *activity-dependent*, as has already been stressed for the emergence of collective goods in general.

First qualification: The structural and cultural contexts in which different levels of the social order (particularly the macro and meso) work today are ones that are systemically skewed towards promoting relational evils rather than goods. This is what underlies the decrease in 'social integration' noted by most commentators in the developed and developing parts of the globalized world today. Although this decline in social integration is frequently attributed to different factors by those writing from different schools of thought, what is striking is that no one defends the opposite thesis – that social integration is on the increase.

Even those who give most attention to the undoubted growth in 'connectivity' – throughout the world and in particular areas – would be making a big mistake if they equated *quantitative* growth in, for example, telecommunications, transportation, and trans-national production with an equivalent *qualitative* increase in social integration between their users. Although none of these changes are *sui generis* predisposed towards fostering relational goods or evils, their mode of operation, the vested interests they serve, and the unequal 'bargaining positions' of those involved mean that their workings are far from neutral where the relationality of all those involved (now meaning everyone) is concerned. Another way of putting this is that although many would characterize such 'connectivity' in empiricist terms as 'the Network Society', this says nothing at all about 'who benefits'. The skewed nature of 'beneficiaries' – those most powerful in commandeering 'networks' to their own ends – spells a bias towards the generation of relational evils and a consequential RSV that is explored further later.

Second Qualification. Throughout this book, all relational goods and evils have consistently been held to be *activity-dependent.* Despite this universally being the case, we have periodically signalled that the generation of relational goods is more difficult at the macro-level because of the (current) impersonality involved in representative rather than participatory democracy; the impenetrability of the increasingly pivotal finance market; the inaccessibility of supra-national bodies and lack of control over their regulative governance, even by national polities; and the capacities for surveillance of large organized bodies on one another and upon citizens at large. Usually, we only know about the impact of such activities *post hoc* and that means after they have wreaked havoc, as in the current economic crisis. What then follows are attempts to deal with their negative consequences (by austerity measures to quantitative easing) rather than a radical reversal such that they are transformed into promoters of relational goods, all of which is well known.

Nevertheless, such macro-level influences should not lead us to forget that *activity dependence* can and does mean that agents and actors *also* generate relational evils at meso- and micro-levels, many of which today are intertwined with the macro-issues just touched upon, without this being *necessarily the case*.

In other words, there are forms of organizational relations and types of interpersonal relations that themselves fuel relational evils, that is, those forms of relations whose outcomes are deleterious to social integration and, ultimately, to human flourishing. Acknowledgement of these relatively autonomous sources of relational evils is important in preventing the picture and arguments presented in this book from drifting into a form of relational utopianism or gloom.

Moreover, this recognition does not entail any kind of collapse into the individualism of the everyday type that attributes relational evils to the unalterable fact that 'there will always be a few rotten apples in the basket' that contaminate the rest. It would simply be the equivalent of those individualists who hold that a few rapacious bankers are accountable for the current crisis and should be dealt with by confiscation of their bonuses and strong doses of virtue ethics.

Instead, recognizing that agents and actors have their own properties and powers also invites us to scrutinize how these can be exerted to pervert and to stymie plans, projects, and interventions whose aim was the production of 'relational goods' into precisely the opposite. In other words, we need to explore further the mechanisms at lower levels that contribute to and can cumulate in 'relational evils', because these are therefore at least partly responsible for the emergence of RSV rather than ASV. This is the obverse of holding 'the System' (any system) to be exclusively and universally responsible for the loss of social integration and its negative consequences, which entails a lapse into holism.

The context of relational evils and the resulting reduction in social integration

It is worth acknowledging that in our discussion of relational goods, most of the examples and illustrations given were 'bottom up' in kind.

This is a tendency, not a law, although good reasons can be given for why they are currently most unlikely to be 'top down' (see Chapter 6). In high and late modernity, relational evils tend to show the reverse tendency to work from the 'top downwards' and, again, there are good reasons for this trend.

All action takes place in a prior context and there is no possibility of 'context-less' action. (For any who dislike the word 'context' – though chosen for its neutrality – the terms 'circumstances', 'situation', or 'environment' may be substituted.) Because the context pre-dates their actions and often the contemporary agents and actors themselves, they cannot be held responsible for it, but neither can they avoid being affected by it, *especially* if they seek to transform it. The many influences that stem from the prior context into which primary agents (those sharing the same life-chances) are born all turn on the distribution of socially scarce resources and the process by which these resources are structurally produced and culturally legitimated.

If a range of large-scale relational evils was inspected empirically – take for example, steep and gross inequalities without relationship to human capabilities, legalized discrimination against particular groups, often normatively devaluing half or more of a given population, or gross infringements of human rights – the *empiricist* would be likely to conclude that such relational evils were correlated with the *asymmetry of resources* characterizing the 'beneficiaries' of versus those suffering from this state of affairs. They would have grasped something, but as empiricists they would have difficulty in accounting for the *sources and origins* of these asymmetries (and of cases such as the [material] exceptionalism of the Jewish diaspora throughout most of Europe, which did not prevent their expulsion and persecution.) This is because empiricists rest content with detecting overt patterns amongst manifest and measurable outcomes rather than seeking for the generative mechanisms causally responsible for them. (Any pattern detected will most likely be the causal outcome of plural and countervailing mechanisms together with intervening contingencies.) Yet, the source of 'top down' relational evils rests in the generative mechanisms at work and how they shape action to the detriment of social solidarity.

As realists, we are very interested in generative mechanisms, particularly in our one global society in the immediate future. Capitalism spread globally in the last three decades of the twentieth century, first through multinational production, then thanks to financial deregulation enabling the emergence of the finance market, and finally because of its growing synergy with information technology. In the slogan of its protagonists, 'there is no alternative', but simultaneously this served to license its intrinsically *competitive situational logic of action*. What does calling this 'a logic' mean, because this concept is not a metaphor? Fundamentally, it derives from the inherent nature of this mode of production to generate 'winners' and 'losers'. The 'free' market is open to all (who can compete) and it does not preclude 'humanistic' entrants from seeking to provide living wages, model villages, better housing, and so on. However, as the costs of the latter produce lower profits, the logic entails that these entrepreneurs will become less competitive if they do not fail altogether.

In other words, the logic of for-profit enterprises is of the 'If – then' variety. If any firm wishes to land on the side of the in-profit winners, then there is, indeed, little alternative to engaging in monetary cost-benefit analysis and endorsing instrumental rationality in decision-making. Competition is intrinsic to capitalism and hostile to sociability: the working class community and educational self-help (e.g. Mechanics' Institutes) were defences against or in opposition to this antipathy. Yet, despite its historical importance and greater yield in profits, this logic is no exception in terms of its negative 'downwards' effect upon social integration.

How any society earns its keep has never been irrelevant to the downward (and outward) influence of its 'relations of production' and their repercussion as relational evils at lower levels. This is not the economic determination of downward causation if only because control, coercion, and containment were always involved, and these may be counteracted internally or by external circumstances. For example, feudal fealty involved passing landholding titles from the Crown to the barony; from barons to local lords and so on downwards, but with 'loyalty' being calculative and frequently contested by force. The System of Legal Estates similarly involved granting juridical taxation privileges to the nobility, oppressive to the Third Estate, which included the people and were a proximate stimulus to revolution. State socialism bought support from the *nomenklatura* by according them scarce access to desirable resources; the same practice divided Party from non-Party members, whilst at the micro-level, neighbour was induced to inform upon neighbour, but it met with resistance. Equally, any form of authoritarianism (classical, slave, or colonial) entailed a downward fostering of social divisions and generally of corruption at lower social levels.[8] In all of these cases, networks existed and were indispensable (Shakespeare's theatrical 'messenger', and the earlier 'messengers' of classical drama served to link the nodes.) They differed only in speed, complexity, and the nature of the traffic carried.

Is neo-capitalism any different in the downward dispersal of its 'situational logic of competition'? During the 'golden' interlude of the post-war years, the formula of 'Social democracy + the welfare state + neo-capitalism' largely operated as a morphostatic mechanism. It was dependent upon the *mutual regulation* of capital and labour, of government and opposition. In short, for the quarter of a century at most after World War II, the state of the one mattered to the other and vice versa. That is, until corporate multinationals freed themselves from national confines to pursue the *situational logic of competition* and to loose themselves from the constraint that the need for legitimacy had previously imposed, now that there was no determinate population of indispensable employees who were also its national legitimators.

As the remit of national governments shrank, so correspondingly party membership and voter turn-out diminished throughout Europe. Politics became increasingly 'centrist', with a withering of political vision and even distinctive Party platforms. In turn, such politics without conviction meant a drastic shrinkage of normativity in political life. Political parties became preoccupied with tactics; with a St Simonian 'administration of things' – the latter day management of austerity and the reduction of public spending with minimum backlash – not the 'government of people' based on a normative conception of the good society. Tactical governance, with its 'about turns', absorption

[8] Here is a novelist's description of the colonial heritage of 'downwards corruption' in the Congo at the time of independence: 'How can I begin to describe the complexities of life here in a country whose leadership sets the standards for absolute corruption? You can't even have a post office box in Kinshasa; the day after you rent it, the postmaster may sell your box to a higher bidder, who'll throw your mail in the street as he walks out the door. The postmaster would argue, reasonably, he's got no other way to support his family – his pay envelope arrives empty each week, with an official printed statement about emergency measures. The same argument is made by telephone operators, who'll place a call outside the country for you only after you specify the location in Kinshasa where you'll leave *l'enveloppe* containing your bribe. Same goes for the men who handle visas and passports. To an outsider it looks like chaos. It isn't. It's negotiation, infinitely ordered and endless.' Barbara Kingsolver, *The Poisonwood Bible* (New York: Harper, 1998).

in today's latest 'scandal', and the announcement of a 'quick fix', behaves like the fire service attending only to emergency calls. It ejects commitment from the political domain, whether in the form of expansive political philosophies or explicitly normative organizations with a broad conspectus on the good life.

Instead, tactical governance works through bureaucratic regulation whose highest aims are manifest (measurable) efficiency and effective control. Ultimately, politics without conviction generates a huge shrinkage of normativity itself within public life as a whole and particularly notable in the main social institutions, resulting in further fragmentation of social integration.

Over the last quarter of a century, all of the traditional professions and the corresponding organizations where they work have become subject to governance by performance indicators. Schools, hospitals, universities, social service departments, and so forth became managed by 'objective' performance indicators with results published in League Tables, which undermined the solidarity amongst 'free professionals' and the relationality between them and those they served. The use of performance indicators represents an extension of the *logic of competition* from the business world to one previously held to consist importantly in the quality of human relations. The indicators deployed could capture measurable quantitative differences in crude empiricist terms (hospital through-put, waiting times for operations, and so forth) but were incapable of assessing the quality of care, of teaching, or of research.

Both internally within each organization and externally between the potential public of users, the *logic of competition* constituted an assault upon solidarity. A new conflict of interests had been introduced between professionals and the growing ranks of administrators; one damaging to the professional ethic and, in turn, to those who were being served. It seems, for instance, that a measurably excessive death-rate was required before the relational evils developing between staff and patients were addressed.[9] Externally, this induced a loss

[9] In extreme cases, such as the report just issued on the Mid-Staffordshire Health Trust in Great Britain, meeting performance targets had taken precedence over patient care. Robert Francis QC, leading the investigation, commented in his report that patients were left 'unwashed, unfed and without water' while staff treated them and their relatives with 'callous indifference'. 'There was a lack of care, compassion, humanity and leadership,' he said. 'The most basic standards

of intergenerational solidarity (given the higher use of health service resources by the old in populations where they were disproportionately represented) and an organized scapegoating of migrants. The effects of austerity policies augmented the deficit in social integration as welfare benefits were rolled further back, unemployment and part-time temporary work increased, and public spending cuts proliferated.

Were we to hold this depressing parade of cases illustrating the derogation of sociability to be inevitable for any social formation beyond relatively undifferentiated early societies, we would be inconsistent realists. This is because no socio-economic generative mechanism to date has been eternal. Another is that countervailing mechanisms, which there has not been the space to discuss, may change in all kinds of ways including their strength of counter-action. The third is not some appeal to contingency, because to rely upon the contingent in attempting to say anything definite about macroscopic social change in the foreseeable future is an oxymoron. In our view, the increasingly popular resort of social theorists to the notion of 'self-organization' merely summons up another hidden hand. Instead, the third reason for not endorsing a historic decline in social integration as an inevitable consequence of size or functional specialization derives from something that the instances mentioned earlier (and too cursorily) in late modernity have in common; all are examples of a social formation which operates (operated) in a zero-sum manner. What we seriously question is the necessity of this itself. Probably, if pushed, we would grant that it is not just the conceivability of win–win generative mechanisms, but the fact some have already been realized that saves us from sociological despair.

The following paragraph attempts to indicate why we have not given up on sociability, without succumbing to utopianism. However, nothing in the lines of thought being pursued by us questions the subordinate hypothesis hinted at in relation to empiricist observations, namely that large asymmetries of wealth, power, or repute are not propitious to social integration or the generation of relational goods, much less the Common Good.

of care were not observed and fundamental rights to dignity were not respected.' The headline of *The Independent* (09.02.2013) read 'NHS's darkest day: Five more hospitals under investigation for neglect as report blames "failings at every level" for 1,200 deaths at Stafford hospital'.

To consider the growth of countervailing mechanisms as (a) a source of relational goods that re-valorize sociability, and also (b) ones capable of significantly moderating the relational evils that undermine both its worth and efficacy, is to signal sources of potential reversal. In practice today, to do so is to dwell upon the burgeoning third sector, the voluntary and 'social-private' sectors, their pro-social ends, uses of alternative currencies, and harnessing of human capacities outside the framework limited to the market exchange of equivalents. This has already been discussed in Chapters 6 and 7. The vitality of this sector is not in question; much more contentious is its ability to moderate relational evils by (i) doing more than supplying window dressing for corporate enterprises (as is already the case, just as 'green' and 'organic' were earlier and effortlessly harnessed to marketing) and (ii) resisting the great temptation to engage in *competitive* counter-institutionalization (the route followed by many 'successful' charities as they develop hierarchies of command, selective criteria for participants, paid lobbyists, and celebrity figureheads).

We cannot re-open this discussion now, but merely underline that the very colonization of the third sector that serves to bring it inside the corporation also places its (diluted) aims on company agendas, holds them to account, and makes a difference to their internal dynamics. Meanwhile, new voluntary initiatives continue to develop outside, fuelling the momentum of gradualist change by acting effectively as freelance Research and Development departments. Perhaps this is a realistic role that can be foreseen for the domestic social economies of the old European developed world, ones that are already losers in the capitalist global competition.

Nevertheless, no such gradualism would fundamentally undercut the *situational logic of competition* and its attendant relational evils. This is the attraction of exploring the potential of an alternative mode of production, whose outcomes are win–win in kind, and that extends a different *situational logic of opportunity*. This depends upon free-giving, flexible involvement, and crowd-sourcing. Crucially it is based upon cultural goods which are not *qua talis* scarce commodities because sharing does not diminish their intrinsic value. In other words, the terms in which it operates are the opposite of restrictive attempts to attach scarcity value to cultural goods by artificial means (such as the increase in patents and the growth of intellectual property rights) that yield competitive advantage. The obverse is general licensing, genuine open access, peer-to-peer production, and the distinctive *modus operandi* on which the success of Wikipedia was built. These show that the goals of free creation and diffusion are possible and a host of organized information and communication technology (ICT) movements are already working to this end.[10]

It is the combination of two factors that makes this win–win scenario worth exploring in general and specifically because together they would work to dispel relational evils. On the one hand, if knowledge is becoming the main factor in production – as those proclaiming the 'Information Age' insist – then in the absence of natural scarcity, the one-time advantages (asymmetries) benefiting those commandeering that which was scarce can begin to decline as the very foundations of competition are undermined. This has not been seriously examined in the social sciences, because it tends to be assumed that those with contemporary competitive advantages in the market will be able to prolong them by simply annexing digital advances – as, indeed, they try to do. On the other hand, the intensity of morphogenetic change fostered by digital science and technology has been trivialized by being presented as the simple 'acceleration thesis'.[11] Its basic defects are a failure to specify clearly what *kinds* of things are 'accelerating' (other than life experiences) and what generative mechanism is causally responsible. Yet, if the two factors are considered in conjunction, then digital diffusion, without loss of value, and the intrinsically transformational nature of digital technology would seriously challenge those forms of *vested interests* (and their reproductory practices) that perpetuate the asymmetries constituting the material cause of gross relational evils. That is why the notion of a morphogenic society merits our attention.[12]

[10] See Archer, 'How Agency is Transformed in the course of Social Transformation', in her (ed.), *Generative Mechanisms Transforming the Social Order* (Dordrecht: Springer, 2015), chapter 7.

[11] H. Rosa, 'Social Acceleration: Ethical and Political Consequences of a Desynchronized High Speed Society', in H. Rosa and W. E. Scheuerman (eds.), *Social Acceleration, Power, and Modernity* (University Park: Pennsylvania State University Press, 2009), pp. 77–111; H. Rosa, W. E. Scheuerman (eds.), *High-Speed Society. Social Acceleration, Power, and Modernity* (University Park: Pennsylvania State University Press, 2009).

[12] This is the concept being examined by ten social scientists, among them ourselves, in a book series on 'Social Morphogenesis' producing a volume each year: Archer (ed.), *Social Morphogenesis* (2013); *Late Modernity: Trajectories towards Morphogenic Society* (2014); and *Generative Mechanisms Transforming the Social Order* (forthcoming 2015), Dordrecht: Springer.

Some 'activity-dependent' cautions about the reversal of relational evils

The last section dealt with macroscopic contexts of action that in different ways were systematically skewed against the production of relational goods and thus contributed to the production and usually continuation and sometimes exacerbation of relational evils. However, what about contexts which are 'neutral' in this respect or even those designed to generate relational goods and reverse relational evils? Is there not a sense in which desirable outcomes (ASV) are predicated upon the interactions of already 'fully fledged' Relational Subjects? Is there not also an argument to be made about how persons can be Relational Subjects but that the kind of relationality they value can be at variance with that valorized by other Relational Subjects? These two considerations are introduced as cautions against over-precipitous social policy interventions, ones based upon good intentions to harness sociability towards increasing relational goods but which can have the unintended consequence of producing relational evils instead.

To facilitate discussion, let us briefly revisit those Family Group Conferences that are increasingly employed in many countries and legislated for in a few. Note the cautiousness with which these were introduced earlier in this Conclusion; at best the network's capacity to increase sociability as an ASV requires monitoring and sometimes, at the end of a given morphogenetic cycle, it must be concluded that the extent of reciprocity, trust, co-operation, and affinity has not been enhanced and neither has bonding, bridging, and linking been increased for those in difficulties – so, a different approach should be taken.

Let us recall that those taking part will include the network of family, perhaps friends and neighbours, and the social workers who facilitate dialogue between them. Recall too that the range of problems includes youth offending, educational issues, and domestic violence. The process is dialogical and aims to synthesize the various perspectival accounts in a manner acceptable and helpful to the subjects involved. Thus, the proximate network represents the context of the intervention. What takes place when a Conference is convened depends upon the actions of those present but partially shaped in the past.

As Tolstoy put it, 'each unhappy family is unhappy in its own way',[13] and this forms the *leitmotif* alerting us to some of the *relational factors* that themselves could prevent the dialogical dynamics from approximating to a remedial 'ideal speech situation'. These are at least threefold.

First, and perhaps most important, the FGC seems to be predicated on a collective form of Communicative Reflexivity, that is, upon the readiness of subjects in difficulties to accept the Conference's participants as their interlocutors in external conversation and to hold that their own deliberations (as singular subjects, a couple or a small group) need to be confirmed and completed by dialogical exchanges with these others. Yet, this is not the sole mode by which reflexivity (individual or collective) is practiced, and it appears from empirical research to be on the decline. However, not only would taking part in an FGC be uncongenial to those who mainly practice other modes of reflexivity (especially to Autonomous Subjects), but also those who are 'Communicatives' themselves select their interlocutors and often are found, for example, to avail themselves of one parent rather than the other or one group of friends rather than another for various reasons. Moreover, the subjects in difficulties have *already* had the chance to turn (selectively) to their family members and those in their proximate environment for dialogical assistance, but they have not chosen to do so or it has been to no avail.

Perhaps protagonists of this scheme of intervention would reply that the Conference supplies a novel forum for sharing and harnessing support that is not dismissed at least by Communicative Subjects, especially when they do recognize that they confront problems. Nevertheless, participation may still be resisted and rejected by Autonomous and some Meta-Reflexives as constituting 'enforced Communicative Reflexivity' (particularly when the FGC has the backing of the law) and one that is alien to them. Autonomous Subjects value their independence highly and would be inclined to walk away from imposed relational involvement. Meta-reflexives are likely to be disengaged 'meta-participants' who are constantly evaluating the procedure and questioning the value of their participation in it. 'One size does not fit all' and it seems that the FGC would be more suited to those practicing Communicative and Fractured Reflexivity as their dominant mode,

[13] Leo Tolstoy, the opening line of *Anna Karenina*, p. 1.

given that as Relational Subjects they tend towards high dependency upon others.

Second, it has also been found that external interlocution (in ordinary conversation) with the subject's *confidantes* operates to reinforce normative conventionalism. It seems plausible that this would also mark the small group dynamics of exchanges within a FGC. Yet, a different attitude towards the conventional norms might sometimes be the 'solution' to a problem. For example, children deemed to be in difficulties at school and who have, say, a record of truancy, may have encouraged their parents (conjointly) to consider 'home schooling' as a way forward. However, schooling at home is still far from being a common or generally accepted practice. It takes much effort and skill to organize and has to confront some serious reservations about domestic educational resources and the child's loss of mixing with its peers. In consequence, the conventionalism manifested at the FGC could strike out 'home schooling' as a route to explore, thus reinforcing the tentativeness with which the parental couple had ventured this course of action (even to one another as Relational Subjects). It could lead the couple to discard it, when it is possible that their radical and demanding solution would have worked better than the Conference's consensus.

Third, the manner in which unhappy families are unhappy in their own ways will be brought into their dialogical exchanges as Conference participants. Old grievances and jealousies, disparities in education and differences in belief, and the tendency of parents-in-law each to defend their own child in a couple-issue cannot simply be set aside, if only because they will have been selectively but relationally reinforced among different parts of the family. Friends or neighbours may have heard only one version of events, so 'taking sides' will affect their dialogical contributions, and it is hard to see how such well-rehearsed perspectival interpretations could be eradicated. For example, the children's problems could be attributed to the mother by her in-laws because she is in employment, whilst the father's in-laws might dwell upon his unwillingness to share in child care. How could this log-jam be resolved, because the couple is probably fully aware of this issue, but she needs and wants to work and he may have been marginalized from or lacks the skills or inclination to care for young children? Perhaps, here, the FGC could break deadlock by encouraging the participants to regard themselves as a group resource that is able to cooperate by offering some more hours of paid child care and fostering greater paternal involvement, thus alleviating something of the problem – in which case they will, indeed, be helping to produce a relational good.

That would represent an upward spiral towards ASV. Alternatively, for the couple and some of the family having their 'dirty linen' washed in public could intensify a downward spiral, resulting in separation or divorce, thus culminating in RSV for the small group concerned. For young offenders, particularly resolute Autonomous Reflexives, only too familiar with the intervention of social workers in their lives, it is conceivable that such an experience of a FGC could precipitate a choice of their gang over what is seen as humiliation and surveillance on their block. In other words, for upward spirals of sociability to engage, Relational goods have to be very robust to offset relational evils.

Moreover, there does remain the danger of 'relational authoritarianism', especially if such approaches lose their intended dialogical and interactive character, based on voluntary participation, and become institutionalized as normal social service practice. 'Beneficent authoritarianism' already characterizes some applications of preventative medicine. For example, it is routine practice in certain countries for health centres or authorities to write informing patients that being over 65 they are strongly advised to have an injection protecting against 'flu and an appointment has been made for them to receive this jab. Of course, some subjects simply put this in the bin, but the assumptions that they are not working, that their diaries are empty, and that a public service administrator has the right to dispose of their time still rankles. Greater sensitivity would lead such a service to be issued as an invitation rather than presuming to deprive subjects of agency and capacity to evaluate the offer, which medical research shows not to be universally beneficial.

There are many pitfalls to 'enforced relationality', which is obviously an oxymoron because it traduces reciprocity by rendering one party passive. Its implementation would constitute a blatant relational evil for some and result in reduced trust in the service providers and reluctance to call upon them when needed. True respect of human dignity entails an acceptance of human diversity. Relational Subjects are not homogeneous, and neither are the conditions on which they can embrace and engage in reciprocity, cooperation, and trust. Planned interventions can only be positive for ASV as invitations to participate in a variety of initiatives; otherwise they themselves can generate relational evils that contribute towards RSV.

A final word

Social relations are inherently ambivalent. They can be untieable knots that entangle people and lead them to the worst possible situations or be valuable encounters that provide good experiences and help people to flourish. They are sources of conflicts as well as of cooperation, and not infrequently at the same time. They can be constraints upon human dignity or, conversely, resources that enhance human rights. They can reflect social and cultural structures that subtly bring with them forms of social alienation or, under certain conditions, can offer opportunities for actions that empower people. In sum, they can work for relational goods or relational evils. All depends on how social relations are seen and managed. This is why social agents, both individual and collective, must continuously redefine themselves as Relational Subjects. To some extent, they realize that their life depends on the properties and powers of the social networks to which they belong. But in most cases they lack the capacity – in particular, adequate reflexivity – to think in this manner about their sociability and manage it in such a way as to generate relational goods rather than relational evils.

Emphasizing the positive as well as the negative aspects of social relations, their divergences or convergences, is too easy. Much more difficult and fruitful is the task of clarifying the morphostatic/morphogenetic character of social relations which may trouble or enhance what we have called here 'the Relational Subject'. In this book we have tried to understand the winding processes through which the Relational Subjects have to pass in order to find their way forward and realize themselves by discerning which of their opportunities are positive, deliberating upon their life courses, and dedicating themselves to the kind of sociability that helps them to flourish rather than to wither in the emerging society where habitual action has become an inadequate compass.

Index